GLOBAL POLITICS

for A-level

Robert Murphy
John Jefferies
Josie Gadsby

SERIES EDITOR:
Eric Magee

HODDER
EDUCATION
AN HACHETTE UK COMPANY

Hachette UK's policy is to use papers that are natural, renewable and recyclable products and made from wood grown in sustainable forests. The logging and manufacturing processes are expected to conform to the environmental regulations of the country of origin.

Orders: please contact Bookpoint Ltd, 130 Park Drive, Milton Park, Abingdon, Oxon OX14 4SE. Telephone: (44) 01235 827720. Fax: (44) 01235 00401. Email: education@bookpoint.co.uk

Lines are open from 9 a.m. to 5 p.m., Monday to Saturday, with a 24-hour message answering service. You can also order through our website: www.hoddereducation.co.uk

ISBN: 978 1 4718 8941 7

© Robert Murphy, John Jefferies, Josie Gadsby, Eric Magee 2017

First published in 2017 by

Hodder Education,
An Hachette UK Company
Carmelite House
50 Victoria Embankment
London EC4Y 0DZ

www.hoddereducation.co.uk

Impression number   10 9 8 7 6 5 4 3 2 1

Year   2021 2020 2019 2018 2017

Photos reproduced by permission of: **p. 3** Lazyllama/Alamy, **p. 8** US Army Photo/Alamy, **p. 16** Sueddeutsche Zeitung Photo/Alamy, **p. 23** Wenn Ltd/Alamy, **p. 26** World History Archive/Alamy, **p. 27** Friedrich Stark/Alamy, **p. 32** Vario images GmbH & Co.KG/Alamy, **p. 33** Vario images GmbH & Co.KG/Alamy, **p. 34** dpa picture alliance/Alamy, **p. 42 (top)** TopFoto, **p. 42 (bottom)** ZUMA Press, Inc/Alamy, **p. 48** jamdesign/Fotolia, **p. 51** Richard Human/Alamy, **p. 55** Penny Tweedie/Alamy, **p. 62** brianeuro/Alamy, **p. 74** Europa Newswire/Alamy, **p. 77** Jim West/Alamy, **p. 81** 360b/Alamy, **p. 86** Spencer Platt/Staff/Getty Images, **p. 91** Sean Pavone/Alamy, **p. 99** Xinhua/Alamy, **p. 109** Picture Partners/Alamy, **p. 116** Delphotostock/Fotolia, **p. 122** 508 collection/Alamy, **p. 125** igotvenocom/Fotolia, **p. 130** Norman Chan/Fotolia, **p. 133** Photomac/Fotolia, **p. 137** Topfoto, **p. 160** REUTERS/Alamy, **p. 161** REUTERS/Alamy, **p. 167** Living Legend/Fotolia, **p. 172** TopFoto, **p. 175** AWesleyFloyd/Fotolia, **p. 178** REUTERS/Alamy, **p. 182** dpa picture alliance archive/Alamy, **p. 187** jgolby/Fotolia, **p. 197** Ben Flavell/Alamy, **p. 203** Stocktrek Images, Inc./Alamy, **p. 206** john wreford/Alamy, **p. 210** Topfoto, **p. 217** dpa picture alliance archive/Alamy, **p. 219** Alexander/Fotolia, **p. 221** Olli Geibel/Alamy, **p. 226** estherpoon/Fotolia, **p. 236** SPUTNIK/Alamy, **p. 239** carabay/Fotolia, **p. 248** olga_nosova/Fotolia, **p. 249** magicbones/Fotolia, **p. 252** gilbertc/Fotolia, **p. 256** Xinhua/Alamy, **p. 262** Sasa Kadrijevic/Alamy, **p. 264** Romolo Tavani/Fotolia, **p. 270** Christo Sharpe/Alamy, **p. 281** Claudia Wiens/Alamy, **p. 287** kamasigns/Fotolia, **p. 295** Lulla/Fotolia, **p. 309** US Air Force Photo/Alamy, **p. 312** London pix/Alamy, **p. 316** Zuma Press Inc/Alamy Stock Photo, **p. 319** eyetronic/Fotolia, **p. 321** fotostock/Alamy, **p. 324** Jiang/Fotolia

Typeset by Aptara Inc.

Printed in: Italy

A catalogue record for this title is available from the British Library.

Get the most from this book

This brand new textbook created for the 2017 specification helps you develop an understanding of global politics using a range of features.

Special features

Learning outcomes
A summary of the learning objectives for each chapter.

Key terms
Concise definitions of key terms where they first appear.

Distinguish between
A clarification of the difference between two commonly confused concepts or institutions.

Content box
Outline key facts.

Case study
Topical examples to use in essays.

Debate
The two sides of a controversial question set out to hone evaluation skills.

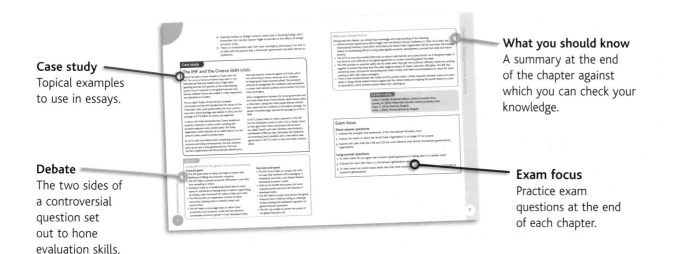

What you should know
A summary at the end of the chapter against which you can check your knowledge.

Exam focus
Practice exam questions at the end of each chapter.

Contents

Answers to the exam focus questions can be found at: **www.hoddereducation.co.uk/GlobalPolitics**

Chapter 1

Theories of global politics

> **Learning outcomes**
>
> By the end of the chapter you should understand:
> - what global politics is
> - what the challenges of modern global politics are
> - the comparative theories of global politics and what they are useful for
> - what realism is and whether states behave in a realist way
> - what liberalism is and whether there is a liberal world order
> - whether the world is experiencing a 'clash of civilisations'

Getting you started

This chapter introduces the key theories of global politics. In doing so, it also covers many themes and debates that are covered in depth in later chapters.

Is global politics under pressure as never before?

Today's global politics is turbulent and unpredictable. States are deeply linked and dependent on each other in terms of politics, trade and shared challenges. Yet, across the world, many of the traditional structures of global politics are under pressure.

Since 2011, Syria has seen one of the bloodiest conflicts of modern times. The international community, including the United Nations (UN) and the major world powers, has been unable to reach agreement or a peaceful solution. Casualties and refugees are being counted in millions.

The 2008 global financial crisis also exposed how interdependent states' economies are. A banking collapse in the USA spread financial chaos across the world, sparking a global downturn in the world economy. Both events demonstrated just how much of a global society we have become, with globalisation, technology, increased communication and easier travel linking peoples, businesses, refugees, students and many more as never before, and impacting economics, politics and security across the world.

The UK's vote to leave the European Union (EU) has also put the world's foremost regional organisation under immense pressure. The election of Donald Trump to the office of US president has been seen by some as a rejection of globalisation, reflecting a possible return to US isolationism in the face of an increasingly hostile and turbulent world. In Europe, too, populist nationalist parties are increasingly challenging traditional parties and their view of the international order.

In addition to all of these pressures, there is an increasing demand for states to work together on common challenges. Climate change, for example, can only be tackled effectively by states working together and by all states committing to action. Similarly, the threat from globalised terror networks and non-state actors demands global action.

The UK voted to leave the EU in a 2016 referendum

Increasingly, global politics is struggling to respond to the scale of these challenges. There are more powerful actors on the international stage than ever before. The major powers of China, Russia and the USA are becoming increasingly matched in terms of power and their willingness to demonstrate this power. Others, such as Brazil and India, are emerging powers with growing economic influence. Others are coming to terms with and seeking to best manage their declining status as world powers. In a globalised economy, some multinational corporations (MNCs) are more powerful than states. And non-state actors, such as the so-called Islamic State and the al-Qaeda network, have been challenging traditional state power. The key challenge for global politics is to manage these competing interests and shared concerns.

National politics is about the ability to resolve disputes, share resources and take decisions legitimately within agreed structures, laws and institutions. However, unlike in national politics, such as that in the UK or the USA, there is no central world government or authority. Global politics has a far more complex and multi-layered range of structures, laws and institutions at regional and international level. Ultimately, the most legitimate and powerful actors in global politics are often nation-states. States are far less bound by structures, laws and institutions than actors in national politics. Agreements are made and achievements gained because nation-states agree to or work towards them. When states do not agree, global politics often experiences gridlock.

What is global politics?

To begin to understand global politics, it is useful to compare global with national politics. Both relate to:

- taking decisions legitimately
- accountability and holding those in power to account
- solving shared problems, such as a domestic or global threat of terrorism
- resolving disputes, such as disagreements over ownership of territory
- sharing resources fairly and peacefully

The differences between national and global politics

There are important differences between national and global politics in terms of power, legitimacy and authority.

Power in global politics is the ability to achieve desired outcomes and to influence others. In national politics, a national or sub-national government, such as Her Majesty's Government in the UK, exercises power. It is legitimately elected by the people with a mandate to implement the manifesto promises it made during an election campaign. In global politics, there is no form of world government. Institutions such as the UN carry some authority, but only as much as individual member states allow. Therefore, states can choose to ignore or defy these attempts at **global governance**.

Legitimacy is the ability to do things fairly and lawfully. This can be achieved through complying with or creating a form of legislation or law. For example, one way of undertaking military action lawfully is through a UN Security Council (UNSC) Resolution, which in itself is a statement of international law. In national politics there is usually a legislature, which holds the legitimacy and powers to create laws, and a judiciary and police force, which apply and enforce the law (see Table 1.1). In global politics, there is rarely such clear authority. Laws are created only when states agree to them. Laws often apply only to those states that have signed up to them. And laws are often enforced only when states permit it.

Authority comes from the possession of both power and legitimacy. The UK Parliament has authority because it is democratically elected and so possesses legitimacy. For example, in September 2013, when the UK Parliament voted against air strikes on the Assad regime in Syria, Prime Minister David Cameron certainly felt the effects of parliament's authority and he had to abandon his plans to carry out the strikes.

In global politics, there is no comparable structure of world government with such clearly defined powers and scope. There is certainly no government structure that has comprehensive power over every state and region of the world. There are institutions that have some authority over certain states or regions, but this authority is not absolute, because states can decide to ignore or withdraw from these institutions. Some states are not even members of these institutions to begin with.

Key term

Global governance
Attempts to bring government structures and authority to world politics in order to deal with common interests and challenges, such as climate change or global terrorism.

Table 1.1 Examples of sources of power and authority in UK and US national politics

Source	UK authority	US authority
Legislature: amends and votes on laws	The UK Parliament has the power and authority to make and unmake laws.	The US Congress has the power and authority to approve presidential appointments and budgets.
Executive: proposes laws	Her Majesty's Government in the UK is made up of the prime minister and his/her cabinet, supported by the civil service. It can propose laws and policies for parliament to vote on.	The US president has powers to negotiate treaties with other states.
Judiciary: interprets and enforces the law	National courts. For example, the UK's Supreme Court in 2017 declared that the UK Parliament, rather than the executive, must trigger Article 50 to begin the process for leaving the EU.	The Supreme Court is the USA's highest court and takes decisions on issues of major constitutional significance. For example, the 1973 Roe vs Wade decision ruled that women had the right to decide whether or not to terminate their pregnancy.

National and global politics

National politics

- There is a government with a clear mandate and authority. Political parties usually compete in elections, are legitimately elected by a defined electorate within the state and then govern with clear authority.
- National laws are usually clearly written down, codified and set out in law, and apply to all citizens without exception.
- Courts and police enforce national laws, and have clear and legitimate authority to do so.
- There are usually clear and authoritative institutions for taking decisions, such as voting on laws and resolving disputes fairly and legitimately, for example national parliaments or assemblies, such as the UK Parliament or the US Congress. A vote in one of these institutions carries clear authority and results in laws being debated, amended and, ultimately, approved or not.

Global politics

- There is no single world government with a clear mandate or authority. States are the most powerful and authoritative actors and, ultimately, a higher authority cannot force states to do anything against their will.
- International law may be written down and codified but often it applies only to states that have formally agreed to these laws (normally by signing and ratifying treaties).
- International law is hard to enforce, particularly if powerful states refuse to comply. Enforcement is possible only through sanctions or military action, and is inconsistently applied.
- There are many institutions capable of making decisions, but none can do so without the consent of member states. Summits and intergovernmental organisations (IGOs) offer states a means of resolving disputes and opportunities to work together (for example, in the UN, the EU, the Group of Seven/Eight (G7/8) and at the Paris Climate Change Conference 2015). They have varying legitimacy and authority, and states can ultimately choose whether or not to join and remain part of these institutions. States can also ignore their decisions or opt out of joint action.

Activity

1 Looking at Table 1.1 and the separation of powers it summarises, are there institutions in global politics that have similar powers and responsibilities to:
   (a) an executive?
   (b) a legislature?
   (c) a judiciary?
2 What differences do you see between the powers of these branches of government in national politics compared with global politics?

Who is involved in global politics?

By the nature of its much larger geographical scope, there are more actors involved in global than national politics. The powers, impact and limitations of each of these actors are covered in greater depth in later chapters.

States are the primary actors in global politics, as they have the most authority and legitimacy to take decisions. States differ widely in terms of their power, which impacts on the amount of authority they have on the world stage, and their ability to achieve their desired outcomes and influence other states. Powerful states, such as China, Russia and the USA, are more likely to achieve their own goals and also to dominate and limit the choices available to less powerful states.

In addition to states, there are a number of non-state actors that contribute towards global decision making. These include:

- IGOs such as the UN and the Bretton Woods Institutions (the International Monetary Fund (IMF), the World Trade Organization (WTO) and the World Bank)
- regional organisations such as the EU, the Association of Southeast Asian Nations (ASEAN) and the North American Free Trade Agreement (NAFTA)
- non-governmental organisations (NGOs) such as Oxfam and Human Rights Watch

Activity

Consider the difference between national politics and global politics.

1 Why might it be more difficult to reach agreement in global politics than in national politics?
2 In global politics, which actors are:
   (a) the most powerful?
   (b) the most legitimate?

Realism and liberalism

Key terms

Realism States are the most important and authoritative actors in global politics, and their primary goal is to protect their own national interests.

Liberalism States' interests in global politics are linked and interdependent, and best advanced through states working closely with each other and with non-state actors in order to achieve common political objectives.

Security dilemma The idea that as one state builds up its defences, others will respond by building up theirs, thereby increasing tensions between the two states or even provoking conflict.

Two of the key theories in global politics are **realism** and **liberalism**. They represent different ways of approaching international problems.

Realism and an anarchical world order

Realism is governed principally by the belief that nation-states are the most legitimate and powerful actors in global politics. The realist viewpoint includes the following:

- The authority of IGOs, such as the EU and the UN, should be limited. In this respect, global politics is an anarchical society, since nation-states retain the exclusive right to act in whatever way they wish. Although nation-states may decide to work through and with other non-state actors, they do not abandon their sovereign right to advance their own self-interest. (Anarchy, in this context, should be understood in its literal sense as the 'absence of authority or government' rather than necessarily a state of chaos and disorder.)
- Since nation-states exist in a state of global anarchy, this creates a **security dilemma**, because they can only rely upon themselves for their own protection. States, therefore, live in a self-help system in which they must build up their own security apparatus through military power and alliances.
- States act rationally and usually prioritise defending their own national interest. Usually, this means that a state's prime motivation is to defend its national security against perceived threats.
- All states are ultimately trying to find ways of increasing their power and influence within the global political order.
- The natural state of the world order is for states to compete with each other, making the most of their power. Therefore, states are often in conflict with each other.

See Box 1.1 for more information on the theories of key realist thinkers.

> **Box 1.1**
>
> ## Important realist thinkers
>
> The titles of the following texts from key realist thinkers all question some of the assumptions of liberalism, for example the inevitable competition for power that exists between states and the idea of an anarchical society where there is no higher authority in global politics above nation-state level.
>
> ### Kenneth Waltz, *Theory of International Politics* (1979)
>
> Waltz was a defensive realist thinker. Bipolarity, where two major powers are competing for power, is more stable than multipolarity, where many rival powers are competing with each other (see page 260). Two major powers can negotiate their way to stability more easily than many powers. The international system is in a state of anarchy, with no central authority above nation-state level.
>
> ### Hedley Bull, *The Anarchical Society* (1977)
>
> Bull identified the idea of an **anarchical society** within which a **society of states** operates in spite of this anarchy. A society of states is formed when states realise that they have common interests and values and will benefit from working together. When this happens, states begin to interact and impact on each others' decisions, so 'they behave — at least in some measure — as parts of a whole'.
>
> ### Hans Morgenthau, *Politics Among Nations* (1948)
>
> Morgenthau is a classical realist thinker. Political man is a naturally selfish creature and will always try to dominate and have power over others. Moral considerations in global politics are less important than the national interest.
>
> ### John Mearsheimer, *The Tragedy of Great Power Politics* (2001)
>
> Mearsheimer is an offensive realist thinker. He explained that conflict and competition for power between the great world powers will continue. States are trying to secure hegemony, meaning they want to dominate all other states within a region.

Key terms

Anarchical society The term used by Hedley Bull in his 1977 book of the same name. It is the idea that global politics is in a state of disorder because there is no higher authority than nation-states with the power to control global politics.

Society of states Global politics is a system in which states attempt to establish order by forming alliances, creating international institutions and laws.

Anarchical world order in action

The Iraq War, 2003

Believing that Iraq still owned, and was prepared to use, weapons of mass destruction (WMD), the USA and a limited number of allies, including the UK, invaded the country in March 2003. The stated objective was to disarm Iraq and its leader, Saddam Hussein, of these weapons.

However, the USA launched military action without a clear UNSC Resolution. In fact, the last resolution before the invasion (UNSC Resolution 1441) offered Iraq 'a final opportunity to comply with its disarmament obligations', and Russia and France did not support US invasion plans and urged UN weapons inspectors (who reported that Iraq was cooperating with inspections) to be given more time for assessments.

A combination of a ground assault and air strikes brought Saddam Hussein's regime to an end within days. Saddam fled, but was later captured and tried by an Iraqi Special Tribunal. He was executed on 30 September 2006. After the invasion, UN weapons inspectors concluded that there were no WMDs in Iraq.

In March 2003, US soldiers invaded Iraq during the 'War on Terror'

The 2003 Iraq War is an example of realism in US and UK foreign policy because of the following.

- **The USA was prepared to 'go it alone', without international support:** military action was launched without clear UNSC approval or wider international agreement and support. The coalition consisted of the USA as the lead player, and military forces from Australia, Poland and the UK.
- **The war's legality was highly questionable:** the UK's Chilcot Inquiry into the Iraq War concluded in 2016 that the case for war was 'unjustified' and that Saddam's regime posed 'no imminent threat'. The UN secretary-general at the time, Kofi Annan, said in 2004 that the invasion did not conform to the laws of the UN's founding Charter and was, 'from our point of view, illegal'.
- **The USA and its allies were acting in what they perceived, and argued, was their national interest:** the USA saw complying with international law as an obstacle to successfully carrying out action it believed to be in its national interest. Prime Minister Tony Blair said that Iraq represented 'a current and serious threat to the UK national interest' because the UK government believed that WMDs were a threat to the middle east region.

However, many realist thinkers opposed the Iraq War. For example, US political scientist John Mearsheimer believed that it was not in the USA's national interest to invade.

Chinese activity in the South China Sea

There has long been disagreement between the nation-states in the South China Sea region — including Brunei, China, Malaysia, the Philippines, Taiwan and Vietnam — over territorial waters (see Figure 1.1). The region is of strategic value because it is thought to contain valuable natural resources, including oil and gas. It is also a key shipping route.

In recent years, China has attempted to expand its territorial waters in the region by building islands and increasing naval patrols. At the same time, it has been investing in building up and modernising its naval forces, including developing new and improved aircraft carriers.

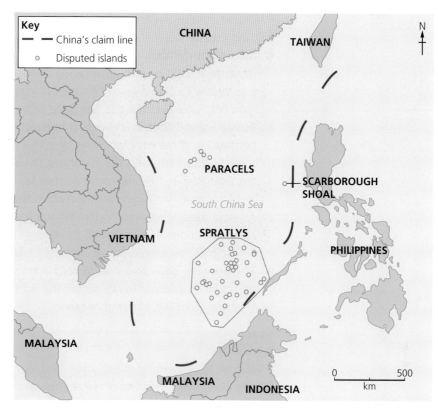

Figure 1.1 Disputed territories in the South China Sea

In response, the US Navy has carried out so-called Freedom of Navigation patrols in what it considers to be international waters, but which China claims as its own territorial waters. As China's naval power increases, the risk of a clash between these two powerful nation-states in the South China Sea increases. In 2013, a UN tribunal ruled that China was not complying with the relevant international law, the UN Convention on the Laws of the Sea. China called the ruling 'a piece of paper that is destined to come to naught'.

The USA has also increased its diplomatic and military influence in Asia. President Barack Obama's administration announced a significant 'pivot to Asia', indicating that it did not want to give the impression that US influence in the Pacific would be reduced. The USA continues to maintain a significant military presence in the Asia-Pacific region. Both China's and the USA's activities in the South China Sea are an example of powerful states wishing to maintain power and influence within a key strategic region.

The Russian annexation of Crimea, 2014

In 2014, Russian-backed militia entered the Crimea region in Ukraine and, within months, Crimea was declared independent. Ukraine, formerly part of the Soviet Union, has long been torn between the West (potentially to join the EU) and the East (Russia offered Ukraine very favourable gas supplies and, since the break-up of the Soviet Union, an agreement with Ukraine allowed Russia to continue to operate from the Sevastopol port in Crimea's Black Sea region, Russia's only warm-water port).

Russia did not invade Ukraine with conventional military forces, but reports suggested the presence of Special Forces wearing uniforms without any identifying insignia (see page 85). Pro-Russian rebel groups then became active in the predominantly ethnically Russian eastern regions of Ukraine, some with Russian government backing.

Russia's actions in Crimea are an example of realist foreign policy for the following reasons.

- **Russia put military forces into Ukraine unilaterally:** it did not discuss the move with IGOs or gain justification through international law. The UNSC was unable to pass a resolution condemning Russia because, as a permanent member, Russia vetoed this (see page 86).
- **Russia argued that it was acting in its national interest:** from a Russian perspective, there were worrying signs that Ukraine might be tilting decisively towards closer ties with the West and, in particular, the EU. Since the end of the Cold War in 1991, ten other former Soviet states, including Estonia, Latvia and Lithuania, had allied themselves and their territories with the North Atlantic Treaty Organization (NATO, see page 119), the pro-Western military alliance founded as a means of countering the military might of the Soviet Union. Moscow judged this as a threat to its national interest.
- **The primary objective was to regain territorial control of Crimea:** in particular, Russia wanted to secure the warm-water port of Sevastopol, a key strategic objective of the annexation.

Activity

Research other events in global politics and examine how they can be explained using the theories and ideas of realism. You could start with the following examples:

- the Syrian civil war (2011–)
- War in Afghanistan (2001–14)
- the UK's decision to leave the EU, known as 'Brexit' (2016)

Distinguish between

Realism and liberalism: human nature

Realism

- Human nature is naturally selfish and egoist and therefore states are interested in their own (national) interests. Human nature is fixed and driven, and cannot be changed, so states too are motivated by a desire to dominate and have power over others.
- States are also motivated by a need to survive, especially in a global 'self-help' system where there is no guarantee that any other state or actor in global politics will help them.

Liberalism

- Liberals believe in a more optimistic vision of human nature than realists. Human nature is not fixed and states can therefore improve and develop.
- Humans, and therefore states, are committed to individual liberty and freedom (for example, human rights).
- Humans, and therefore states, prefer to work in partnership with others and look for opportunities to do so. International cooperation, through IGOs, is therefore possible and desirable.
- It is possible to impose order on humans and states from above, for example through a rules-based system of international law.
- Conflict is a feature of global politics but must always be avoided and exist only as a last resort.

Synoptic links

In Component 2, the multiculturalism option examines how multiculturalist thinkers, such as Charles Taylor, celebrate diversity and endorse the concept of meaningful global citizenship. Such an inclusive approach to global politics challenges the realist belief that global politics is determined by state egoism.

Case study

Realist language in the 'Leave' campaign (2016)

In June 2016, the UK held a referendum on the country's continued membership of the EU. The question on the ballot paper was 'Should the UK remain a member of the European Union or leave the European Union?'

During the morning of Friday 26 June, it was announced that 51.89% of UK voters had voted to 'Leave' and 48.11% to 'Remain'. The UK prime minister, David Cameron, who had called the referendum and campaigned for the UK to remain in the EU, resigned, stating that 'the British people have voted to leave the European Union, and their will must be respected'.

The 'Leave' campaign involved prominent Conservative, Labour and United Kingdom Independence Party (UKIP) figureheads, including Boris Johnson, Michael Gove and Nigel Farage. The language, slogans and key messages of the 'Leave' campaign can all be analysed for realist themes (see Table 1.2). This is an example of theory being used for explanatory purposes — in other words, attempting to explain why something happened in the way that it did.

Table 1.2 Realist language in 'Leave' campaign slogans

Slogan	Realist message
'Vote Leave, Take Back Control'	The central slogan of the 'Leave' campaign emphasised the view that leaving the EU would free the UK from being forced to comply with EU laws.
'While we're in the EU, we can't make trade deals on our own'	The 'Leave' campaign argued that EU membership prevented the UK from negotiating its own trade deals with other key allies, such as the USA.
'EU law overrides UK law'	The 'Leave' campaign argued that the EU has the power to make its own laws and force the UK to adopt these laws (and so bypass sovereignty).
'Vote leave... and we can control immigration and have a fairer system where we welcome people to the UK based on the skills they have rather than the passport they hold'	The 'Leave' campaign argued that because every EU citizen has the right to live and work anywhere in the EU (the principle of 'freedom of movement'), the UK was no longer able to prioritise admitting foreign workers based on their skills.

Source: 'Vote Leave, Take Back Control' campaign leaflet, June 2016

Questions

1 Were the realist arguments of the 'Leave' campaign justifiable?
2 What arguments would liberals use to counter the 'Leave' campaign claims (see page 295)?

International anarchy and its implications

The concept of a world that is in a state of anarchy is worth clarifying. The literal meaning of anarchy is that there is a lack of authority. Anarchy is frequently associated with the idea of conflict or chaotic social unrest, for example riots and lawlessness. In global politics, the realist viewpoint of anarchy may mean both:

- a simple lack of authority, and
- the potential for conflict between states in the absence of a higher authority above states.

An analogy frequently used to explain realism and the idea of **international anarchy** is John Dalton's Billiard Ball Model (see Figure 1.2). The billiard balls in the game represent nation-states. The billiard balls' hard shells represent the national sovereignty of individual states. If one billiard ball hits the others, they will spread out across the table. The billiard balls will remain separate entities and will not merge together.

It is important to note that the Billiard Ball Model is a *way of explaining realism* and is not a *theory in its own right*. Therefore, it is better to refer to the theory as 'realism', rather than the Billiard Ball Model, in an exam situation.

Key term

International anarchy
The notion that states are self-contained units that frequently clash with each other, in a world system where there is no authority that is as legitimate, powerful or authoritative as nation-states.

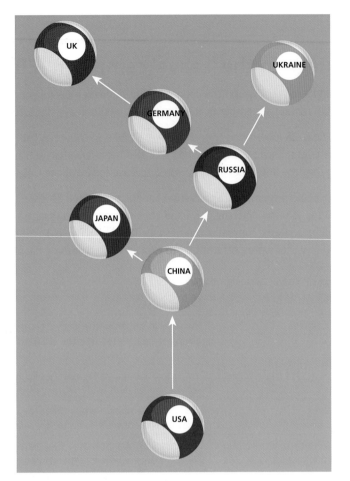

Figure 1.2 The Billiard Ball Model

Consequences of international anarchy

In the eyes of realists, international anarchy leads to the following.

- IGOs such as the EU and the UN will be limited in their impact and effectiveness. This is because states determine the success or failure of these international efforts. States have created IGOs, and IGOs ultimately serve state interests. (When they no longer do this, they collapse — such as the League of Nations — or states leave, as seen in the UK's decision to leave the EU.)

- States will also want to prevent IGOs from making decisions that are not in their national interest. This is often most clearly seen in the veto powers that the five UNSC permanent members (China, France, Russia, the UK and the USA) wield, which frequently prevent coordinated action on matters ranging from the Israel and Palestine conflict to the Syrian civil war (see page 101).

- Unlike national law, rules in global politics — known as international law — do not always apply. In an anarchical world system, no international body can force states to sign up to international law. Customary international law, which in theory applies to states regardless of whether or not they have signed and ratified a law, does exist for abuses of humanitarian law. The Geneva Conventions for example, are customary international law and apply to all states, but the decision to enforce the law is ultimately the political decision of international bodies, such as the UN, or individual, especially powerful states.

- International courts may be ignored, or may not have decisive powers to investigate at all. The International Criminal Court (ICC, see page 180) has limited powers to hold states to account for the most serious crimes against humanity. But, in reality, states that have not fully agreed to the ICC's founding Rome Statute (see page 180) are able to escape justice, as there is no authoritative global force to bring states and those responsible for international crimes before the court. The European Court of Human Rights (ECtHR, see page 184) experiences similar difficulties.

Given that global politics lacks a single commanding authority, Hedley Bull suggested that the world order was built on a society of states. Within this otherwise orderless society, states attempt to create the best and safest order they can. They form IGOs, which sometimes solve problems but other times do not. They attempt to make international laws, which are sometimes observed, other times not.

Synoptic links

In Component 1, the concept of liberalism is addressed. According to John Rawls, a liberal world order must have moral foundations and therefore depends upon the shunning of illegitimate 'outlaw states' that do not conform to universally accepted principles of global cooperation.

Distinguish between

Anarchical society and a society of states

Anarchical society
- An anarchical society is a state of global politics without an ordering authority above nation-state level.
- The most powerful actors are states. No other actor can compel states to do anything against their will. In this sense, the world is anarchical.

A society of states
- Global politics lacks any central authority. States are, therefore, the most authoritative bodies.
- States use their authority to negotiate the best possible global society and world order that they can. These attempts have their successes and failures, but they are the only means of avoiding chaotic and disorderly global politics.

Realism and the superiority of states

Realists believe that states are the most important actors in global politics, and that they are more powerful and significant than other actors, such as IGOs, NGOs and MNCs.

- **IGOs only exist because states created them:** this further reflects the power of states. States have the ultimate power to decide to join or leave IGOs. It is rare, but not unprecedented, for states to decide to leave IGOs. The most obvious example is the UK deciding to trigger Article 50 of the Treaty of Lisbon, enabling it to leave the EU. In 1966, France withdrew its troops from NATO (but remained a member state of NATO) in protest against perceived US dominance of the alliance. More recently, the African Union (AU) states threatened to withdraw from the ICC (see page 181) in protest at a perceived bias against African states in the courts' investigations and judgments. States are, therefore, the fundamental building blocks of IGOs.

- **IGOs succeed or fail based on member-state actions:** the success or failure of IGOs is down to the decisions and agreement of their member states on matters large and small. Most IGOs are intergovernmental forums in which state governments conduct and negotiate business. When a UNSC Resolution is passed on matters of international peace and security, this is because states have negotiated the text between them, made amendments and then a majority of states has agreed to it. Equally, when the UNSC fails to agree a resolution, this is because a majority of states has not agreed to it. Criticism of the UN for 'failing to act' — for example, in the Syrian conflict — may be considered unfair. The UN is only able to act when a majority of its member states agrees to a particular course of action.
- **States often act outside IGOs:** states often make agreements with each other outside IGOs, by negotiating treaties with each other. States have complete freedom to agree to or opt out of these treaties.
- **Free trade only exists because states have agreed to it:** free trade could not exist without states' consent. As with IGOs, states are the 'building blocks' (see page 305) of the global system of international trade. States have the power to create protectionist laws that could make trade more difficult, for example by raising national taxes on foreign imported goods. States also have the power to abolish or reduce the amount of laws, making trade easier, for example by granting tariff-free access to another state that wishes to export to the other. States have the power to enter into free-trade agreements with groups of countries (such as in the EU and the Trans-Pacific Partnership (TPP)) or to negotiate individual trade agreements with individual states (for example, China has negotiated specific bilateral trade agreements with other states in the region, including Australia and Pakistan). As part of the process of leaving the EU, the UK will need to negotiate new trade agreements with many other states, since its previous agreements were based on its being a member of the EU bloc.
- **States still have the power to act unilaterally, regardless of IGOs or treaties:** for example, Russian action in the Crimea (2014) and UK and US action in Iraq (2003) went ahead without clear UNSC mandates. These actions show the overwhelming power of nation-states to act alone. When states do this frequently, it is often called isolationism.

Realism and the inevitability of conflict

Realists believe that conflict is inevitable and is the most natural, or usual, state of affairs in global politics. This is because they believe the following:
- States are likely to try to maximise their power and influence, resorting to, or provoking, conflict if necessary.
- States are inherently selfish and are likely to promote their own national interest, even if that means resorting to conflict.
- The world system is anarchical, so there is no authority capable of preventing conflict unless states judge that conflict is not in their interests. For example, international efforts through the UN and Geneva peace talks failed to restrain the various actors from pursuing their perceived interests during the Syrian conflict.
- States put their own security at risk and make conflict more likely when they build up their own military defences to counter a perceived threat. This in turn encourages the opposing state to increase its own security or military infrastructure. This is known as the 'security dilemma'.

Distinguish between

Realism and liberalism: order, security and the likelihood of conflict

Realism

- Conflict is an unavoidable feature of global politics.
- Conflict is sometimes necessary, both to defend vital national interests and to increase a state's power and influence.
- Defending internal security and stability is crucial. This is best done through well-defended borders, and clear and enforced laws.
- Every state is potentially a threat to other states.

Liberalism

- Conflict is avoidable and efforts should be made to prevent and reduce conflict.
- IGOs, such as the UN, offer a forum for conflict resolution.
- States being bound together in deep economic cooperation reduces the likelihood of them fighting each other. The EU is a good example of economic cooperation leading to limited conflict (for this it was awarded the Nobel Peace Prize in 2012).

Synoptic links

In Component 2, the feminism option examines the way in which power has, historically, been expressed in a patriarchal fashion. Male domination of the state is exploitative, undermining the potential for cooperation. The masculine ideal of power and dominance therefore undermines the core collectivist principle of global liberalism.

The security dilemma

According to defensive realism, all states want to protect themselves against threats from other states and, increasingly, non-state actors. States may:

- decide to invest in their military power, by increasing the number of troops, warships or aircraft that they are able to deploy
- keep or acquire nuclear weapons (for example Iran, North Korea). Others may want to acquire new technology to gain a strategic advantage, such as missile-firing drones.

However, other states may see this military build-up as a threat and respond by building up their own military resources. What was intended perhaps as a defensive strategy may even provoke other states to respond with aggression. It will be difficult for other states to trust the intentions of states in building up their military resources. This can perhaps best be seen in the tensions between Russia and those former Soviet states that have now joined NATO. These states have calculated that their security interests are best served by joining a US-backed collective security alliance. NATO has required these states, such as Estonia and Latvia, to increase their military spending because it is fairer if all NATO members make an equal contribution to the collective military alliance rather than states simply benefiting from the military strength and resources of the richest and most powerful NATO member states.

It is possible to identify the security dilemma in today's global politics in the middle east. Saudi Arabia and Iran are the region's major powers, and each represents key sects within the religion of Islam (Saudi Arabia is the major Sunni power, Iran is the major Shia power). Both compete for power in the region and continue to challenge each other.

Case study

NATO and Russia tensions

In 2015, President Vladimir Putin approved a new Russian National Security Strategy. The strategy declared that NATO's enlargement, in terms of member states, meant that the alliance was getting closer to Russia's borders and now represented an 'external threat'. It also stated that the build-up of NATO forces in countries bordering the Russian Federation was not consistent with international law and that Russia's foreign policy had triggered a 'counter-action' from the USA and its allies.

With the end of the Cold War in 1991, it might have been expected that relations between Russia and the NATO member states would ease. During the immediate aftermath of the Cold War, with Russia's territory much decreased and its power significantly

Russian president Vladimir Putin

weakened, NATO expanded to include ten former Warsaw Pact (the Moscow-led military alliance during the Cold War) or Soviet states. Some analysts suggest that Western powers missed an opportunity to reassure Russia and to try to influence it to seek greater partnership with its European neighbours. Instead, the conclusion is that NATO and the West decided to expand their power and influence when Russia was at its weakest.

From a Russian perspective, NATO's military build-up is the security dilemma in action. As Russia rebuilt after its defeat in the Cold War, and attempted to regain its power and influence in global politics, so it has increased its military power and influence in its immediate neighbourhood. The most significant and destabilising demonstration of this came in 2014, with the annexation of Crimea from Ukraine. Russia also intervened decisively in the Syrian conflict (to which the USA and its allies were unwilling to commit), when it backed President Bashar al-Assad with its air power from the autumn of 2015.

The security dilemma is perhaps most obvious in the actions and reactions of states of similar potential power as they try to match each other. Russia feels that it is in the country's national interest to match NATO's military power on its Western borders.

Interestingly, US president Donald Trump has been criticised for potentially weakening NATO's power and placing the future of the alliance in doubt. Trump said during his election campaign that NATO was 'obsolete' and that member states could no longer be guaranteed safety under the US security umbrella, and that they would need to pay their fair share (2% of their GDP) towards the alliance's defence costs. Critics say that this risks weakening the alliance at a time when Russia is demonstrating increasing willingness to challenge NATO.

Balance of power

Given that a key goal of realists is to protect their own security from rival state attacks, it is no surprise that realists are preoccupied with how power is distributed in the global system. Is there one state that is much more powerful than all the others (a unipolar system, see page 265)? Are there lots of states and actors competing for power (a multipolar system, see page 271)? Or are there only two major powers, which are roughly equal to each other, with no other potential rivals (a bipolar system, see page 260)?

The best guarantee of security for some realists is the first of these scenarios — to dominate all other potential rivals in a unipolar system. The USA experienced this to some degree in the immediate aftermath of the fall of the Soviet Union in 1991. Other realist viewpoints believe that a balance of power in a bipolar world order is better for security.

If a unipolar system is not possible, because another rival state is also powerful, then realists believe that the most stable outcome is for the powerful states to roughly match each other's power. In this scenario, realists believe that the states will balance each other out. Neither will want to risk attacking or challenging the other, because they would run the risk of retaliation by a state with similarly threatening military resources to its own. This could lead to the following:

- States may try to balance power by trying to match the military and economic resources of their rival. There may be an arms race, with both states trying to acquire similar amounts of weapons or types of technology.
- Smaller states may try to join alliances with more powerful states or other smaller states.

We can contrast this aspect of realism with the security dilemma (see page 15), where some liberals believe that when states try to match each other in terms of their military power, they can actually risk provoking the other state by appearing to represent more of a threat.

The most obvious example of a balance of power in global politics was between the USA (including its NATO allies) and the Soviet Union during the Cold War. With the knowledge that both were equally matched and that a nuclear weapons attack would only result in deadly retaliation, the two states engaged in a nuclear weapons arms race. This concept of mutually assured destruction (MAD) successfully ensured that there was no nuclear confrontation between the USA and Soviet Union during this period. Neither did the two rivals fight each other on the battlefield — both instead engaged in proxy wars using other actors to fight each other (for example, the USA arming the Mujihadeen in Afghanistan to fight the Soviet Union, without actually deploying troops of its own).

Since the terror attacks of 9/11 in the USA, a more multipolar global order has emerged, with many states and non-state actors, such as al-Qaeda, challenging each other for power. Therefore, power is currently imbalanced in global politics (see Box 1.2).

Box 1.2

Russia and the USA: a balance of power?

Table 1.3 compares the balance of power between Russia and the USA by examining types of power and tactics in response to recent global crises.

Table 1.3 Russia vs the USA: a balance of power?

	Russia	USA
Military power	Weaker than the USA in terms of troop numbers and naval and air power. One aircraft carrier (which is unreliable and needed to be escorted through the English Channel with a tug on stand-by).	Technologically more advanced than Russia. Drone technology highly effective, as proved in Afghanistan, Iraq, Pakistan and Syria in degrading al-Qaeda.
Nuclear warheads	Estimated at 7,300 (2016).	Estimated at 6,970 (2016).
Willingness to use military power	President Putin appears to have made a strategic decision to replace the USA as the major global power willing to use its military on the international stage. Putin is prepared to use 'boots on the ground', drone and naval power.	Under the Obama administration, there was great reluctance in the USA to use military power. There was little support for new military action in Congress or among the general public. The USA shied away from military action in Syria and very reluctantly agreed to air strikes in Libya.
Cyber power	The CIA accused Russia of interfering in the 2016 US presidential elections when it leaked embarrassing Democratic Party emails. Germany has also accused Russia of using offensive cyber power. Russia denies the allegations.	There is little evidence in the public domain of the USA employing offensive cyber power. However, the USA has used defensive cyber power to protect key cyber interests.
Economic power	The Russian economy is very weak. Economic sanctions have caused significant damage. Falling oil prices hit Russia's significant oil export industry hard.	The US economy has recovered from the global financial crisis of 2008–9. It is, however, losing ground, though its nearest rival, China, is yet to overtake it.
Tactics	Russia has favoured unilateral action above seeking approval from the UN for action in Syria and has outright breached international law in its incursion into Crimea.	The Obama administration was highly cautious in using military resources. Drone strikes, rather than boots on the ground, were the weapon of choice. On 13 April 2017, President Trump unleashed the Mother Of All Bombs (MOAB) for the first time in combat against so-called Islamic State in Afghanistan. The Trump administration also launched air strikes against the Assad regime in 2017 in response to alleged chemical weapon attacks.
Conclusion	Russia's power is derived from its overwhelming willingness to use its otherwise much weaker resources. It has decisively increased its use of military power in spaces ceded by Western powers (notably Syria). There are signs that Russia is increasingly willing to use cyber power offensively.	Under Obama, the USA remained the predominant military power in terms of resources, but it was unwilling to use them. Instead, it resorted to economic sanctions, rather than military power, to stem Russian aggression. Even these economic sanctions were restrained. The USA uses cyber power predominantly defensively.

Activity

Using the information provided in this chapter and Box 1.2, what evidence is there that there is a balance of power between Russia and the USA? Base your assessment on:
- their respective military resources and their willingness to use them
- the effectiveness of their use of military power
- their respective responses to demonstrations of power

How is this balance of power consistent with a multipolar order in today's global politics?

Distinguish between

Realism and liberalism: power

Realism

- Powerful states will always be able to overcome weaker states.
- Threats and the use of force are particularly important types of hard power (see page 255) to possess and maximise, especially in a self-help system where no other actor can be guaranteed to protect a state's security.
- The primary goal and motivation of states is to increase their power.
- When power is shared equally between states it can create stability (the balance of power, see page 17).
- States are aware of the limits of soft power (see page 255), though they may use smart power (see page 255), by combining hard and soft power to achieve their intended outcomes.

Liberalism

- The use of power, particularly military, can often be counterproductive (the security dilemma, see page 15).
- Military power is not the only form of significant power. Economic power and free-trade links can enable states to become richer, and also more stable and secure. As states become more economically interdependent, the risk of conflict decreases. In this way, economic interdependence makes the entire global system more stable and peaceful.
- Soft power and smart power are important means by which states can achieve their intended outcomes. They should be the first option, with hard power used only as a last resort.

Activity

Spend some time thinking about the realist viewpoint on global politics.
1 Do you agree that conflict between states is an inevitable, even natural, state of affairs?
2 To what extent was President George W. Bush a realist president?
3 Do all states try to become as powerful and influential as possible, or does this only apply to states that are already powerful?

Liberalism and a cooperative world order

Liberalism is governed principally by the belief that states can, and should, work together, and that international agreements, laws and institutions are both helpful and possible. The liberal viewpoint includes the following:

- States are not the only actors in global politics — a wider range of non-state actors has a positive role to play, including IGOs and NGOs. They can help states become aware of different viewpoints and policy choices, adding to a richness of ideas and debate.
- International law is possible and desirable. Global politics and world order should be based in clearly agreed international rules. These can help to hold states accountable for their actions and ensure that all states conform to basic standards. For example, the Universal Declaration of Human Rights (UDHR) sets out basic principles of human rights that all states should respect.
- A state's primary aim should not merely be to become more powerful, particularly not at the expense of other states. Liberals reject the idea of a zero-sum game, where global politics is a question of one state winning and another losing.
- On the contrary, there is mutual benefit in states cooperating and working together on matters such as security, trade and development. IGOs, such as the EU and the UN, offer clear rules and forums for achieving this.

- Democracy plays a key role in keeping states safe and peaceful. Democratic states are less likely to fight each other.
- International trade binds states together in common interests, making them more dependent on each other and reducing the likelihood of conflict.

See Box 1.3 for more theories of key liberal thinkers.

Box 1.3

Important liberal thinkers

The following texts from key liberal thinkers each question some of realism's assumptions, for example hegemony (Keohane), history (Fukuyama) and the nation-state (Ohmae).

Robert Keohane, *After Hegemony* (2005)

Keohane was one of the proponents of the idea of complex interdependence, which argues that states and their individual fortunes are inextricably linked. He challenges the idea that realists will always reject international cooperation because of their preference for protecting their national interest, arguing that it is more rational and indeed increasingly in states' national interests to find more ways of cooperating with each other. Keohane agrees that states are inherently egoistical. But international law and institutions that try to persuade and enable states to reach shared solutions, rather than enforce decisions on states, can still be successful.

Francis Fukuyama, *The End of History and the Last Man* (1992)

Fukuyama argues that, with the end of the Cold War and the defeat of the Communist Soviet Union, liberal democracy would become the undisputed form of human government, which he calls the 'endpoint of mankind's ideological development'.

Kenichi Ohmae, *The End of the Nation State* (1995)

Globalisation has brought about a deep and revolutionary set of economic, cultural, technological and political shifts that have dramatic implications for state sovereignty. Ohmae argues that states are losing their economic power and are no longer the main participants in the global economy.

Case study

Liberal language in Hillary Clinton's election speeches (2016)

During the 2016 US presidential election race, former US secretary of state (the US Cabinet's equivalent of the UK's foreign secretary) Hillary Clinton tried to present an image of competence and experience in foreign policy, in comparison with her election rival, Donald Trump. Much of the language she used implied that her foreign policy as president would be liberal in its nature, and that she would retain partnerships with IGOs and defend the international deal struck with Iran to limit its nuclear weapons programme.

Clinton argued that nation-states working together to protect each other's national security through a collective military alliance such as NATO (see page 119) was in the US national interest:

> NATO... is one of the best investments America has ever made... from the Balkans to Afghanistan and beyond, NATO allies have fought alongside the United States, sharing the burdens and the sacrifices.

Clinton also argued that a combination of military power, economic sanctions and diplomatic negotiation (often known as 'smart power', see page 255) had paid off in successfully persuading Iran to halt its nuclear weapons programme:

> We brought Iran to the negotiating table. We began talks. And eventually, we reached an agreement that should block every path for Iran to get a nuclear weapon.

Finally, Clinton emphasised the importance of diplomacy and negotiation in resolving conflict, and cautioned against conflicts that might become lengthier and more costly. She argued that investing in development and diplomacy would help tackle problems at their source:

We need to embrace all the tools of American power, especially diplomacy and development, to be on the frontlines solving problems before they threaten us at home.

Diplomacy is often the only way to avoid a conflict that could end up exacting a much greater cost. It takes patience, persistence and an eye on the long game — but it's worth it.

Source: Speech given by Democratic presidential candidate Hillary Clinton, San Diego, California, 2 June 2016

Liberalism, complex interdependence and globalisation

This is the idea that states and their fortunes are inextricably linked. Globalisation is seen as a key factor in increasing states' links to and dependence on each other.

Globalisation can be thought of as increased links between and dependence on states and all other non-state actors in global politics. It has primarily occurred due to improved communications links and technology. Liberals are convinced that globalisation is a reality that needs to be managed through increased cooperation. They believe that greater interconnectedness and cooperation is the direction of travel for global politics.

- **Economic:** much-improved communication and transportation have increased trade between states. There is greater economic interconnectedness because more states are trading with each other as it becomes easier to do so. International economic organisations, such as the WTO (see page 141), have played their part in this expansion of new trade agreements. Developed economies have invested heavily in many developing economies.
- **Political:** political decision making has become increasingly globalised, through the increase in international and regional governmental organisations. The increasing number of political challenges that require a collective response has also increased, including climate change, organised crime, health pandemics (such as the 2015 Ebola crisis) and global terrorism. The number of international and regional political institutions managing shared interests has increased, as has their membership.
- **Social:** communities that were previously relatively self-contained have become increasingly connected in terms of shared media and culture. Increased global immigration has created much more diverse societies, although some argue that this has led to an erosion of national culture. It has also enabled ideas to travel quickly across borders. For example, the speed with which the Arab Uprisings spread from Tunisia to Egypt and other middle eastern and north African states has been attributed to the power of social media (such as Facebook and Twitter) and satellite news channels (such as Al Jazeera).

Key term

Complex interdependence The idea that states and their fortunes are inextricably linked.

An analogy often used to explain **complex interdependence** and liberalism is that of a cobweb. In contrast to Dalton's Billiard Ball Model (see page 11), the Cobweb Model represents the links between states (see Figure 1.3). If one strand breaks, the cobweb may begin to disintegrate. This demonstrates the extent to which states are dependent and rely on each other.

Figure 1.3 The Cobweb Model

Just as with the Billiard Ball Model, it is important to note that the Cobweb Model is a *way of explaining liberalism and complex interdependence*, rather than it being a *theory in its own right*. Therefore, it is better to refer to the theory as 'liberalism', rather than the Cobweb Model, in an exam situation.

Complex interdependence and the global financial crisis

In 2008–9, a house price crash sparked a lending crisis in US banks, which spread around the world. The effects were felt in the global banking system, as banks became nervous about taking on risk and stopped lending to each other. In some cases, customers began withdrawing their savings, putting banks under even greater pressure. It led to what has been described as the worst global financial crisis since the Great Depression in the 1930s.

Economic growth slowed across the world and unemployment rose. North America and Europe were particularly severely affected. Economic growth in China slowed. A crisis was sparked in the Eurozone single currency area, as several indebted economies, notably Greece, were unable to borrow from international markets and required other Eurozone member states and the European Central Bank (ECB, see page 315) to bail them out.

The financial crisis fallout dominated UK prime minister Gordon Brown's time in office. As part of international efforts to deal with an international crisis, in April 2009 Brown hosted a Group of Twenty (G20, see page 147) summit in London. The meeting resulted in national governments and the IMF agreeing a financial stimulus to inject much-needed funds into the international banking system. While facing domestic problems of a different nature, Brown led the international summit effectively. Humiliatingly, he later misspoke in the House of Commons, claiming that 'we saved the world...', much to the mockery of MPs.

In April 2009, Gordon Brown hosted a G20 summit in London, as part of international efforts to deal with the global financial crisis

The crisis raised questions of whether or not the international financial system needed tighter regulation and if the IMF could have done more to both prevent and react to the crisis (see Chapter 4).

Distinguish between

Realism and liberalism: states and sovereignty

Realism
- States remain the primary and most powerful actors in global politics.
- Sovereignty is an absolute concept — it should not be violated, limited or given away, except...
- ...another state's sovereignty may be infringed upon if one's own national interest requires it. For example, the USA's unauthorised 2011 operation to assassinate Osama bin Laden was argued as a justifiable incursion into Pakistan's sovereign territory.
- States should be wary of giving up too much sovereignty to IGOs. Powers of veto are a useful means of protecting one's national interests while retaining one's ability to use the IGO as a forum for influencing other states towards one's own desired outcomes.

Liberalism
- States are important actors in global politics but they work within a complex web of interdependence and with other non-state actors, such as IGOs and NGOs.
- Sovereignty exists to be used to a state's advantage — this may mean pooling sovereignty with other states in an IGO, such as the EU.
- Another state's sovereignty may be infringed if it is necessary to uphold the values and interests of the international community, for example under the doctrine of the UN Responsibility to Protect (R2P, see page 195), if human rights abuses are taking place.

Constraints on conflict

Unlike realists, who believe that global politics is naturally prone to conflict, liberals — notably the philosopher Immanuel Kant — identify three strands of liberalism that act as constraints on conflict.

1   **Democracy:** some analysts note that conflict between democratic states is very rare and that democracy acts as an important restraint on states fighting each other. Certainly, governments in democratic states are more accountable to their citizens than in undemocratic states. Usually governments of democratic states have to seek the permission of their national legislature to engage in military action. For example, in 2013 the UK Parliament voted against military action against the Assad regime's chemical weapons programme in Syria. (It has become increasingly common — but not compulsory — for the UK Parliament to be consulted before UK armed forces are committed to military action. The refusal of the UK Parliament to support military action was considered to be a factor in the Obama administration later deciding not to put possible military action in Syria to a vote in Congress.) Leaders and governments in democratic states also have to bear in mind that military action may be unpopular (particularly if there are large numbers of casualties) and that they may be voted out in elections if this is the case. This is not a concern that leaders of undemocratic states necessarily need to worry about.

2   **IGOs:** liberals believe that IGOs act as a restraint on conflict because they are a means of peaceful dispute resolution between states. While IGOs do not have full authority over nation-states (and states can ignore them or opt out, or they can be locked in gridlock on more complex problems), liberals believe they are the closest possible challenge to the dangerous notion of an anarchical system of global politics. They may not resolve every dispute, but they offer a forum to defuse some disputes altogether, reduce tensions in some and keep open the possibility of dialogue in others.

3   **Economic interdependence and trade:** liberals believe that the more states are trading with each other, the more they are dependent on each other and the more likely it is that conflict would be mutually harmful. Liberals also believe that free trade in a global system governed by rules has formalised and legitimised the global sharing of resources. Previously, states fought each other for territory and resources, but in modern times, widespread global free trade has offered a peaceful means for states to gain from each other's resources.

These three restraints on conflict are visualised through the Kantian Triangle (see Figure 1.4). Even before IGOs and free trade existed in the sense that we know them today, liberal philosopher Immanuel Kant identified that:

> republican constitutions [democratic states], commercial exchange [economic interdependence] and a system of international law would help foster peaceful relations between states.

The Kantian Triangle helps us to understand the relationship between the three core elements, and how each:

(a) helps to strengthen the others

(b) contributes towards the overall outcome of a more peaceful status quo

For example:

■   Membership of IGOs often helps to build democracy within states. The EU, for example, makes it a requirement for member states to meet certain

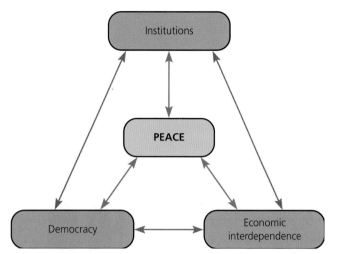

Source: Adapted from Russett, B. & Oneal, J. (2001) 'International Systems: Vicious Circles and Virtuous Circles', *Triangulating Peace*. Norton.

Figure 1.4 The Kantian Triangle

democratic criteria. Turkey has so far failed to be accepted into the EU, partly because of weaknesses in its democracy.

■ Democratic states offer a more stable base with which other states can trade. They are more transparent and are less prone to corruption, which is a factor that puts off potential foreign investors. Democratic states are more likely to be peaceful and more stable, making them more attractive to foreign investment.

■ Many IGOs have been founded to make economic interdependence easier. IGOs such as the EU and the ASEAN offer their members a framework within which they can trade with each other freely, based on a commonly agreed set of rules. One state can potentially open up more trade links more quickly with other states through joining a bloc of nations, rather than acting alone.

Debate

Does democracy contribute to peace?

Yes

■ Wars must be seen as legitimate, and governments that initiate conflict are held accountable for the legitimacy, success and failure of military conflicts they initiate.

■ Democratic governments need to win elections and are unlikely to enter into conflict if said conflict does not have domestic support.

■ Intra-state conflict, or civil war, is less common in states that are internally democratic. The rise in the number of democratic states has been accompanied by a fall in global conflict (both civil wars and inter-state conflicts).

No

■ During the 2003 Iraq War, two of the most well-respected democratic states (the USA with the backing of the UK, commonly known as 'the cradle of democracy') initiated wars that were later declared to have been illegal.

■ Both President George W. Bush (in 2004) and Prime Minister Tony Blair (in 2005) won elections despite signs of early difficulty in the Afghanistan and Iraq Wars, though both conflicts became significantly more difficult and unpopular after these elections.

■ A democratic decision to avoid conflict may not result in peace. Many suggest that the UK and the USA should have initiated military action against President Assad in 2013 and that failure to act also has consequences (specifically, the USA's failure to take action against Assad's use of chemical weapons, something that President Obama had called a 'red line').

■ No democracy is perfect, so some states that appear democratic may offer insufficient safeguards against conflict or poor decision-making. The UK Parliament voted to invade Iraq in 2003 because the government and the opposition agreed on the need for conflict.

President Barack Obama: a liberal president?

Within a year of becoming President of the United States, Barack Obama was awarded the Nobel Peace Prize, in recognition of his 'extraordinary efforts to strengthen international diplomacy and cooperation between peoples'. The quote includes two key features of liberalism, but how liberal a president did Obama turn out to be?

President Barack Obama's election campaign was focused on ending the USA's involvement in Afghanistan and Iraq, closing the controversial Guantánamo Bay detention centre for terrorist suspects and re-engaging with the middle east, the Muslim world and the UN.

Ending wars

Obama ended the wars in Afghanistan and Iraq, but was not able to declare decisive victory in either country. A troop surge in Afghanistan in the final year of the conflict failed — US forces withdrew in 2014, with the Taliban insurgency undefeated.

Drone strikes increase

The drone was the Obama administration's weapon of choice. Highly effective at 'degrading' al-Qaeda in the mountainous regions between Afghanistan and Pakistan,

Former US president Barack Obama

US drones have also been used in Iraq, Somalia, Syria and Yemen. They were considered to be a useful alternative to 'boots on the ground' in the wake of Obama's reluctance to deploy troops. Drone strikes have been particularly effective against non-state actors.

Libya

Obama reluctantly committed the USA to air strikes over Libya in order to prevent a humanitarian crisis when Libyan leader Colonel Muammar Gaddafi threatened to kill civilians rebelling against his regime. The US intervened with both UNSC approval and the support of the Arab League, in contrast to the conflict in Iraq. Once again, the aftermath of intervention proved problematic and longer-lasting peace elusive. A power vacuum and violent civil war developed, as the government in the capital, Tripoli, was unable to command authority across the country.

Syria

In 2013, Obama failed to uphold a self-declared 'red line' when President Assad's forces used chemical weapons against civilians. The USA did not respond with military force and instead struck a deal with Russia to disarm Assad of chemical weapons.

Iran nuclear deal

In striking a deal with Iran, in which devastating economic sanctions were lifted in return for Iran halting its nuclear ambitions, many hailed Obama's use of smart power (see page 255) and caution to prevent military confrontation. However, critics argue that the deal has upset the delicate balance of power between Iran and Saudi Arabia, and that Iran cannot be trusted to comply.

Closure of Guantánamo Bay terrorist detention centre

The camp in Cuba remains open, despite Obama calling it 'a sad chapter in American history'.

A detention centre in Guantánamo Bay, Cuba

Strategic withdrawal from the middle east

The Obama administration made very few attempts to resolve the Israel–Palestine problem. Israel continues to build settlements in areas from which the existing UNSC Resolution 242 requires Israel to withdraw.

Arab Uprisings

During the Arab Uprisings (2010–12), which affected several nation-states in the middle east and northern Africa, the Obama administration decided to side with the protesters (and popular opinion) and ditch US support for strong-men leaders such as Egypt's president Hosni Mubarak.

Little appetite to breach international law

The Obama administration showed little appetite to uphold international law. For example, it decided that there was no means by which the USA could prevent Russia from annexing Crimea in 2014.

Conclusion

Some analysts conclude that Obama managed the limits of US power. Others judge that Obama was unwilling to use US power abroad, and that he exhibited huge reluctance to start new wars (for example, he was indecisive over increasing troops numbers in a so-called surge against the Taliban in Afghanistan).

Activity

Using the information in the Case study, and your own knowledge and research, assess whether Barack Obama's presidency was liberal or realist.

Liberalism, the international community and liberal interventionism

While realists believe that states should only act when their national interest requires it, there is a strand of liberal thinking that believes states should act regardless of their national interest. The media and political leaders often employ the phrase 'international community' to describe a coordinated response to a crisis, often referring to what the international community believes or what it 'should do'. It is a notoriously vague expression, with no clear definition. Who is the 'international community'? Do those using this term have a defined group of states in mind?

For liberals, the idea of an 'international community' does exist as an aspiration to work towards. They believe states share interests, values and attitudes. For example, human rights apply to all human beings regardless of where they live in the world. Consequently, liberals believe that human rights are worth defending, since they are a globally shared value and interest. Therefore, if a state abuses basic human rights, the 'international community' should do something to prevent the abuse. Why? Because preventing human rights abuses is in the global interest — if human rights abuses go unchecked, the argument runs, the entire global system of human rights would be weakened.

Of course, realists disagree that there are shared global attitudes and values. They believe that attitudes, interests and values come primarily from states themselves and are not always aligned.

Tony Blair's Chicago speech

The idea of an international community with shared interests and values to be defended was underlined in a key speech given by former UK prime minister Tony Blair, in Chicago in 1999. The speech came after the successful NATO-led military intervention in Kosovo, in former Yugoslavia, where Serbian forces' expulsion of ethnic Albanians had prompted a humanitarian crisis. Blair argued that such an international community *did* exist, stating that 'just as within domestic politics, the notion of community — the belief that partnership and cooperation are essential to advance self-interest — needs to find an international echo'. Blair argued that national interest and international interest were increasingly difficult to separate. Military intervention in another state should not be decided purely on whether there was a threat from that state to the outside world, but on the basis of the nature of the threat to the state's own domestic population. Put simply, other states should intervene for humanitarian reasons, in order to prevent human suffering in its own right, rather than for narrow self-interest alone.

Synoptic links

In Component 1, socialism celebrates the principles of global fraternity and cooperation. According to socialist thinkers such as Karl Marx and Friedrich Engels, human beings are rational and gain more from working together, both domestically and globally, than from competing. This supports liberal attempts to establish a harmonious world order based upon mutual support and understanding.

The UN and the Responsibility to Protect

Around this time, the UN also gave its backing to the idea that states had a responsibility to intervene in other states in order to prevent human suffering. The failure of UN peacekeepers to prevent a genocide from taking place in the African state of Rwanda in 1994 prompted the UN's interest.

There was also agreement that the legitimacy of intervening in other states to protect lives needed to be made clearer. The Responsibility to Protect (R2P) doctrine, agreed by the UN World Summit in 2005, confirmed that states had a 'responsibility to protect' (see page 195) the populations of other states if they were suffering, or were likely to suffer, serious harm.

Military action would be justified by several core principles of liberalism:

- The purpose of military action was solely to protect civilians, rather than to pursue narrow self-interest.
- The state/s could only intervene once it/they had made every effort to resolve the situation through non-military means, such as diplomacy and negotiation.
- Intervention could only take place if a UNSC Resolution authorised it (thereby making the intervention legitimate in the eyes of international law).
- The military action must be proportionate, must be likely to succeed and must not make the situation worse.

Liberalism and the likelihood of global governance

Liberals disagree that global politics is naturally without order and instead believe that global governance is possible and desirable. They do not necessarily agree that a form of world government, with full authority to force states to comply, is possible. But they point to the huge number of IGOs that have been created since the end of the Second World War as evidence that a more informal type of governance can indeed work.

Impact and growth of intergovernmental organisations

IGOs are a feature of the post-Second World War global order. Before 1945, very few IGOs existed. Apart from the League of Nations, states worked together by agreeing ad-hoc treaties with a flexible, rather than fixed, number of partner states.

After the horrors of the Second World War, during which nationalism had once again given rise to global conflict, world leaders believed that security and stability would be best delivered if states tried to find more ways of working together in a more formal and sustained manner.

Several of the world's now most-established and influential IGOs emerged during the time immediately after the end of the Second World War. The UN, the IMF and the World Bank were all founded in 1945. NATO was founded in 1949, as divisions between the Soviet Union and the USA and its allies deepened.

Since the Second World War, international organisations:

- have increased in number
- have increased in the range of policy areas with which they are involved (for example, military, economic, trade and development objectives)
- have seen the number of states joining them (member states) increase
- have prompted the founding of other regional organisations (for example, the ASEAN, the AU and the Gulf Cooperation Council). (See Table 1.4 for further information.)

Table 1.4 Post-Second World War IGOs and their impact

Date founded	Organisation and purpose	Impact
1945	The United Nations (UN) was founded to advance international peace and security, human and economic development.	The UN expanded from 52 to 193 states. The UN Security Council (UNSC) has authorised military action, sanctions and peacekeeping missions around the world. The UN agreed and drove forward the most comprehensive and coordinated set of international development targets in the Millennium Development Goals (MDGs). It is now considered the most authoritative and legitimate global political institution.
1945	The International Monetary Fund (IMF), founded at the Bretton Woods Conference (see page 131), aimed to create institutions that would stabilise and organise the global economy after the Second World War. A key objective was to move the global economy towards more free trade and greater economic cooperation.	The IMF's role has expanded to make it a key institution in resolving financial crises that have an impact on more than one state, in order to minimise their impact on the global economy. It played an important role in the international response to the 2008 global financial crisis (see Chapter 4).
1944	The World Bank was also founded at the Bretton Woods Conference (see page 132). Member states contribute to a fund, which provides loans to developing countries.	The World Bank has focused its work increasingly on international development. It played a major role in the UN's MDGs.
1949	The North Atlantic Treaty Organization (NATO) was founded as a collective military alliance to act as a counterweight to the Soviet Union.	NATO has grown from 12 to 28 signatory states. It is increasingly involved in military operations outside western Europe, including in Afghanistan, and counter-piracy operations in the Indian Ocean.
1958	The European Union (EU) was founded to bind states that had been at the centre of two world wars in an economic and political union.	The EU has widened its membership to 28 member states (pre-Brexit) and in 2000 deepened its integration to establish a single currency. The UK's 2016 vote and issuing of Article 50 to leave the EU, however, will see a powerful and influential member state become the first member to exit the union.
1963	The African Union (AU) (established 2001 and launched 2002) was founded as the Organisation for African Unity in 1963 to act as a political and economic union for all African states. Today, the only African state outside the union is Morocco.	The AU does not compare with the EU in terms of depth of integration and impact on state sovereignty. Instead, it has remained a forum through which African states can speak with greater influence on the world stage. For example, in 2013, the AU threatened to withdraw as a bloc from the founding treaty of the ICC. The AU, with UN funding and training, has carried out mostly successful peacekeeping operations in Somalia and Darfur, Sudan.
1967	The Association of Southeast Asian Nations (ASEAN) was founded primarily to promote economic cooperation and development in southeast Asia.	ASEAN has enabled southeast Asian nations, each economically powerful in its own right, to form a much more powerful bloc in a region dominated by China's economic might. Trade and connectivity between ASEAN states has been made easier. In 2002, the ASEAN bloc negotiated a free-trade agreement with China, which, together, is worth 10% of the global economy, giving the states greater bargaining power and influence than if they had negotiated alone.

Debate

Does conflict or cooperation dominate global politics?

Conflict

- Conflict continues to exist in all its forms.
- Civil wars are increasing. The Syrian civil war, which began in 2011, has seen nearly half a million killed and led to 12 million refugees. Non-state actors, such as the militant organisations Boko Haram, al-Shabaab and so-called Islamic State, are engaged in struggles against state governments and have seized state territory.
- Conflict between states has reduced significantly but continues, as seen with Russia and Ukraine since 2014. Some states, such as Iran and Saudi Arabia, are not directly fighting each other, but instead engage in proxy wars, for example in Syria and Yemen.
- Since the 9/11 terror attacks in the USA, non-state actors, such as al-Qaeda and so-called Islamic State, have created significant conflict. These conflicts point to an increase in tensions between violent Islamic extremism and the Western world.

Cooperation

- The number of international and regional governmental organisations has increased, as has the number of states joining them. These bodies offer a means of peaceful dispute resolution.
- States cooperate deeply and are extremely interdependent on matters of trade, which have expanded with the forces of economic globalisation, decreasing regulation, improved technology and communications.
- Extensive international efforts have been made to resolve shared challenges, ranging from climate change (see Chapter 6), the global financial crisis (see Chapter 4) and global poverty (see Chapter 4). States have chosen to work through IGOs and also through more informal means, such as ad-hoc summits like the 2015 Paris Climate Change Conference and groups such as the G7/8 and G20.

Distinguish between

Realism and liberalism: intergovernmental organisations

Realism

- IGOs are useful as a means of enhancing state power and sovereignty, and conducting business with other states, if it is possible to get outcomes that are the same as a state's national interest.
- They are not useful, and are even dangerous, if it is not possible to achieve one's national interest.
- They are very dangerous and undesirable if the IGO has powers to compel states to do things. States should be able to veto decisions that do not fit with their national interest.

Liberalism

- IGOs are a key part of establishing a world order governed by rules. They are the most powerful and authoritative source of international law. They are also likely to be the most comprehensive and even universal source of international law if IGOs have lots of members.
- They offer states a means of peaceful dispute resolution (for example, through the UN). They provide a forum for discussion and negotiation.
- They offer states a means of deepening economic integration and free trade (for example, through the EU and the ASEAN).
- They offer states the opportunity to work together and be more powerful than if they acted alone (for example, through NATO).

Activity

Spend some time thinking about the liberal viewpoint on global politics.

1   Do you agree that states and their fortunes are inextricably linked? What evidence is there for this idea of complex interdependence?
2   What evidence can you find from recent events in global politics that a sense of 'international community' exists?

The end of history?

In 1989, US political scientist Francis Fukuyama wrote an essay titled 'The End of History?', in which he proposed the thesis that mankind's ideological evolution had come to an end. With the end of the Cold War and the collapse of the Communist Soviet Union, the battle of ideas between liberal democracy and communism had been resolved, with liberal democracy the unchallengeable winner.

Fukuyama expanded his theory in his 1992 book *The End of History and the Last Man*. He claimed that liberal democracy had become the unchallenged universal global model of government. Democracy had been established as the undisputed governmental system of choice, even if it had temporary setbacks. Liberal models of free trade and capitalism were becoming an irreversible global norm. Fukuyama's ideas have provoked much debate over the extent to which the ideological world order is settled.

With such a provocative title, it is worth considering the precise detail of what Fukuyama outlined in his book. For students of global politics who are assessing whether or not a theory is valid, rather than referring to a broad phrase such as 'the end of history', it is always worth keeping precise arguments in mind. Therefore, to expand, Fukuyama argued the following.

- Global politics was witnessing the 'endpoint of mankind's ideological evolution and the universalisation of Western liberal democracy as the final form of human government'.
- The failure of communism and the collapse of the Soviet Union had confirmed the victory of liberal democracy and capitalism.

The collapse of the Berlin Wall in 1989 signalled the end of the Soviet Union

- To be prosperous, even communist states would need to adopt some aspects of capitalism.
- There would be an end to ideological struggle, but there would not be an 'end of history' in the sense that there would no longer be conflict or crises.
- There would be a 'capitalist creep', through which greater democratic and economic freedoms would eventually be accompanied by greater individual freedoms.
- An ideological challenge from radical Islam would not be widespread in its effect because of its religious and cultural limitations to predominantly Islamic states.

His ideas have been criticised for the following reasons:
- They suggest that a US model of government is the best form of government and should be replicated across the world. Critics say that this represents a potentially dangerous attempt to impose a Western-dominated viewpoint of the 'best' democratic model across the world, one that was arguably attempted in unsuccessful nation-building efforts in Afghanistan and Iraq in 2001 and 2003 respectively.
- Fukuyama's thinking directly challenges Marxist ideology, which argues that communism will replace capitalism as the ideal system of world government.
- In the aftermath of the 9/11 attacks, some critics pointed to a continuing clash of ideology between states and non-state actors such as al-Qaeda, even if clashes of ideology between states may be reducing. US political scientist and academic Samuel P. Huntington countered that the clash of ideologies had been replaced by a clash between civilisations (see page 35).

The 9/11 terror attacks on New York and Washington, DC raise the question of a new 'clash of civilisations'

China's Marxist capitalism: resisting the end of history?

Despite Fukuyama's arguments, China, the world's second-largest economy, is neither a liberal democracy nor does it fully conform to a capitalist free-market economy. It is worth examining the system of political and economic government that has delivered exceptional economic growth for China.

China is a single-party state. The Communist Party of China governs it, there is no accepted political opposition and, consequently, there are no democratic elections. The government controls all news media — no independent media outlets exist. In its 2016 Annual Report, Human Rights Watch declared that 'China remains an authoritarian state, one that systematically curtails a wide range of fundamental human rights, including freedom of expression, association, assembly, and religion'.

While political freedoms are almost entirely absent, China does have considerable economic freedoms. These were initiated in the late 1970s by reformists within the Communist Party of China, and led by the eventual president Deng Xiaoping. As part of these reforms:

- agriculture was moved from collective ownership to private ownership
- China was opened up to foreign investment
- private individuals were allowed to set up their own businesses

The Chinese government has defended its lack of political freedom as a so-called China model, where it is possible to have economic freedom leading to spectacular economic growth but without political freedom holding this back. Certainly, the Chinese economy has seen huge growth (by an annual average of close to 10% since 1989). Furthermore, China's growth has been a major contribution to worldwide economic growth. While this growth has slowed since the global financial crisis, it continues to outstrip the USA. Many economic forecasters predict that China will overtake the USA as the world's largest economy by around 2020.

Despite this economic success, the proceeds of economic growth remain very poorly spread among the Chinese population compared with the USA. In 2016, gross domestic product (GDP) per capita (the value of goods and services produced by a state) in the USA was seven times that in China.

Political unrest is rare in China. Government forces ruthlessly suppressed pro-democracy protests in 1989 in major Chinese cities and, most notably, in Tiananmen Square, Beijing, resulting in the deaths of over 200 civilians. In response, the government reversed some political freedoms that had come with China's economic liberalisation, including clamping down on media freedom.

China's educated and economically empowered middle class is growing fast. Some analysts believe that as much as 75% of China's population will be earning middle incomes by 2022, driven on by the growing economy. However, there is still discontent, with demonstrations against issues such as government land seizures leading to protesters being arrested and imprisoned.

But for the time being China's system of so-called Marxist capitalism seems secure enough. A growing educated and empowered middle class was one key factor in the Arab Uprisings of 2010–12. Whether China's burgeoning middle class will respond with similar calls for political

Tiananmen Square, 1989, where government forces ruthlessly suppressed pro-democracy protests

freedom, proving Fukuyama's theory decisively correct, remains to be seen.

Debate

Was Fukuyama right about the end of an ideological struggle?

Yes

- The number of states that are liberal democracies increased from 35 in 1974 to 120 in 2013, which accounts for 60% of world states.
- Former communist states, such as China and Russia, have adopted some aspects of capitalism. Although China is not a liberal democracy, it subscribes internationally to free-market principles.
- Communism was explicitly abolished in the newly formed Russian Federation, which arose out of the Communist Soviet Union after the end of the Cold War. Former Soviet states in eastern Europe have enthusiastically adopted liberal democracy and liberalised their economies, joining the EU and even the Eurozone.
- The world economy has quadrupled since the late 1990s. This is clear evidence that capitalism is delivering benefits to the global economy.
- Democracies may be either fragile or imperfect, but longer-term trends are more important, especially when considering that democracy can take decades to properly embed. The long-term trend is that the number of liberal democracies is increasing and that liberal democracy in itself offers the best conditions for liberal democracy to improve.
- Fundamental Islam has been limited to non-state actors such as al-Qaeda and so-called Islamic State — no state has adopted this extremist ideology as a form of government.

No

- The world's second-largest economy, China, remains authoritarian and is not a liberal democracy. Furthermore, its power is rising and increasingly challenging its rival, the liberal democratic and capitalist flag-bearer, the USA.
- Communist parties are still in power in single-party states in China, Cuba, Laos and Vietnam.
- The Arab Uprisings did not give rise to an increase in democracy, except for Tunisia. Many states took a backwards step, such as Egypt, which has returned to military rule.
- Many democratic states have significant weaknesses. India has been democratic since 1947, but a third of its elected candidates in the 2014 elections have criminal indictments against them.
- Russia's democratic elections have been questioned for being neither free nor fair. Russia may have moved towards liberal democracy and away from communism, but it remains in many aspects an authoritarian state, with little government scrutiny and accountability.
- Other democracies are fragile. There have been military coups in Turkey (2016) and Thailand (2006), suggesting that liberal democracy is still under threat.
- There is increasing concern that capitalism has created wide inequality. Some have seen the 2008 global financial crisis as a failure of the capitalist model. Economists, including Thomas Piketty, suggest the election of left-wing governments in Greece (and, to some extent, the move to the left by the UK Labour Party under Jeremy Corbyn) reflect a growing movement that believes capitalism is in need of reform.
- Radical Islam has emerged as an ideological challenger to both the West and secular governments in the middle east and north Africa.

Activity

Spend some time thinking about Fukuyama's key arguments in *The End of History and the Last Man*.

1. To what extent do you agree that Western liberal democracy has become the universal form of government?
2. What actors, or actions, in global politics might put the dominance of Western liberal democracy at risk?

A clash of civilisations?

In 1993, Samuel P. Huntington wrote an essay that appeared in *Foreign Affairs* magazine, entitled 'The Clash of Civilizations?' (sometimes abbreviated to COC). Huntington argued that the source of global conflict in the twenty-first century would not be political or economic, but cultural. Specifically, conflict would be fought between civilisations. He later expanded his thesis in the 1996 book *The Clash of Civilizations and the Remaking of World Order*.

Huntington argues that states' desires for territorial or economic gain had been the motivation for conflicts. As a result, nation-states had been created from these conflicts and had gone on to become the principal actors in global politics. Western powers, Huntington argued, had driven most of these conflicts. Colonial wars of the nineteenth and twentieth centuries, for example, reflected states' desires to acquire new territory and expand their economic sphere of influence. With these gains now settled, Huntington argued that the space was created for a clash between the West and non-Western civilisations, and among non-Western civilisations (see Figure 1.5 in Box 1.4).

Distinguish between

Ideology and civilisation

Ideology
- Ideology is a set of political ideas agreed, championed or implemented by a group within society (for example communism, capitalism).

Civilisation
- Civilisation is a group of humans that has organised into a settled, urban and literate community with a shared culture and often religion.
- It is not defined by a single political ideology but rather by a shared sense of culture and organised society.

Huntington made several other important arguments in his article:
- Post-Cold War global politics would be multipolar (see page 271) and consist of multiple civilisations.
- A revival of religion, particularly in the Islamic world, would come to represent a challenge to the West in terms of a rejection of Western values and institutions.
- The age of conflict over political or economic ideology had ended. Key political ideas, such as free trade, would no longer be widely challenged. In contrast to Fukuyama's theories, cultural differences would now replace ideological differences. As the product of centuries, cultural differences would remain and be more deeply embedded than differences of political ideology had ever been.
- With globalisation and increased human interactions, people will become more aware of their civilisation roots and of their differences with others, and will try to defend, rather than merge, these differences.
- There are some civilisations that are 'swing civilisations' (notably Russia and Turkey), which appear to be torn between adapting to Western civilisation and developing their Orthodox or Islamic identities (see Box 1.4).
- Forces of globalisation have eroded national identity. Religion is the only remaining cultural identity.

To prevent a potential clash of civilisations, Huntington argued for the West to do the following:
- Pursue greater political, economic and military integration, so that other civilisations cannot exploit differences among the West.
- Expand NATO and the EU to include states that might otherwise fall into the Russian civilisation's sphere of influence. (This advice was followed in the case of the Baltic states, who joined NATO, but not Ukraine, which remains outside NATO.)

Box 1.4

Which civilisations did Huntington identify?

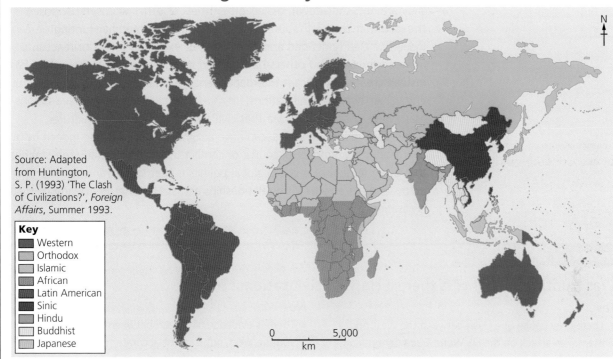

Source: Adapted from Huntington, S. P. (1993) 'The Clash of Civilizations?', *Foreign Affairs*, Summer 1993.

Key
- Western
- Orthodox
- Islamic
- African
- Latin American
- Sinic
- Hindu
- Buddhist
- Japanese

Source: Adapted from Huntington, S. P. (1993) 'The Clash of Civilizations?', *Foreign Affairs*, Summer 1993.

Figure 1.5 Huntington's civilisations

Huntington identified eight major civilisations, and a possible ninth (Buddhist):

- **Western:** including Australasia, the USA and western Europe
- **Orthodox:** including most of Russia and the former Soviet Union
- **Islamic:** including north Africa, the middle east as far as Pakistan and the islands to the south of the South China Sea, including Malaysia
- **African:** including most of Sub-Saharan Africa, but not north Africa
- **Latin American:** including all of Central and South America
- **Sinic:** including most of China
- **Hindu:** predominantly India
- **Japanese:** Japan
- **Buddhist:** including Tibet, most of southeast Asia and Mongolia

- Restrain the military advancement of the Islamic nations. This could be said to have been heeded in the USA's desire to prevent Iran from developing nuclear weapons and potentially encouraging Saudi Arabia to also develop its own nuclear weapons in response (see the security dilemma, page 15).
- Understand that intervention in the affairs of other civilisations would be 'the single most dangerous source of instability and conflict in a multi-civilisational world'. Arguably, the West did not heed this advice through its many interventions in the Islamic world during the so-called War on Terror.

There are a number of criticisms of Huntington's theory:

- US academic Edward Said, who published an article entitled 'The Clash of Ignorance', criticised Huntington for attempting to make civilisations 'what they are not: shut-down, sealed-off entities'. In other words, he opposed the idea that the civilisations as defined and delineated by Huntington can indeed be clearly defined and delineated, or expected to act or react in a unified way. Said and others have argued that history and globalisation has instead created significant interdependence, exchange and sharing of culture and values between civilisations.

- Many have criticised the idea that civilisations and cultural structures, rather than individual states, can have a significant impact and indeed be a coordinated and impactful source of conflict. Many (particularly realists) argue that a key feature of modern global politics is that states remain the primary actors and are able to form relationships across Huntington's clearly defined civilisations.

Debate

Was Huntington right? Is there a clash of civilisations?

Yes

- There is evidence of a clash between the West and Islam. The attack on the US World Trade Center and the Pentagon — the most devastating to occur on US soil since Pearl Harbor (1941) — was a demonstration of violent Islamic extremism attacking the most iconic symbols of Western power and values.

- Although internally divided, the Islamic world represents an increasing threat to the West from multiple sources.

- Global terrorism has since increased, with new groups, such as al-Shabaab (in Somalia), Boko Haram (Nigeria) and so-called Islamic State (Iraq and Syria) emerging. All of these groups have attempted to challenge Western values — the literal translation of Boko Haram is 'Western education is forbidden'.

- The rise of China and its potential to overtake the USA as the world's largest economy represents a stunning increase in the power of the Sinic civilisation, which Huntington identified. We still do not know whether China's rise will be peaceful or not.

No

- There is evidence of a clash between violent Islam and the West, but it is not accurate to say that all of Islam is in conflict with Western values. Large Muslim populations in non-Muslim states testify to greater diversity and cohesion.

- There is little evidence of unity in many of the civilisations that Huntington identified. The Islamic world is divided in terms of policy responses to the outside world and to the West. Iran has, until recently, distanced itself from the USA, while Saudi Arabia has been a close ally.

- The Islamic civilisation is divided internally between the Sunni and Shia sects. This has notably been reflected in the Syrian civil war, with Shia Iran and Sunni Saudi Arabia backing different sides. It has also been seen in deeply sectarian conflict in both Iraq and Syria, where Sunnis and Shias are often in violent conflict.

- Many of the civilisations that Huntington identified show little interest in a clash with the West. India, Japan and Latin America are all deeply interdependent on the West and a clash would not be in the interests of these civilisations.

Activity

Spend some time thinking about Huntington's key arguments in 'The Clash of Civilizations?'.

1 What are the most likely causes of any clash between civilisations?
2 Which is the most powerful force in global politics: culture or ideology?

What you should know

Having read this chapter you should have knowledge and understanding of the following:

- Global governance is the process by which states and intergovernmental organisations try to bring order and security to global politics. It does not try to create a world government, as this is not possible. Instead, states try to create institutions and laws that allow them to solve shared problems and seize international opportunities that are in their national interest.
- The United Nations (UN) was founded to maintain global peace and security, improve economic development and advance human rights. Its role has since expanded to include preventing environmental degradation and increased responsibilities for UN peacekeepers.
- One of the most powerful bodies in international relations is the UN Security Council (UNSC). Its permanent members have a powerful right to veto proposed resolutions. Sometimes this results in stalemate. Nevertheless, the UNSC has still had a considerable impact, even if it cannot always resolve crises in which its permanent members wish to block action.
- The North Atlantic Treaty Organization was founded to act as a collective security alliance against the Soviet Union. It has since expanded both its membership and the scope of its operations. Today, it is more actively involved in combating global threats outside Europe, and has led offensive operations in Afghanistan and Libya. Its military stance against Russia is more defensive and is intended to act as a deterrent.
- International efforts, through the UN and the Treaty on the Non-Proliferation of Nuclear Weapons, have proved successful in preventing states from developing nuclear weapons. The major nuclear weapons powers, however, have not disarmed and have only very slowly reduced their stockpiles of weapons.
- Global political governance depends ultimately on states' agreement. States use intergovernmental organisations and sign treaties primarily to pursue their own national interest. Sometimes, national interest and international interest are the same. This is when global governance efforts are most successful.

Further reading

Bull, H. (1979) *The Anarchical Society: A Study of Order in World Politics*. Columbia University Press.

Fukuyama, F. (1992) *The End of History and the Last Man*. Free Press.

Fukuyama, F. (6 June 2014) 'At the End of History Still Stands Democracy', *Wall Street Journal*. www.wsj.com/articles/at-the-end-of-history-still-stands-democracy-1402080661

Huntington, S. P. (2002) *The Clash of Civilizations and the Remaking of World Order*. Simon & Schuster.

Kissinger, H. (2015) *World Order: Reflections on the Character of Nations and the Course of History*. Penguin.

Mearsheimer, J. (2003) *The Tragedy of Great Power Politics*. W. W. Norton & Company.

Exam focus

Section A

1 Examine the validity of the argument that a balance of power creates order in global politics. *[12 marks]*

2 Examine the criticisms that have been made of Samuel P. Huntington's 'Clash of Civilizations' theory. *[12 marks]*

3 Examine the arguments that support Francis Fukuyama's views in his book *The End of History and the Last Man*. *[12 marks]*

Section C

1 Evaluate the extent to which contemporary world order tends towards anarchy and chaos. *[30 marks]*

2 Evaluate the extent to which war and international conflict are inevitable features of global politics. *[30 marks]*

3 Evaluate the divisions regarding human nature that exist between liberals and realists. *[30 marks]*

Chapter 2

The state and globalisation

Learning outcomes

By the end of this chapter you should be able to:
- understand both the meaning and the significance of the Westphalian nation-state-centred approach to global politics
- be able to define economic globalisation and explain why and in what ways free-trade economic liberalism has impacted the world
- understand why economic globalisation is so controversial
- appreciate the ways in which political globalisation has impacted the centrality of the state in global affairs
- understand the meaning of 'cultural globalisation' and the way in which it has challenged the nation-state's cultural hegemony
- understand why the impact of political and cultural globalisation has been limited
- identify contrasting approaches to the impact of globalisation on international relations
- understand to what extent globalisation has successfully challenged the fundamental importance of the state in global relations

Getting you started

Key terms

Sovereignty The principle of absolute and unlimited power and the defining characteristic of a state. National sovereignty means that a state has absolute authority over all its citizens within its borders.

Nation-state An autonomous political organisation defined by the common ties of a shared nationality and citizenship based upon a recognisable culture manifested through, for example, a common ancestry and language. State borders broadly match a relatively homogenous culture.

'The report of my death was an exaggeration'

In 1992, the prominent Japanese-American academic Francis Fukuyama published *The End of History and the Last Man*. Fukuyama argued that war would eventually become a thing of the past due to the rise of liberal democracies and their unwillingness to engage in conflict with each other. He indicated that the close connectivity between democracies could evolve to challenge the primacy of the state and that the European Union (EU) could provide a model for the future relationship between nations. As states worked more closely together, supranational governance would increasingly challenge the absolute **sovereignty** of the **nation-state**.

Fukuyama provided no time frame for what he termed the 'end of history', but the book's publication, just as the Cold War was ending, persuaded many that Fukuyama was providing a clear insight into what the world of the future could look like. In 1989, the Berlin Wall was torn down, leading to the reunification of Germany as a liberal democracy. Elsewhere, in eastern Europe Communist dictatorships were overthrown with extraordinary rapidity to be quickly replaced with democratically elected governments. In 1991, the Soviet Union collapsed and a year later, in Maastricht, the leaders of the European Economic Community (EEC) pledged themselves to a common citizenship and currency. Significantly, the community was renamed a union. The popularity of the economic liberal principles of the Washington Consensus (see page 45)

41

Japanese-American academic Francis Fukuyama

further encouraged trust and cooperation between states. Even in China it seemed that free-market reforms would so empower a new middle class that they would demand democratic reforms that would challenge Communist rule.

However, history has not moved in the way many liberals predicted. The internet has provided unheard of opportunities for the integration of peoples across the world through shared online experiences. Global free trade has created greater global wealth than ever before. And yet the internet has also facilitated insularity. The television network RT (formerly Russia Today), for example, deploys its global outreach not to break down barriers but to provide Russian nationalism with a global audience. Fox News is deeply partisan. The rapid advance of regionalism has, far from undermining national citizenship, provoked a backlash, especially in Europe where most countries have seen a rise in Euro-sceptic nationalist parties, a phenomenon that Brexit is likely to encourage. In the USA, the driving force behind free-trade liberalism, President Trump stated in his inaugural speech that it is the 'right of all nations to put their own interests first'.

Mark Twain is alleged to have remarked on reading his obituary in the newspaper that 'the report of my death was an exaggeration'. The same may be true today of the nation-state. This chapter will explore to what extent globalisation, in its diverse forms, has really transformed the world. Are we moving into what has been called the 'post-sovereign state' world or does the nation-state still remain the key player in international relations?

President Donald Trump was inaugurated as the 45th President of the United States on 20 January 2017

The state: nation-state and national sovereignty

Characteristics of a nation-state and national sovereignty

Since the seventeenth century, the state has increasingly become the main player in global relations, providing the foundation for domestic peace and international relations. According to the Dutch scholar Hugo Grotius, the state is 'a complete association of free men, joined together for the enjoyment of rights and for their common interest', while both Jean Bodin and Thomas Hobbes argued that adherence to the authority of the sovereign state provided the most effective way of protecting society from mankind's potential for anarchy. Bodin lived through the St Bartholemew's Day Massacre in 1572, when vengeful Catholics murdered French Protestants in their thousands as royal governance broke down. Hobbes had first-hand experience of the destruction wrought by the English Civil War. Both appreciated that a powerful sovereign state, with the ability to control its subjects, provided the best way of ensuring peace and stability.

The Westphalian state system

The Peace of Westphalia in 1648, which ended the Thirty Years' War, is particularly important in the development of the principle of state sovereignty. It finally ended the Holy Roman Emperor's claim to possess sovereign authority over virtually independent German states. This meant that each individual state would be sovereign over its own internal affairs and no other state or, supposedly, superior body could intervene within its borders. By establishing the principle of the territorial integrity of sovereign states, Westphalia also defined the theory of the sovereign equality of states as follows:

- No state has the legal right to intervene in the sovereign affairs of another state.
- All states, whatever their size, possess the same legal right to independence.

The Congress of Vienna, 1814–15

The state, as the absolute provider of security both from internal rebellion and outward aggression, would provide the foundations for both domestic and global politics. The expansion of French power during the revolutionary and Napoleonic period (1793–1815) challenged this principle. However, the Congress of Vienna reasserted the primacy of sovereign states in determining European affairs, establishing a balance of power that would last for almost 100 years.

The nation-state in the twentieth century

During the twentieth century, Westphalian principles dominated across the globe. In his Fourteen Points (1918), US president Woodrow Wilson established the principle that nation-state sovereignty should be founded upon the right of self-determination based on a shared ethnic heritage. This led to the creation of new states such as Austria, Czechoslovakia, Hungary and Poland after the First World War.

The Montevideo Convention (1933) determined that a sovereign state must possess:

- a defined territory
- a permanent population
- a viable government
- the capacity to enter into diplomatic relations with other states

A state would possess a monopoly of law-making powers within its borders, while outside interference could not legally change a state's borders.

Post-Second World War decolonisation

Following the end of the Second World War there was yet more nation building, as former colonies of the great powers (the Allied victors) gained independence. In 1947, the independent states of India and Pakistan were established, while the British prime minister Harold Macmillan referred to a 'wind of change' blowing through Africa as old empires crumbled in the face of nationalist movements. In the middle east after the Second World War, Egypt, Iraq, Israel, Jordan, Lebanon and Syria all achieved independence. In the far east, China (in 1949) and Vietnam (in 1975) were unified under Communist rule. Finally, from 1989 to 1991, as communism collapsed throughout eastern Europe, new nation-states, including the 15 constituent parts of the Soviet Union, were established based upon Wilsonian principles of self-determination. By 2017, of the 193 members of the United Nations (UN), only 15 had existed as independent nation-states in 1910.

The UN and state sovereignty

The nation-state as a political community bound together by citizenship, nationality and culture therefore became an increasingly powerful force in global politics. It provided states, old and new, with a common identity and determined the main structures by which international relations are still conducted to this day. Article 2 of Chapter 1 of the UN Charter recognises this fact by noting that 'The Organization is based on the principle of the sovereign equality of all its Members'.

No state, however powerful, has the right to intervene in the affairs of another state, since all states can claim the same right to determine policy within their own borders without fear of outside interference. All states can claim equal territorial integrity. Loyalty to the state and the use of its economic,

Distinguish between

External and internal state sovereignty

Internal sovereignty
- Internal sovereignty is the location of sovereignty within a state.
- In the UK, the Westminster Parliament possesses legislative sovereignty. However, the devolved Scottish and Welsh assemblies may be in the process of achieving de facto sovereignty in their domestic affairs.
- The consequences of the UK's EU referendum suggest that popular sovereignty weighs more than legislative sovereignty, since parliament was unprepared to ignore the vote.
- The UK's withdrawal from the EU will further change the location of sovereignty within the UK.
- In certain circumstances the prime minister exercises sovereignty on behalf of the monarch through the use of the royal prerogative.
- It can be a fluid concept since, within the state, the location of sovereignty may change. In 2017, the Supreme Court determined that parliament, not the government, had the sovereign authority to trigger Article 50 of the Lisbon Treaty.

External sovereignty
- External sovereignty means that all states are equally sovereign in their relations with each other.
- The least powerful state is as sovereign as the most powerful state and so its territorial integrity is as legally valid.
- The cover of sovereignty is an equally strong protective cover for all states.
- According to Westphalian principles, one state may disagree with the way in which another is governed. However, because all states possess sovereign independence, this gives that state no excuse to interfere with another state's sovereign affairs.
- Article 2 of Chapter 1 of the UN Charter recognises this fact (see page 185).

political and military power to achieve its objectives underpin the realist interpretation of global affairs. States act out of self-interest in order to achieve the best possible outcome for themselves.

The legitimacy of a nation-state also derives from its acceptance as a nation-state by other nation-states. Palestine, for example, claims nation-statehood. However, since the UN does not accept these claims it remains unrecognised.

The process of globalisation

The widening and deepening of interconnectedness and interdependence

Globalisation has had a dramatic impact on the influence of the state. It has created a complex web of interconnectedness that challenges the state's sole authority to make decisions affecting the lives of its citizens. This process of growing interconnectedness has manifested economically, financially, politically, technologically and culturally. It has created a world in which nation-states cannot insulate themselves from what is happening elsewhere in the world.

The significance of economic and financial globalisation

Since the end of the Cold War, economic liberalism, often referred to as the 'Washington Consensus', has led to the dominance of free-market principles in global trade. This means that:

- states need to establish the sort of conditions that global investors find attractive, which includes policies of low corporate taxation and light regulation, since too much taxation and/or bureaucracy is likely to repel investment
- any state that seeks to act in defiance of economic globalisation will risk loss of investment and capital flight

Governments do not, in reality, exert absolute control over the macro-economic decisions that they make. For example, in order to encourage foreign business, Vietnam has offered extremely competitive financial incentives to businesses, such as a 0% withholding tax on dividends remitted overseas and corporate income tax of just 20%.

The globalisation of markets

The globalisation of financial markets, facilitated by the instantaneous communication the internet provides, means that global events can affect a state's economic wellbeing. This is seen in a number of ways:

- In 1997, global capital flight from Thailand gravely threatened southeast Asian prosperity, as it led to the contagion spreading throughout the region when investors withdrew capital from its neighbours.
- In 2007–8, the sub-prime mortgage crisis in the USA, precipitated by bankruptcy of US bank Lehman Brothers, provoked a global banking crisis. This led to stock markets throughout the world plummeting and a global recession, in which the value of global trade declined by 9%.

The influence of non-state actors

Global interconnectedness has also been advanced through the rise of myriad non-state actors. As the problems that the world faces become more complex, from climate change to international terrorism, a 'collective security dilemma' is created, which states cannot resolve on their own. Therefore, they increasingly

Key terms

Interconnectedness
The way in which states become more linked through their shared membership of intergovernmental and regional organisations. Through cooperation, states no longer approach global relations in terms of maximising their own power.

Economic globalisation
Process by which states across the world become more closely connected and interdependent according to the principles of free trade, which leads to the greater transnational flow of goods, services and capital.

Key term

Non-state actors Entities, such as NGOs, IGOs, transnational corporations and even criminal and terrorist networks, that wield significant influence over global affairs.

need to work together in intergovernmental organisations (IGOs) in order to try to resolve problems.

For example, in 2009, the G20 responded to the global financial crisis by implementing a global strategy of reflation and continued commitment to free trade. The Intergovernmental Panel on Climate Change (IPCC) provides an international forum in which recommendations for action are agreed (see page 233). The International Atomic Energy Agency is designed to ensure that its signatory states abide by the terms of the Treaty on the Non-Proliferation of Nuclear Weapons (NPT, see page 122).

The influence of intergovernmental organisations

The Bretton Woods Institutions

The Bretton Woods Institutions are the:

- World Bank
- International Monetary Fund (IMF)
- World Trade Organization (WTO)

All of them impact on state sovereignty by advancing global free markets and free trade. The structural adjustment programmes (SAPs) that the World Bank and IMF implement are founded on the core premise that economic growth is maximised through free-market reforms and free trade. Governments should encourage foreign investment by adopting economic policies conducive to foreign investment.

At the beginning of 2017, the WTO had 164 states as members, including both China (2001) and Russia (2011). The WTO is also closely associated with globalisation, since it encourages free trade by seeking to persuade nations to reduce import tariffs. It tries to resolve trade disputes between countries and it provides a forum for the resolution of trade wars. Economic globalisation has created a neoliberal consensus that free trade creates greater wealth and so all states should engage with this economic model in order to achieve prosperity.

The United Nations

The UN is the most significant of all IGOs. Established in 1945, it is based on the liberal principle that the international community needs to work together to resolve 'collective dilemmas'. Nation-states do not sacrifice their sovereignty as members of the UN. However, by cooperating, nation-states create a more peaceful and prosperous world that they each benefit from.

UN agencies include the following.

- **World Health Organization (WHO):** responsible for the eradication of smallpox and the near total elimination of polio. The WHO also spearheads and coordinates the global response to epidemics such as Ebola and the Zika virus.
- **International Atomic Energy Agency (IAEA):** monitors states' fulfilment of the terms of the NPT (1968).
- **United Nations High Commission for Refugees (UNHCR):** the world's most important tool in seeking to alleviate the plight of refugees. In 2017, there were 65 million refugees worldwide: the highest number since the end of the Second World War.
- **United Nations International Children's Fund (UNICEF):** spearheads childhood immunisation programmes in the developing world and globally promotes the rights of the child.
- **World Food Programme (WFP):** provided food relief to 76.7 million people in 81 countries in 2015.

The UN has also been responsible for:

- the Millennium (2000–15) and Sustainable Development Goals (2015–), which have made considerable progress in reducing poverty.
- climate change conferences, which have provided an opportunity for states to work together on limiting carbon emissions and reducing the impact of climate change.

Regional organisations

Many regional organisations have been established in order to take advantage of the opportunities globalisation offers. These include the following.

- **1957:** EEC (the EU since 1992)
- **1967:** Association of Southeast Asian Nations (ASEAN)
- **1991:** Mercosur
- **1994:** North American Free Trade Agreement (NAFTA)

These regional IGOs function as mini-free trade areas, encouraging trade and specialisation within them. This cooperation provides these regions with greater influence in international trade. By establishing regional customs unions, or 'fortresses', this also protects them from the rigours of global competition. In the process, economic (and in the case of the EU considerable political) sovereignty is pooled. This means that nation-states accept limits on what their governments can do so that they can achieve a greater collective benefit.

The influence of non-governmental organisations

NGOs can have considerable soft-power influence on states by enriching the political debate. They include pressure groups such as:

- Amnesty International
- Greenpeace
- Human Rights Watch
- Médecins Sans Frontiéres

In 1997, the International Campaign to Ban Land Mines was awarded the Nobel Peace Prize for the successful way in which it had worked with governments. Global celebrities, such as Emma Watson in her 'He For She' speech at the UN, have also played an increasingly important role in focusing global attention on issues such as female equality. Bob Geldof and Bono performed an indispensable role at the 2005 Gleneagles Summit in persuading G8 leaders to commit 0.7% of their GDP to overseas development and to support debt relief. This illustrates how decision making within the global community has been dispersed to new stakeholders whose influence may, ultimately, count for more than that of governments. In 2005, when Nelson Mandela announced that his son had died of AIDS, this dramatically focused attention on a disease that many African governments had sought to ignore than did the work of any government.

The internet's impact

The internet has transformed global communication, impacting states across the world. It has led to the instantaneous trading of shares and movement of capital, creating a global marketplace for business and commerce. It has also created a global marketplace of ideas, in which people anywhere in the world are able to access a limitless supply of information and ideas. The consumer opportunities the internet offers would have been unthinkable even in recent memory.

These technological advances have created the potential for a more global culture in which the same goods, fashions and ideas penetrate anywhere in

Political globalisation
Process by which the nation-state no longer solely takes decisions affecting its citizens. Instead, decisions are more polycentric, involving a variety of non-state actors (e.g. IGOs, NGOs and regional organisations).

Global governance The way in which the nation-state increasingly shares decision making with non-state actors, such as IGOs, NGOs and TNCs. Global collective dilemmas have made the principle of global governance increasingly important in international relations.

The internet has transformed global communication, trade and technology

the world. In 2016 Apple announced that it had sold its billionth iPhone, and Coca-Cola, Microsoft, Google and Facebook are among the most instantly recognisable brands in the world.

In terms of the spread of ideas, the internet has made it more difficult for states to control the information its citizens receive. Facebook and Al Jazeera played an important role in provoking the 2010–12 Arab Uprisings by undermining states' abilities to control the flow of information to their people. The internet has also provided a global platform for Islamic fundamentalism to radicalise Muslims and non-Muslims across the world, so making it more difficult for national governments to defeat both external and internal terrorist threats.

Distinguish between

Economic and political globalisation

Economic globalisation
- Economic globalisation is the process by which the world's economy becomes more closely connected. This leads to the greater transnational flow of goods, services and capital.
- A greater global commitment to free trade and free markets has encouraged this connectivity. This is closely associated with the principles of the Washington Consensus advanced by the Bretton Woods Institutions (the World Bank, IMF and WTO).
- Technological advances, including greater capacity for transportation and instantaneous communication via the internet, have further encouraged economic globalisation, linking most countries in the world into a global supply chain.
- Economic globalisation is closely associated with liberalism. This derives from nineteenth-century liberal thought, which regarded free trade as a moral good, since it encourages cooperation between states. According to liberalism, free trade between nations reduces the risk of war between states.

Political globalisation
- Political globalisation involves the participation of non-state actors in decisions affecting the nation-state. This means that the state is no longer autonomous in decision making — its centrality is challenged by a variety of other stakeholders (IGOs, regional organisations, international lobbying groups, TNCs). Domestic governments increasingly need to react to these challenges to sole authority in decision making.
- Political globalisation creates the potential for global governance based upon increasing inter-reactions among states and non-state actors.
- Since states still value domestic political hegemony, political globalisation has not penetrated as deeply as economic globalisation.

To what extent does globalisation address and resolve contemporary issues?

The contemporary world faces numerous challenges, such as poverty, climate change, terrorism and extremism, and the role of globalisation in resolving such problems has proved extremely controversial. Some political commentators regard globalisation as part of the solution, while for others it is actually part of the problem.

Poverty

In what ways has economic globalisation reduced poverty?

Supporters of globalisation argue that it has done more than anything else in history to address and resolve the problem of global poverty.

Convergence between the Global North and South

The Brandt Reports in 1980 and 1983 first coined the term 'the North/South divide'. It highlights the economic and social divisions between the developed world (the Global North) and the developing world (the Global South). According to this definition, living standards, high wages and industrial productivity are mostly to be found in the northern hemisphere. Poverty, low wages, agriculture and structural disadvantage are mostly concentrated in the southern hemisphere.

Supporters of economic globalisation argue that free-trade liberalism has done more than anything else in history to challenge this 'stereotype' by creating new jobs in manufacturing across the world. As a result of greater trade than ever between countries, gross world production has dramatically increased, as the following figures show.

- **2000:** US$41,016 trillion
- **2014:** US$77,868 trillion

The number of people living in extreme poverty has also dramatically decreased, as people across the world gain higher-paid jobs and have access to cheaper food and medical equipment. According to the World Bank, the numbers living on less than US$1.25 a day (the global measure of poverty) have dropped.

- **1980:** 1.9 billion
- **2015:** 702 million

This statistic is even more remarkable when we take into account that the global population has increased by almost 3 billion since 1980.

As a result of the enhanced trading opportunities that free trade creates, developing countries have been able to break into global markets and use their comparative advantage in cheap labour in order to lift millions of their citizens out of extreme poverty. In the developing world, output per person almost doubled between 2000 and 2009, with an average annual rate of growth over that decade of 7.6%. This was 4.5% higher than the rate seen in rich countries.

Tariffs may seem to provide an immediate answer to domestic prosperity by protecting producers from foreign competition. However, this encourages them to charge higher prices in a protected environment. Free trade encourages countries to specialise in what they produce most cheaply, so reducing the cost to sell it globally, while providing them with their own niche market to exploit.

As a result, the developing world has made huge advances:

■ In 1980, 84% of China's population lived in extreme poverty. This number had decreased to 12% by 2010.
■ In 1980, 60% of India's population lived in extreme poverty. This number had decreased to 33% by 2010.

The relative success of the Millennium Development Goals (MDGs) (see page 166) can also, to a great extent, be attributed to the way in which globalisation has lifted more people out of poverty than ever before in history. By opening up their markets to foreign investment less-developed countries have been able to climb the development ladder to prosperity. In the process, this has created greater convergence between them and the developed world, challenging the relevance of a division of the world into a prosperous Global North and a poverty-stricken Global South.

■ China has used its enormous supply of cheap labour to manufacture low-cost goods, which it sells globally. In 2015, exports from China amounted to US$2.282 trillion. This was an increase of 20.2% from 2011, while 26.3% of the total exports were in electronic equipment.
■ In 2015, South Korea was the sixth-largest exporter specialising in computers, cars and wireless telecommunications equipment. Its companies, including Hyundai, Kia and Samsung, have global recognition. In the 1970s the economies of North and South Korea were roughly equal. Today, South Korea's engagement in global free trade means that its industrial output is 17 times larger than that of its neighbour. It is also estimated that because of better diet and living conditions, the average 20-year-old South Korean stands 6cm taller than a North Korean contemporary.
■ Since the 1950s, Taiwan has focused on export markets. Initially, this was in cheap toys and textiles. The capital this created was then used to diversify into more high-price goods. In 2016 Taiwan's technology-intensive economy was ranked 22nd in the world in terms of gross domestic product.
■ Vietnam is increasingly focusing on the development of its world export market. Its specialisation is in low-cost manufacturing, with labour costs just 50% of those in China.

Many African countries have also been able to take advantage of new trading opportunities by concentrating on those sectors in which they possess comparative advantage:

■ Botswana (diamonds)
■ Côte d'Ivoire (cocoa, coffee, palm oil)
■ Ethiopia (coffee)
■ Ghana (gold and cocoa)
■ Kenya (tea)

Significantly, investors are increasingly investing in Africa's non-commodities sector, as they appreciate the potential value of its growing urbanised and better-skilled workforce. The Chinese, in particular, have been quick to appreciate the value of the cheap outsourcing of labour in Africa's new urban centres. Industrial parks have opened in a number of east African countries — for example, the Huajian Group, which manufactures Ivanka Trump-branded

Coffee is one of Ethiopia's main exports

shoes, has moved production to Ethiopia, since it estimates that production costs will be dramatically lower there than in China. Its president, Zhang Huarong, has said that he intends to create 30,000 new jobs in Ethiopia by 2020. The Hawassa Industrial Park in Ethiopia is also now estimated to be the largest in the world.

As a result of such confidence in Africa's future as a manufacturing hub, foreign direct investment in the continent in 2015 reached US$60 billion — five times higher than in 2000 — making it second only to the USA in terms of investor attraction.

Globalisation and consumers

Globalisation has also driven down the cost of consumer goods, providing most people in the world with the opportunity to own the sort of sophisticated material possessions that were once confined to only the very wealthiest. In the developing world, 8 out of 10 people own a mobile phone and in 2016, the world's cheapest smartphone, the Ringing Bells Freedom 251, was launched on the Indian market at a cost of just £2.79.

Breaking out of the poverty cycle

The employment opportunities that economic globalisation creates also provide people in the developing world with the chance to break out of a cycle of rural poverty. Protected economies stagnate, since markets are restricted, and a lack of competition encourages complacency and inefficiency. Jobs in factories may not, of course, seem very attractive, but they can provide the opportunity for people, for the first time, to enjoy a regular wage, have the potential for career development and accumulate the capital necessary to give their children a better education. As Paul Collier states in *The Bottom Billion* (2007): 'globalisation provides virtually infinite possibilities of expansion ... this expansion creates jobs, especially for youth'.

In what ways has economic globalisation entrenched poverty?

Greater inequality

Critics of economic globalisation argue that although globalisation has created greater wealth than ever before, it has also had dramatically negative consequences. Too often the wealth that is generated through global free trade is concentrated in the hands of the elite. This dramatically increases the gap between the rich and the poor. In China, in 2016, it is estimated that the poorest 25% owns just 1% of the country's total wealth, while the richest 1% of households owns a third of the country's wealth. Thus, globalisation may be raising all boats but it is not raising all boats equally. Amy Chua in *World on Fire* (2002) has argued that by obviously concentrating wealth in the hands of a very small number of individuals, resentment and dissatisfaction is created among the majority who, although they may be becoming practically better off, do not feel as though they *are* better off. This undermines social cohesion and can encourage the rise of destabilising political movements.

A race to the bottom?

As global capitalism is based upon the maximisation of profit, so it suits the interests of international business to seek out the lowest costs in which to do business. This can create a 'race to the bottom', as states compete to attract business by keeping regulations as minimal as possible.

In recent years a number of shocking incidents have shown how developing countries can 'cut corners' in order to attract business (for example, the deaths of 1,129 employees through the collapse of the Rana Plaza garment factory in Bangladesh in 2013 due to structural failings). Chinese companies in particular are alleged to have very low standards of corporate social responsibility and to exploit workers in the developing world. Human Rights Watch has accused Chinese mining firms in Africa of countenancing appalling human rights abuses. Elsewhere, Cambodia's attempts to break into the global export market depend upon the sale of cheap textiles, and the Cambodian government has systematically ignored labour rights and working conditions in order to maximise profitability.

According to anti-globalisers, globalisation gives too much power to TNCs, which are undemocratic and unaccountable. It also undermines the ability of the state to protect its own citizens from exploitation. In this way, globalisation takes real power from the people and gives it to TNC directors, who too often wield the whip hand over governments, especially in the developing world. Economic globalisation may even be seen as a form of violence against the poor — through exploiting cheap labour, TNCs weaken the industrial and democratic rights that over generations have been built up to protect these people.

Activity

The Gini coefficient measures the extent of inequality within a state. The higher the level of income inequality, the higher the Gini coefficient. Therefore, such a society may be less harmonious than a society with a low Gini coefficient.

As a result of the proceeds of economic globalisation being shared unequally, major players in globalisation, such as China and the USA, have remarkably high scores on the Gini coefficient. The World Bank regards a coefficient above 0.40 as representing severe income inequality. It estimated China's score as 0.42 in 2012 and the USA's as 0.41 in 2013.

Critics of economic globalisation argue that the resentment inequality creates has a damaging impact on social cohesion. This leads to a rise in crime, class antagonism and even an increase in populist movements. According to the business academic C. K. Prahalad, the gap between the top and the bottom of the 'economic pyramid' has dramatically increased as a result of globalisation.

For right-wing politicians like former UK prime minister Margaret Thatcher, income inequality does not matter, so long as everyone is getting wealthier as a result of free-market reforms. In her last Prime Minister's Question Time in November 1990, the Liberal Democrat MP Simon Hughes asked Thatcher if she regretted that the gap between rich and poor had considerably increased in the UK since 1979. Her reply was unequivocal:

> What the honourable member is saying is that he would rather that the poor were poorer, provided that the rich were less rich. So long as the gap is smaller, they would rather have the poor poorer. You do not create wealth and opportunity that way. You do not create a property-owning democracy that way.

To what extent do you agree with Mrs Thatcher that growing income inequality does not matter, so long as society overall is becoming richer?

Activity

According to the right-wing novelist, playwright and political philosopher Ayn Rand, in *Capitalism: the Unknown Ideal* (1966), 'Capitalism did not create poverty, it inherited it'.

Using the interpretations below and your own research, to what extent do you think that economic globalisation has benefited the world's poor?

Globalisation is good

- Economic globalisation is based upon the principle that the reduction of trade barriers and import tariffs encourages greater global trade and stimulates foreign investment. This provides nation-states throughout the world with the opportunity to use their advantages in a global free market, so giving them access to literally any market in the world.
- Developing countries in particular have benefited from new export opportunities, leading to greater convergence between the economies of the Global South and the Global North.
- The expansion of global trade also provides consumers with a wider variety of goods at lower prices, since TNCs constantly seek out the cheapest and most cost-efficient place in which to manufacture.

Globalisation is bad

■ Globalisation enables powerful TNCs to open factories wherever they like in the world. They will seek out the least regulated economy with the cheapest workforce, thereby leading to a 'race to the bottom'. Since TNCs lack any commitment to the workforce they employ, workers' rights and job security are undermined.

■ As a result of globalisation, poorer countries are swamped with cheaply made foreign imports so that they remain in a peripheral stage of development, mainly producing raw materials and allowing foreign investors to exploit their workforces.

■ Globalisation exacerbates greater inequality both between and within countries, creating destabilising social tensions.

> ### Synoptic links
>
> Ayn Rand's influence on the development of economic liberalism can be found as a core political idea (conservatism) in Component 1. Rand's laissez-faire approach to the economy also has similarities with the free-market ideology of Milton Friedman and the Chicago School.

Democratic deficit

Economic globalisation gives too much power to intergovernmental bodies such as the IMF, World Bank and WTO, which are severely lacking in democratic accountability. Too often the free-market/free-trade reforms these agencies encourage damage the interests of the poorest, and yet there are no democratic means of opposing them.

It could be argued that the same is also true of regional bodies, such as the EU. The way in which the EU negotiates treaties on behalf of its member states, such as the proposed Trans-Atlantic Trade and Investment Partnership (TTIP), demonstrates how far removed the public is from decision making. Even though the TTIP has been accused of lowering European standards of protection for workers, consumers and the environment in return for tariff reductions, there is no democratic mechanism by which to oppose the deal.

Destruction of local cultures and the environment

TNCs' success in reducing labour costs and prices can lead to the destruction of traditional local industries, such as rice in Ghana, ground nuts in Sierra Leone or small-scale peasant agriculture in Jamaica. In terms of cost-efficiency, this is economically sound. However, opening up local markets to global competition, as the IMF, World Bank and WTO advocate, can have an appalling social cost. Sudden global challenges to small-scale industry and agriculture can lead to family breakdown, crime and prostitution.

The materialism that globalisation encourages also undermines traditional cultural observances. The spread of factories throughout the developing world breaks up families, as young people head for big cities in search of work. In China, a spate of suicides among lonely young workers at Foxconn factories demonstrates how such 'proletarianisation' can have devastating consequences.

Some have criticised TNCs for abusing the environment and showing little responsibility towards indigenous cultures. For example, Shell has faced scrutiny for its degradation of the Niger Delta. In 2010, the UN estimated that TNCs had caused US$2.2 billion of damage to the environment annually.

Reducing labour costs and prices can lead to the destruction of traditional local businesses, such as in the rice paddy fields of Ghana

Lack of job security

Since global capitalism seeks the cheapest workforce, it also undermines the long-term job security of workers around the world. TNCs withdraw their factories from countries in which labour costs have risen. For example, Chinese firms are increasingly moving operations to lower-cost Africa and Vietnam. In the 2016 US presidential election, both Bernie Sanders and Donald Trump generated massive vocal support among blue-collar workers who felt that they were losing their future to cheaper factories in China and Mexico. Indeed, during the campaign, Trump argued that the impact of globalisation had been to leave 'millions of our workers with nothing but poverty and heartache'. Subsequently, in his inaugural speech, Trump argued that global competition had created 'carnage' in the USA's manufacturing heartlands.

Anti-globalisation resentment is also likely to have encouraged some of the extreme nationalistic attitudes deployed towards the EU during the 2016 Referendum. Especially among the working class, there was the conviction that Brexit would stop the free flow of goods, capital and labour that threatened job security.

World systems (dependency) theory

Left-wing globalisation sceptics, such as Immanuel Wallerstein in his 'world systems' theory, also argue that globalisation can lock developing states into permanent dependency status. This is because if they open their borders to trade too early, the 'dumping' of cheap manufactured products on them means they become 'dependent' on cheap foreign imports and so never develop their own industries. This can be termed 'neocolonialism', since developing countries are condemned to a peripheral status in global trade. Developing states therefore end up providing markets and a workforce for TNCs, without developing their own business interests.

According to the Prebisch–Singer hypothesis, exporting the primary products that fuel economic globalisation means that developing countries face declining terms of trade in the long run. This then traps them into permanently low levels of development. The Cambridge economist Ha-Joon Chang argues that the developing world, at least initially, should be prepared to protect its vulnerable industries with subsidies and tariffs. If it does this, it will be able to achieve a sufficient stage of development as to be able to withstand foreign competition.

Activity

On 24 April 2013, the Rana Plaza factory in Bangladesh collapsed, killing 1,129 employees and injuring 2,500 due to structural failings in the construction of the eight-floor factory that manufactured low-cost garments for the world market, including brands such as Benetton, Monsoon Accessorize, Primark and Walmart. Even though employers had discovered cracks in the building, employees were ordered to carry on working as usual. The building collapsed during the morning rush hour.

To what extent do you think disasters such as this undermine the case for economic globalisation?

Case study

The Dell Theory of Conflict Resolution

During the nineteenth century, liberal economists and politicians were keen to point out the close connection between free trade and peace. British liberals such as John Bright, Richard Cobden and William Gladstone viewed free trade not only as an economic good but as a moral good, according to the principle that 'if goods do not cross borders, armies will'.

More recently, Thomas Friedman, in his Dell Theory of Conflict Resolution, has argued that not only does economic globalisation encourage greater global prosperity, it also greatly reduces the risk of conflict between nation-states. This is because such a complex web of economic interconnectedness is established between states, that it would be irrational for any state to go to war with another in the same supply chain. The USA's and China's reliance on each other for both trade and foreign investment has therefore created such a symbiotic relationship that it would be self-defeating for them to go to war with each other.

However, realists have criticised this theory, pointing out that states are primarily 'power-maximisers' as well as risk-takers, and that they do not always act according to rational principles. In 1910, Norman Angell published *The Great Illusion*, which argued that war between Germany and the UK was inconceivable because it would be economic suicide for both sides. After all, in 1913 there was a greater volume of trade between the two countries than ever before. The following year, of course, the First World War broke out as a result of these great powers' struggle for strategic influence. This suggests that we ought not to be too confident about the extent to which free trade really does make war unthinkable.

Synoptic links

Left-wing criticisms of free-market capitalism are also covered under 'socialism' in Component 1. Marx and Engels warned that the capitalist system is based upon institutionalised exploitation and so cannot meaningfully benefit the working class.

Does economic globalisation resolve the issue of global poverty?

Yes

- Developing countries attract investment by engaging in free trade, so allowing them to break out of a cycle of subsistence agriculture.
- Nation-states are able to use their 'comparative advantage' within a global market, so creating limitless opportunities for expansion.
- Developing countries have an incentive to provide a better-trained and educated workforce in order to attract investment.
- Global capital flows encourage the rise of a job-creating entrepreneurial class.
- Globalisation reduces the global cost of imports, enabling the world's poorest to purchase subsistence and consumer goods more cheaply.
- The internet facilitates global investment and the spread of new knowledge-skills, so creating a commercial environment from which no country needs to be excluded.
- TNCs outsource employment to countries with the lowest labour costs, creating diversification in developing countries that export raw materials and/or manufacture products.
- There has been a dramatic decrease in levels of global poverty since developing countries have engaged in globalisation.
- There is greater convergence between the GDP of the Global North and the Global South.
- The MDGs have been largely successful due to the effect of economic globalisation.

No

- Economic globalisation creates a 'race to the bottom', as governments reduce costs by limiting workers' rights through organised commercial violence against workers.
- Proletarianisation leads to the disintegration of communities, with a corresponding rise in crime.
- Job security in both the developed and developing worlds is threatened, as businesses move production in order to take advantage of the lowest-cost environment in which to produce.
- Social harmony is undermined as the income gap between rich and poor increases both within and between countries.
- Core states 'dump' cheap manufactured products on peripheral/developing states so that they continue producing raw materials. This ensures that they remain in a state of neocolonial dependency (Prebisch–Singer hypothesis), trapping them in low levels of development.
- Global capitalism is volatile, encouraging crises such as the sub-prime mortgage recession of 2007–9 and the euro crisis. Instability threatens stable socioeconomic progress in states.

Human rights

In what ways has international law advanced human rights?

Respect for the rule of law provides the basis for liberal democracy within a nation-state. In the same way, the acceptance of international law is a prerequisite for adherence to a global standard of human rights.

The state as the source of civil liberties

Westphalian principles of non-interventionism enshrine the concept that states determine civil liberties. This means that the cultural heritage of the nation-state influences the rights that its citizens enjoy. Realists support this interpretation, arguing that it is the sole right of national communities to decide these rights. Not only does the diversity of cultural traditions throughout the world justify this, but it also encourages global stability by making states the moral arbiters of what occurs within their borders. This removes any legal justification for outside powers destabilising sovereignty.

The rise of international human rights-based law

Liberals claim that human rights are universal rather than relative. There is such a thing as a global community and there are certain human rights that, by virtue of our common humanity, we all possess. In 1948, the UN, responding to the horrors of the Second World War, issued the Universal Declaration of Human Rights (UDHR). This established certain human freedoms that all human beings have a right to enjoy. The UDHR recognises 'the inherent dignity' and 'equal and inalienable rights of all members of the human family' as 'the foundation of freedom, justice and peace in the world'. It also sets out the core civil, political, social and religious rights that we should all enjoy, whomever we are and wherever we live.

The UDHR does not represent hard international law, since states are not bound to obey it (see Box 2.1). However, it possesses great moral persuasive power and provides a standard of human rights accountability by which the international community can judge states. Human Rights Watch, in particular, uses the UDHR to measure the extent to which governments abuse the rights of their citizens.

Box 2.1

The Universal Declaration of Human Rights (1948)

The UDHR embodies the following principles:

- 'All human beings are born free and equal in dignity and rights. They are endowed with reason and conscience and should act towards one another in a spirit of brotherhood' (Article 1)
- Freedom from discrimination (Article 2)
- The right to life, liberty and security of person (Article 3)
- The banning of slavery in all its forms (Article 4)
- Prohibition of 'torture' and 'cruel', inhuman or degrading treatment or punishment (Article 5)
- Equal recognition before the law (Article 6)
- Equal protection by the law (Article 7)
- The right to a fair trial (Article 8)
- Protection from 'arbitrary arrest, detention or exile' (Article 9)
- The right to 'full equality to a fair and public hearing by an independent and impartial tribunal' (Article 10)
- The right to be 'presumed innocent until proved guilty' (Article 11)
- The right to privacy (Article 12)
- The right to freedom of movement (Article 13)
- The right to asylum from persecution (Article 14)
- The right to a nationality (Article 15)
- The right to marry whom you wish, and have a family (Article 16)
- The right to own property (Article 17)
- Freedom of thought, conscience and religion, and freedom to change one's religion (Article 18)
- The right to 'freedom of opinion and expression' (Article 19)
- The right to 'freedom of peaceful assembly and association' (Article 20)
- The right to 'democratic involvement' (Article 21)
- The right to 'social security' (Article 22)
- The right to work, a fair standard of employment and the right to join a trade union (Article 23)
- The right to 'rest and leisure' (Article 24)
- The right to an adequate standard of living (Article 25)
- The right to education (Article 26)
- 'The right freely to participate in the cultural life of the community' (Article 27)
- 'Everyone is entitled to a social and international order in which the rights and freedoms set forth in this Declaration can be fully realized' (Article 28)
- The right to limited interference by government in one's life (Article 29)
- 'Nothing in this Declaration may be interpreted as implying for any State, group or person any right to engage in any activity or to perform any act aimed at the destruction of any of the rights and freedoms set forth herein' (Article 30)

The 1950 European Convention on Human Rights (ECHR) also dates from the aftermath of the Second World War. Inspired by former UK prime minister Winston Churchill, the Conservative politician David Maxwell-Fyfe played a key role in drafting its terms. The convention enumerates what rights European citizens may claim by virtue of their humanity rather than by means of their national citizenship (see Box 2.2). It also established the European Court of Human Rights (ECtHR).

The ECHR has established a powerful standard of human rights, which has greatly impacted the development of European domestic law. The ECtHR's rulings on member states are binding (although they are not enforceable). In a number of significant cases, European states have changed their domestic laws to conform to ECtHR rulings:

- In 1981, after the Royal Ulster Constabulary questioned Jeff Dudgeon about his sexual preferences, the ECtHR declared that Northern Ireland's criminalisation of homosexual acts was in violation of the ECHR. In 1982, Northern Ireland's domestic law was altered to decriminalise male homosexual sex.
- In 1999, the ECtHR ruled that the dismissal of two gay men from the military was in breach of their right to a private life. As a result of the ruling, the UK recognised the equal rights of gay people to serve in the UK military.
- In 2010, the ECtHR ruled that Section 44 of the Terrorism Act 2000, which authorised police to stop and search people without grounds for suspicion, was contrary to the ECHR. Theresa May, as home secretary, immediately complied with the ruling, and the law was changed.
- The rise of more authoritarian governments in Turkey and Russia, as well as claims by individuals (often Roma) in eastern European states that their human rights are being ignored, demonstrate the importance of the ECtHR's existence, since it provides plaintiffs with the opportunity to achieve justice beyond the confines of the nation-state. In 2016, the ECtHR delivered 993 judgments. There were 222 judgments against Russia, 77 against Turkey, 71 against Romania and 70 against Ukraine. The greatest number of violations of the ECHR involved the right to liberty and security (286) and inhuman or degrading treatment (193).

Box 2.2

The European Convention on Human Rights (1950)

The ECHR consists of three parts. The main rights and freedoms (Articles 2 to 14) are contained in Section I:

- Right to life (Article 2)
- Freedom from torture (Article 3)
- Freedom from slavery (Article 4)
- Right to liberty and security (Article 5)
- Right to a fair trial (Article 6)
- No punishment without trial (Article 7)
- Respect for private and family life (Article 8)
- Freedom of thought, conscience and religion (Article 9)
- Freedom of expression (Article 10)
- Freedom of assembly and association (Article 11)
- Right to marry (Article 12)
- Right to an effective remedy before a national authority (Article 13)
- Freedom from discrimination (Article 14)

The New World Order

The ending of the Cold War, an ideological conflict that had divided the world since the end of the Second World War, provided further impetus for the development of a universal standard of human rights. Dramatic steps were also being taken to resolve seemingly intractable conflicts, such as those in Northern Ireland, Palestine and South Africa. Such optimism was reinforced in 1993, when the UN General Assembly voted unanimously to establish the post of a UN High Commissioner for Human Rights. Globally influential political figures, such as former UN secretary-general Kofi Annan, South African president Nelson Mandela, US president Bill Clinton and Prime Minister Tony Blair, also focused the world's attention on human rights as an issue of defining importance in international relations.

Instant news

The internet's globalisation of information has also meant that human rights abuses can be instantly publicised, so that atrocities captured on mobile phones can be flashed around the world in seconds. Global pressure groups, such as Human Rights Watch and Amnesty International, have further raised the profile of human rights abuses. The UN's failure to intervene during the Rwandan genocide in 1994 and its hesitancy over how to react to the Bosnian Civil War (1991–95) also heightened the sense that the global community could and must do more to enforce an international standard of human rights.

UN war crimes tribunals and the International Criminal Court

In the 1990s, a number of international courts were established to try war crimes. In 1993, the UN Security Council (UNSC) established the International Criminal Tribunal for the former Yugoslavia to deal with war crimes that took place during the Balkan conflict. War crimes tribunals to investigate human rights abuses committed in Cambodia, Rwanda and Sierra Leone followed.

In 2002, the Rome Statute treaty established the International Criminal Court (ICC) as a permanent body prepared to try all those (including heads of state) indicted for either war crimes or crimes against humanity. This court, it was hoped, would dramatically increase the influence of human rights-based law by establishing a global consensus that an internationally recognised court could now challenge the Westphalian principles of state sovereignty. In 2017, 124 nation-states recognised the authority of the court, and it has so far secured three convictions (see page 180).

> **Synoptic links**
>
> Many of the liberal thinkers covered in Component 1 wrestled with the relationship between human rights and the rights of society as a whole. John Locke focused on the extent to which citizens should obey government and John Stuart Mill on the extent to which individuals can determine their own moral preferences.

In what ways has international law failed to advance human rights?

The rival claim of state sovereignty undermines the scope of international justice. The UDHR only amounts to soft persuasive power, while the authority of the ICC requires the cooperation of nation-states to be effective. Thus, international human rights-based law only works if nation-states are prepared for it to work. Often states will decide to pursue their own perceived best interests, confident that they will not be punished if they act in defiance of international law.

The International Criminal Court

The unwillingness of nation-states to accept the ICC's jurisdiction considerably undermines its authority:

■ Three (China, Russia and the USA) of the permanent five members of the UNSC have hardly set a good example of global cooperation through refusing to accept the ICC's jurisdiction.

■ The USA has enacted the American Service Members' Protection Act (2002), which states that the US government can use 'all means necessary' to free its servicemen if the ICC detains them.

■ In 2016, Russia withdrew its signature from the Rome Statute when the ICC claimed the country's forces had illegally annexed Crimea.

■ A number of African leaders, such as Sudan's Omar al-Bashir and Kenya's Uhuru Kenyatta, have ignored indictments to attend the ICC. In 2016, South Africa, one of the ICC's most significant members, notified the UN that it was beginning the official process of departing from the ICC's jurisdiction, since membership no longer served its national interests.

The European Convention on Human Rights

As we have seen, member states may 'derogate' from the ECHR in public emergencies. The ECHR also lacks the coercive powers to enforce its judgments on states if they do not obey its rulings:

■ The UK is in defiance of the ECHR by not allowing prisoners voting rights. As home secretary, Theresa May argued for the replacement of the Human Rights Act, by which the UK accepted the jurisdiction of the ECHR, by a British Bill of Rights.

■ In 2016, Russia asserted the primacy of domestic law over the ECHR.

■ Turkey suspended its membership in the aftermath of the failed military coup in 2016 when many outside observers condemned what they saw as President Erdogan's brutal suppression of opposition.

The problems that the ECtHR and ICC face in establishing a more rules-based approach to global justice demonstrate the continued importance of the state as the final arbiter of human rights. The growing influence of increasingly nationalist leaders, such as Donald Trump in the USA, Vladimir Putin in Russia, Recep Tayyip Erdogan in Turkey and Xi Jinping in China, suggests that the centrality of the state in determining the rights of its citizens is likely to continue. This illustrates the limitations of international courts of justice, but also their increasing importance in putting forward the case for human rights in an increasingly authoritarian world order.

Conflict

In what ways has the international community attempted to resolve conflict?

Post-Cold War idealism

At the end of the Cold War, the rise of human rights-based international law led to a number of humanitarian interventions in order to protect people from war crimes, ethnic cleansing or crimes against humanity, including:

■ Iraq, 1991

■ Somalia, 1992

■ Bosnia, 1995

By the end of April 1999, half of the 2 million residents of Kosovo were refugees or internally displaced people

- Kosovo, 1999
- Sierra Leone, 2000
- East Timor, 2000

Following the First Gulf War, in 1991, UN Resolution 688 condemned Saddam Hussein's retribution against Shia and Kurdish rebels. This led to France, the UK and the USA establishing 'no-fly zones' within Iraqi airspace to protect Saddam's opponents from his retribution. In 1992, President George H. W. Bush sent US troops into Somalia 'to stop the starvation'. In 1995, as a result of the escalating humanitarian disaster, the North Atlantic Treaty Organization (NATO) intervened against the Bosnian Serbs during the Bosnian Civil War. In 1999, NATO bombed Serbia in order to stop the 'ethnic cleansing' that Serb forces were carrying out in Kosovo, a constituent part of the Serbian state. During this conflict, former prime minister Tony Blair, who had pushed especially hard for military action, defined the principles of this new internationalism in his Chicago speech. In it he stated that mass murder could not be 'a purely internal matter'.

Other such humanitarian, rather than strategic, interventions were also made by UN peacemakers in East Timor from 1999 and by the UK in Sierra Leone in 2000. In 2005, the UN published the Responsibility to Protect (R2P), a global political commitment declaring that sovereignty is conditional upon a nation-state protecting its citizens from 'genocide, war crimes, ethnic cleansing and crimes against humanity'.

In what ways has the international community failed to resolve conflict?

The decline of humanitarian interventionism

Although it had seemed as though the more globally connected world would prioritise humanitarian interventionism, this increasingly proved not to be the case. Liberals had hoped that increasing economic, political and cultural exchanges between states would establish the UN as the ultimate arbiter of peace and war, and that a newfound global respect for human rights would restrain the brutality of dictators. Yet, even during the euphoria of the immediate post-Cold War period, there were unmistakable signs that the influence of the state in determining the wellbeing of its citizens, together with its relationship with other states and NGOs, was still paramount.

When the Yugoslav Federation broke up in 1991 and the Balkans were plunged into civil war, both the UN and the EU were paralysed by indecision, only hesitantly intervening to ease the suffering without being seen to take sides. In Chechnya, during two brutal wars, Russian forces succeeded in quelling independence at the cost of, some have estimated, 160,000 lives. In Rwanda, 800,000 Tutsis were killed during the 1994 genocide while the UN dithered. In all these cases the global community failed to confront mass killings, since these were going on within states and so, it could be claimed, were outside the jurisdiction of any other body.

Failings of intervention

- In 2003, the US and UK invaded Iraq without the UN's explicit endorsement, primarily in order to achieve strategic objectives in the region. The resulting humanitarian disaster, in which some estimates suggest half a million may have died, together with the rise of militant Islamism and the consequent destabilising of the region, further challenged both the justification and the effectiveness of interventionism.
- The limits of interventionism have been further illustrated by the lack of progress made in Afghanistan. In spite of years of 'nation-building' by Western powers, the Taliban continues to wield immense influence as NATO forces have gradually been withdrawn.
- Although it helped to topple Colonel Muammar Gaddafi, NATO's 2011 intervention in Libya has left the country in a state of anarchy.

All of these failures have undermined much of the practical case for humanitarian interventionism. In addition, the conflicting strategic interests and declining trust between China, Russia and the USA have discouraged action. Therefore, even though the civil war in Syria has led to an unparalleled humanitarian disaster, Western powers, scarred by failings in Iraq, Afghanistan and Libya, have been wary of fully committing themselves to the overthrow of the Assad government. The way, too, in which Russia, sensing Western lack of resolve, then militarily intervened to support its long-time ally President Assad against the rebels suggests that the great powers may, once again, be putting realist self-interest before liberal idealism.

Realism as a guide to foreign policy

When the Cold War ended in 1991, the future seemed to be one of greater global cooperation. States increasingly embraced the sorts of common values that led then-US president George H. W. Bush to speak of a 'New World Order' based on a global community increasingly working together to resolve the problems it jointly faced. Former UK foreign secretary Douglas Hurd recalls that there were, 'no more enemies — just new friends to be made', while 'out went ideology — in came idealism'. Initially, influenced by liberal idealists like Tony Blair and the dominance of Western power, it had seemed as though a determined effort was being made to create an 'empire of the good'. Westphalian principles of state sovereignty would no longer be used to excuse mass murder within states.

Such liberal optimism now seems misplaced, especially since Donald Trump's inaugural speech in January 2017 in which he promised that the USA would 'not seek to impose our way of life on anyone' and that his only principle will be 'America first'. The way in which Trump has endorsed self-interest as the guiding principle for a nation-state suggests that the future of liberal interventionism is now seriously in doubt.

> ### Activity
>
> The contrast between Tony Blair's Chicago speech (1999) and Theresa May's Philadelphia speech (2017) illustrates how attitudes are changing. When Blair delivered his speech, at the height of the Kosovo intervention, he remarked that:
>
> > In the end, values and interests merge. If we can establish and spread the values of liberty, the rule of law, human rights and an open society then that is in our national interests too. The spread of our values makes us safer.
>
> In contrast, on her first meeting with Donald Trump in February 2017, Theresa May stated that:
>
> > The days of Britain and America intervening in sovereign countries in an attempt to remake the world in our own image are over.
>
> Do you agree with Theresa May or Tony Blair on whether Western powers should be prepared to intervene abroad in order to confront wickedness? Explain using specific examples.

Without a commitment to humanitarianism from either the UK or USA, it is highly unlikely that other countries will have the authority to take a moral lead on humanitarian intervention. Liberal principles of a global community of nations are in more doubt than ever before. It seems likely, therefore, that barbaric states, at least in the immediate future, will have less to fear than before from outside interference.

> ### Activity
>
> The Syrian civil war, which began in 2011, has proved to be the biggest humanitarian disaster of the twenty-first century so far. Out of a pre-war population of 22 million it is estimated that almost 5 million refugees have fled the country and over 6 million are displaced internally. The UN also estimated that by December 2016, 220,000 people had lost their lives in the civil war.
> Given the enormous scale of this human tragedy and the UN's declaration in 2005 of the R2P, why has the international community failed to work together to resolve the crisis?

In what way has globalisation impacted on environmental issues?

'Collective dilemma'

The challenge of 'man-made' climate change provides a classic example of a 'collective security dilemma', which can only be resolved if states cooperate in order to lower carbon emissions and protect the environment. The way in which the members of the UN's IPCC have worked together to highlight the

Case study

The influence of the internet

The internet has made it possible for people virtually anywhere in the world to communicate with each other in ways that would, until very recently, have been unthinkable. This globalisation of communication challenges the power of the state in determining the political allegiance and cultural preferences of its citizens. For example, the use of Facebook and Twitter helped to provoke the Arab Uprisings, as citizens succeeded in organising themselves electronically, so undermining the authority of repressive governments.

Liberals optimistically hope that the internet can become a way of creating a genuinely global dialogue in which people exchange ideas and shared experiences beneath the radar of government. International pressure groups, such as Make Poverty History, also use the internet to coordinate 'global people power', which further illustrates how instantaneous electronic communication has the potential to create new supranational movements and allegiances. More negatively, the internet has enabled extremist ideologies, such as Islamic fundamentalism, to challenge national allegiances.

However, what liberals have failed to appreciate is that there is no reason why states should not use the internet to advance their own nationalistic world view at the expense of others. RT (formerly Russia Today) illustrates how the power of the internet can be deployed to advance a highly nationalistic interpretation of world events. The Chinese government has successfully used the internet to advance its own nationalistic agenda, while restricting outside electronic influences through its 'firewall'. World leaders have also become adept at tweeting their opinions, sometimes criticising other nation-states, in a way that mobilises national support. Both India's prime minister Narendra Modi and President Donald Trump are inveterate tweeters and use Twitter to advertise and advance the interests of their own nations rather than the global community.

dangers of a rise in global temperature demonstrates that IGOs can play a key role in developing a global response to cross-border problems.

National responses

Although the IPCC has focused global attention on the risks of climate change, nation-states remain the key players in determining how to respond to this challenge. For example, the China/US joint climate change agreement in 2014, in which both countries agreed to work together to combat climate change, proved vital in establishing an optimistic framework in which climate change could be debated at the Paris Conference in 2015. In order for Paris to be a success, it was vital to achieve agreement on action between states, which had not been the case at Copenhagen in 2009. Significant progress was made, with the vast majority of the world's countries agreeing to limit their carbon emissions, as well as accepting international reviews of their progress.

However, the UN possesses no coercive power if states refuse, or fail, to reduce their carbon emissions. In June 2017, for example, President Trump announced that the USA would withdraw from the Paris climate change agreement. According to Trump, it would cost the USA US$3 trillion and 6.5 million jobs. As the president put it, 'I was elected to represent the citizens of Pittsburgh not Paris.' This demonstrates that even collective dilemmas as fundamental as climate change still depend upon states agreeing to work together for the common good.

Synoptic links

Ecologism is covered as an optional political idea in Component 2. Radical ecologists, such as Carolyn Merchant, argue that political globalisation has approached environmental issues from too anthropocentric a position. As a result, progress towards restoring the environment has been slow and ineffective.

To what extent has globalisation created a global monoculture?

'Cultural homogenisation'?

It has been claimed that the spread of a global consumer culture based upon a common adulation of certain products and brands has undermined the significance of national boundaries in determining the culture of a nation-state. The resulting 'cultural homogenisation' of once diverse cultures has created a global monoculture, as the differences between cultures are ironed out. What makes a society, culture or civilisation unique is therefore lost through conformity to certain global cultural norms.

'Coca-Colonization'

Sociologist Brendan Barber has termed the materialism that cultural globalisation encourages as 'Coca-Colonization'. Author and filmmaker Naomi Klein has referred to 'commodity fetishism', whereby we become so obsessed with materialism and brand culture that we undermine the uniqueness of our own culture.

In the UK, the most popular attraction for Chinese tourists travelling outside London is Bicester Shopping Village. The adulation of brands such as Hollister, Nike, Apple, Microsoft, Gucci, Prada, Dior and Armani is global. Globally, 50% of internet traffic and 40% of radio programmes are in English. According to Barber, this has created a 'McWorld' culture, in which people all over the world crave the same sort of materialistic fulfilment, enjoy the same sort of entertainment and eat the same sort of Americanized food. The ten most successful global restaurant chains and the ten most profitable films in history are all American. According to *Fortune*, in 2015 eight of the top ten most admired brands in the world were American. Michael Jackson's *Thriller* is the best-selling album of all time. The global domination of certain brands and a desire to emulate US standards of dress, food and entertainment has therefore led to a diluting of distinct cultures. In its place is a bland, shallow and vulgarised faux global culture, which ultimately represents nothing of permanent value.

A global marketplace

Cultural globalisation also has the potential to provide us with greater choice than ever before, creating a rich global diversity of opportunity rather than a 'one size fits all' experience. Therefore, rather than creating a monoculture, it actually creates a more globally diverse culture, as people anywhere in the world select from a global array of choices. For example:

- Japanese manga comics have a global audience.
- In Russia, the most popular television show in 2015 was the UK-made *Sherlock*, while *Doctor Who* and *Downton Abbey* are hugely popular in the USA.
- Real Madrid and Manchester United are two of the most popular sports teams in the world, while Chelsea has a strong following in Latin America.
- 'Scandinavian noir' detective fiction and television programmes have a worldwide appeal.

Walking down any high street in the UK provides further evidence of the diversity of experience that globalisation offers. In 1960, there were 500 Indian

Key terms

Cultural homogenisation The process by which those characteristics that make the cultures of nation-states different from each other are flattened out, encouraging the establishment of a more uniformly similar global culture.

Monoculture Result of cultural homogenisation, in which the similarities between the lives of people in countries across the world are greater than their differences (also relates to the terms 'Coca-Colonization', 'McDonaldization' and 'McWorld').

Cultural globalisation The process by which people anywhere in the world participate in the same homogenised global culture (e.g. food, clothes, entertainment, brands, products), so that our cultural differences become less striking than our cultural similarities.

Debate

Is globalisation another name for Americanization?

Yes

- The USA dominates the world in terms of its cultural outreach: casual American-style clothing is ubiquitous, while US festivals such as Halloween now have a global following, challenging national festivals such as Bonfire Night.
- The ten most profitable films in history, led by *Avatar*, are American.
- The top ten restaurant chains globally are all US-led, including McDonald's (1), KFC (2) and Subway (3).
- The ten most admired companies in the world are US-led, including Apple (1), Google (2) and Berkshire Hathaway (3).
- Four of the top five most visited websites are American, including Google (1), Facebook (2) and YouTube (3).
- The equivalent of 20% of the world's population drinks a Coca-Cola product every day.
- The USA is the dominant global economy, representing 22% of global GDP in 2016. The free-trade principles that have dominated the global economy since the end of the Cold War are firmly rooted in the principles of the Washington Consensus.
- The World Bank, IMF and WTO have each advanced the interests of the Washington Consensus.
- US principles of liberal democracy were hugely influential in leading to the collapse of Communist power in Russia and eastern Europe.
- US global troop deployments are unparalleled, further extending US interests and ideals. A total of 130,000 US troops are stationed throughout the world, including 38,000 in Japan, 34,000 in Germany, 24,000 in South Korea and 6,000 in Kuwait (2016).

No

- The internet has provided new opportunities to challenge the USA's cultural outreach. It provides a level playing field on which the USA now competes equally with other nation-states and ideologies.
- The mega-hit 'Gangnam Style', by South Korean pop star Psy, received 2.74 billion hits (January 2017), making it the most watched video on YouTube. The most popular global television show in 2015 was the UK's *Top Gear*.
- The most popular global sports are Association Football (3.5 billion fans), followed by cricket (2.5 billion fans).
- British 'values' have a global appeal through the worldwide popularity of television programmes *Downton Abbey* and *Sherlock*, and most powerfully the Harry Potter books and films.
- The USA's soft-power influence is regularly challenged by the UK (first place, 2015) and Germany (first place, 2013).
- Rival news channels such as the BBC, RT and Al Jazeera now challenge the influence of CNN.
- The carnage that resulted from the Anglo-American invasion of Iraq in 2003, including detention at Guantánamo Bay and the atrocities at Abu Ghraib, have undermined US global influence. Islamic fundamentalism, rather than liberal democracy, influenced the Arab Uprisings.
- The USA's global popularity is changing: in 2015, 44% of Chinese had a positive view of the USA and 49% had a negative view, while in Russia just 15% had a positive view, while 81% had a negative view.
- As a result of economic globalisation, China has become the biggest global investor in other countries. The establishment of the Asian Infrastructure Investment Bank (AIIB) is designed to challenge the dominance of the World Bank in the developing world.
- The Chinese firm Sinopec is now the world's wealthiest business (2017).
- President Trump's commitment to 'America first' and his executive order withdrawing the USA from the Trans-Pacific Partnership (TPP) suggests that the country now feels that it has become the victim of, rather than the driving force behind, economic globalisation.

restaurants in the UK — now there are around 9,500. One of the fastest-growing restaurant chains in the world is Nando's, a South African company with Portuguese/Mozambique influences — in 1992, it had one branch in the UK, but by 2017 there were 339. Carne Argentina Unica (CAU) now provides an Argentinian dining experience in a growing number of British cities. Pret A Manger trades on its continental appeal and yet it was founded in the UK in 1986.

Glocalisation

A process known as 'glocalisation' has also enabled local communities to mould global brands to their own culture, which demonstrates that globalisation may be more subtle than mere 'Coca-Colonization'. The Balti curry was developed in Birmingham, and is a mixture of Indian and British-Asian influences. Chicken tikka is similarly British in origin and has frequently topped polls as the UK's favourite food. Famous brands such as McDonald's have adapted to local conditions, serving lobster burgers in Canada and vegetarian burgers to the Hindu market in India. Bollywood has taken from Hollywood epic and dramatic influences, while adding distinctly Indian glamour and romance to the mix.

> ### Activity
>
> In 2012, a group of Eton sixth-formers posted a clip called 'Eton Style' on YouTube. By 2017, it had had over 3 million views.
> 1 Why might this be used as an example of glocalisation?
> 2 What other examples of glocalisation can you discover?
> 3 To what extent does glocalisation challenge the argument that globalisation is creating a global monoculture?

The limits of materialism

Cultural globalisation can also create a negative backlash, which, far from contributing towards a global monoculture or encouraging tolerance and diversity, has actually reinforced ethnic and national identities, so undermining global cosmopolitanism. In that case, rather than bringing the world closer together, globalisation is doing exactly the opposite by stirring up resentment against what many regard as the vapid consumerism that the 'McWorld' culture represents.

As early as 2 November 2001, the veteran Labour politician Tony Benn noted in his diary that because of the uncertainties and blandness of globalisation, 'when things go wrong everyone rallies round their own tribe or religion or village or town and fights off anyone else'. The way in which globalisation advances ultimately unfulfilling consumerism and the instant gratification of social media do not, therefore, create true fulfilment. Instead, it creates a cultural void based on greed and narcissism. More compelling ideologies can step into this void, offering deeper and more profound cultural experiences based upon shared cultural, ethnic and religious experiences.

The rise of identity politics

This can be seen today across Europe, with the rise of political parties and leaders who achieve popularity by emphasising the distinctiveness of their own culture, with promises to safeguard it from alien influences.

In Hungary, Viktor Orbán has generated huge appeal by emphasising the country's Christian heritage as a frontier state resisting Muslim advance. In the Netherlands, Geert Wilders has said that Islam can have no place in Dutch society. In France, Marine Le Pen and the National Front claim to represent France's unique cultural identity. In the UK, the surge in support for UKIP during the 2015 general election indicated a more nationalistic mindset among voters (although it lost its only seat in the 2017 general election). The subsequent 2016 vote to leave the EU suggests, too, that many voters saw European integration as a threat to the 'British way of life'. Even in the USA, the driving force behind globalisation, President Trump has emphasised US exclusivity in marked contrast to the cosmopolitanism of President Obama. His executive order to build a wall on the Mexican border, as well as indefinitely banning Syrian refugees and prioritising the rights of Christian over Muslim refugees, have been justified as issues of national security. Equally they could be seen as a way of preserving those traditional American values that make the USA special.

A clash of civilisations?

In his 1996 hypothesis 'The Clash of Civilizations', Samuel Huntington acknowledged the paradox that the popularity of Western-influenced consumer goods can actually create a reaction rather than a global monoculture. This is because threatened cultures then seek to reassert their own values in defiance of 'Coca-Colonization'. We must therefore beware of assuming that just because there are 36,615 McDonald's restaurants across the world (2016), our eating habits impact on our attitudes.

Instead, other civilisations may seek to protect their own identity through characterising their values as superior to those of the West. The right to determine one's sexuality is, for example, now acknowledged throughout much of western Europe and Latin America. However, gay sex is still illegal in 72 countries and in ten is punishable by the death penalty. President Museveni of Uganda, for example, has condemned Western tolerance of homosexuality, declaring that it is 'disgusting' and 'un-African'. In Russia, there has been a resurgence of national identity during the Putin years closely associated with Slavic pride and the moral conservatism of the Orthodox Church. In his State of the Union address in 2014, President Putin accused American liberalism and consumerism of leading to a 'path of degradation'. Therefore, the way in which Americanization and materialism has contributed towards a cultural backlash should not be underestimated. Huntington, in particular, focuses on the way in which the globalisation of Western liberalism can be seen as a threat to Islam, leading to its rejection of Western values. Critics of Huntington's thesis argue that he unhelpfully generalises Islam, however it is clear that some militant branches of Islam have, rather than accommodating Western values, sought to oppose them.

Islamic fundamentalism

The most striking example of the rise of identity politics as a reaction against cultural homogenisation has been the growth of Islamic fundamentalism. It is inspired by the writings of Sayyid Qutb, who, when he lived in the USA from 1948 to 1950, was shocked by what he saw as that culture's moral depravity and materialism. Islamic fundamentalism contrasts the purity of Islam with the decadence and moral relativism of liberalism and consumerism. For Qutb, the USA was living in *Jahiliyyah*, a state of barbarous ignorance.

Having spread in north Africa and Afghanistan from the 1980s onwards, fundamental Islam's appeal has broadened as a result of the Western invasions of Afghanistan and Iraq and the instability provoked by the Arab Uprisings. So-called Islamic State is, in its own violent fashion, another manifestation of how cultures that may feel threatened seek to restore their sense of uniqueness in response to the seductive appeal of global consumerism.

Has cultural globalisation created a 'McWorld'?

Yes

- American-inspired products and styles dominate global brand culture and monopolise global markets.
- Cultural homogenisation flattens out differences between nation-states, creating a 'McWorld' based upon borderless food and entertainment.
- The 'Coca-Colonization' of previously distinctive cultures creates a 'race to the bottom' in terms of cultural preferences.
- The internet has further reinforced the potential for a global monoculture by creating a worldwide audience for popular celebrities, trends and products.

No

- Cultural diversity, more than cultural uniformity, encourages greater global choice than ever before.
- Glocalisation allows global influences to adapt to local conditions, so creating a new, distinctive culture.
- The reaction against cultural homogenisation leads to the rise of identity politics, through which nation-states, ethnic groups and religious movements seek to define themselves according to their own unique characteristics.
- Fear of loss of identity in a more uniform globalised community reinforces traditional principles of 'otherness'.

Synoptic links

In Component 2, the options on nationalism and multiculturalism focus on the ways in which individuals seek to identify themselves. Is it possible to integrate within a multicultural group based on diverse allegiance and experience, or does nationalism provide the ultimate form of allegiance?

What is the difference between the liberal and realist approaches towards globalisation?

Liberalism and globalisation

Liberals are globalisation optimists. Given their emphasis on the importance of global cooperation, liberals see globalisation as a way of encouraging greater connectivity between states and peoples, thereby creating greater trust and understanding. According to the Dell Theory of Conflict Resolution, the way in which economic globalisation has dramatically increased global trade binds countries into the same global supply chains, preventing conflict. Political globalisation also develops cooperation between states and non-state actors over issues such as climate change, conflict resolution, nuclear non-proliferation and terrorism. Liberals therefore regard globalisation positively, since it establishes foundations for global governance in which states see greater value in cooperation than in conflict.

The advance of regionalism also challenges the primacy of the nation-state, so reducing the risk that nationalist hatreds and resentments may lead to war. A more globalised world will be a safer world in which states are motivated less by egotistical principles of power maximisation than by working together to resolve collective security dilemmas. Since liberals argue that state egoism caused the wars of the twentieth century, the only way of avoiding war in the future, as well as safeguarding the future of the planet, is to embrace globalisation as a method of enhancing common humanity.

Realism and globalisation

Realists are sceptical about the extent to which globalisation can, or should, challenge the primacy of the state in global relations. Realists state that the nation-state should act according to the interests of its citizens. In a dangerously anarchic world, attempts to pretend that we all pursue the same interests are both hopelessly idealistic and ultimately self-defeating. Therefore, attempts to put constraints on states' freedom of action and to pool sovereignty through regional or intergovernmental organisations are dangerous and undermine the absolute right of the state to determine policy itself.

Realists doubt the extent to which liberal cooperation works. They are wary of attempts to develop universal human rights, since this can dangerously challenge Westphalian principles of state sovereignty, the bedrock of global stability. Realists also dismiss attempts to create greater regional integration, most notably in the EU, since only the nation-state can meaningfully lay claim to the loyalty of its citizens. Humanitarian attempts to intervene in the affairs of other states, although they may be guided by the best of intentions, are also likely to cause more harm than good and so, as former US secretary of state Henry Kissinger said, you may 'with a bleeding heart have to let it go'.

Realists also argue that states should advance the interests of their own citizens in global trade and so are generally less ideologically committed to free trade than liberals. President Trump's commitment to protectionism therefore provides a highly realist approach to international trade, in which his focus on protecting US workers' jobs contrasts with liberals' ideological commitment to free-trade economic globalisation. As the Victorian prime minister Lord Palmerston once put it, 'We have no eternal allies, and we have no perpetual enemies. Our interests are eternal and perpetual, and those interests it is our duty to follow.'

To what extent has globalisation transformed the world?

Hyper-globalisers

Hyper-globalisers argue that globalisation is creating a revolutionary shift in the structures of global power, which will ultimately make the nation-state obsolete. Greater economic integration, worldwide capital flows, instantaneous global communication, the growing influence of TNCs and the rise of influential non-state actors have combined to challenge the centrality of the state in international relations. So much of modern life is so inextricably connected through trade and capital flows that the nation-state can no longer determine its own future and must work within economic and financial parameters established through globalisation. As a result, hyper-globalisers infer that an increasingly 'borderless world' is being created — state borders are more permeable than ever before to goods, people, capital and ideas.

In this 'post-sovereign state' world, irresistible global trends dilute the unique characteristics of states. The end result tends towards greater global governance and potentially, at some distant point, world government. According to this thesis, the impact of economic globalisation has been so great that it is making the state primarily a depot through which global trade and capital flows. Academic and lawyer Philip Bobbitt has referred to the state being 'hollowed out' by globalisation, as supraterritorial interests and decisions challenge the importance of territorial integrity and nation-states' authority.

Key term

World government The concept that all political decision making becomes centralised within one supranational authority that would possess sovereign authority over citizens of the world.

Globalisation sceptics

Globalisation sceptics question the extent to which globalisation is new and whether it really has challenged the authority of the state. Sceptics point out that the world has experienced globalisation before. For example, between 1870 and 1913 dramatic advances in telegraphic communication, the size and speed of ships, Great Britain's commitment as global hegemon to advancing free-trade liberalism and the role of the Royal Navy in policing the world's sea lanes established a first wave of globalisation. A global commitment to the gold standard, the monetary system in which a country's currency or paper money has a value directly linked to gold, further encouraged the necessary stability to encourage overseas investment. However, although this combined to generate more global trade than ever before, it did not undermine state sovereignty. Indeed, rival nationalisms would help provoke the outbreak of the First World War in 1914.

Modern-day globalisation has also failed to create a more global community. For instance, when nation-states have embarked upon regionalism, this has been so that member states can use globalisation to their advantage by pooling their influence on the world stage. The collapse of the Doha Round of WTO negotiations (see page 143) shows that developing countries are not prepared to accept that they should continue to open up their markets without reciprocal Global North arrangements for agriculture. Theresa May's post-Brexit commitment to controlling UK borders even at the expense of losing access to the European Single Market challenges the theory that nation-states are bound by economic forces they cannot control. The election of Donald Trump on a protectionist manifesto further illustrates the way in which nation-states can still act in defiance of what had been perceived to be unchallengeable economic principles. One of President Trump's first executive actions was to withdraw the USA from the TPP, which had been designed to deepen economic ties between member states and dramatically reduce tariffs.

Transformationalists

Transformationalists acknowledge that globalisation has had a deep impact on state sovereignty. They emphasise the totality of the globalisation experience. Economic, political and cultural developments have been so profound that states have to engage with a new set of rules in an increasingly closely connected world. According to this interpretation, new stakeholders such as TNCs, IGOs and NGOs continually challenge states' sovereign authority.

However, transformationalists do not agree that globalisation signals the decline of the state. Rather, the state is continually having to adapt to the challenges globalisation presents. Membership of regional bodies, such as the ASEAN and the EU, and the influence of the World Bank and the IMF, have challenged state sovereignty and yet states still retain sovereignty and can use this as a negotiating tool. Although greater economic and financial integration has increased the influence of TNCs, states retain the right to determine fiscal, trade and monetary policy, as illustrated by the bilateral trade deals President Trump favours.

States' sovereign authority may even be *enhanced* by globalisation. China's global influence has dramatically increased as a result of globalisation, giving its government's economic decisions worldwide significance. The internet, as well as creating a global marketplace of ideas, has also been used by states to advance their own political ideologies, as the intense Russian nationalism of RT demonstrates.

The implications of globalisation for the nation-state and national sovereignty

The way in which globalisation has impacted state sovereignty is very controversial. Realists have generally argued that by challenging the nation-state's centrality in international relations, globalisation is dangerously destabilising. Liberals, however, argue that it creates greater prosperity and makes the resolution of global collective dilemmas easier.

In what ways has globalisation challenged the nation-state?

Economic globalisation

Since the world is so economically closely connected, states cannot insulate themselves from global financial crises such as the 2008 collapse of US bank Lehman Brothers. The huge financial influence of TNCs, such as Apple, Google and Microsoft, also means that states need to shape policy in such a way as to attract investment from TNCs. A nation's policymakers are therefore primarily concerned with creating conditions favourable for foreign investment, which significantly reduces its freedom of manoeuvre. A global consensus in favour of the guiding principles of economic liberalism further restricts governments' freedom of action since, in order to attract trade and investment, governments are forced to adopt policies of low corporate taxation and free-market reforms, sometimes at the expense of workers' rights.

Intergovernmentalism

In an increasingly interconnected world, the interests of nation-states are bound together with IGOs such as the IMF, World Bank and WTO. Nation-states have to accept the authority of these bodies even if governments perceive them to be against their national interests. Member states have to adopt WTO judgments. As lenders of last resort, both the IMF and World Bank impose conditions on recipient states that they have little choice but to accept.

UN war crimes tribunals and the establishment of the ICC have also been instrumental in developing universal standards by which nation-states should be expected to abide in relation to their citizens. Increasingly it is IGOs, rather than sovereign states, that take the lead in addressing collective dilemmas such as climate change, global crime and terrorism, and nuclear proliferation.

Regional organisations

The spread of regionalism has impacted state sovereignty. The EU provides the most advanced example of regionalism, as decisions, made by a qualified majority voting on the Council of Ministers, are legally binding to all member states. The European Central Bank (ECB) sets a common interest rate for Eurozone members and the Treaty of Lisbon provides the EU with a legal identity so that it can negotiate with sovereign states, as it has done with the signing of the TTIP. The majority of EU members still adhere to the Schengen Agreement, which allows passport-free travel between member nations. Other regional organisations, such as Mercosur, NAFTA and ASEAN, have also imposed certain free-trade rules on their members, thereby limiting member states' sovereignty.

The internet

The increasing reach of the internet compromises states' physical borders. Access to anti-government websites and the organising power of social media contributed to the Arab Uprisings. The internet can also create new supranational allegiances through, for example, radicalisation, which challenges national identity. Cyber terrorism and cyber warfare further challenge the ways in which a state protects its citizens — computer hackers can now penetrate right to the heart of government, making the protection of territorial state borders irrelevant to a state's survival.

Non-governmental organisations

Myriad NGOs are challenging the influence of the nation-state on its population as their transnational influence, which the internet facilitates, reaches across borders. NGOs include global pressure groups such as Human Rights Watch and Greenpeace, which now inform political debate across the world. Celebrities play an increasingly key role in global issues. For example, Angelina Jolie is a UN Special Envoy for Refugees and has addressed the UNSC on the Syrian refugee crisis. Global foundations such as the Bill & Melinda Gates Foundation and the Clinton Foundation play a huge role in fighting poverty in the developing world, while the near total eradication of guinea-worm disease has been due to the Carter Center.

Challenges from below

Forces from within also challenge the integrity of the nation-state. Instead of nationalism declining in importance, it is noteworthy how people still wish to define themselves according to ethnic and nationalist identities, even if these ideals threaten existing state allegiances. Kosovo's and East Timor's recent independence has been justified on the grounds of self-determination, while the Russian annexation of Crimea in 2014 is based upon the nationalist principle that Crimeans view themselves as Russians rather than Ukrainians.

Actress Angelina Jolie is also a UN Special Envoy for Refugees

In 2014, Scotland only narrowly voted not to secede from the UK, and in 2015, the Scottish nationalism peaked when the SNP won 56 of the 59 parliamentary seats in Scotland.

In what ways is the nation-state still important?

The limits of liberalism

The nation-state remains the key decision-maker when negotiating with other states. Although there are more opportunities for global cooperation via IGOs than ever before, nation-states choose the extent to which they will work with other countries. The UN is based on the principle of the 'sovereign equality' of all its members (Article 2). The permanent five members of the Security Council exercise their national vetoes on whether or not to engage in conflict resolution and war. Nation-states negotiated the Paris climate change agreement and its success depends upon states being prepared to fulfil their obligations. Meetings of the G7/8 conclude with communiqués of intentions, but member states retain the right of whether or not to fulfil them.

Even in the EU, the most advanced example of regionalism in the world, member states retain the right of veto on key issues that define a sovereign state, including foreign policy, defence, taxation and non-EU immigration. Article 50 of the Treaty of Lisbon also provides a mechanism by which nation-states may reclaim their sovereignty.

President Trump unilaterally withdrew from the TPP. In January 2017, he also caused international outrage by seeking to suspend the US Refugee Admissions Program for 120 days, which placed an indefinite ban on Syrian refugees and established a 90-day suspension on anyone arriving from seven predominately Muslim countries. He also capped the number of refugees that the USA would accept in 2017 at 50,000.

Whether or not nation-states choose to cooperate with each other therefore remains at the core of global relations.

Activity

Although liberals claim that IGOs and regional organisations provide unprecedented opportunities for states to work together, others claim that powerful states can actually use these organisations to further their own sovereign interests. Anti-globalisers have often accused the IMF, World Bank and WTO of being agents of American free-market imperialism, while it is claimed that China, as the major shareholder in the AIIB, will use the loans it provides as a way of advancing its economic influence across Asia. Critics claim that the establishment of the Eurasian Customs Union in 2010 represents a way for Russia to regain strategic influence in its 'near abroad' (the newly independent republics, other than Russia itself, that emerged after the dissolution of the Soviet Union). To what extent do you think that globalisation has increased or decreased the power of the state?

Policy and the state

The state still retains power over most issues that determine the life of its citizens. National governments determine fiscal and tax policy. The UK government has, for example, decided to focus on developing the country's infrastructure by expanding Heathrow and constructing HS2. President Trump's radical programme of tax cuts will have a dramatic impact on US citizens. The state also determines the way in which citizens are educated, and cared for in old age, while defence policy, immigration and foreign policy are decided and implemented at a national level.

The state can also police the internet. The Chinese 'firewall' is highly effective and the Chinese Ministry of Culture has warned that video-streaming sites will be punished if they do not remove 'violent' and 'erotic' Japanese cartoon video clips. Russia has enacted legislation that bans 'undesirable' foreign NGOs from operating in the country if they are perceived to threaten 'the foundations of the constitutional system of the Russian Federation, its defence capabilities and its national security'.

States are not, therefore, simply the depots through which foreign capital and goods pass — they remain crucial in determining the sort of lives their citizens lead. Government leaders' decisions have defining importance, as shown by the enthusiasm with which the UK government arranged the successful state visit of China's President Xi Jinping, which resulted in £30 billion worth of negotiated contracts. The speed, too, with which Prime Minister Theresa May sought to reaffirm the UK's 'special relationship' with the USA following the inauguration of President Trump further demonstrates the importance of bilateral relations between nation-states.

Activity

In 1968, the controversial Conservative politician Enoch Powell told the Conservative Party Conference:

> Too often today people are ready to tell us: 'This is not possible, that is not possible.' I say: whatever the true interest of our country calls for is always possible.

To what extent do you think nation-states should remain the key decision-makers in global politics?

National borders and security

Although liberals predicted that globalisation would reduce the significance of state borders and gradually replace them with supraterritorial flows of goods, capital and people, the opposite has in fact proved to be true. Terrorist atrocities since the events of 9/11 have instead made states much more determined to protect their borders. The US Department for Homeland Security was established in 2002 in order to better police US borders, and it is now the third-biggest federal employer, with 240,000 employees (2017). President Trump has also promised to fulfil his manifesto commitment to build a wall on the Mexican border and within days of taking office he banned travel to the USA from seven Muslim countries. The Syrian refugee crisis has also threatened passport-free travel within the Schengen Agreement zone. In 2015, Russia tightened its visa requirements by demanding fingerprints from foreign visitors from certain countries, including the UK.

Liberal hopes that a borderless world would one day become a reality seem as distant as ever before, while the threat of terrorism has often increased state power over its citizens. In the UK, for example, the Investigatory Powers Act (2016) requires web and phone companies to store everyone's web-browsing histories for a year and, if required, to provide the security services with access to this information.

President Trump has committed to building a permanent wall on the 3,100 km US–Mexico border

Human rights and civil liberties

Liberal hopes that the end of the Cold War could lead to the universalisation of a human rights culture have not been realised. States continue to determine the extent of civil liberties they grant their citizens, and these depend more upon religious/cultural traditions than universality. 'Asian Values' focus more on the rights of the community than those of the individual and in most Muslim countries the moral codes of the Qu'ran inform the nature of one's human rights. In Russia, the conservative values of the Orthodox Church have increasingly influenced political decision making. Indeed, the emphasis of the UDHR on individual human rights and self-fulfilment is seen in many parts of the world as encouraging a form of Western cultural imperialism.

Therefore, states continue to be the main arbiters of human rights. In the USA, for example, the death penalty is legal and yet it is not within the EU. In western Europe, attitudes towards homosexuality have dramatically liberalised and yet homosexuality is still illegal in a third of the world's countries. The UK does not allow prisoners to vote and yet, according to the ECHR, this is denying prisoners their human rights. Where one resides therefore determines the sort of private life one is able to live, rather than any objective standard of human rights.

International law

When the ICC was established in 1998, China refused to join, arguing that 'the statute is an attempt to interfere with the domestic affairs of a sovereign nation'. The USA, another non-signatory, signed a number of bilateral trade agreements with other countries, obliging them not to submit US personnel to the ICC's jurisdiction. Although human rights have gained greater international coverage in recent years, nation-states still determine the extent to which they will abide by international standards of human rights and accept the international arbitration of disputes.

The judgments of the International Court of Justice (ICJ), sometimes referred to as the World Court, require states to accept them if they are to be enforced. For example, in 1992, El Salvador and Honduras agreed to accept the ICJ's settlement of a border dispute between the two countries. However, Israel has consistently ignored the ICJ's opinion that the wall separating Israel from Palestinian territories is illegal according to international law. In 2016, the UNSC condemned Israel's building of settlements in the occupied territories, but Israel's prime minister, Benjamin Netanyahu, has refused to recognise this decision in spite of international condemnation.

International law is therefore 'soft' law. For example, when India and Pakistan reneged on their obligations to the Treaty on the Non-Proliferation of Nuclear Weapons by announcing they had achieved nuclear defence capability, they were criticised but no international action was taken against them. In 2014, the Organization for Security and Co-operation in Europe declared that the Crimea referendum on whether it should replace Ukrainian with Russian sovereignty was illegal, and yet it still went ahead, with Russia declaring the result as binding.

The limits of international law on state sovereignty are nicely illustrated by former US president George W. Bush's dismissive response to criticism that the Iraq invasion had infringed international law: 'International law? I'd better call my lawyer — he didn't bring that up to me'.

National allegiance

Although liberals anticipated that globalisation would lessen citizens' allegiance to their nation-state state loyalty continues to be remarkably potent. National identities still matter in determining an individual's sense of who they are. President Putin has reasserted Russia's sense of its own unique destiny, stating that 'we will be sovereign or we will dissolve in the world'. President Trump has expressed his commitment, at the expense of all other considerations, to 'the American people'. Across Europe, the dominance of pro-European parties is being challenged by the likes of the French National Front, the Freedom Party and Alternative for Germany, all of which want to restore national self-determination. Scottish, Palestinian and Basque nationalist movements further illustrate how important nationhood is to those who do not possess it.

Case study

Embassies under fire

On 17 April 1984, demonstrations against the Libyan leader Colonel Muammar Gaddafi were held outside the Libyan embassy in London. During the demonstrations, automatic gunfire was discharged into the crowd of protesters, killing Metropolitan policewoman Yvonne Fletcher. The Metropolitan Police Service laid siege to the embassy for the next 11 days and eventually embassy staff were expelled from the UK. However, nobody was ever charged with Yvonne's murder, even though it is clear that the gunfire had come from within the embassy.

Julian Assange gained worldwide fame as the founder of WikiLeaks, a website he set up to enable 'whistle-blowers' to release classified information to the internet. He spoke at numerous conferences, but in 2010 was accused of rape and molestation while in Sweden. In 2012, the Swedish government demanded that he be extradited from the UK to Sweden to answer these charges. Fearing that the USA might then seek his extradition from Sweden, Assange claimed asylum in the Ecuadorian embassy in London. The embassy's sovereign immunity has thus far protected him from prosecution — Assange knows that if he leaves the embassy, he will be arrested.

These cases illustrate that respect for state sovereignty is still at the root of global relations, since it would be the gravest possible offence to challenge the diplomatic immunity of another nation's embassy. An example did occur in 1979, when Iranian 'students' overran the US embassy in Tehran, but this provoked international condemnation, demonstrating that such actions remain morally and diplomatically unacceptable.

State egoism

States still generally act out of sovereign self-interest rather than according to more liberal cosmopolitan values. The UN did not provide a mandate for the Anglo-American invasion of Iraq in 2003, and both countries ignored calls for international restraint in order to achieve their strategic objectives in the region. In 2014, Russia annexed Crimea from Ukraine in defiance of international condemnation that it had illegally infringed Ukrainian sovereignty. Defence spending by China, Russia and the USA is dramatically increasing, and China is increasing its presence in the South China Seas by militarising reefs and expanding the reach of its naval manoeuvres. The main players in the Syrian civil war — Iran, Russia, Turkey, the UK and the USA — each have their own strategic objectives in the region, which have undermined attempts to achieve a humanitarian solution acceptable to all. Examples such as these suggest that states are primarily 'power-maximisers' and that realist principles of self-interest still play the key role in determining the relationship between states.

Debate

Is state sovereignty becoming less important?

Yes

- Global acceptance of free-market liberalism, encouraged by the Bretton Woods Institutions, restricts the economic choices that governments can take. According to Susan Strange, 'Markets are now masters of governments'.
- States now share power with non-state actors, the decisions of which directly impact on the job prospects and living conditions of working people globally.
- The internet influences citizens and potentially creates new, supranational allegiances.
- There is pooling of sovereignty within regional organisations such as the EU, ASEAN and NAFTA.
- Collective dilemmas such as climate change, nuclear proliferation, terrorism and international crime require intergovernmental solutions.
- States accept legal limitations on their domestic jurisdiction in the ECtHR, ICC and IJC. According to Kofi Annan, sovereignty must be 'responsible', suggesting that it can be forfeited by unjust acts (UN R2P, 2005).

No

- Nation-states choose whether or not to cooperate with non-state actors. Globalisation has involved many more 'stakeholders' in political debate, but nation-states retain their exclusive rights of sovereign decision making.
- Nation-states enter into relationships with other nation-states in regional organisations and international treaties that limit their absolute freedom of action. However, states are free to withdraw their involvement.
- It is difficult to enforce international law or international standards of justice within nation-states. The USA has not closed down Guantánamo Bay, in spite of international condemnation, while the UNSC has unsuccessfully prevented Israeli settlement policy in the occupied territories.
- The Syrian government's human rights abuses have not triggered a response from the international community according to the principles of 'conditional sovereignty' outlined in the UN's R2P.
- State allegiance still determines the loyalty of a state's citizens — such loyalty seems to have increased rather than lessened in the face of the growing uncertainties globalisation provokes.

Is globalisation a new phenomenon?

A global village?

Hyper-globalisers assume that our experience of globalisation is unique in the way in which it has established such interconnectedness between states and citizens across the world. Indeed, some liberal critics of the nation-state have even speculated that we are now living in a 'global village', in which what binds us together outweighs our differences. The internet penetrates almost everywhere in the world and global capital flows are instantaneous, creating a supraterritorial world in which state sovereignty and borders matter less than ever before.

Global governance and world government

Global governance

- Global governance exists today. It refers to the complex web of interconnectedness through which nation-states work with each other and with non-state actors.
- The UN, WTO, IMF, World Bank and various regional and international judicial bodies all facilitate this interconnectedness.
- States retain sovereignty and choose the extent to which they cooperate with each other and stakeholders through a complex array of diverse relationships. Global governance therefore involves interconnectedness, rather than the centralisation of global power within one single, supranational body.
- Liberals encourage the further development of global governance, since by connecting the global community it reduces 'state-egoism' and, consequently, the possibility of war.

World government

- World government does not exist. If it did, it would mean that the nation-state, either voluntarily or involuntarily, would abandon the right to govern its own citizens.
- Power would, therefore, be centralised in one location rather than diffused among various states and non-state actors.
- The closest the world has yet come to world government is the UN, but this organisation is based upon the sovereign equality of its member states and so is primarily intergovernmental rather than supranational.
- Realists oppose the principles of world government, since they argue that states are the most important players in global relations. Liberals, too, are cautious of endorsing the principles of world government, since it is often associated with a lack of democratic accountability and the empire-building tendencies of dictators.

The lessons of history

However, we should treat such far-reaching theories with scepticism. Globalisation is in the process of transforming the relationship between states, and between states and non-state actors, and yet many historians would argue that 'we have been here before'. As we have seen, the first great age of modern globalisation lasted from 1870 to 1913, when global trade dramatically expanded and British hegemony guaranteed the world's sea lanes. British values, such as free trade, a meritocratic civil service, opposition to slavery and even cricket have had a global influence significantly more profound than today's commercialisation and materialism. Mahatma Gandhi played a key role in ending British rule in India, but his autobiography demonstrates how deeply he had absorbed British values. Today, the British Commonwealth is, after the UN, the biggest organisation in the world. British principles of parliamentary democracy have also globally penetrated as deeply as more modern Americanization, without provoking the same sort of cultural backlash as 'Coca-Colonization'.

Activity

Socrates is quoted to have said: 'I am not an Athenian or a Greek, but a citizen of the world'. Since then, many idealistic writers, from Desiderius Erasmus to Lord Tennyson, have dreamed of national identities being subsumed within a global citizenship.

To what extent do you think modern-day globalisation has taken us close to, or further away from, Socrates' ideal?

Recep Tayyip Erdogan, President of Turkey

Pre-twenty-first-century global cosmopolitanism

It would also be misleading to suggest that states and peoples are more connected today than ever before in history. In reality, the way in which leaders such as Vladimir Putin, Donald Trump, Narendra Modi and Recep Erdogan have deployed nationalistic rhetoric and policies to win public support indicates that nationalism is, if anything, becoming more important in global relations. This is a far cry from earlier periods of history, when one's nationality was significantly less important than it is today.

The great age of migration was actually the nineteenth century, when millions sought a new life in the USA and there was extensive movement of peoples within the British Empire. So rapid was the expansion of continental railways that in 1861 France even abandoned the passport, and passport-free travel became the norm across Europe until the First World War. In the eighteenth century, intellectuals crossed borders in a way that would be surprising even today — the English radical Thomas Paine, for example, advised both US and French revolutionaries.

The universality of the Roman Catholic Church also challenged state sovereignty and transformed the cultures of indigenous populations. King Henry VIII broke with Rome and declared himself Head of the Church of England because he lacked the sovereign authority to divorce Catherine of Aragon. Missionaries spread the Catholic faith from Japan to South America.

During the Roman period, a single language, culture and citizenship dominated western Europe and the near east. In the Acts of the Apostles (22:25), for example, St Paul is not flogged when he declares his Roman citizenship.

Has globalisation changed the world?

Yes

- Economic globalisation has dramatically increased global trade, lifted millions out of poverty and created the potential for greater convergence between the Global North and Global South. According to the World Bank, as a result of globalisation, more than 85% of the world's population can now hope to live to at least 60, which is double the global life expectancy of 100 years ago.
- As a result of economic globalisation, China is on course to become the world's biggest economy, challenging US economic, political and military hegemony. This represents a shift of the global balance of power eastwards towards emerging economies.
- The pace of regionalism has increased as regions work more closely together in order to take advantage of new global opportunities for trade.
- Since the world is so economically and financially interconnected, no state can avoid financial crises, such as the collapse of Lehman Brothers in 2008.
- As a result of the internet, global capital flows are now instantaneous, interlinking economies all over the world. National borders have become more porous as goods and capital flow more freely between states, and TNCs rather than nation-states increasingly determine employment opportunities and labour rights, especially in the developing world.
- Personal laptop possession enables anyone to become an entrepreneur (Thomas Friedman has used the metaphor of 'The Rise of the Windows' to illustrate how ownership of a Windows PC/Apple Mac provides anybody, anywhere with limitless opportunities for business success).
- There are few truly national products remaining, as TNCs such as Adidas and Nike manufacture and sell across the world.
- Cultural globalisation has homogenised global culture, encouraging a more rootless and superficial 'McWorld' culture.
- Nation-states work more closely together in IGOs, and the UN R2P has encouraged a more universal standard for human rights.
- NGOs such as Greenpeace have added another layer to global decision making, further challenging the exclusivity of nation-states.
- The internet has facilitated the spread of radicalisation and terrorism, undermining national allegiances.

No

- Global interconnectedness is not entirely new. The first wave of modern globalisation occurred in 1870–1913. Previous periods of history experienced remarkable degrees of integration.
- The Global North still dominates ownership of global wealth. North America and Europe contain 18% of the world's adult population and yet they possess 67% of total household wealth (2015).
- Since the 2007–9 global recession, cross-border trade has actually decreased — this represented 53% of world economic productivity in 2007, but just 39% in 2016.
- Nation-states remain the key players in global politics, but IGOs require states to work together if they are to be successful. South Africa's decision to leave undermined the ICC's influence.
- The global impact of the 1929 Wall Street Crash and even the South Sea Bubble in 1720 demonstrate that the global economy is not uniquely interconnected today.
- Citizens still identify with their nation-state — globalisation has not created a global citizenry and there is a rise in nationalist parties across Europe.
- Realist self-interest, rather than liberal cooperation, determines nation-state policy, for example the Russian annexation of Crimea, the ongoing dispute between China and Japan over the ownership of the Senkaku/Diaoyu islands, and President Trump's executive order withdrawing the USA from the TPP.
- Regionalism is under threat from the nation-state, for example Brexit (2016) and President Trump's criticisms of the NAFTA.
- Cultural globalisation has reinforced nationalist, ethnic and religious identities as a reaction to homogenisation and materialism.
- The extent of one's human rights is still determined within states and cultures — the universalisation of human rights is undermined by continuing allegiance to 'Asian', 'Muslim' or 'Russian' values, for example.
- Terrorist threats and migration have led to the reassertion of national control over borders — the migrant crisis threatened the Schengen Agreement and President Trump is committed to building a wall along the Mexican border.

What you should know

Having read this chapter you should have knowledge and understanding of the following:

- The extent to which rumours of the death of the nation-state might have been exaggerated. In the euphoria following the end of the Cold War, remarkable advances were made in global trade and political interconnectivity, which did suggest that the authority of the nation-state was being challenged.
- The nation-state does now have to compete with many more stakeholders, and political dialogue is no longer primarily between states. Instead, states and non-state actors increasingly work together, both formally and informally.
- The urgency with which collective dilemmas need to be resolved has further encouraged intergovernmental solutions to world problems.
- A global acceptance of the principles of economic liberalism and the rising importance of transnational corporations has limited the socioeconomic solutions that nation-states can deploy to address domestic problems.
- Instantaneous capital flows have encouraged the rise of supraterritorial global capitalism.
- The internet has 'flattened out' many of the cultural differences that have made nation-states unique.
- However, the state has actually proved much more resilient than many liberals and hyper-globalisers anticipated.
- States remain the key players in decision making and, although they may cooperate with non-state actors, ultimate authority still lies with the state.
- States have frequently acted in defiance of international law and yet the international community has been slow to punish them. The establishment of a supranational universal standard of human rights is as distant as ever.
- The Trump administration challenges the extent to which states act within the boundaries of free-trade liberalism. Protectionism may now be reasserting itself in defiance of the Washington Consensus.
- The regional and global implications of Brexit for the nation-state have yet to be fully understood.
- The internet, far from transforming the world into a global village, has encouraged the resurgence of national pride, resentments and prejudice, reinforcing rather than challenging state autonomy.
- We should be careful of suggesting that globalisation has transformed the world, especially since history suggests that there have been earlier, possibly even more profound, periods of globalisation.
- Modern-day globalisation is, nonetheless, in the process of changing the world, and yet rather than the nation-state succumbing to new challenges, it has adapted to them. In some ways the new challenges and uncertainties of the twentieth century have even strengthened the nation-state. As Mark Twain suggested, rumours of the death of the nation-state may indeed have been 'much exaggerated'.

Further reading

Chang, H. (2011) *23 Things They don't Tell You about Capitalism*. Penguin.
Collier, P. (2008) *The Bottom Billion*. Oxford University Press.
Friedman, T. (2007) *The World is Flat*. Penguin.
Stiglitz, J. (2003) *Globalisation and its Discontents*. Penguin.

Section A

1 Examine the difference between economic globalisation and political globalisation. *[12 marks]*

2 Examine the effectiveness of the international courts and tribunals in protecting human rights. *[12 marks]*

3 Examine how successful humanitarian interventions have been in achieving their objectives. *[12 marks]*

4 Examine the view that cultural globalisation is creating a monoculture. *[12 marks]*

5 Examine why economic globalisation is so controversial. *[12 marks]*

Section C

1 Evaluate the extent to which cultural globalisation has had a greater impact on the world than any other form of globalisation. *[30 marks]*

2 Evaluate the extent to which economic globalisation has benefited the world's poor. *[30 marks]*

3 Evaluate the extent to which human rights-based law has challenged the principle that states determine the human rights of their citizens. *[30 marks]*

4 Evaluate the validity of the view that 'The nation-state remains the key player in global politics'. *[30 marks]*

5 Evaluate why and in what ways there has been growing opposition to globalisation. *[30 marks]*

Global governance: political

Getting you started

Key terms

United Nations (UN)
The world's principal intergovernmental organisation, founded in 1945 and comprised of 193 member states. It has a wide range of responsibilities and powers (e.g. international peace and security, economic development, human rights and social progress).

North Atlantic Treaty Organization (NATO) A military alliance consisting of the USA and its key allies in western Europe, with the purpose to protect western Europe from military threats from the Soviet Union.

This chapter explores various ways in which the **United Nations (UN)** and the **North Atlantic Treaty Organization (NATO)** attempt to manage the shared challenges that many states face together. Ranging from peace and security to the environment, we consider whether global political governance is an achievable ideal.

Ukraine, 2014: was the UN powerless to stop Russia annexing Crimea?

During a series of nights in February 2014, in the region of Crimea, Ukraine, unidentified, heavily armed men in green uniforms blockaded the international airport, took over the regional parliament buildings and secured several military bases. The soldiers wore uniforms without any identifying insignia. At first, neighbouring Russia claimed that the soldiers were local 'self-defence groups'. Later, Russia confirmed that these so-called little green men were in fact Russian Special Forces, known as 'Spetznatz', who had arrived to annex, or separate, Crimea from the state of Ukraine (see Figure 3.1).

Figure 3.1 Crimea

In February 2014, 'little green men' without identifying insignia, later confirmed to be Russian Special Forces, blockaded several locations in Crimea

This Russian aggression raised an immediate challenge for the UN — namely, how would it respond to such an obvious incursion by a sovereign state into another, in the borderlands of Europe?

The UN's primary responsibility for upholding international peace and security, and resolving international crises such as this, lies with the **UN Security Council (UNSC)**. Therefore, the UNSC was expected to respond to this incident, but with Russia being one of the five UNSC permanent members, action would be difficult, if not impossible. Russia's status as permanent member would lead it to veto (block) any UNSC resolution challenging its actions in Crimea.

In March 2014, a referendum, which Russia strongly backed, was held in Crimea to ask the population if they wished to remain part of Ukraine or become part of Russia. The UNSC attempted to pass a resolution condemning the referendum as illegal, invalid and illegitimate, noting that the presence of Russian troops meant that the vote could not be free or fair. Russia, however, vetoed the resolution and the referendum went ahead. Despite the concerns of independent international observers over the vote's conduct, and whether the referendum question even allowed voters to back the status quo, it was reported that a majority of 96% had voted to become part of Russia.

With the UNSC vote vetoed, the UN General Assembly (UNGA) — with its one member, one vote equality and no veto powers — successfully passed a resolution condemning Russia's actions in Crimea. Despite passing the resolution by a large majority (100 states were in favour, 11 states against), the UNGA's resolutions are not binding in international law. Consequently, the UNGA vote was largely symbolic and could not force Russia to change course.

As a result, the Crimea region became a subject of the Russian Federation, meaning that it was no longer under the sovereign control of the state of Ukraine. Russia gained full control of Crimea, with Russia's prime minister Dmitry Medvedev confirming in July 2015 that 'Crimea has been fully integrated into Russia'.

Russia's actions raise challenging questions for the UN and NATO, the military alliance founded to protect western European states from the aggression of Russia's predecessor, the Soviet Union. Ukraine was not a member of NATO, but had shown ambitions to join the organisation, as well as the European Union (EU). Had the prospect of Ukraine joining a military alliance

UN Security Council (UNSC) The UN's supreme decision-making body on matters of international peace and security, able to issue binding resolutions with the full force of international law.

with the USA and becoming part of a western European, rather than remaining under the Russian sphere of influence, spooked Russia into intervening?

It was not the first time the UNSC had been powerless to control the actions of its permanent members. In 2003, the UK and the USA were alone in proposing military action in Iraq. They launched said military action without UNSC approval. Both episodes confirm that, when they wish to, powerful states can defy the UN.

Synoptic links

In Component 1, the nationalism option explores the different types of nationalism and how they relate to the way in which nation-states see their responsibilities and interactions with other states. Liberal internationalism sees the benefits of states working with other states, through the kinds of political global governance outlined in this chapter, to solve common challenges.

What is global governance?

The government of a sovereign state is relatively easy to identify: it has a leader, often elected and in the form of a president or prime minister. Usually, the leader and his or her government have to follow clear rules that set out what their powers are and the limits of their power, often in the form of a constitution. If elected directly by the population, the government is usually seen as legitimate and the population accepts its actions. The government usually makes laws that its population must follow. Courts and a police force enforce these laws and there are clear consequences when people break them. The government proposes policies to manage the state effectively, for example public services such as health and education.

In the most stable states, these combined activities are called 'governance', whereby the state is managed effectively, resources are distributed fairly and challenges are met with decisive solutions. There is good governance, broadly following the principles set out above, and bad governance, where power may be held illegitimately and resources are scarce, or managed corruptly or incompetently (for example, in the case of failed states).

Increasingly, states have recognised the need for some form of global governance. Challenges such as the global financial crisis, international terrorism, climate change, world poverty, global human rights abuses and violent conflict can only be resolved by states working together. These threats affect many states and many states contribute to these threats. Only by states working together are they likely to have any impact on reducing these threats. Just as national governance seeks to exploit opportunities and manage threats experienced at the national level, global governance seeks to do exactly the same at a global level.

Distinguish between

Government and governance

Government
- This is an executive body that is in power, usually of a sovereign state.
- Often elected, a government's leadership and authority is usually clear.

Governance
- The act of governing and trying to command authority over a particular territory or group.

The lack of world government

However, attempts at global governance are much harder and less successful than national governance. This is because nation-states remain powerful and decisive actors in global politics. They are sovereign, meaning that they are usually able to take their own decisions, and it is rare for a higher authority to force states to do something against their wishes (see Chapter 4).

It is difficult to insert a layer of formal authority above nation-states because there is no recognised 'world government', in the sense of a government that nation-states accept as legitimate to act on their behalf, and which has sovereign power and the authority to act. These difficulties include the following.

- **States are the principal actors:** they make or break global governance initiatives. Nothing is agreed unless states agree to take action. They are the building blocks of unified action. Some states can opt out of or block agreements (for example, the Kyoto Protocol, see page 239), making these agreements meaningless or end in failure.
- **International law is largely unenforceable:** in the case of most nation-states' laws, every citizen is required to comply and is held accountable in the courts if they break the law. By contrast, international law is often optional and requires states to actively sign up in order for the law to cover them (states can choose not to sign and ratify key treaties, such as the Rome Statute, which created the International Criminal Court (ICC)). States can also change their minds and withdraw from treaties that they have signed. Customary international law (see page 171) is law that is so widely accepted that it applies to states regardless of whether they have signed up to it or not. However, the same difficulties arise if powerful or rogue states simply ignore attempts by, for example, international courts to hold them to account.
- **Lack of international enforcement:** even if states have signed up to international law, there are few means of international enforcement (for example, international or regional human rights courts) that can hold states accountable and force them to change their behaviour.

How far states are willing, or able, to participate in global governance is linked to the different types of power that they have and the way that they use their power (see Chapter 7).

- **Rogue states:** these states, particularly those in which there is an illegitimate government that is exceeding its powers (such as North Korea), often have no desire to be part of, and therefore influenced and persuaded by, any systems of global governance.
- **Failed states:** these states are not fully in control of their internal governance (such as Somalia). They are rarely effective participants in global governance, as they cannot yet hold authority over their own populations. Insurgent groups, such as Boko Haram in Nigeria or so-called Islamic State in Iraq and Syria, often take over regions within failed states, meaning that the government does not exercise full control over all of its territory.
- **Powerful states:** these states can pick and choose which global agreements they are part of and simply ignore international pressure (as seen in the example of Russia's actions in Ukraine, but also the refusal of the USA to sign climate change agreements such as the Kyoto Protocol).

Since no single, authoritative world government exists, states work within global institutions or intergovernmental organisations (IGOs) and negotiate treaties between two or more states so that they can reach agreements on

Table 3.1 Types of global governance

Type of global governance	Why is it needed?	Examples
Political global governance (Chapter 3)	Political global governance covers all forms of collective decision making between states. When states come together to make decisions on matters of peace and security, human rights or climate change, they are doing so within political institutions or processes. In this way, environmental, judicial and economic global governance are all subsets of political global governance.	This chapter focuses on the key IGO, the UN, and its most powerful decision-making body, the UNSC.
Economic global governance (Chapter 4)	The 2008 global financial crisis, in which a lending crisis in the USA sparked a global economic recession, is a recent example of the need for global financial governance to regulate and manage an increasingly interconnected global economy.	A number of key financial IGOs, such as the International Monetary Fund (IMF) and the World Trade Organization (WTO), have long been established to help both rich and poor states with their economic development.
Human rights global governance (Chapter 5)	Since the UN Universal Declaration of Human Rights (UDHR) was agreed in 1946, human rights have been thought of as universal and having global relevance, irrespective of national borders and different cultures. Alongside this, global governance has made various attempts to agree global human rights laws and established the ICC to hold states and others abusing human rights to account. The principal aim is to ensure that states cannot hide behind national sovereignty and abuse human rights without punishment.	The International Court of Justice (ICJ) and the International Criminal Court (ICC) are key institutions that have judicial global governance as their aim. They use codified documents, such as the UDHR, and international law as the basis for their judgments.
Environmental global governance (Chapter 6)	Global warming and climate change are increasingly recognised as global responsibilities requiring urgent action. Global conferences and agreements have attempted to take action to reduce the harmful effects that states have on the global commons (see page 218). It is perhaps the most obvious example of a challenge that cannot be resolved by states acting alone and one in which all states (developed and developing alike, where there is a key clash on which states bear the greatest responsibility) must take action.	Global action to tackle environmental degradation is primarily driven through international summits such as the Copenhagen and Paris summits of 2009 and 2015. States sometimes sign international agreements, such as the Paris Accords, when they commit to taking joint action.

Key term

Non-governmental organisations (NGOs)
Not-for-profit organisations that are independent from states and IGOs, and are engaged in a wide range of activities. They are usually funded by donations but some are primarily volunteer-run.

issues of shared importance. **Non-governmental organisations (NGOs)** are increasingly important in global governance initiatives, but the work of global governance is primarily conducted between nation-states, either within IGOs or working together in more informal, ad hoc discussions.

Types of global governance

There are four main types of global governance (see also Table 3.1):
1   Political (examined fully in this chapter)
2   Economic (Chapter 4)
3   Human rights (Chapter 5)
4   Environmental (Chapter 6)

Activity

Think about national governments around the world, their roles and responsibilities:
- List the duties and responsibilities that national governments carry out.
- What might the duties and responsibilities of a world government be?
- Why is it unlikely that a world government would ever be formed?
- Is it impossible for a world government to carry out all of these duties and responsibilities?
- With no world government in existence, how do actors in global politics attempt to carry out some of these duties and responsibilities?

Political global governance

There are three main ways in which states can work together in political global governance, each of which we will examine in this chapter. Which of these approaches is used, in any particular context, depends on the nature of the issue and the motivations of the states involved in tackling the issue.

1 **IGOs:** these organisations — principally the UN — provide a permanent and formal rules-based framework in which states can negotiate and form agreements. Most IGOs are intergovernmental in the sense that nation-states negotiate and agree upon their decisions. It is only in regional organisations (principally the EU, see Chapter 8) that supranational powers are to be found, meaning that this IGO can force states to do things that they may not agree with.

2 **International treaties:** a means of creating international law more flexibly on specific issues, either within or independent of IGOs, and between two (bilateral treaties) or more (multilateral treaties) states.

3 **Ad hoc meetings:** states can meet in informal meetings and undertake negotiations and agreements on a more ad hoc basis.

Each of these methods of political global governance carries a number of different features and functions, which states can use to their advantage. However, sometimes states can also suffer from the methods' disadvantages (see Table 3.2).

Table 3.2 Advantages and disadvantages of possible approaches to global political governance

Approach and examples	Advantages	Disadvantages
IGOs (e.g. the UN (page 91), NATO (page 119))	A permanent forum for debate and negotiation, in which long-term projects can be pursued (such as the Millennium Development Goals (MDGs)) and long-term relationships built. An authoritative and legitimate actor in global politics, based on clear rules and international law (for example, the founding UN Charter). Good for smaller countries, if all countries have an equal voice (such as in the UNGA). Membership itself can be made dependent on states becoming part of key agreements (for example, all UN member states must sign and ratify the UDHR).	Can become gridlocked, particularly if powerful states are given veto powers (for example, the veto power of the five UNSC permanent members). Less meaningful for smaller countries, if they have no clear powers and are out-muscled by more powerful states. Effectiveness is dependent on the collective determination of an IGO's member states. If this, collectively, becomes weak, the IGO becomes weak (for example, declining defence spending of NATO countries). States are likely to find ways of limiting the IGO's power if they feel it threatens state sovereignty.
International treaties (e.g. the Treaty on the Non-Proliferation of Nuclear Weapons (NPT) (page 122), the North Atlantic Treaty (page 119))	Allow like-minded states to create binding international law on any issue in which they have a common interest. Outside IGOs, states can sometimes be more flexible and responsive than by working within IGOs.	States can choose not to sign and ratify treaties, meaning that they are not covered by them. For example, key states that have acquired nuclear weapons either did not sign or withdrew from the NPT. Even when states have signed treaties, their cooperation largely remains a choice and there is little means of forcing states to comply with treaty obligations.
Informal meetings/ negotiations/ agreements (e.g. the 2015 Paris Summit (page 244))	Allow states to respond very quickly to crises and form agendas with maximum freedom. For example, the London Group of Twenty (G20) Summit in 2009 quickly developed an agenda designed to tackle the global financial crisis.	Sometimes seen as less legitimate, or even illegal in international law (for example, the US-led invasion of Iraq in 2003). Decisions or agreements are not binding in international law, and are therefore even less enforceable. States are at liberty to make their own independent choices and protect their sovereignty, making blockages more likely.

The United Nations

Former US ambassador to the UN Henry Cabot Lodge stated that:

> This organization is created to prevent you from going to hell. It isn't created to take you to heaven.

The UN is the world's most comprehensive and powerful IGO. It has more member states and it carries out a wider range of activities in more places across the world than any other IGO. Since it was founded in 1945,

it has become a highly respected international organisation, seen as legitimate in its own right and a source of legitimacy for other actions and actors in global politics. For example, for a newly independent state, becoming a member of the UN is an important confirmation of statehood, while UNSC-authorised military action is widely accepted to be legitimate.

The UN has its central headquarters in New York and has a global presence in offices and regional headquarters across the world. Its objectives range across a wide number of responsibilities, including tackling global conflict, reducing poverty and upholding human rights. It is the most important institution and forum for global political governance that exists in modern global politics.

However, the UN is not without its critics. Some analysts argue that it is powerless to deal with international crises effectively. For example, some say that the USA's foreign policy during the War on Terror sidelined the UN and rendered it powerless, while others say the organisation has turned a blind eye to recent atrocities in Syria.

This section will examine the UN's founding objectives and its relevance today, and how the major organs of the UN — including the UNSC — work. It will also evaluate how effective the UN really is at dealing with the major challenges of conflict, human rights and global poverty.

The UN headquarters in New York

In Component 1, some of the ideas of nationalism do not necessarily conflict with political global governance. The concept of general will, as argued by philosopher Jean-Jacques Rousseau, that nations have the right to govern themselves, does not conflict with UN principles. Indeed, the right of nations to govern themselves is made clear in the founding UN Charter.

How and why was the UN founded?

Signed just months after the end of the Second World War, the language of the UN Charter — the UN's founding document and constitution — is heavy with the regret and determination of a war-weary world (see Box 3.1).

Box 3.1

Preamble to the UN Charter

The UN Charter was signed on 26 June 1945 in San Francisco, USA, at the conclusion of the UN Conference on International Organization. It came into force on 24 October 1945.

We, the peoples of the United Nations, determined...

... to save succeeding generations from the scourge of war, which twice in our lifetime has brought untold sorrow to mankind;

... to reaffirm faith in fundamental human rights, in the dignity and worth of the human person, in the equal rights of men and women from countries large and small;

... to establish conditions under which justice... and international law can be maintained;

... to promote social progress and better standards of life in larger freedom.

... have agreed to the present Charter of the United Nations and do hereby establish an international organization to be known as the United Nations.

The UN Charter's Preamble demonstrates the key priorities of world leaders in 1945. The Second World War had caused huge human and economic destruction and suffering across the world. In 1945, there was a united global desire to create an international organisation aimed at preventing future conflict and similar human rights abuses as those seen during the war. There was also an urgent need to coordinate efforts to rebuild shattered economies and infrastructure crippled by war.

After the First World War, several nation-states created the League of Nations (1920–46), which had similar objectives to prevent another global conflict. The outbreak of the Second World War confirmed that the League of Nations had utterly failed. The League had, in fact, consisted of only a limited number of nations, with nothing like the universal membership of today's UN. Major powers had joined and left (Germany and Japan left in 1933), failed to join (the USA never joined) or were expelled (the USSR, in 1939). The League of Nations' replacement needed to make sure that major powers stayed the course in order to solve challenges collectively, rather than leaving at the first sign of crisis or challenge to state sovereignty. Above all, it needed its members to be able to stick together, and take effective and decisive action to deal with major international crises.

> **Distinguish between**
>
> ## The League of Nations and the United Nations
>
> **The League of Nations**
> - Founded in 1920 as the first attempt at global political governance.
> - Its membership was unstable, as major powers left when they felt their national interests could not be protected.
> - It failed in its founding objective after the First World War to prevent another global conflict, and was replaced by the UN after the Second World War.
>
> **The United Nations**
> - Founded in 1945 to replace the League of Nations.
> - Its membership and functions have grown consistently since its founding.
> - It remains the world's most comprehensive IGO and the pinnacle of global governance efforts.
> - The use of the UNSC veto protects the national interests of major powers (the five permanent members — China, France, Russia, the UK and the USA).

The UN Charter

To form the UN, member states agreed and then signed the UN Charter, the UN's constitution. The charter is the multilateral treaty that sets out UN powers within international law and outlines how the UN works and carries out its key functions. It also sets out member-state rights within the UN, the powers of its organs (see page 95) and the relationships between the various organs. The founding objectives in Chapter 1 of the charter were, and remain, as follows:

- To maintain international peace and security and 'to take effective collective measures for the prevention and removal of threats to peace'.
- To maintain friendly relations among nations.
- To promote and encourage respect for fundamental human rights.
- To uphold respect for international law.
- To promote social progress and better standards of life.

Other key parts of the charter include Chapters 6 and 7, which are often referred to in UNSC decisions and resolutions.

- **Chapter 6:** sets out the UN's powers to resolve disputes between nation-states using peaceful means. This can include negotiation and peace talks.
- **Chapter 7:** sets out the UN's powers to resolve disputes between nation-states and, increasingly, non-state actors using the military force of its member states. A UNSC Resolution (see page 98) that invokes (that is to say, makes use of for legal purposes) Chapter 7 will legitimise the use of member-state force. Chapter 7 also includes Article 51, which allows states to use force in self-defence. Article 42 is the clause that specifically allows for military action if peaceful means have not been successful.

Current challenges

The UN's role has expanded considerably from its initial founding purpose to focus on a number of specific challenges or threats.

Climate change

The UN has taken more action to reduce environmental degradation, conscious that the global commons (see page 218) requires collective action to be adequately protected. The UN's key task has been to get a majority of member states to agree on the existence and impact of climate change. The Intergovernmental Panel on Climate Change (IPCC, see page 233) helped with this task.

The UN also organises key international summits within the UN Framework Convention on Climate Change (UNFCCC, see page 232). The first major environmental summit was the 1992 UN Earth Summit held in Rio de Janeiro. Subsequently, the UN has made painstaking progress to encourage states to take collective action and make international agreements to limit emissions. The Kyoto Protocol was a UN treaty that was signed in 1997 and enhanced the UNFCCC. Subsequent major summits have been held annually, including the Copenhagen Summit (2009) and the Paris Summit (2015). These are discussed in more depth in Chapter 6.

Nuclear weapons and proliferation

The UN has also developed a leading role in limiting the spread, or proliferation, of nuclear weapons and other weapons of mass destruction. The Treaty on the Non-Proliferation of Nuclear Weapons (NPT, see page 122) was first opened for willing states to sign in 1968. The UN provided a vital forum for states to decide on, codify and sign the NPT. Although four UN member states have not signed the treaty (and it is not a requirement of UN membership to sign it), the UN played a key leadership role. The UNGA has a dedicated Disarmament Commission (UNDC) and within the UN Secretariat, the UN Office for Disarmament Affairs takes a lead. The UN's impact on nuclear issues is explored further on page 122.

Peace and security

UN peacekeeping activities have expanded hugely in scope and number during the organisation's lifetime (see page 110). The UNSC became more active on matters of peace and security after the Cold War ended in 1991. Before this, gridlock between the USA and the Soviet Union made decision-making in the UNSC difficult.

Furthermore, the 1990s saw the biggest increase in UN-approved military intervention, especially in Somalia (1992), Rwanda (1994) and Bosnia (1995). The UN's impact on matters of peace and security is explored further on page 111.

Reducing poverty

The UN has also expanded its role in reducing global poverty. The Millennium Development Goals (MDGs, see page 166), agreed at the UN's Millennium Summit in 2000, represented a huge increase in focus and scope for the organisation's development efforts. The UN continued this focus by reshaping the MDGs into the Sustainable Development Goals (SDGs) when the MDGs reached their agreed endpoint in 2015.

Key UN institutions

The UN's main headquarters is in New York. The main deliberative bodies of the UN, including the UNGA and the UNSC, are based and have their meetings there. Other major UN offices are in Geneva, The Hague (the ICJ), Milan, Nairobi and Vienna.

The UN is notorious for its complex structure and the relationships between its many agencies, secretariats, councils, assemblies and courts (see Figure 3.2). The second UN secretary-general, Dag Hammarskjöld, lamented in 1955 that people thought of the UN as a 'weird Picasso abstraction', so complicated was its organisational structure.

There are five main institutions, often called 'organs', of the UN, each of which has specific functions and powers (see Table 3.3). The most powerful organ is the UNSC.

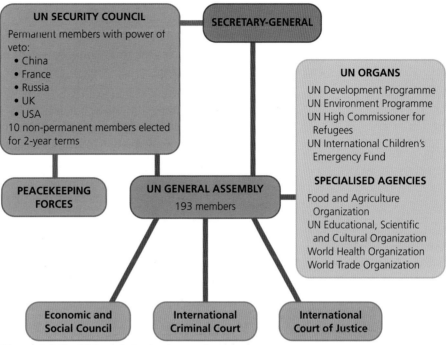

Figure 3.2 The UN's main institutions and organs

Table 3.3 The UN and its principal organs

Principal organ	Function and related bodies
UN Secretariat	The UN's 'civil service', or bureaucracy, led by the UN secretary-general.
	Staffed by UN officials from across the world.
	Includes branches such as the Department for Peacekeeping Operations (DPKO), the UN Development Programme (UNDP) and the Office for the Coordination of Humanitarian Affairs (OCHA).
UN Security Council (UNSC)	The UN's executive committee, responsible for peace and security, and for passing binding resolutions under Chapters 6 and 7 of the UN Charter.
	Its five permanent members (China, France, Russia, the UK, the USA) have veto powers and can block any proposed resolutions with which they disagree.
	It has a further ten non-permanent members chosen by regional quotas, who serve 2-year terms.
UN General Assembly (UNGA)	The UNGA can be thought of as the UN's Parliament. Every member state can participate in debates and is represented equally, with one vote per state.
	Its annual meeting is held at the UN Headquarters in New York each autumn. It allows world leaders to address the UN and there are often votes on major issues (such as the 2012 vote on Palestine's observer status membership of the UN).
International Court of Justice (ICJ)	The ICJ makes judgments principally on territorial disputes between states, and not on human rights matters (the ICJ should not be confused with the ICC (see page 180)).
	In 2013, China did not accept that the ICJ could decide on whether its expansion of Chinese territory in the South China Sea was lawful.
UN Economic and Social Council (ECOSOC)	Responsible for economic security and development, and human rights.
	ECOSOC is made up of 54 members states, elected by the UNGA for 3-year terms.
	It oversees the work of the World Health Organization (WHO) and the UN International Children's Emergency Fund (UNICEF). The World Bank, the IMF and the WTO are related bodies, which arguably wield more power and influence than ECOSOC itself.

UN membership

Initially, 51 states signed the UN Charter and became the founding members of the organisation. As of 2017, the UN has 193 member states. The most recent full member of the UN was South Sudan, which gained independence from Sudan in 2011 and joined the UN in the same year. The UN's membership increased dramatically in the 1950s and 1960s, as many former colonies achieved independence. All undisputed nation-states in the world are UN member states. Indeed, there is a direct link between being recognised as an independent nation-state and becoming a UN member state.

Where a state's sovereignty is not internationally recognised, it may be given non-member observer status if it is agreed by a vote of the UNGA. Palestine, whose independence is still disputed, has been given non-member observer status (the Vatican is the only other). This allows its voice to be heard at the UNGA, but stops short of giving it full recognition as an independent state or allowing it voting rights.

The UN was founded on the basis that all member states would be equal, regardless of their size or power (see Chapter 2). The UN Charter states that the UN will operate on the basis of the 'sovereign equality of all of its members'. From the beginnings of the UN and its charter, it was recognised that the UN would respect state sovereignty and the independence of states. Chapter 1 of the charter states that the UN 'should not intervene in matters which are essentially within the domestic jurisdiction of any state'. This was an early indication that the UN would focus its activities only on those issues that required a unified, global approach and not interfere with anything best left for states to deal with independently. The UN is therefore dependent on states consenting to the activities it proposes — nothing is forced on states (except in rare circumstances, with UNSC authorisation).

While the UN Charter commits to treating all member states equally, regardless of power or size, the same charter gave additional powers to the five permanent members (frequently abbreviated to the P5) of the UNSC. These additional powers are explored in greater detail later in the chapter.

The UN Secretariat and secretary-general

The UN Secretariat is the UN's civil service or administrative body, overseeing the work of the entire UN and its subsidiary bodies and agencies. It has 9,000 staff across the world, under the overall leadership of the UN secretary-general at the headquarters in New York. The secretary-general's role includes the following:

- Acting as the UN's public spokesperson. Former secretary-general Kofi Annan spoke of the need for the UN to have 'someone with a status that governments would recognise, someone with authority to speak to humanity as a whole. Who could that be, if not the secretary-general of the United Nations?'
- Leading the UN Secretariat and setting the UN agenda, to be approved by consensus with the member states in the UNGA.

The UNGA appoints the secretary-general on the recommendation of the Security Council, for a 5-year term (see Table 3.4). The secretary-general is

Case study

Palestine's observer status at the UN

In November 2012, the UNGA voted by 138 to 9 (with 41 abstentions) to approve Palestine as a non-member observer state at the UN. Granting Palestine any form of recognition as an independent territorial and political body has been controversial, as the Palestinian territories lie within the state of Israel (see Figure 3.3).

The president of the Palestinian Authority, Mahmoud Abbas, reacted to the vote by saying that it was the first step in Palestine achieving independence:

> We did not come here seeking to delegitimise a state established years ago, and that is Israel; rather we came to affirm the legitimacy of the state that must now achieve its independence, and that is Palestine.

In contrast, the Israeli government reacted with disappointment. The ambassador to the UN, Ron Prosor, declared that the UN should not have been used as a means of trying to secure Palestinian statehood:

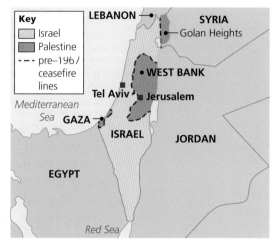

Figure 3.3 Israeli and Palestinian territories

> there's only one route to statehood and that route does not run through this chamber in New York. It runs through direct negotiations between Jerusalem and Ramallah [the capital of the Palestinian territories].

The vote came as peace talks between the Israelis and Palestinians had stalled for 2 years. UN Secretary-General Ban Ki-moon saw the vote as a means to kick-start those peace talks. He said:

> we must give new impetus to our collective efforts to ensure that an independent, sovereign, democratic State of Palestine lives side by side with a secure State of Israel.

The secretary-general was referring to the so-called two-state solution to the Israel and Palestine issue, which both the Israelis and Palestinians had agreed to in principle.

Questions
1 What is the significance of Palestine being given non-member observer status at the UN?
2 Why do you think that so many members of the UNGA backed Palestine's bid for observer status?

Table 3.4 Recent UN secretaries-general

Period in office	Secretary-general	Nationality
1946–52	Trygve Lie	Norway
1953–61	Dag Hammarskjöld	Sweden
1961–71	U Thant	Myanmar (Burma)
1972–81	Kurt Waldheim	Austria
1982–91	Javier Pérez de Cuéllar	Peru
1992–96	Boutros Boutros-Ghali	Egypt
1996–2006	Kofi Annan	Ghana
2007–16	Ban Ki-moon	Republic of Korea (South Korea)
2017– (elected for a 5-year term)	António Guterres	Portugal

expected to represent the interests of the UN, and not any single nation-state or group of nation-states. In reality, the secretary-general's powers are limited, but the role usually carries considerable persuasive or soft power (see page 255), enhanced through being seen as neutral and defending the UN's founding values. Both Hammarskjöld and Annan were awarded the Nobel Peace Prize for their UN leadership. Of course, this does not prevent the public statements of the secretary-general from sometimes being ignored, particularly if the UNSC does not back those statements (significant power in the UN resides in the decisions of the UNSC and the consent of the UNGA).

However, some secretaries-general have used the role to set a decisive agenda for the UN. For example, Kofi Annan led the Millennium Summit and Report, which culminated in the agreement of the MDGs. The same report also adopted the suggestion of a doctrine known as the Responsibility to Protect (R2P), which recognised the need to legitimise external intervention when states abuse human rights. Previously, Secretary-General Dag Hammarsköld was the driving force in creating the UN peacekeeping forces, famous for their blue helmets or berets.

The secretary-general's power also depends on the prevailing geopolitics of the time. During the Cold War, secretaries-general found it difficult to project a distinctive agenda during the bipolar standoff between the Soviet Union and the USA. After the 9/11 terror attacks, Secretary-General Kofi Annan attempted in vain to persuade the USA, motivated to protect its perception of its national interest, to pursue its interest through the UN. Annan expressed his regret that the 2003 invasion of Iraq was launched unilaterally, without a specific UNSC Resolution, declaring the military action illegal and contrary to the UN Charter.

The UN Security Council

The UNSC is the UN's executive committee and is responsible for maintaining international peace and security. It is the most powerful branch of the UN, with powers to:
- issue binding resolutions in international law, by which all UN member states must abide
- issue economic sanctions and call upon other UN member states to adopt them
- authorise military action, ranging from humanitarian intervention to no-fly zones

The UNSC is the supreme decision-making body for dealing with international crises. It is comprised of five permanent members and ten elected, non-permanent members. The UN Charter grants special powers to its permanent members, such as the right to veto UNSC Resolutions, thus preventing them being adopted.

The UNSC's streamlined membership is designed to make it an active and decisive body on international security matters. The larger membership of the League of Nations, with powerful states and less powerful states seen as equals, had led to the powerful states leaving in order to protect their national interests. The UNSC allows the possibility of joint action where there is agreement and also allows the most powerful states the right to veto and

The UNSC in session

protect their national interests. Its effectiveness is, therefore, dependent on what its members, particularly its permanent members, are able to agree.

Membership

The UNSC is made up of five permanent members: China, France, Russia, the UK and the USA. The permanent members were the most powerful states when the UN was founded, the victors of the Second World War. There are also ten non-permanent members, which the UNGA elects for 2-year terms (see Table 3.5).

The permanent members are given the right to veto any resolution with which they disagree. Non-permanent members have no veto power.

Functions and powers

Some have called the UNSC the most powerful body in international politics, owing to the powers it possesses. Its resolutions represent binding international

Table 3.5 UNSC permanent and non-permanent membership, September 2017

Permanent members	Non-permanent members
France China Russia UK USA	Regional allocation, overlapping **Africa:** 3 seats **Western Europe and Oceania, Asia, Latin America and the Caribbean:** 2 seats each Egypt, Italy, Japan, Senegal, Ukraine, Uruguay (until end of 2017) Bolivia, Ethiopia, Kazakhstan, Sweden (until end of 2018)

law and other states must comply with them. Moreover, it can authorise military action against other states.

For a resolution to be passed, the UNSC requires:

- no veto from a permanent member
- a two-thirds majority of permanent and non-permanent members

The non-permanent members are, therefore, significant and diplomatic efforts are frequently required to persuade non-permanent members to support resolutions if they are to succeed. If seven non-permanent members vote against a resolution, it will not pass, even if all five permanent members vote in favour (the so-called sixth veto). The non-permanent members therefore give the UNSC a more balanced, regional membership, including quotas for each continent.

The veto: vital safeguard or cause of paralysis?

The UNSC veto power was created to prevent the problem that had plagued the League of Nations, namely that decisions had to be made unanimously among a group much larger than the five permanent members of the modern-day UNSC.

The idea of 'great power unanimity' recognises that some states are (or were) more powerful than others. The more powerful states needed to have their superiority recognised and for decisions on peace and security matters to be taken in a smaller group, where these states could defend their interests using the veto. The veto therefore recognises the importance of powerful countries remaining within the UN. States may also abstain if they do not agree with a UNSC Resolution but do not feel strongly enough to veto.

Whether or not and how often the permanent members use their veto depends on how powerful they are, and on the balance of power in the UNSC itself, at any time:

- Russia is the most frequent user of the veto — it has used the veto more than 100 times since 1945. It also used the veto more times than any other state during the Cold War period.
- The USA is the second most frequent user of the veto. It also vetoed frequently during the Cold War period, although it vetoed less frequently than the Soviet Union during the Cold War as it was less isolated in the UNSC.
- The Cold War saw the Soviet Union and the USA frequently use the veto, reflecting the bipolarity of the world order in which both nation-states were equally powerful and intent on challenging each other.
- After the Cold War, with the USA the dominant hegemon in a unipolar world order, the USA became the most frequent user of the veto. A defeated former Soviet Union, now the Russian Federation, did not veto as much as it had during the Cold War.
- Since 2001, a more multipolar world order has frequently seen Russia use the veto and, for the first time, increasingly China. This has been especially problematic in the UN's response to the conflict in Syria, where disagreements between Russia and France, the UK and the USA have seen frequent vetoes of resolutions on both sides.
- France and the UK have not vetoed since 1989. This arguably reflects the fact that, as less powerful permanent member states, they have fewer national interests at stake in the matters the UNSC discusses.

Often just as important as the permanent members' use of the veto are the occasions when a resolution was not put to a vote because it was known in advance that a permanent member intended to use its veto. For example, in 2003, France and Russia made it clear that they would veto a UK/US-led resolution seeking final authorisation for the military invasion of Iraq. The UK and the USA knew that their resolution would be vetoed and that there was a fundamental difference of opinion since France and Russia believed that Iraq should be given more time to comply with UN weapons inspections. Therefore, they abandoned their resolution and instead took military action unilaterally.

Case study

The UNSC: powerless on Syria?

The UN and specifically the UNSC have come under significant criticism for their response to the war in Syria, which began in 2011. Critics say that the UNSC should have done more to prevent government forces led by President Bashar al-Assad from committing what UN Secretary-General Ban Ki-Moon called 'systematic torture' and 'barrel bombing of neighbourhoods'. In his final speech to the UNGA, Ban Ki-Moon said that Assad's forces were responsible for the deaths of 300,000 people because of a 'failure of leadership'. Strong criticism from the secretary-general, but by 2016 what had the UN and the UNSC done to help in Syria?

Use of chemical weapons

After the Assad regime used chemical weapons against civilians in 2013, some expected that the USA would lead military action against the regime. President Obama had previously stated that the use of chemical weapons represented a 'red line'. By September 2013, it was clear that Russia, Syria's ally, and the UK and US public would not support a resolution for military action. Therefore, UNSC Resolution 2118 set out a plan to disarm Syria of its chemical weapons. Weapons were shipped out under neutral observers, but barrel bombings using toxic chemicals continued.

Action against rebel groups, including so-called Islamic State

UNSC agreement for condemning the activities of so-called Islamic State heightened after the 2015 Paris terrorist attacks. A UNSC Resolution was approved in December 2015, condemning the activities of so-called Islamic State, al-Qaeda and affiliated organisations in the middle east, north Africa and beyond. The resolution took action to freeze the bank accounts and other financial assets of these groups. It did not authorise any military action against Islamic State but was clear in its condemnation and also highlighted a number of other activities (such as a travel ban for individuals associated with Islamic State and a ban on the sale of weapons).

Peace talks

The UNSC has passed several resolutions supporting peace talks that took place in Vienna. The International Syria Support Group is 15 states, including several major global and regional powers that have an influence on the conflict (Iran, Iraq, Jordan, Qatar, Russia, Saudi Arabia and the USA are among its members). The Support Group has secured only temporary ceasefires but has nevertheless provided a forum for influential actors to keep the dialogue open.

Humanitarian assistance

The UN has provided humanitarian assistance through its Office for the Coordination of Humanitarian Affairs (OCHA), which is responsible for the UN's emergency humanitarian responses. As of 2016, there were 13.5 million people in need of humanitarian assistance. Difficulties in accessing key areas of need, such as the besieged city of Aleppo, have hampered the UN's efforts. In 2016, an air strike attacked a UN humanitarian convoy, killing 18 civilians. Ban Ki-moon later condemned the strike as 'sickening, savage, and apparently deliberate'.

Questions

1 What factors or actors have limited UN action on Syria?
2 To what extent is criticism of the UN's response valid?
3 Is the UNSC an institution designed with liberalism or realism in mind?

Despite the focus on the veto, it is important to consider the actions that the UNSC has successfully agreed and achieved. Against the many examples of restriction by permanent members' use of the veto, the UNSC has been remarkably active and is capable of acting decisively when there is agreement among its permanent members.

UN Security Council achievements

The UNSC has achieved many significant successes during its operation (see Table 3.6). It has authorised peacekeeping forces across the world in more than 69 operations. It approved a comprehensive package of economic sanctions against Iran between 2006 and 2015 with the ultimately successful aim of forcing Iran to the negotiating table and to dismantle its nuclear weapons programme.

When Syrian government forces used chemical weapons in an attack in Gouda in August 2013, it was not UNSC paralysis that prevented military action against the Syrian regime but sceptical domestic publics and legislatures, principally in the war-weary UK and USA. Instead, the UNSC agreed a comprehensive international disarmament process that disarmed and removed chemical weapons from Syria (see Case study). The UNSC is, therefore, a busy council, taking action on a range of crises.

A further UNSC success story is that the most powerful states, the permanent members, have all remained within the UN system and have, without any interruption, maintained the UNSC as a forum for negotiation and diplomacy since 1945. This record contrasts with the League of Nations' failures, where the most powerful states felt that the only way to protect their national interests was to leave the organisation altogether. The UNSC is especially weak, indeed powerless, when a permanent member misbehaves or decides to take unilateral action in defiance of the UNSC (for example, the US-led invasion of Iraq in 2003 and Russian forces' annexation of Crimea in 2014).

Table 3.6 Significant UNSC Resolutions

Date	UNSC Resolution	Effect
22 November 1967	242	The UNSC calls on Israel to withdraw from territory that it occupied in the Six Day War, including the Gaza Strip, Golan Heights and West Bank. Israel has not complied with this resolution and has occupied the territory since 1967.
8 November 2002	1441	The UNSC unanimously gives Iraq and its leader Saddam Hussein a 'final opportunity with its disarmament obligations', stating that the country was in material breach of previous UNSC ceasefire resolutions. It warns of 'serious consequences' in the event of future violations. The UK and US governments claimed that this authorised the 2003 invasion of Iraq. Many experts in international law — including the UN Secretary-General Kofi Annan — disagreed.
31 March 2005	1970	The UNSC refers Libya to the ICC for investigation, the first time it had unanimously agreed to use its powers to refer countries that have not signed the Rome Statute to the ICC (see page 180).
17 March 2011	1973	The UNSC demands a ceasefire in Libya and agrees 'all necessary means short of foreign occupation' for the protection of civilians. It also establishes a no-fly zone. China and Russia abstain. NATO then begins an air campaign that includes bombing key Libyan government targets.
27 September 2013	2118	The UNSC requires Syria to disarm itself of chemical weapons, establishing a process successfully overseen by the Organisation for the Prohibition of Chemical Weapons (OPCW).

Debate

Does the veto prevent the UNSC from getting anything done?

Yes

- Permanent members are too powerful and are able to veto anything that threatens their national interests and prevent action from being taken — the UNSC has been powerless to act meaningfully on Syria, for example.
- Powerful permanent members can misbehave and veto any action against them (for example, Russia's actions in Crimea in 2014).
- The UNSC is powerless to stop powerful countries from acting alone (or unilaterally) to pursue their interests (for example, the US-led invasion of Iraq in 2003).

No

- The UNSC achieves a lot, passing many resolutions successfully.
- Under its Chapter 6 powers, it can settle disputes peacefully and has authorised 69 peacekeeping missions around the world since 1948. Under Its Chapter 7 powers, it has authorised military action (most recently in Libya in 2011) and has imposed successful sanctions on regimes posing a risk to international security.
- Allowing powerful states to have a veto has meant that major powers have stayed within the UN system and the UNSC remains relevant. Without it, there is a risk that powerful permanent members would leave the UN, as happened with the League of Nations.

Arguments for reform

Many criticise membership of the UNSC as outdated, saying that it represented the most powerful states at its creation in 1945, but not the major powers of today. While it can still be argued that China, Russia and the USA are major world powers, whether France and the UK still deserve great power status and the veto rights that come with it is debatable. British and French membership is still largely linked to their status as nuclear weapons states, their power at the end of the Second World War and their subsequently high-profile roles in international diplomacy.

There have been calls for newly risen, and some long-established, powers to be included as permanent members. Brazil, Germany, India and Japan — all of which are much more powerful than they were in 1945 — have been the most widely suggested new permanent members. There have also been calls for an African state, such as Nigeria or South Africa, to gain permanent membership — the continents of Africa and South America are currently entirely unrepresented.

These changes would require amendments to the UN Charter. The current permanent members would be able to use their veto to prevent any new permanent members that were not to their liking or if they feared these new members would diminish their own influence. Even agreeing on potential new permanent members is fraught with difficulty. Pakistan would be likely to oppose a permanent membership for India. Choosing which of Africa's main economic powers, Nigeria or South Africa, gets membership is not an obvious or easy choice. With a majority of UN member states accepting the authority of the current UNSC, reforming the council potentially puts at risk the widespread legitimacy and stability the council largely enjoys.

Options for reform include:

- new permanent members with veto power
- new permanent members that do not have veto power
- removing veto power from some or all of the current permanent members
- increasing the number of non-permanent members, or having them serve longer terms than the current non-permanent members

Should the UNSC be reformed?

Yes

- France and the UK are no longer significant world powers and should either be replaced or supplemented with other powers that have emerged since 1945.
- The UNSC's composition reflects a view that the major powers in global politics have not changed since 1945. The UNSC, therefore, does not reflect the current geopolitical realities in its membership, especially in not taking into account newly emerged powers such as Brazil, Germany, India and Japan.
- More non-permanent or permanent members without veto power could be a compromise that would allow for greater diversity without giving new members too much power. While they cannot veto resolutions, they are not powerless. If seven non-permanent members vote against a resolution, it will not pass. Permanent members have to make efforts to persuade non-permanent members to support their resolutions.
- The UNSC was already successfully reformed in 1965, when the number of non-permanent members increased from six to ten.

No

- It would be impossible for the permanent members to agree on new permanent members, as they have power of veto. Attempts at reform would be doomed to failure.
- Agreeing on new members would be fraught with difficulty. Pakistan would likely oppose India's membership, seeing this as a direct threat to its interests.
- More states having veto power would further increase the likelihood of resolutions being vetoed and, therefore, the UNSC being unable to act. Even with only two states, Russia and the USA, active users of the veto (see Figure 3.4), the UNSC is often in stalemate.
- Measures such as abolishing the veto altogether, or otherwise restricting the ability of the major powers to protect their national interests, could see the UN return to the problems of the League of Nations, where the major powers withdrew because they had no facility to defend their national interests.

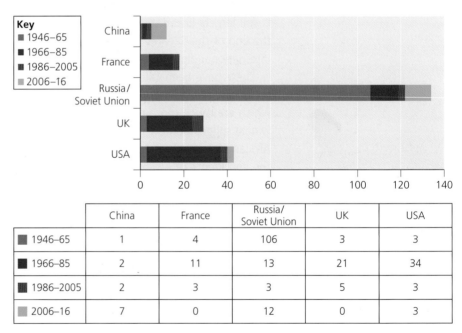

	China	France	Russia/ Soviet Union	UK	USA
1946–65	1	4	106	3	3
1966–85	2	11	13	21	34
1986–2005	2	3	3	5	3
2006–16	7	0	12	0	3

Figure 3.4 UNSC permanent members' use of the veto, 1946–2016

Military power

The UN does not have a military force of its own. The UN Charter attempted to set up a Military Staff Committee that would take charge of planning military operations. However, the UNSC permanent members did not provide the military forces needed to set up an independent military contingent. This partly reflected nervousness and the fractured nature of the Cold War period.

However, it was also clear that the permanent members did not wish to divert and dilute their own military resources to a UN force.

Consequently, the UN and the UNSC have had to rely on organisations such as NATO and the African Union (AU) to carry out military operations on its behalf. The African Union Mission in Somalia (AMISOM) operates under a UNSC Resolution, and is funded and supported by the UN Department for Peacekeeping Operations. The UNSC authorised military action in Libya in 2011, but NATO carried out the action.

The UN General Assembly

Often called the UN's parliament, the UNGA is the UN forum in which all 193 member states have an equal voice and vote (see Figure 3.5). It is the only UN organ in which every member state has permanent representation. NGOs are often allowed to attend and address UNGA meetings, further widening the accessibility and inclusivity of the UNGA as a forum for debate.

The UNGA's main occasion is its annual meeting, held every September at the UN Headquarters in New York at the UNGA's debating chamber. This equality of representation is notable for allowing countries to have a voice regardless of their size or power, but it does mean that the UNGA is relatively weak in its powers. Unlike those of the UNSC, its resolutions are not binding and carry no force in international law. Member states can therefore ignore these resolutions, meaning they carry mostly symbolic status. The UNGA also has no authoritative voice on matters of international security, which are largely left to the UNSC to deal with alone.

Functions and powers

The UNGA's primary functions include:
- electing UNSC non-permanent members
- appointing the secretary-general on the basis of the UNSC's recommendation

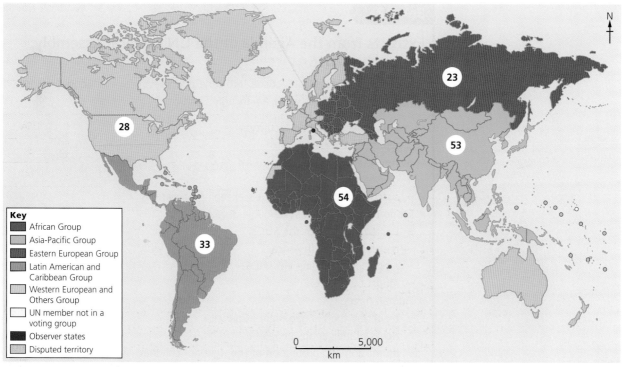

Figure 3.5 Division of the UNGA

- considering and debating reports from ECOSOC and the ICJ
- approving the UN's budget
- electing judges to the ICJ

Decision making in the UNGA can be challenging and time-consuming, given that every member state can take part in debates. UNGA decisions on resolutions relating to peace and security, admission of new members and the UN budget need a two-thirds majority, making it difficult to reach consensus on the most controversial issues.

However, the UNGA can take decisive action. Its most enduring achievement was the UN's Universal Declaration of Human Rights (UDHR), signed in 1948. The UDHR remains the foundational and guiding global human rights framework, and it has influenced subsequent international and domestic human rights law. More recently, in 2000, the UNGA approved the Millennium Declaration, which agreed a unified set of global economic and human development targets, the Millennium Development Goals (MDGs). The UNGA agreed the successor to the MDGs, the Sustainable Development Goals (SDGs), in September 2015. The SDGs set out a new series of targets for development that will run until 2030 (see Box 3.2, which sets out further aspects of the 2016 UNGA agenda).

More controversial decisions are also not beyond the powers of the UNGA. Palestine was granted non-member observer status in 2012, despite powerful and vocal opposition from Israel and the USA, which both voted against the resolution (138 states voted in favour, 41 abstained, including the UK, and 9 voted against). This recognition of the State of Palestine at the UN subsequently allowed it to successfully become the 123rd signatory to the Rome Statute, whereupon it formally joined the ICC. This meant that, for the first time, it was within ICC powers to investigate Israeli security forces in Palestinian territory for alleged war crimes.

Box 3.2

Extracts from the Agenda of the UN General Assembly, September 2016

The UNGA Agenda is categorised into nine main sections for discussion, some of which, from the 2016 Agenda, are included below.

- International peace and security:
  - report by the UNSC
  - the situation in the middle east
  - question of Palestine
  - comprehensive review of peacekeeping operations
- Economic growth and sustainable development:
  - implementation of the SDGs
  - tackling malaria in Africa
  - progress on tackling HIV/AIDS
  - report by ECOSOC
- Human rights:
  - report by the Human Rights Council
  - rights of indigenous peoples
  - promotion and protection of the rights of children

- Humanitarian and disaster relief assistance:
  - assistance to the Palestinian people
  - strengthening the coordination of UN emergency humanitarian assistance
- Justice and international law:
  - report by the ICJ
  - report by the ICC
  - oceans and law of the sea
- Disarmament:
  - establishment of a nuclear weapons-free zone in the middle east
  - nuclear disarmament
  - drug control, international terrorism and crime prevention
  - measures to eliminate international terrorism
- Organisational and administrative matters:
  - report of the secretary-general
  - appointment of the UN secretary-general
  - election of the five non-permanent members of the UNSC

Activity

Across the world, many students take part in Model United Nations (MUN), a simulation of the UN's debates and procedures. This provides an excellent way of understanding the UN's processes and how individual states make their views known and shape cooperative policies on issues of importance to them. Many MUN conferences replicate the UNGA's sub-committees, which then propose ideas for the entire UNGA to vote on.

1 Research how UNGA Resolutions are written here: **http://bestdelegate.com/ model-un-made-easy-how-to-write-a-resolution**.

2 Working in groups, write your own UN Resolution on an issue in global politics that you care about.

3 As a class, you could come up with your own agenda of different issues to be discussed and then debate them together, using this resource as a guide: **http://bestdelegate.com/how-to-debate-resolutions**.

Committees

The UNGA committees (see Table 3.7) are a means of streamlining the work of the assembly into specific, focused committees. The committees have much smaller membership and put forward proposals for resolutions to be voted on, and therefore adopted by, the full UNGA. During the course of a year each committee will submit as many as 60 draft resolutions for the UNGA to consider.

The committees are an important means for states to call for action on specific issues and apply pressure on other actors in global politics. The Human Rights Council is another subsidiary body of the UNGA (see page 105).

The Economic and Social Council

ECOSOC is one of the principal organs of the UN and is responsible for economic security and development across the UN's member states. Unlike the UNGA's Economic and Financial Committee, which is more of a forum for

Table 3.7 UNGA committees and their functions

Committee	Functions and key decisions
Disarmament and International Security Committee	Considers all disarmament and international security matters, including matters ranging from preventing the proliferation of nuclear weapons to the illegal small arms trade. The committee reports to the UNGA, which can vote on ideas the committee discusses. For example, an UNGA Resolution was passed in 2010 pressing for a nuclear weapons-free zone in the middle east.
Economic and Financial Committee	Considers issues relating to economic development, including international trade and poverty reduction. In 2015, for example, the UNGA adopted the committee's recommendations on development cooperation with middle-income countries. This is an excellent example of the specifics that the sub-committees are able to get into, ensuring that the UN system hears the interests of a very specific group of states.
Social, Humanitarian and Cultural Committee	This committee debates specific areas of human rights concern, such as the rights of women and refugees. The committee is able to call for action relating to specific human rights abuses in specific countries. In 2015, the UNGA adopted a resolution calling on states to protect the human rights of migrants and to prevent human trafficking.

Table 3.8 ECOSOC: major specialised agencies and funds

Specialised agencies	Programmes and funds
Specialised agencies have their own budgets, leadership and organising assemblies made up of a small number of member states. They include: ■ the UN Educational, Scientific and Cultural Organization (UNESCO) ■ the World Bank (see page 139) ■ the IMF (see page 133)	ECOSOC directly administers and manages programmes and funds while UNGA supervises them. They are less autonomous than the specialised agencies, and include: ■ the WHO ■ the UN Development Programme (UNDP) ■ the World Food Programme (WFP)

generating ideas and policies, ECOSOC is much more active and carries out a wide range of projects aimed at improving economic development and growth. ECOSOC does this through 14 major branches, which include well-known, specialised agencies and funds that are allocated large amounts of the UN's budget in order to carry out their work (see Table 3.8).

ECOSOC itself, which oversees all of these agencies and funds, is made up of 54 member states, elected for 2-year terms. Since the UNGA adopted the SDGs, ECOSOC now focuses much of its work on economic, social and environmental sustainable development.

ECOSOC's specialised agencies have the power to set their own agenda and some, for example the IMF, are highly influential players on the world stage. The leaders of these agencies, for example the IMF's Christine Lagarde, speak with real independence and authority. Its programmes and funds also bear huge responsibility for actually delivering much of what the UNGA pledges to do. For example, the UNDP has led all of the UN's work on human and economic development across the world, with a large budget of over US$5 billion.

The International Court of Justice

The ICJ is the principal judicial organ of the UN. Based in the Peace Palace at The Hague, in the Netherlands, it has two key functions:

1 To settle legal disputes between member states.
2 To give advisory opinions on legal questions submitted by authorised agencies.

The court has 15 judges, all of whom the UNGA elects for 9-year terms and are independent, rather than representing their home state. Unusual for the legal process, the court does not have automatic authority to hear

Chapter 3 Global governance: political

The ICJ is based in the Peace Palace at The Hague

cases between states — rather both sides have to agree that the court has jurisdiction (or the legitimate legal authority to make a ruling) on the matter. This has allowed states simply to declare lack of jurisdiction on cases that are not to their liking.

However, the ICJ has made rulings on contentious cases and carries out an important role in arbitrating between states that are in dispute with each other. For example, in 2004, it ruled that the security fence Israel constructed around the Palestinian West Bank, in territory that a UNSC Resolution continues to call for Israel to withdraw from, was illegal under international law. However, Israel chose to ignore this ruling and continued to build the barrier, stating that it was vital to its internal security.

In theory, ICJ rulings are binding on UN member states. If they do not comply, the UN Charter allows for the matter to be referred to the UNSC for enforcement. However, again action is entirely dependent on the UNSC issuing a resolution forcing states to comply.

Distinguish between

The International Court of Justice and the International Criminal Court

The ICJ
- Cases can be heard against all UN member states provided they recognise the court's jurisdiction.
- Cases heard largely involve territorial disputes between nation-states, and not international criminal law.

The ICC
- Cases can only be heard against states that have signed and ratified the Rome Statute, or those the UNSC has referred to the court.
- Cases heard relate to breaches of international criminal law, including crimes against humanity.

How effective is the UN?

Evaluating the effectiveness of the UN in its key areas of responsibility — resolving conflict, reducing poverty, safeguarding the environment (see page 218) and upholding human rights (see page 171) — is not a simple matter. The UN works in every country in the world, with huge budgets devoted to thousands of individual projects, and it has been working to these objectives across many decades (see Figure 3.6). The UN is not responsible for everything, good or bad, that happens in the world. Equally, there are many events and factors in global politics that are outside the UN's control.

Points to bear in mind when evaluating the effectiveness of the UN include the following:

- Who is responsible for its successes and failures — the organisation and institutions themselves or the member states (particularly its most powerful members)?
- What can be defined as 'effectiveness'? This is a subjective term. If the UN organises peace talks but the peace talks do not succeed, is that a failure? Could the peace talks have been organised without the UN's influence? Is the success of peace talks only judged on whether or not they succeed in the ultimate goal of ending conflict, or do they serve a more subtle and meaningful purpose?
- From a realist perspective, if states are the most authoritative and powerful actors in global politics, is it reasonable to expect the UN to be more effective?

To come to a fair evaluation of its effectiveness, we cannot consider all that the UN has tried to do in its history. Instead, we can look at some key moments, crises and ideas in which the UN might have been expected to be effective.

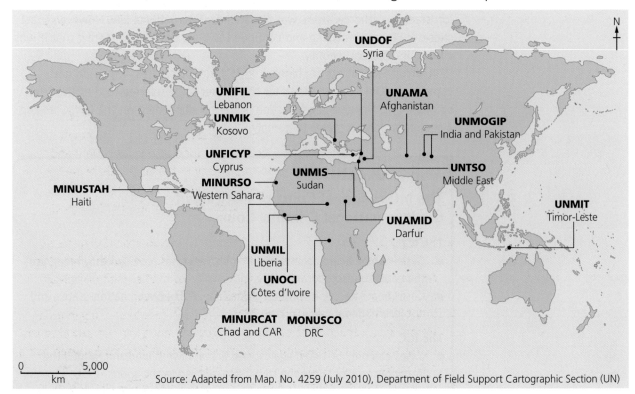

Source: Adapted from Map. No. 4259 (July 2010), Department of Field Support Cartographic Section (UN)

Figure 3.6 UN peacekeeping operations in 2017

Maintaining international peace and security

One of the central objectives of the UN when it was founded in 1945 was to:

> maintain international peace and security and 'to take effective collective measures for the prevention and removal of threats to peace'.

Clearly, the UN has not managed to prevent conflict altogether, and it would be unreasonable to expect it to have done so. In any case, the founding objectives are more nuanced and realistic, committing the UN to removing 'threats to peace'. What influence *has* the UN had in some of the major threats to peace and security that have emerged since 1945? To evaluate, it is helpful to divide the post-1945 period into several key periods. These divisions are also a useful way of thinking about key periods in the balance of power in global politics.

The Cold War (1945–91)

A military standoff between the Soviet Union and the USA dominated the early decades of the UN, from 1945 until the fall of the Berlin Wall in 1989 and the collapse of the Soviet Union in 1991. The UN — in particular, the Security Council — was powerless to influence the conflict, given that two UNSC permanent members were, in effect, at war with each other.

More influential during this period was NATO, which created a specific security alliance for the USA and its western European allies, like-minded states that felt a shared threat.

The NPT was also influential during this period in preventing a major spread of nuclear weapons beyond the Soviet Union and the USA. However, the Cold War did not prevent the UN from agreeing to send peacekeepers to conflicts, for example in Africa, which the two countries felt did not affect their core security interests.

Post-Cold War: instability in Africa and Europe (1991–2001)

The Cold War's aftermath saw the collapse of the Soviet Union and of Russian power. Fifteen new and independent states split from Moscow's control. With the USA now the predominant world power (hegemon) and Russia less inclined to oppose its former enemy in the UNSC, there was the prospect of the UN being more decisive and activist. However, the UN's limitations became apparent in a series of high-profile peacekeeping failures during this period:

- In 1992, UN peacekeepers in Somalia were unable to defend themselves against a rebel attack and were forced to retreat. US troops attempted to rescue the situation by fighting back against the militias with disastrous results, as portrayed in the 2001 film *Black Hawk Down*.
- In 1994, UN peacekeepers in Rwanda were powerless to stop a genocide from taking place in front of them. The UN had not given the peacekeepers permission to intervene with force against the tribal fighters. Between half a million and a million civilians lost their lives.
- Peacekeeping operations in Bosnia (1992–95) failed to prevent Serb forces from executing 8,000 Bosnian Muslims in Srebrenica, when Serbian forces overran a UN-declared 'safe haven'.

The War on Terror (2001–9)

The UN was largely sidelined during the War on Terror. The US government, under President George W. Bush, was determined to protect what it saw as its own national interest, having suffered in the 9/11 terror attacks the most serious attack on US soil since Pearl Harbor. A UNSC Resolution authorised and created the International Security Assistance Force (ISAF) and the UN was heavily involved in reconstruction and development work in Afghanistan throughout the conflict. However, ISAF was under US, not UN, military command.

Furthermore, military action in Iraq in 2003 was launched without a UNSC Resolution, after France and Russia indicated that they would not support the invasion. UN Secretary-General Kofi Annan later condemned the Iraq War as being:

> illegal and not in conformity with the UN Charter … I think that in the end everybody is concluding that it is best to work together with allies and through the UN to deal with those issues.

Post-War on Terror: the Arab Uprisings (2010–12) and the present

During this period, the US government under President Barack Obama stopped using the term 'War on Terror' and began to focus on withdrawing US troops from conflicts in Afghanistan and Iraq.

The Arab Uprisings sparked in Syria one of the bloodiest conflicts seen in recent years, with over 500,000 killed and more than 6 million refugees. The UN has been powerless in the face of a determined Syrian government under President Bashar al-Assad. Russia decided to intervene unilaterally, without UN consent, with controversial military action in support of the Assad regime. The USA and its allies were initially reluctant to intervene, partly due to scepticism and war-weariness at home. Eventually France, the UK and the USA began air strikes against so-called Islamic State in Iraq and Syria, at the request of the Iraqi government.

The only meaningful UNSC action during this period was the resolution to disarm Syria of its chemical weapons. Even still, human-rights observers reported that Syrian government forces were using barrel bombs with chlorine gas against rebel forces. Indeed, on 4 April 2017, a suspected government forces chemical attack took place on the Syrian town of Khan Shaykhun, killing at least 74 people, including many children, and injuring around 550.

Another key challenge of the period since 9/11 has been the emergence of non-state actor threats from terrorist groups such as al-Qaeda and so-called Islamic State. The UN was established to deal principally with security threats from nation-states and has found it harder, if not impossible, to counter non-state actor threats.

We can see, therefore, that during periods where there are major threats to international security, such as the Cold War or the so-called War on Terror, the major powers have tended to prioritise their own national interests. During these periods, the effect of protecting that national interest has been that the UN has at best been overlooked and at worst deliberately bypassed.

Case study

Rwanda and Srebrenica: failures of UN peacekeeping?

The UN peacekeeping missions in Rwanda (1994) and Bosnia (1995) have been much criticised for failing to prevent two major genocides. In Rwanda in April 1994, the Hutu majority government attacked the Tutsi minority, killing as many as 1 million in just over 100 days. In Srebrenica, Bosnia, in July 1995, Serbian forces killed 8,000 Bosnian Muslims in just over 10 days. In both cases, UN peacekeepers were present. How, then, did these atrocities happen?

Rwanda

- A 1999 inquiry concluded that not enough was done to respond to indications that a genocide was likely to happen.
- 2,500 UN peacekeepers were withdrawn after ten Belgian peacekeepers were killed earlier in the conflict.

Bosnia

- Bosnian Muslims had surrendered their weapons to UN peacekeepers days before the massacre took place. Serbian forces exploited this. The UN peacekeepers refused a request from the Bosnian Muslims to have their weapons returned.
- Srebrenica was a UN-declared 'safe zone', but Serbian forces ignored this. They overwhelmed UN peacekeepers, who did not have sufficient resources to defend themselves so they stood aside.

Successes

It is relatively straightforward to identify major failures of, and gridlock within, the UN system in failing to prevent conflict. Harder to judge is the UN's effectiveness in less high-profile peacekeeping operations around the world, where peace has been successfully retained or conflict prevented from getting worse. By definition, it is harder to identify what has been responsible for something not happening.

Also harder to judge is the impact of the much lower-profile, day-to-day discussion, pressure and debate that takes place within the UNSC every day at UN Headquarters in New York. These discussions will not always result in a headline-grabbing UNSC Resolution. However, since 1945 the UNSC has been there as a forum for debate and diplomacy. It is not possible to know how global peace and security would have fared without such a forum.

The list of UNSC peacekeeping successes includes the following:

- UN peacekeepers in Sierra Leone from 1999 to 2005 successfully prevented the country relapsing into conflict while a peace agreement was put in place. UN blue-helmet soldiers helped to destroy thousands of weapons and disarm thousands of fighters, including child soldiers. Sierra Leone, a former recipient of peacekeeping assistance, now itself provides peacekeeping troops in Somalia.
- UN military observers have been monitoring the disputed border region of Kashmir between India and Pakistan since 1949. The region has suffered from crises, and even short periods of outright conflict. But it is difficult to assess how the region might have fared without independent UN observers present, reporting on Indian and Pakistani military activity and holding these two nuclear weapons states accountable for their actions.

The balance of power

Equally, the balance of power in world politics, and within the UNSC, has played a major part in determining whether the UN has been able to act or not. The balance of power becomes more obvious the more that major powers see a particular issue as affecting their core national interests (see Table 3.9).

Table 3.9 Power distribution and its impact on the UN's effectiveness

Period	Nature of power distribution	Impact on the UN and its effectiveness
1945–89	Bipolarity (two major powers opposed to each other)	It is difficult, even impossible, for the UN to act if permanent UNSC member states are at war or disagreeing with each other. In these circumstances, the use of the veto becomes so frequent or likely that many issues are simply dealt with outside the UN system.
1989–2001	Unipolarity (a single hegemon)	There is the potential for the UN to be very active on the issues that the single major power (in this period, the USA) favours. Less powerful states may be disinclined to use their veto power.
2001–date	Multipolarity (many world powers competing with each other)	Arguably, this is the current balance of power in global politics, with a resurgent Russia increasingly challenging Western power and the emergence of powerful non-state actor threats (al-Qaeda and so-called Islamic State). UNSC agreement has once again been difficult on major issues, with both China and Russia increasingly wielding their veto power.

The UNSC has, however, been able to agree action in states and regions where the permanent members do not have a clear national strategic interest at stake (see Box 3.3). Most UN peacekeeping operations have been in Africa and states of less geopolitical importance to the major world powers. Consider the following statement from the UN Department for Peacekeeping Operations (2016), highlighting its most successful peacekeeping operations:

> Since 1948, the UN has helped end conflicts and foster reconciliation by conducting successful peacekeeping operations in dozens of countries, including Cambodia, El Salvador, Guatemala, Mozambique, Namibia and Tajikistan. UN peacekeeping has also made a real difference in other places with recently completed or ongoing operations such as Sierra Leone, Burundi, Côte d'Ivoire, Timor-Leste, Liberia, Haiti and Kosovo.

Box 3.3

What factors are required for success in peacekeeping operations?

The following factors all contribute to success in UN peacekeeping operations. There must be:

- genuine commitment to a political process from all parties in working towards peace (there must be a peace to keep)
- clear, credible and achievable mandates, with matching personnel, logistical and financial resources
- unity of purpose within the UNSC, with active support to UN operations in the field
- host-country commitment to unhindered UN operations and freedom of movement
- supportive engagement from neighbouring countries and regional actors
- an integrated UN approach, effective coordination with other actors on the ground and good communication with host-country authorities and population
- the utmost sensitivity towards the local population and upholding the highest standards of professionalism and good conduct (peacekeepers must avoid becoming part of the problem)

Source: UN Department for Peacekeeping Operations

Activity

Research the UN peacekeeping operations in:

- Somalia (1992)
- Rwanda (1994)
- Bosnia (1995)

Which of the factors in Box 3.3 contributed the most to the difficulties UN peacekeepers experienced in these conflicts?

Debate

Has the UN been effective in maintaining international peace and security?

Yes

- The UNSC has been extremely active, approving peacekeeping operations, military intervention and sanctions across the world.
- Nuclear proliferation has been controlled and few new nuclear weapons states have emerged.
- The UN is limited in what it can do by what its member states agree. The UN is not always unable to act, it merely has to operate within the constraints of what its most powerful members perceive as their national interest.
- The UN has so far succeeded where the League of Nations failed in preventing another world war. Inter-state war has decreased considerably since the UN was founded and democracy has spread.

No

- The UN has struggled to respond to security threats from non-state actors, including al-Qaeda. The UN was largely sidelined during the early stages of the War on Terror.
- UN peacekeepers have seen tragic failures in Somalia, Rwanda and Bosnia. Unless there is peace already in place, UN peacekeepers are unable to have a positive impact.
- Civil wars have increased, even while inter-state war has decreased. The UN has been less able to respond to internal conflict, as it was designed to deal with inter-state conflict.

Reducing poverty

The UN was also founded with the specific objective of reducing poverty and promoting economic development among all its member states. The Preamble to the UN Charter (see page 92) states that the UN will 'promote social progress and better standards of life in larger freedom'. In 2000, UN Secretary-General Kofi Annan published the Millennium Report, attempting to refocus the UN for the challenges of a new century. Annan conceded that the UN needed to confront 'the central challenge that we face today … ensuring that globalisation becomes a positive force for all the world's people, instead of leaving billions of them behind in squalor'.

Annan's proposal, later endorsed by the UNGA, was to focus the efforts of the UN and its member states on eight specific development themes and targets (see Box 3.4). The targets, called the Millennium Development Goals (MDGs), would be time-bound, to be measured annually and delivered within a 15-year target (by 2015). The MDGs were powerful because it was the first time human development objectives had been internationally agreed. A total of 189 member states and 23 international organisations committed to the goals, reflecting a huge international consensus.

The MDGs created the potential for the UN, member states and NGOs to coordinate their development efforts on MDG priorities. Previously, there had been no international coordination of this kind. For the next 15 years, many global and national aid budgets were aligned with MDG priorities. In the first

The MDGs were committed to reducing global poverty, particular in poor regions such as Sub-Saharan Africa

5 years, foreign aid budgets doubled from US$6 billion to US$12 billion. The MDGs were clear and measurable, and the UN Development Programme (UNDP) led rigorous monitoring and reporting of global, regional and national progress.

> ### Box 3.4
>
> ## The eight Millennium Development Goals
>
> Goal 1   Eradicate extreme hunger and poverty
> Goal 2   Achieve universal primary education
> Goal 3   Promote gender equality and empower women
> Goal 4   Reduce child mortality
> Goal 5   Improve maternal health
> Goal 6   Combat HIV/AIDS, malaria and other diseases
> Goal 7   Ensure environmental sustainability
> Goal 8   Develop a global partnership for development

By 2015, the UN called the MDGs 'the most successful anti-poverty movement in history'. Indeed, there were some clear successes to report. These successes were particularly obvious when seen as part of the overall global picture:

- The number of people living on less than US$1.25 per day had been reduced from 1.9 billion in 1990 to 836 million in 2015.
- The global number of child deaths under the age of five had fallen from 12.7 million to 6 million.
- New HIV infections had fallen from 3.5 million to 2.1 million, with 13 million people receiving anti-retroviral treatment in 2015, compared with just 0.8 million in 2000.
- The number of people with access to clean drinking water doubled between 1990 and 2015.

However, when looking at specific regions, countries and genders, the MDGs' success was varied:

- Sub-Saharan Africa had not met the MDG for extreme poverty reduction, as it is still 12.5% behind the MDG target.
- By contrast, economic growth in China distorted the overall global figures, where it had contributed to a reduction in extreme poverty in eastern Asia, from 61% in 1990 to 4% in 2015. The UN conceded that 'China and India played a central role in the global reduction of poverty'.
- The UN found that in 2015, women were still more likely than men to live in poverty. Globally in the same year, women earned 24% less than men.

The MDGs have now been followed by the Sustainable Development Goals (SDGs), which the UNGA agreed in 2015. Sustainable development is frequently defined as 'development that balances the needs of today with those of tomorrow, ensuring that future generations and resources are not put at risk'. The SDGs therefore have an increased focus on protecting the environment and reducing climate change. The number of targets has also been increased considerably, from just eight MDG targets to 169 SDGs. All of the MDGs, for example poverty reduction, gender equality and clean drinking water, have a corresponding SDG to ensure that progress on these issues continues (see Box 3.5).

Box 3.5

The SDGs in the long term

In general, the UN's long-term efforts aimed at reducing poverty have been more successful than efforts to maintain peace and security. This perhaps reflects the fact that the UN member states have been more united in their desire and approach to tackling development. The UN's development work has been backed up by a large aid budget (the UNDP alone has a budget of US$5 billion) and many other UN agencies, such as the WFP, the WHO and UNICEF.

The UN has at times been less successful in delivering emergency aid or humanitarian relief, as opposed to the longer-term efforts of the MDGs. This has not always been the UN's fault. Providing humanitarian aid in conflict zones is not straightforward and is often, for example in Syria, restricted by heavy fighting and blocked by armed groups. Some criticised the UN emergency assistance to Haiti in response to the 2010 earthquake for being too slow and failing to adequately target relief efforts. These examples demonstrate that, at times, emergency relief can be hampered by similar logistical and political challenges as peacekeeping operations.

Debate

Has the UN been effective in reducing world poverty?

Yes
- The MDGs have been a highly effective, coordinated international effort to tackle poverty, with considerable successes (see page 166).
- A total of 1 billion people have been lifted out of extreme poverty. The number of people living on less than US$1.25 per day has decreased, from 1.9 billion in 1990 to 836 million. These were both key targets of the MDGs.

No
- Other factors, such as the rapid growth of China, have been responsible for some of the seemingly impressive MDG figures.
- Poverty in Sub-Saharan Africa continues to lag behind other regions.
- Global inequality has continued to rise.

International organisations such as the UN are not the only way in which states try to tackle shared threats and opportunities. Treaties have been used since medieval times to allow states to come to formal, tailored agreements with other states, usually allowing major powers to come to peace settlements or agreements. One of the most notable treaties in studies of modern global politics is the Treaty of Westphalia, signed in 1648 at the end of the Thirty Years' War (see Chapter 2). The treaty marks the beginning of the modern idea of the sovereign nation-state, with respect for internal and external sovereignty being key principles of the treaty.

In modern global politics, treaties are frequently the legal basis on which IGOs are founded (for example, the UN Charter and the Treaty of Rome, which founded the European Community, now the EU). Furthermore, states frequently come together to agree treaties on specific issues, such as arms control, international justice, climate change or free trade. They offer a flexible means of agreeing action on any matter between two or more like-minded states. Treaties between two states are known as bilateral treaties, and those between many states are multilateral treaties.

Are treaties an effective means of global governance?

Treaties can be very targeted and aimed at specific issues. There are many examples of successful international treaties (see Table 3.10).

Treaties are a useful tool in modern global politics for the following reasons:

- They allow states to form agreements on any issue, ranging from the environment to world health.
- They are targeted and specific, unlike IGOs, which may cover a range of policy areas and competencies. This is attractive to states that wish to retain more control over their sovereignty, as they essentially get to pick and choose the international agreements that suit their particular interests.
- They represent formal international law, increasing (but not guaranteeing) the likelihood of enforcement and accountability.

Table 3.10 Successful international treaties

Treaty	Function	Effectiveness
Treaty of Rome (1957) (political governance)	Founded the European Community (EC), later the EU	Six countries signed the founding treaty and the EC has since become the EU, with 28 member states (although the UK decided in 2016 to become the first EU member state to leave the union).
ASEAN Free Trade Area agreement (1992) (economic governance)	Founded the ASEAN Free Trade Area, which has now become the regional trading bloc known as the Association of Southeast Asian Nations (ASEAN)	The ASEAN has rapidly moved towards creating a free market, reducing tariffs on imports and exports.
Kyoto Protocol (1997) (environmental governance)	Committed its state parties to reduce emissions	Major polluting states did not sign up, notably the USA.
Rome Statute (1998) (judicial governance)	Created the ICC, signed and ratified by 121 states (although it is not signed and ratified by three of the permanent five members (China, Russia and the USA))	The ICC has successfully convicted three individuals, however there is criticism that its conviction rate is too low. Non-participation of the most powerful states undermines its legitimacy.

A weakness of treaties is that states can choose whether or not to sign and ratify them. For example, three out of the five UNSC permanent members (China, Russia and the USA) have not ratified the Rome Statute (the treaty that established the ICC). The fact that the most significant military powers in the world have been able to opt out of a major treaty represents a serious weakness.

Similarly, while the NPT (see page 122) is the most widely signed arms control treaty in the world, key states have opted not to sign it, or have signed and then later withdrawn from the treaty (North Korea), or have developed nuclear weapons (India, Israel, North Korea and Pakistan). However, it should not be taken for granted that the 190 states that signed the treaty made a conscious decision in international law to agree not to pursue their own nuclear weapons programmes. Clearly, a state could simply withdraw from the treaty and develop nuclear weapons, but the overwhelming majority has stayed within a powerful collective and mutually assuring framework.

The North Atlantic Treaty Organization

One of the most significant treaties of the post-Second World War era has been the North Atlantic Treaty, signed in 1949, which founded the North Atlantic Treaty Organization (NATO). The North Atlantic Treaty is a collective military security agreement that was signed at the start of the Cold War, with the aim of protecting its members from the threat of military (especially nuclear) attack from the Soviet Union and the Warsaw Pact countries.

NATO is therefore an example of a collective security alliance. In order to prevent the spread of the Soviet Union into western Europe, and recognising that the war had both economically and militarily weakened these countries who were potentially unable to defend themselves, NATO created a formal alliance backed up in international law by a treaty.

The key principle of NATO is Article 5 of the treaty, which states that an attack on one member state shall be regarded as an attack on all member states. When Article 5 is triggered, it means that there is a collective military response from NATO member states. NATO has only used Article 5 once, when NATO allies indicated their support for the USA after the 9/11 terror attacks on New York and Washington, DC.

While Article 5 has only ever been invoked in support of its most powerful member state, one of NATO's founding objectives was to protect smaller states (particularly those in western Europe and bordering the Soviet Union). Being part of NATO, a formal military alliance with many nation-states, makes smaller states more powerful than they would be alone. In reality, the USA has always been the dominant military power within NATO, and NATO membership can also be seen as an alliance with the USA.

The NATO headquarters are located in Brussels, Belgium. NATO has a civilian secretary-general (currently former Norwegian prime minister Jens Stoltenberg), who acts as the organisation's chief executive and main spokesperson. There are 28 members (see Figure 3.7).

Is NATO still relevant?

Since the end of the Cold War, some have questioned the continuing relevance of NATO. Certain US politicians have questioned the USA's commitments to NATO, sentiments that President Donald Trump expressed in the 2016 US presidential election campaign. The USA currently accounts for 70% of NATO

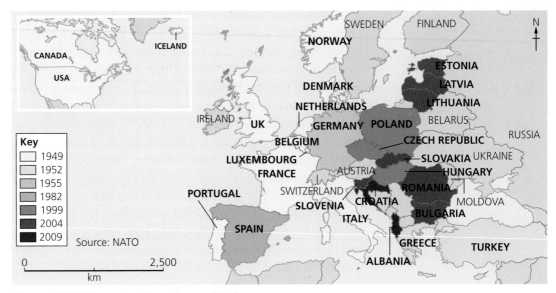

Figure 3.7 NATO membership and year of joining

member states' defence budgets, reflecting its far larger military power and historic influence. Critics in Washington, DC complain that NATO is over-reliant on the USA and that the USA is subsidising European defence budgets. Despite NATO countries agreeing to spend 2% of their GDP on defence, and this being a condition of membership, in 2015 only five states — Estonia, Greece, Poland, the UK and the USA — met this commitment.

While the Cold War may have ended, those arguing for a continuing role for NATO point to Russia's incursion into Ukraine as evidence of renewed Russian power and its desire to recapture territory lost after the fall of the Soviet Union. Former Soviet states and now EU and NATO member states Latvia, Lithuania and Estonia all have borders with Russia. NATO has responded by expanding its European Response Force from 13,000 to 40,000 troops, creating a new 'spearhead force' of 5,000 troops and establishing new headquarters in its member states in the Baltic and eastern European regions. NATO hailed this as 'the largest reinforcement of collective defence since the end of the Cold War'.

From a Russian perspective, in 2016, President Vladimir Putin claimed in his New Year address to the Russian people that NATO represented a key national security threat to the Russian Federation. Putin pointed to the 'intensification of military activities, further expansion of the alliance and moving military infrastructure closer to Russia's borders' as evidence of the perceived threat.

It is clear that NATO–Russia relations are in a 'sensitive period'. The tensions are a relevant example of the so-called security dilemma in global politics. The security dilemma reflects the fact that when one world power feels a threat from another, it increases its security defences, which in turn leads to the other power feeling a growing threat and increasing its own security defences accordingly. In the Cold War, this was seen most powerfully through the nuclear arms race between the Soviet Union and the USA.

Do NATO member states pay their way?

During his election campaign, President Donald Trump pledged that he would consider withdrawing the USA from NATO, calling it 'obsolete' and stating that the alliance was 'costing us a fortune'. Criticism was aimed at member states that were not meeting NATO's target of spending 2% of GDP on defence. Current estimates suggest that the USA accounts for 22% of NATO's budget.

Who is not paying enough?

As of 2016, it is easier to identify who *is* paying enough. Only five member states — Estonia, Greece, Poland, the UK and the USA — met the 2% target. Canada, France, Germany, Italy and Turkey are among those member states that have not met the agreed targets.

Activity

Review the interactive map showing NATO's military operations at this link: **www.nato.int/nato-on-the-map/#.**
1 Where is NATO currently deployed?
2 What current threats is NATO focused on?

Military operations

Despite being founded with the objective of countering the threat from the Soviet Union at the end of the Second World War, NATO's first military operations did not take place until 1995. Humanitarian concerns primarily motivated two operations in the 1990s, both in former Yugoslavia:

- In 1995, Operation Deliberate Force included air strikes against the Bosnian Serb army, which had carried out massacres in so-called UN safe zones, including in Srebrenica, where in July 1995 Bosnian Serb forces killed some 8,000 Bosnian Muslims. A UNSC Resolution had authorised this military operation, making this a good example of the UNSC using the forces of another international organisation (NATO) to carry out its objectives.

- In 1999, NATO launched nearly 80 days of air strikes in Kosovo, in former Yugoslavia. Operation Allied Force was primarily a humanitarian mission to protect Kosovar Albanians from the armed forces of the Federal Yugoslav Republic and its leader Slobodan Milošević. This operation was not backed by a UN Security Council Resolution, with Russia opposed and condemning the campaign as a breach of international law.

It is important to note that NATO's first military operations came in a theatre of conflict and with objectives very different to those initially intended. Neither of these two campaigns in former Yugoslavia was carried out to protect a fellow NATO member state, as the collective security alliance intended. In the immediate aftermath of the Cold War, NATO focused on humanitarian crises within Europe and was able to do so both with and without the support of Russia.

Since NATO invoked Article 5 in 2001, the organisation's operations have further expanded beyond their original geographical space, moving beyond Europe to the middle east and south Asia. Military operations in Afghanistan (2001–14) were conducted under NATO's leadership. Similarly, the military

NATO conducts anti-piracy operations off the coast of Somalia

no-fly zone and subsequent campaign of air strikes against Colonel Muammar Gaddafi's regime in Libya in 2011 was a NATO-led operation.

NATO has also conducted counter-piracy operations in the Indian Ocean off the coast of Somalia, in order to protect international shipping lanes. These operations confirm that NATO is now a military alliance with its widest range of deployments, and indeed NATO has to some extent rebranded itself, by leaning towards a more humanitarian role in order to remain relevant. With a resurgent Russia, NATO is also rediscovering and redefining its role as a collective security alliance to counter Russian aggression.

Nuclear weapons

Since the nuclear attacks on Hiroshima and Nagasaki in 1945 which ended the Second World War, a major global political challenge has been to control the spread and amount of nuclear weapons. Specific international treaties have been agreed, such as the Treaty on the Non-Proliferation of Nuclear Weapons (NPT), which aims to control the proliferation of nuclear weapons to states that have not yet acquired them, and to bring about gradual disarmament of states that have already acquired these weapons. Other treaties have been attempted, such as the Comprehensive Test Ban Treaty (CTBT), which aims to prevent the testing of nuclear weapons.

Currently, there are eight states known to possess nuclear weapons (see Figure 3.8). The five permanent members of the UNSC all possess nuclear weapons and have signed and ratified the NPT. This confirms in international law that they are nuclear-weapons states and commits them to not sharing nuclear technology except for peaceful purposes (such as nuclear power) and, ultimately, disarmament. These states are:

- the USA (since 1945)
- Russia (since 1949)
- the UK (since 1952)
- France (since 1960)
- China (since 1964)

Three states possess nuclear weapons and have not signed the NPT:

- India (since 1974)
- Pakistan (estimated to be since the mid-1980s)
- North Korea (since approximately 2006, when it carried out the first official test).

It is also widely suspected, but not confirmed, that Israel has possessed nuclear weapons since perhaps as early as the 1960s.

Nuclear weapons have various delivery methods. The UK's nuclear weapons are submarine-based, with Trident nuclear missiles constantly patrolling anywhere in the world at any time (see Case study). The USA's and Russia's nuclear weapons have three delivery methods (a so-called nuclear triad), including strategic air bombers, intercontinental ballistic missiles (with a range of up to 5,500 km) and submarine-launched missiles. The USA has strategic nuclear air bombers based in Belgium, Germany, Italy, the Netherlands and Turkey.

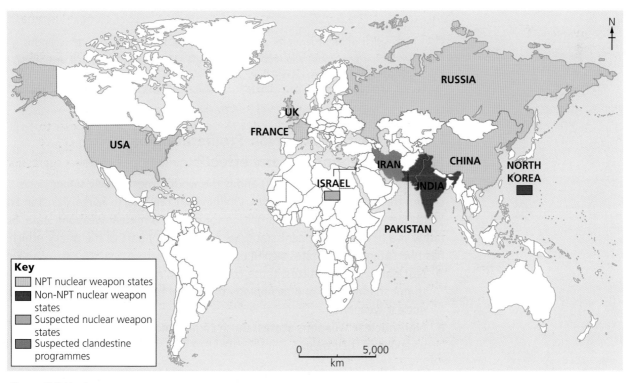

Figure 3.8 Nuclear weapons states

The UK's nuclear weapons

Prime Minister Winston Churchill first set British scientists to work on developing an atom bomb in 1941. By 1952, Operation Hurricane was the first successful test of a British nuclear weapon, on remote islands off western Australia. In the 1950s and 1960s, British nuclear weapons were air-based, launched from RAF Vulcan bombers (known as V-bombers). Concerned that the V-bomber fleet could be pre-emptively attacked, a submarine-based Polaris nuclear weapons system was developed and became operational in 1968. By 1994, the weapons system had been upgraded to the Trident missile system used by Royal Navy submarines today.

One of the first duties of a new UK prime minister is to write final instructions to Royal Navy Trident submarine commanders in the event that a nuclear attack has wiped out the UK government. Historian Peter Hennessy commented that 'the nuclear bit shakes them all. Then you realise you are prime minister at a deeper level'.

The future of the UK's nuclear weapons, often referred to as a nuclear 'deterrent', came up for debate again in July 2016. The UK Parliament voted overwhelmingly to renew the Trident missile system, which would see the building of four new submarines at an estimated cost of £31 billion. Prime Minister Theresa May said that it would be an 'act of gross irresponsibility' to abandon a continuous at-sea nuclear deterrent. At the same time, the UK committed to reducing its stockpile of nuclear warheads to 180 by 2020.

The current UK government sees the retention of nuclear weapons as an important symbol of its continuing relevance and power in global politics. Without nuclear weapons, the UK would be the only non-nuclear member of the UNSC permanent five, and some say that its permanent member status would be open to greater question.

Activity

Consider the Case study on the UK's nuclear weapons programme, and your own knowledge and research.
1 Make a list of arguments for and against the UK keeping its nuclear weapons.
2 What changes would you recommend to the UK's policy on nuclear weapons? Justify your recommendations.

Has the Treaty on the Non-Proliferation of Nuclear Weapons had any effect?

The NPT came into force in 1970 and is the world's most widely signed arms control treaty, with 190 signatories. Only India, Israel, North Korea, Pakistan and South Sudan (which shows no ambition to become a nuclear weapons state, but rather is a newly independent state) are not currently part of the treaty, which has two categories of states signed up to it.

- **Nuclear weapons states:** those committed to nuclear disarmament and to not sharing skills and technology that could help other states to possess nuclear weapons.
- **Non-nuclear weapons states:** those committed to not developing nuclear weapons of their own.

One of the NPT's successes is that, apart from North Korea, no state has successfully developed nuclear weapons since the mid-1980s. Non-nuclear weapons states that signed the treaty have, therefore, kept to their promise. One former nuclear weapons state, South Africa, successfully gave up its nuclear weapons entirely when it signed the treaty and disarmed itself.

Apart from North Korea, no state is known to have successfully developed nuclear weapons since the mid-1980s

Of course, states that have wanted to develop nuclear weapons, and then avoid commitments to disarming themselves, have simply chosen not to sign the treaty or be bound by its regulations. None of India, Israel or Pakistan is likely to sign the treaty and commit to nuclear disarmament. North Korea withdrew from the treaty in 2003 (the only state ever to do so) and 3 years later tested its first nuclear weapon, showing that states can quickly opt out and develop nuclear weapons.

However, there has been mixed success in disarming the nuclear weapons states. There were dramatic reductions in Russian and US stockpiles of nuclear warheads directly after the end of the Cold War, but progress has slowed since 2007. The most dramatic reductions in US and Russian warheads occurred between 1986 and 2006. However, these two states still possess 90% of the world's nuclear warheads. Both Russia and the USA signed a specific treaty in 2010 – the Strategic Arms Reduction Treaty (START 2) — pledging to reduce their warheads to 1,500 deployed warheads and no more than 700 strategic deployed missiles and bombers by 2018. Currently, neither country has moved to reduce their nuclear arsenal (see Figure 3.9). In the same period, France, the UK and the USA have all invested in improving their existing nuclear weapons technology.

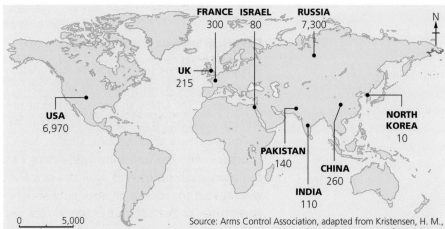

Source: Arms Control Association, adapted from Kristensen, H. M., Norris, R. S., and the US Department of State (2017)

Figure 3.9 Operational nuclear warheads

Most worrying is North Korea's development of nuclear weapons. Since withdrawing from the NPT in 2003, it has developed nuclear weapons that *The Economist* estimates will be able to reach New York and Washington, DC by 2021. North Korea regularly threatens its neighbours, South Korea and Japan. In 2016, some estimated that the country added 20 new warheads to its stockpiles every 6 weeks, spending a huge proportion of its GDP on developing its nuclear arsenal. Even China, usually a trusted ally of the North Korean regime, agreed to strict sanctions against North Korea at the UNSC in response to the growing threat.

Case study

Iran's nuclear weapons programme: halted or paused?

Iran's apparent intent to develop nuclear weapons has been a major concern in recent decades. However, these ambitions were dealt a significant blow in 2015, when Iran and the UNSC's permanent five members (plus Germany) agreed a major deal whereby Iran committed to halting its nuclear weapons programme. In return, the permanent five and the EU agreed to end decades of economic sanctions against the country, which had crippled its economy.

Former US president Barack Obama hailed the Joint Comprehensive Plan of Action (JCPOA) as a triumph of diplomacy, which had achieved 'something that decades of animosity [had] not, a way to prevent Iran from getting a nuclear weapon.'

Critics of the deal, including President Donald Trump, say that it is too trusting of Iran. During the 2016 US presidential election campaign, Trump said, 'They are laughing at us back in Iran', and that the deal was a 'one-sided, lopsided disgrace'. Iran might attempt to continue clandestine nuclear programmes — sceptics warn of a 'cat and mouse' chase between Iran's regime and international nuclear inspectors for years to come. Much also depends on whether the reformist faction in the Iranian government holds power over the security hardliners.

Questions
1   What are the potential benefits of the JCPOA?
2   What are the potential risks of the JCPOA?

Realist and liberal views on global political governance

It is essential to link all these examples and evaluation of the effectiveness of global political governance to the realist and liberal theories considered in Chapter 1.

Realist views

It is possible to see realist tendencies in nation-states within global political governance, particularly powerful ones, being very obstructive to global political governance. The UNSC in particular has at times been paralysed by states seeking to protect their national interest in line with realist principles.

Equally, treaty organisations, such as NATO, have been founded on realist principles, with the states involved aiming to protect their national security and build up their defences against a perceived threat. Global governance goes against the idea of an anarchical society, beyond any form of orderly governance, or the Billiard Ball Model (see page 11) as described by Hedley Bull and others.

Liberal views

The UN was founded on liberal principles, namely that states can achieve more by working together in the common interest than they can achieve alone. The liberal principle hopes that states will be prepared to subordinate state sovereignty to achieving success at a global level. Global political governance is a core ideal of liberalism, but while there have been major successes, the successes of global governance have tended to be when states have seen this to be aligned with their core interests.

The UNSC is an excellent example of an international institution created with both liberal and realist ideals at its heart. It allows states to work together in the common interest when they agree. It allows states the means to protect their national interest when they cannot agree. Whether states agree or not is largely a matter of detail and relative power between them. Global political governance is essentially the art of the politically possible and is entirely dependent on states (particularly the most powerful states) as the ultimate decision-makers.

Debate

Is political and global governance an unachievable ideal?

Yes

- Conflict (particularly violent conflict) is still a dominant force within global politics.
- Securing agreement within international institutions is still very difficult, especially when states choose to protect their national interests. The UNSC is frequently unable to reach agreement except on issues of less strategic importance.
- Many important actors in global politics are now outside of global political governance organisations. Multinational companies, NGOs, civil society groups and violent non-state actors are all minor (or entirely excluded) players in formal, perhaps outdated, global political governance institutions.

No

- Conflict is much less prevalent *between* states, while conflict *within* states is much more prevalent. International institutions and trade links provide many means of non-violent dispute resolution. Globalisation means that states' interests are increasingly aligned and interdependent.
- An unprecedented number of IGOs now exist in which states can discuss and come to agreements on matters of shared importance. These IGOs are geographically diverse (ASEAN, the AU, the EU, the UN) and policy diverse (economic, environmental, judicial, political). An expansion in forums for global political debate and discussion has accompanied the rise of globalisation.

What you should know

Having read this chapter you should have knowledge and understanding of the following:

- Global governance is the process by which states and intergovernmental organisations try to bring order and security to global politics. It does not try to create a world government, as this is not possible. Instead, states try to create institutions and laws that allow them to solve shared problems and seize international opportunities that are in their national interest.
- The United Nations (UN) was founded to maintain global peace and security, improve economic development and advance human rights. Its role has since expanded to include preventing environmental degradation and increased responsibilities for UN peacekeepers.
- One of the most powerful bodies in international relations is the UN Security Council (UNSC). Its permanent members have a powerful right to veto proposed resolutions. Sometimes this results in stalemate. Nevertheless, the UNSC has still had a considerable impact, even if it cannot always resolve crises in which its permanent members wish to block action.

- The North Atlantic Treaty Organization was founded to act as a collective security alliance against the Soviet Union. It has since expanded both its membership and the scope of its operations. Today, it is more actively involved in combating global threats outside Europe, and has led offensive operations in Afghanistan and Libya. Its military stance against Russia is more defensive and is intended to act as a deterrent.
- International efforts, through the UN and the Treaty on the Non-Proliferation of Nuclear Weapons, have proved successful in preventing states from developing nuclear weapons. The major nuclear weapons powers, however, have not disarmed and have only reduced their stockpiles of weapons very slowly.
- Global political governance depends, ultimately, on states' agreement. States use intergovernmental organisations and sign treaties primarily to pursue their own national interest. Sometimes, national interest and international interest are the same. This is when global governance efforts are most successful.

Further reading

Goldin, I. (2013) *Divided Nations: Why Global Governance is Failing and What We can Do About it.* Oxford University Press.

HanhimÖki, J. M. (2008) *The United Nations: A Very Short Introduction.* Oxford University Press.

Murphy, R. (2015) 'Is the UN Security Council fit for purpose?', *Politics Review Online*, Vol. 24, No. 4, April 2015.

Exam focus

Section A

1 Examine the effectiveness of the United Nations in international peacekeeping. *[12 marks]*

2 Examine the differences between current NATO operations and its founding objectives. *[12 marks]*

Section C

1 Evaluate the extent to which the United Nations has been successful in achieving its founding objectives. *[30 marks]*

2 Evaluate the extent to which NATO is still relevant and useful. *[30 marks]*

3 Evaluate whether the UN Security Council is fit for purpose. *[30 marks]*

Chapter 4

Global governance: economic

> ## Learning outcomes
>
> By the end of this chapter you should understand:
> - the role and significance of key economic intergovernmental organisations including the World Bank, the International Monetary Fund and the World Trade Organization
> - the role and significance of the Group of Seven/Eight and the Group of Twenty in economic global governance
> - the significance of world trade in global politics and how it is managed
> - the causes of poverty and how poverty is measured
> - the effectiveness of attempts to resolve poverty
> - the impact of globalisation on world poverty

Getting you started

In 2008, a deep recession in the USA brought about a worldwide economic downturn, the worst since the Great Depression in the 1930s. During the 1920s, a rapid expansion of credit had encouraged people to buy shares, expecting an easy profit. The problem was that this new 'gold rush' was based on speculation. When a sudden loss of confidence encouraged some major investors to sell, panic ensued and shareholders across the USA rushed to cash in their shares. This caused the Wall Street Crash.

On Black Tuesday (29 October 1929) share prices fell by a staggering US$40 billion in just one day. In 2008, banks providing ever-greater mortgages without sufficient proof they could be repaid caused the 'great recession'. Having over-lent, some banks started running out of money. House prices began to fall, and there was a loss of consumer confidence, resulting in a global downturn in trade.

The global financial crisis: a failure of economic global governance?

This 2008 global financial crisis was exactly the kind of situation that intergovernmental organisations (IGOs), such as the **International Monetary Fund (IMF)** and the **World Bank**, had been founded to deal with. An economic crisis had spread beyond any single nation-state and it required the collective action of many states to bring the world economy back from the brink. Exactly how well did these IGOs respond and could they have done more to prevent the financial crisis in the first place?

One of the key causes of the financial crisis was a lack of strict regulations in the global financial system. Many economists concluded that banks were able to take too many risks, lending large amounts that borrowers eventually could not pay back. Both states and the world's economic IGOs had shown no desire for a global effort to tackle this lack of regulation. Indeed, there was general agreement that minimal regulation was to the benefit of the world economy.

The IMF admitted that it had failed to see the global financial crisis coming. It did not predict the risks that dangerous levels of lending in the USA posed.

Key terms

International Monetary Fund (IMF) Established following the Bretton Woods Conference in 1944. It aims to encourage global financial stability by providing technical advice, support and loans to its 189 member states.

World Bank Established as a result of the Bretton Woods Conference in 1944. It focuses on long-term development and provides conditional loans to developing countries.

The global financial crisis of 2008 was the worst economic downturn since the Great Depression

In fact, until April 2007, the IMF was forecasting that 'world growth would continue to be strong'. Many have since criticised the IMF's monitoring of the global financial system's health as being too reliant on states' self-assessment of their own financial position. Monitoring — or surveillance, as the IMF calls it — is a key part of its role.

Economists have also blamed a global imbalance between states in the world economy. For example, China held a large **currency** surplus and its financial institutions were able to lend easily to the USA, which was running a large deficit. This imbalance ultimately led to large amounts of lending and created an economic bubble in which house prices rose quickly. When house prices fell, mortgage holders could not pay back loans that had become more valuable than their homes, creating the so-called credit crunch.

Could economic global governance have prevented the 2008 economic crisis?

Could economic global governance have done anything to prevent this situation? A combination of global agreement and enthusiasm among states for such an economic model and a lack of any forecasting that this economic model might risk a global economic downturn makes this unlikely. The global imbalance also created a complex interdependence between a Chinese economy with an enormous capacity to lend and a US economy with an enormous need for loans.

Did global economic governance do any better once the crisis hit? Informal forums, including the **Group of Twenty (G20)**, provided an essential means by which the world's most economically powerful states could discuss measures to tackle the crisis. The London G20 summit in 2009 saw states take important decisions to inject capital into their banking systems in order to prevent the collapse of the entire global banking system. This was arguably the most important action taken to resolve the crisis, as it provided protection to banks that were regarded as 'too important to fail'. Most states took this action themselves. For example, the UK government decided to place one failing private bank, the Royal Bank of Scotland, under state ownership. The USA took the same measure to save the banks Fannie Mae and Freddie Mac. Both bailouts cost the national governments billions.

The IMF mobilised its funds to lend up to US$700 billion to states that were most affected by the downturn, including Greece, Portugal and Spain. It also required states to donate more to IMF funds, to act as a 'firewall' in order to prevent future crises from spreading. Belatedly, the IMF also supported tougher regulation of the banking sector, which many states agreed to. The World Bank tripled its lending, primarily to middle-income states, in order to prevent prolonged economic recession spreading further in the global economy.

The global financial crisis was a crucial test for global economic governance. The IMF and the World Bank played a significant role in resolving the financial crisis but, ultimately, nation-states played a larger role in bailing out failing banks and reforming their own systems of financial regulation. The crisis demonstrates the complex network of actors involved in economic global governance and the impact that an economic shock in one state can have globally.

What is economic global governance and why is it needed?

In an interdependent world, states need to work together on economic matters as well as political matters. Globalisation has quickened this process. International trade has increased as communications and transport have created better links between states. The number of states involved in international trade has also increased. The impact, both positive and negative, of individual states' economic fortunes is increasingly felt in other states.

The Bretton Woods Conference

The need for more effective economic global governance was first seen close to the end of the Second World War at the Bretton Woods Conference, held in the USA in 1944. The 44 nations of the Second World War Allies met in a remote mountain resort in New Hampshire, to consider how the world's financial systems and trade could be managed in peacetime. Many of today's global economic governance institutions were founded at the conference, including the IMF and the World Bank.

There was also agreement among the Allies that economic pressures had played a part in the rise of fascism in Germany, where the Nazi Party had mobilised a domestic financial crisis as a rallying issue. Just as the world had turned to the League of Nations and then the United Nations (UN) for political global governance, so economists of the Allied nations began to think about how greater international order could be brought to the global economic order.

The aims of the Bretton Woods Conference were to:
- create an agreed system of rules for international economic matters, including world trade
- stabilise world currencies and reduce wide fluctuations in the value of currencies
- prevent a repeat of the Great Depression that occurred in the 1930s
- bolster capitalism against the rise of communism as a competing economic model in the Soviet Union

The Bretton Woods Conference created the following economic global governance IGOs and arrangements.
- **The IMF (1947):** established the US dollar as the basis against which all other states' currencies would be valued, thereby stabilising world currencies from major fluctuations in their value.

131

Key term

World Trade Organization (WTO) Established in 1995 and is the successor to the GATT (1947). It has a membership of 164 states and is designed to facilitate free trade by encouraging global trade deals and resolving trade disputes between member states.

Key term

Group of Seven/ Eight (G7/8) An intergovernmental forum comprising the leaders of seven (and eight, including Russia) highly industrialised countries.

- **The International Bank for Reconstruction and Development (1946):** later known as the World Bank. Its aim is to provide a pool of investment for middle-income states.
- **The General Agreement on Tariffs and Trade (GATT) (1947):** later known as the World Trade Organization (WTO). It is an international forum in which states can make trade deals and international rules on trade.

Collectively, these institutions and the principles on which they were founded (free trade) are known as the Bretton Woods System. This refers to the forums and institutions of global economic governance that states have put in place to manage the global economy. All three of these founding institutions still exist today, although they have been modified and their roles have developed considerably.

In more recent decades, global cooperation on economic governance has focused on the following.

- **Poverty/development:** the value of international coordination through the UN and other forums has progressed considerably. Developed states have increased spending on development. The Millennium Development Goals (MDGs), agreed in 2000 (see page 166), represent the most coordinated effort of IGOs and states to work towards common development targets.
- **Free trade:** there has been an increase in multilateral free trade agreements, most notably the Single Market of the European Union (EU) but also the North American Free Trade Agreement (NAFTA) between Canada, Mexico and the USA. The Trans-Pacific Partnership (TPP), agreed in 2016, established a free-trade agreement between most countries of the Pacific Rim, although President Trump's unilateral withdrawal of the USA from the deal in 2017 means that its future is now in doubt.
- **Single currency:** the economic debate in the EU in the 1990s focused on developing a single currency, the euro. The euro came into circulation in 2002 and is now the currency of 19 of the 28 (pre-Brexit) EU member states. While most economic global governance in global politics is entirely intergovernmental in nature, the Eurozone countries have agreed to strict economic rules and given up significant freedom to make economic decisions nationally (such as setting their own interest rates) to supranational institutions, notably the European Central Bank (ECB).
- **Forums:** there is a need for a forum for discussion and decision making to enable states to resolve international economic crises. The global financial crisis of 2008 posed a particular challenge for key economic IGOs, notably the IMF. In response to the crisis, the IMF dramatically increased the loans it makes to bail out failing economies.

Economic global governance involves many of the same actors as other forms of global governance.

- **IGOs:** principally the World Bank, the IMF and the UN (including the UN Development Programme (UNDP)).
- **Informal intergovernmental forums:** such as the Group of Seven/Eight (G7/8) and the G20, which include the world's most industrialised states and the biggest global economic powers.
- **Multinational corporations (MNCs):** privately owned companies that operate in more than one state.

- **Multilateral forums:** such as the World Economic Forum (WEF), which provides an opportunity for world leaders, IGOs, business leaders, non-governmental organisations (NGOs) and economists to discuss the challenges facing the global economy.

The International Monetary Fund

The IMF was one of the key global economic governance institutions agreed in 1944 at the Bretton Woods Conference. It became fully operational in 1947 and its headquarters are in Washington, DC.

Role

When the IMF was founded, its main role was to encourage stability in world exchange rates. During the Great Depression in the 1930s, many currencies had been devalued, causing great uncertainty and ultimately deep economic recession. The IMF oversaw a system of fixed exchange rates, linked to the US dollar, which in turn was fixed to the price of gold. This system brought much increased stability and prevented unsettling fluctuations in currency value. States and traders in the international financial system knew how much currency was worth and could make investments with a greater degree of stability, rather than being buffeted by variations in the value of a currency.

The fixed exchange rate system broke apart in 1971, when US president Richard Nixon abandoned the fixed link between the value of the US dollar and gold. The decision reflected the USA's desire to have greater flexibility over the value of its currency.

The IMF arose from the Bretton Woods Conference held at the Mount Washington Hotel in 1944

With the collapse of the IMF's founding purpose, from the 1970s onwards its role changed to that it retains today (see Table 4.1):

- The IMF provides economic stability by giving financial support or loans to states that are suffering, or a likely to suffer, from debt crises (when a state is unable to repay loans that it owes to financial institutions such as the IMF or private banks). This has predominantly seen the IMF focusing on the developing world, but it has also made loans to developed countries. In 1976, the UK borrowed US$3.9 million from the IMF as it struggled to deal with a deep financial crisis. More recently, Greece, Portugal and Spain have received IMF loans in order to help save their economies from bankruptcy.
- It monitors the economic outlook of both the world economy and individual member countries, including forecasting and commenting on potential threats and weaknesses.
- It advises member countries on how best to manage their economies, particularly less-developed member countries in which technical economic expertise may be lacking.

Table 4.1 IMF functions

Functions	How it does this
Surveillance and monitoring	Reviews country policies and national, regional and global economic and financial developments through a formal system known as surveillance. The IMF advises its 189 member states, encouraging policies that foster economic stability, reduce vulnerability to economic and financial crises, and raise living standards.
Lending	A member country may request IMF financial assistance if it suffers or is likely to suffer a debt crisis — that is, if it lacks or potentially lacks sufficient financing on affordable terms to meet its net international payments (e.g. imports, external debt redemptions).
Capacity building	IMF experts provide training to member states to help them manage their economy more effectively. For example, experts on tax collection may advise a state that is not taxing its population adequately on how to implement a fair and effective taxation system. It has established Regional Training Centres in Africa to help build expertise in Sub-Saharan African states.

Structure

The IMF has 189 member states, therefore including the majority of the world's states. Aside from very small states such as Andorra and Monaco, only North Korea is not a member country.

A managing director leads the IMF. As of 2017, this is the former French minister of finance Christine Lagarde. The managing director makes frequent interventions and commentary on the global economy as a whole, and the economic fortunes of IMF member countries. During the 2016 referendum on the UK's membership of the EU, the IMF and Lagarde provoked criticism from the 'Leave' campaign by publishing a report a week before the referendum that predicted Brexit would lead to increased inflation and reduce the UK's GDP by 5.5%, pushing the UK into recession. Critics argued that this was unnecessary interference in a decision that should have been left to the British people. On the other hand, some argue that the IMF acts as a useful additional source of economic advice and forecasting to help states and their populations make informed decisions.

Resources

The main source of the IMF's financial resources is payments made to the fund by its member countries. These so-called quotas broadly reflect members' relative positions and wealth in the world economy. The IMF increased the amount of funds available for lending to its member countries in 2008 in response to the global financial crisis, with member states asked to pay more in their quotas. Box 4.1 gives an indication of the funds available to the IMF and where it has focused most of its lending.

Some have criticised the IMF for being undemocratic, as voting power is weighted according to how much states contribute financially in the quota. This means that the most economically powerful states pay the most to the IMF and in return are allocated more power over decision making. One argument is that it is legitimate that those states that contribute the most have influence over how their contributions are allocated. Less economically powerful and less developed states argue that this leads to the powerful states dominating the goals, terms and conditions of the IMF's lending.

Box 4.1

IMF resources and current loans (2016)

The following is a list of IMF resources and current loans.

- **Additional pledged or committed resources:** US$668 billion
- **Committed amounts under current lending arrangements (as of 9 August 2016):** US$159 billion, of which US$144 billion has not been drawn
- **Biggest borrowers (amounts outstanding as of August 2016):** Greece, Pakistan, Portugal, Ukraine
- **Biggest precautionary loans (amounts agreed as of August 2016):** Colombia, Mexico, Morocco, Poland

Source: www.imf.org/external/np/exr/map/lending

Activity

Do the objectives and activities of the IMF conform more to a liberal or realist view of global politics? Draw up arguments for each view.

Response to crises

A key role of the IMF is to respond to financial crises that impact on one, and often many, states. The key aim is to try to keep afloat the economies that are suffering the most, and to prevent them collapsing or getting into so much debt that they are unable to pay it back. The other key aim in an interdependent global economy is to prevent a financial crisis from spreading to other countries.

Apart from the global financial crisis of 2008, the IMF has assisted with three other recent financial crises:

1　The Asian financial crisis (1997)
2　Emergency lending to Brazil (1998) and Argentina (2000)
3　The Eurozone crisis (from 2008 onwards)

Structural adjustment programmes

When the IMF makes a loan to a member country that is in need, it is often conditional. Specifically, the state must undergo economic reforms to overcome the problems that led it to request help in the first place.

For example, this might include:

- cutting wasteful public spending and raising taxes, in order to eliminate the **budget deficit**
- selling government-owned assets to private ownership, known as privatisation
- increasing the amount of taxes that the state collects in order to help it pay for its own public services
- reducing public sector wages

These initiatives are called **structural adjustment programmes (SAPs)** (see Table 4.2). A criticism of SAPs is that they make excessive demands on states, and that this infringes on state sovereignty, often imposing a Western-driven idea of economic management along the lines of the Washington Consensus (see page 45). In defence of SAPs, it is argued that states that have got themselves into financial difficulty should not be given unconditional loans and should have an incentive to prevent economic difficulty from recurring in the future.

SAPs have become so controversial that the IMF and the World Bank no longer use the term 'structural adjustment programmes', replacing it with 'poverty reduction strategies'.

Key terms

Budget deficit When a state spends more than it raises in revenue (for example, through tax revenue), it is said to be running a budget deficit.

Structural adjustment programme (SAP) A programme of economic reform usually following a neoliberal agenda, including government spending cuts and privatisation, which is imposed on a state as a condition of it receiving an IMF loan.

Table 4.2 Examples of SAPs

Member country	Example of SAP requirement	Impact of SAP
Pakistan	Increase the amount of taxes the central government raises in order to help ease government debt. In 2009, it was estimated that 3.2 million Pakistanis who owned multiple properties and bank accounts were not registered for paying tax. Privatise the national airline and 67 other state-owned companies that had accumulated losses amounting to billions of dollars.	Removing tax breaks created progress, but the IMF assessed tax revenue collection in 2016 as still 'below Pakistan's potential'. Pakistan received several new loans despite not making progress on privatisation.
Greece	Reduce public spending on government wages and welfare benefits. The Greek system of state pensions was costing 17.5% of Greece's GDP. The Greek government was required to make €1 billion of savings through pension reforms alone.	The Greek Parliament voted in 2016 to approve reforms to income tax and generous state pension schemes. Greece's governing anti-austerity party, Syriza, proposed the reforms in the face of public protests. Pensions have been cut many times and are now estimated to be worth 25–55% less than at the beginning of the debt crisis.

The Greek government has faced fierce protests in response to its handling of the country's economic crisis

Frequently, the IMF does not act alone in helping states with emergency loans. In the case of the Greek sovereign debt crisis (see page 138), the IMF worked in partnership with the ECB and the European Commission to agree a joint loan package. This three-way partnership, dubbed the 'Troika', required negotiation and agreement between the three institutions on the amount and conditions of the loans.

Specific criticisms of SAPs include the following:

- Economic reforms, such as privatisation, see an increase in corporate profits that are not necessarily shared with wider society.
- Some developing countries see increased prosperity but also an increase in inequality and child poverty, suggesting that the programmes disproportionately benefit the richest.
- Tax rises can sometimes hit the poorest the hardest, particularly indirect taxation such as a sales tax, which poor people cannot avoid if they are going to continue to buy goods.
- With many of the poorest working in subsistence activities or the informal sector (such as family-based farming for survival), reform of the formal sector of the economy (such as registered, profit-making companies) has little impact on improving their lives.
- Opening markets to foreign investors clearly aids in boosting foreign direct investment, but can also expose fragile economies to the effects of foreign economic crises.
- There is a fundamental clash with state sovereignty, particularly if an SAP is at odds with the policies that a democratic government has been elected to implement.

137

The IMF and the Greek debt crisis

Greece has been a major recipient of IMF loans. The country had accumulated large debts in the international financial markets due to high public spending and low GDP growth. As the world banking system froze in response to the global financial crisis, heavily indebted Greece was unable to make repayments and defaulted on its debts.

The so-called Troika of the ECB, the European Commission and the IMF decided that the impact of the Greek debt crisis could spread within the euro currency zone and a rescue package was needed. In 2010, the first package of €110 billion to Greece was approved.

In return, the Troika demanded that Greece implement austerity measures to reduce public spending and privatise expensive state-owned assets. The Troika negotiated a 50% reduction (a so-called haircut) on the amount Greece owed to private banks.

By 2014, with two bailouts, a deepening economic recession and rising unemployment, the anti-austerity party Syriza won a snap general election. This pitched a legitimately and democratically elected party rejecting austerity measures against the Troika, which was demanding the measures as its condition for keeping the Greek economy afloat. It prompted attempts to renegotiate the conditions, and represented a unique clash between political and economic IGOs and state sovereignty.

When renegotiations between the Syriza government and the Troika broke down, Prime Minister Alexis Tsipras called a referendum, asking the Greek people directly whether they supported the conditions of the bailout package. They overwhelmingly rejected the package by 61% to 39%.

In 2015, Greece failed to make a payment to the IMF, the first developed country ever to do so. Banks closed as fears grew that Greece would leave the Eurozone (so-called Grexit) and cash machines were limited to withdrawals of €60 per day. Ultimately, the imperative of preventing 'Grexit' prevailed, with a new bailout deal agreed later in 2015 in order to keep the Greek economy afloat.

Debate

Is the IMF a force for good in the world economy?

Force for good

- The IMF gives loans to states and helps to reduce their likelihood of falling into economic recession.
- It helps to prevent economic difficulties in one state from spreading to others.
- Pooling of funds as a fundamental liberal idea for many states to contribute to helping those in need is a good thing, providing a clear framework for states to help each other.
- It provides an independent monitor of state economies, helping states to identify threats and opportunities.
- It helps to encourage states to reform their economies to an economic model that has delivered considerable economic growth in most developed states.

Not a force for good

- The IMF forces states to comply with SAPs in a way that interferes with sovereignty. It relentlessly promotes a neoliberal, Western-dominated economic model.
- SAPs do not benefit the poorest, but boost corporate profits and serve the interests of developed states.
- It failed to predict and prevent the global financial crisis in 2008 by failing to challenge reckless lending and inadequate regulation of global financial institutions.
- It was unable to prevent the spread of the global financial crisis.

Activity

Are the interventions that the IMF made in Greece and Pakistan an unjustifiable interference in state independence and sovereignty? Debate the arguments for and against.

The World Bank

The World Bank was founded at the Bretton Woods Conference in 1944. Its headquarters are in Washington, DC. The founding objectives of the World Bank were, as the name suggests, to focus on reconstruction of states whose infrastructure and economies the Second World War had destroyed. Much of the World Bank's early work complemented the Marshall Plan, in which the US government funded reconstruction and recovery in war-damaged western Europe.

Objectives

Gradually, as western Europe recovered both economically and in terms of its infrastructure, the World Bank's focus shifted to the developing world outside Europe. In the 1980s, it used SAPs as part of its conditions for lending (see page 136). However, it has since moved its focus away from encouraging economic reform to an emphasis on human and social development.

There are two key institutions within the World Bank.

1 **The International Bank for Reconstruction and Development:** provides loans and assistance to middle-income countries. Some of these loans include conditionality and elements of SAPs (see page 136).

2 **The International Development Association:** provides loans to the poorest countries. These loans tend to have very low rates of interest and sometimes no interest at all.

The World Bank is the world's leading organisation on development and poverty reduction. It focuses on the following:

- It provides loans, technical and financial assistance to support reconstruction and development. It allocates US$20 billon of loans annually.
- It has a growing emphasis on reducing poverty, linked strongly to the MDGs and now to the Sustainable Development Goals (SDGs). The overarching goal of the World Bank is to end poverty within a generation and boost shared prosperity.
- It funds specific development projects (see Table 4.3).
- It provides technical assistance to states, with this advice focusing on human and social development (in contrast to the IMF, where the technical assistance is focused on economic growth and management of public finances).
- It carries out analytical work on development matters, which is made freely available to states and NGOs working on development, adding to global research on the factors that aid and impede development.

Table 4.3 Examples of World Bank projects (2017)

Objective	Country	Project
Higher education in Africa	Eastern and southern Africa	US$140 million was invested in Higher Education Centres of Excellence in higher education institutions, to improve training and research in key sectors including health, education and agriculture.
Renewable energy and provision of electricity	Ghana	The World Bank provided US$700 million for developing offshore natural gas resources in Ghana's territorial waters, helping it to exploit natural resources and generate up to 40% of Ghana's domestic power.
Reconstruction in Afghanistan	Afghanistan	Since 2002, the World Bank has invested over US$3.3 billion for development and reconstruction in Afghanistan. This has been mostly through grants and no-interest loans, and the Afghanistan government has also part-funded many projects.

The World Bank Board agrees new loans, programmes, budgets and priorities. These decisions are then put to a member vote. There are 189 World Bank member states and membership of both the World Bank and IMF is linked (states must first be a member of the IMF before being accepted to the World Bank).

As with the IMF, voting power is weighted according to the amount that states contribute to the bank. The USA carries 16% of the voting power. No other state has more than 5% voting power.

The USA has traditionally dominated the World Bank — every president since its creation has been a US citizen. The current president, Jim Yong Kim, spent his career prior to his presidency working on new treatments for HIV/AIDS and limiting the impact of tuberculosis.

Effectiveness

Since the World Bank's focus has changed towards human development and shifted away from a focus on SAPs, it has achieved considerable success in its aim of reducing world poverty:

- Its programmes have contributed to the success of MDG 1, to reduce world poverty.
- It focuses on direct grants to poorer states, rather than loans, which prevents the creation of additional debt pressures on poorer states.

However, the World Bank does have its critics:

- Its contributions are dwarfed by those of private investors, which amounted to as much as US$900 billion for China and India in 2011. The World Bank's resources reached only US$8 billion in the same year. Consequently, the World Bank should focus only on the poorest or most conflict-ridden states that are unattractive to private investors.
- The imbalance in voting powers is outdated in an increasingly globalised world economy where rising powers, including Brazil, India and China, have less than a third of the voting powers of the USA.

Distinguish between

The IMF and the World Bank

The IMF
- The IMF emphasises global and national economic growth.
- It assists state governments with loans, often to enable them to pay their debts to private banks.
- It provides states with technical assistance on how to more effectively manage their economies as a whole (macro-economic focus).

The World Bank
- The World Bank emphasises ending extreme poverty.
- It focuses on social and human development.
- It provides grants to state governments for specific development projects. Most projects are funded through these grants.
- It provides technical assistance to states on specific development needs, including health and education.

International trade

The desire for states to trade with each other has existed for centuries. At certain points in history, international trade was carried out by force. States aimed to conquer other territories in order to gain their resources or strategic positions on key transport links. In the eighteenth and nineteenth centuries, Great Britain and other powerful states often went to war, acquiring entire empires of territory in order to maximise their economic output and control of strategic resources and territory. It was not until the late nineteenth century that states began to negotiate formal free-trade deals with each other in an attempt to bring order to international trade.

In the twentieth century, a clash of economic ideology between free-market capitalism and the communist model dominated. The capitalist world organised its trade by creating the WTO to act as a forum for agreeing international rules of trade. With the collapse of the Soviet Union in 1989, capitalism seemed to have won the battle of economic ideas. The post-war period saw a new enthusiasm for free-trade agreements between states. Economic integration was deepest in western Europe, with the creation of the European Economic Community (EEC) and the Single Market.

Synoptic links

In Component 1, conservatism explores those ways in which the individual rather than the state should direct economy activity. Writers such as Ayn Rand and Michael Oakeshott provide intellectual foundations for the principles of economic liberalism and free trade.

In an interdependent world, states have therefore moved from challenging each other for economic power through force to making the most of their economic power and trading opportunities peacefully, through international agreements.

Today's economic global governance arrangements concerning world trade therefore push states to work together in a more liberal and cooperative manner. This should not be surprising, since the reality of international trade forces all but the most isolationist of states to work together because it is in their economic interest to do so. States may choose a particularly liberal approach, such as that demonstrated by EU states, which have given up significant sovereignty over matters of trade. Or they may choose a more protectionist approach, by entering into agreements but also trying to protect their own interests, via tariffs or restrictions, against competition from elsewhere in the global market.

The World Trade Organization

The General Agreement on Tariffs and Trade (GATT) was the third of the institutions created at the Bretton Woods Conference in 1944. In 1995, this agreement was established as what we know today to be the WTO, and it is responsible for agreeing the rules of trade between states. In the Second World War era there was no international forum for states to negotiate with each other, but there was a desire to simplify negotiations by creating a specific and permanent institution.

Based in Geneva, the WTO's key goal is to reduce barriers on trade in both goods and services, which usually include tariffs that states might impose on imports. The WTO is not the only means by which states can reduce tariff barriers — states are free to enter into agreements with one or more other states. What the WTO does offer is the opportunity to put together extremely comprehensive trade agreements that will involve nearly all international trade.

The WTO also:

- checks that states are following trade agreements
- produces research on global trade and economic policy
- helps to resolve trade disputes between states

The WTO has 164 member countries, fewer than both the IMF and the World Bank. The member states account for 97% of world trade. It can take years to go through the process of joining the WTO — Algeria applied to join in 1987 and still has not become a full member. States currently applying to join include Iraq, Libya, Somalia and Sudan, all of which have recently seen a change in leadership. The EU is a member of the WTO and its member states are also members in their own right, but EU member states have to act together as a unified bloc of states.

Membership of the WTO involves both:

- *rights*, such as the right to export to other countries
- *obligations*, such as the need to limit restrictions on imports

The topmost decision-making body of the WTO is the Ministerial Conference, which meets every 2 years. Decisions are made by consensus and are binding, so every member has to agree to a trade deal or there is no trade deal.

The WTO operates on six key principles.

1 **Non-discrimination:** states should treat their trading partners equally and fairly, and should not discriminate between their own and foreign products.
2 **More open:** there is commitment to free trade in the sense of lowering trade barriers, such as import bans or quotas where the amount of imports is restricted.
3 **Predictable and transparent:** states should not raise trade barriers without warning or arbitrarily. A predictable system of international trade helps with stability and job creation, and allows for steady competition and lower prices.
4 **More competitive:** states should not interfere in order to give themselves an unfair competitive edge, for example by subsidising exports that would otherwise be uncompetitive or unsustainable.
5 **More benefits for less-developed countries:** allows scope for less-developed countries to catch up and transition to becoming full participants in international trade.
6 **Protection of the environment:** environmental protection must be respected both nationally and internationally.

WTO rules

At its simplest, the WTO is a set of rules that its members agree to abide by. The founding rules of the WTO, agreed in the original GATT in 1947, still stand today and have been added to in subsequent years through specific negotiating 'rounds'. Every member must agree for the round to be successful. There have been nine negotiating rounds, some of which have taken many years to agree, the most recent being in 2001 (see Table 4.4). The WTO has not been able to agree a new set of rules since then.

Table 4.4 Examples of GATT and WTO rounds of agreement

Agreement	Rules included and scope
General Agreement on Tariffs and Trade (GATT), 1947	45,000 tariff removals were agreed, which still stand today and impacted US$10 billion worth of international trade.
Kennedy Round, 1962–67	Expanded the removal of tariff barriers worth US$40 billion. For the first time, this negotiating round dealt with an issue not related to tariffs — that of states 'dumping' products cheaply in other states to dominate the market in that state.
Uruguay Round, 1986–94	The longest successfully concluded negotiating round of the WTO. This was also the WTO's largest trade agreement, as 123 countries were involved. The WTO was formally created in this round. There was a particular focus on reducing agricultural subsidies, although the EU's system of agricultural subsidies, the Common Agricultural Policy (CAP), was largely unaffected.
Doha Round, 2001–date	The WTO's current negotiating round has been ongoing since 2001. A so-called Development Round, it was intended to make progress in widening free trade with developing countries. The talks are in gridlock due to disagreements over further reductions in agricultural subsidies, which developed states are defending in the face of a perceived threat from cheaper agricultural imports. The Organisation for Economic Co-operation and Development (OECD) has estimated that the agricultural subsidies give an unfair advantage worth US$300 billion annually. The USA in particular has been criticised for not challenging its powerful farming lobby.

Criticisms and gridlock: the Doha Round

The failure of the Doha Round to reach agreement has raised criticism of the WTO's effectiveness. Critics say that the powerful nations, including the EU and the USA, are blocking less-developed nations and attempting to preserve the status quo for protectionist reasons. In recent decades, this has led the WTO to become gridlocked (since the WTO was created in 1994, it has successfully agreed only one major international trade deal).

Negotiations in the Doha Round have agreed improvements to customs procedure, but reductions on agricultural subsidies remain a sticking point. The Doha Round was effectively abandoned without agreement in 2015. The *Financial Times* commented that 'having failed to save Doha in the WTO, its members must now save the WTO from Doha', referring to the risk that the failure to agree a new comprehensive trade deal since 2001 has put the entire framework and effectiveness of the WTO in jeopardy. Until new WTO efforts are made, states must resort to negotiating with as many other states as possible in order to agree further liberalisation of tariff barriers.

Other criticisms of the WTO include the following:

- Political power resides with Western powers, and they tend to gain most from deals.
- Decision making is biased towards those countries with large representation in Geneva.
- Workers' rights and environmental protection (sustainable development) is disregarded.
- The WTO is unable to make decisions quickly, its Ministerial Conferences are too infrequent and the need for consensus among all members further slows decision making.

The difficulties in reaching agreement at the WTO might be seen as the reason for states seeking to agree trade deals outside of its forums (see Box 4.2). The TPP (see page 144) and the agreement between the EU and the USA, the Trans-Atlantic Trade and Investment Partnership (TTIP), are examples of states bypassing the WTO.

The EU's Common Agricultural Policy

The CAP is a central part of the EU's trading arrangements. It amounts to 40% of the EU's budget and is used to subsidise farmers to enable them to sell produce at low prices outside of the EU. Agricultural exports from the EU that would otherwise be uncompetitive are given huge EU subsidies to make them competitive.

The CAP is an example of economic protectionism, with the free-market rules of supply and demand largely ignored. In normal free-market circumstances, agricultural production would fall if demand falls. However, because farmers receive income from subsidies as well as from sales, they are therefore able to keep producing even if demand falls. Critics of the CAP say this often results in waste and overproduction. They also say that spending close to half of the EU's budget on a small agricultural sector that represents less than 5% of the EU population is not defensible.

The biggest criticism is the impact on developing countries that are dependent on agriculture, but cannot compete with subsidised EU prices. Such dramatic intervention to manipulate the market and give unfair advantage to EU farmers also goes against the neoliberal nature of international free trade.

Distinguish between

Realism and liberalism: international trade

Realism
- International trade is essential for the economic growth of the nation-state.
- States should be free to make their own trade deals. Negotiating as a bloc of nations (for example, the TPP) negatively impacts state sovereignty.
- States may sometimes need to protect their own vital national economic interests, for example through tariffs on imports that might otherwise harm key national industries.

Liberalism
- International trade is essential for the economic growth of the nation-state and a force for good in the economic development of developing states.
- States may benefit from negotiating trade deals in a bloc.
- International laws that regulate trade mean that states have to stick to the rules and not change the terms of trade arbitrarily. This means that international markets are more predictable, stable and ultimately profitable for all.

The Trans-Pacific Partnership

The TPP is a trade agreement between the states of the Pacific Rim, excluding China. The deal was agreed in 2016 in Auckland, New Zealand. It includes Australia, Brunei, Canada, Chile, Malaysia, Mexico, New Zealand, Peru, Singapore, Vietnam and the USA. Together, the member states amount to 40% of global GDP.

The agreement reduces tariff barriers to trade in the region, cutting 18,000 tariffs.

In one of his firsts acts as president, Donald Trump withdrew from the TPP, stating that membership would have lost US manufacturing jobs to lower-wage nations in Asia. Refusing to be a member of the TPP would therefore, according to Trump, represent 'a great thing for the American worker'.

Those who defend the TPP say that it is designed to create a free-trade zone that will reduce economic protectionism by reducing tariffs on imports. This would therefore encourage greater trade, which would, in turn, generate greater wealth in the region. In terms of geostrategy it would also encourage greater unity among states in the region against China's growing economic influence.

> **Box 4.2**
>
> ### The World Economic Forum
>
> The WEF is an annual conference of world leaders, business leaders, IGOs, NGOs and economists held in Davos, Switzerland each January. The forum allows all of these actors to contribute to setting the agenda for world economic issues. World leaders, for example, give key speeches setting out their government's policies. In 2017, Prime Minister Theresa May spoke at the WEF in a bid to reassure the global economic community that the UK was open for business and would make a success of Brexit.
>
> Some criticise the Davos get-together of the great and the good of the world economy as elitist and out of touch. It does not have a set agenda and is more a forum for discussion than formal agreement. It is also seen as almost a celebration of the capitalist economic model, although China has nevertheless been attending since 1979.

The Group of Seven/Eight

The G7/8 is an informal forum that was founded in 1975 after a successful ad hoc gathering in Paris of the finance ministers of the world's six wealthiest economies (France, Italy, Japan, the UK, the USA and West Germany, the Group of Six). There is no formal application or criteria for membership — it can invite and expel whom it likes. Canada became the seventh member in 1976. In 1997, Russia was invited to join and decided to accept (forming the G8), but was temporarily suspended in 2014 in response to its annexation of Crimea (see Box 4.3).

The G7/8 does not include all of the world's major economic powers, with China a notable absentee. Instead, the group's membership is made up of like-minded historical Western allies. The Council on Foreign Relations has described the G7/8 as a 'steering group for the West'. The group now meets annually to monitor and address developments in the world economy.

Informal forums like the G7/8 (and the G20, see page 147) are different from IGOs because of the following:

- The G7/8 has no formal rules. The UN, by contrast, has the UN Charter, which clearly sets out its purpose and processes.
- It can invite any states, IGOs or NGOs to its meetings.
- It can choose to remove any of its members from meetings, if the presidency state has not invited them to the meetings. In this sense, it has a flexible membership of like-minded allies.

> **Box 4.3**
>
> ### G7/8 members
>
> The current members of the G7/8 include:
>
> - Canada
> - France
> - Germany
> - Japan
> - Russia (joined in 1998, suspended in 2014)
> - UK
> - USA
>
> Representatives for the EU also attend.

Table 4.5 Agenda and outcomes of the 2016 G7/8 meeting (held in Japan)

Agenda item	Outcome
Countering terrorism and violent extremism	The G7 leaders confirmed the G7 Action Plan on Countering Terrorism and Violent Extremism.
Trade	The G7 leaders reconfirmed the importance of free trade and their commitment to fight against protectionism. They agreed to strengthen the multilateral trading system centred on the WTO and to actively promote plurilateral negotiations within WTO-specific areas.
Refugee crisis	G7 leaders expressed unity and solidarity with Europe as it confronted a massive inflow of refugees. They agreed on the importance of short-term humanitarian assistance and efforts to address the root causes.
Russia and Ukraine	The G7 leaders confirmed their intent to call for full implementation of the Minsk agreements by all related parties and encourage Ukraine to conduct comprehensive domestic reforms, and to support Ukraine's reform efforts.

- It has no budget or supporting secretariat, unlike IGOs such as the UN or IMF. If its members want to take action that costs money, the individual member states pay for it (or not).
- The decisions it takes are not binding and rely on the individual will of the participating states to deliver on the commitments they have made.
- There are no defined objectives. This allows it enormous flexibility in tackling any issues that matter to the presidency state and its members.
- It is primarily a forum for world leaders to interact at an annual summit. Between the summits, the G7/8 drives little organised activity.

The G7/8 presidency rotates among members, with the presidency state hosting and organising the annual summit. Russia held the G7/8 presidency in 2014 but the meeting was cancelled due to the other members' opposition to Russia's annexation of Crimea. Japan held the meeting for the sixth time in 2016 (see Table 4.5).

The meetings usually take place outside the capital city of the presidency country, often allowing the leaders to take advantage of a more informal and relaxed setting. During the UK presidency in 2013, members met at the remote Lough Erne estate in Northern Ireland. The previous year, US president Barack Obama hosted the G8 at Camp David, the president's country retreat.

Performance and impact

The first observation about the G7/8 is that its impact on state sovereignty is very negligible. However, this also means that the extent to which its decisions are delivered or enforceable is similarly weak.

Significant G7/8 decisions include the following.

- **2002:** the G7 becomes the G8. This was the first meeting of the G8, having been expanded to include Russia. Russia is invited to host a G8 summit for the first time.
- **2006:** Russia hosts its first G8 summit in St Petersburg. Before the summit, other G8 leaders were critical of Russia's record on human rights and Russia responded by criticising Western 'colonialist rhetoric'. Energy security, including increasing dependence of other G8 members on Russian energy supplies, was a key focus of the summit. Early discussions were also held regarding Russia's membership of the WTO, which was completed in 2012.
- **2007:** the Gleneagles Summit during the UK presidency — G8 leaders agreed to major debt cancellation to heavily indebted poor countries.

Criticism and pressure for reform

There are criticisms of the G7/8:

- Its membership reflects an outdated vision of the world's economic powers. The world's second economic power, China, is excluded. Rising powers such as Brazil and India are also not included.
- It is made up of a group of states that agree with each other. Expelling Russia in 2014 confirms this. There was no attempt to use the G8 as a means of negotiating or persuading Russia to pursue a different course.
- The scope for the G7/8 to achieve major breakthroughs is limited. The issues of the moment tend to dominate summits. The Syrian conflict, for example, dominated the UK's hosting of the G8 in 2013. There is a sense that the G7/8 responds to events, rather than shapes them.
- The G7/8's flexibility and informal approach makes it difficult to hold its members to account for commitments made at the summits.

Arguments for reform suggest that the G7/8 should widen its membership to include other significant emerging and established economic powers. Attempts have been made to broaden the G7/8 by including the so-called Outreach Five, consisting of Brazil, China, India, Mexico and South Africa. However, these attempts have been devalued by the existence of the G20, which already exists as a wider group and has become more powerful, taking a much more significant role in international efforts to address the global financial crisis, for example.

In defence of the G7/8, it is argued that a narrower group of like-minded states is better able to come to agreement and make decisions.

Debate

What are the strengths and weaknesses of the G7/8 compared with IGOs?

Strengths

- For realists, the G7/8 has little impact on state sovereignty. The forum never forces states to do things that they do not agree with.
- Informality allows its members to focus on any issue of importance and to respond to the major issues of the moment.
- A smaller number of member states prevents gridlock in decision making. By contrast, the WTO has a far larger membership but has been unable to agree a new trade deal for its members since 2001.

Weaknesses

- The G7/8 meets less frequently, so it acts in bursts rather than consistently.
- It is a forum for like-minded allies, rather than for active problem-solving and resolving differences of opinion.
- It is a forum for the richest and most powerful states to preserve their own interests.
- It no longer reflects the states that are the most economically powerful.
- There is little accountability — for example, there is no checking that states deliver on the commitments they have made.

G20

The G20 was created in 1999 as a means of expanding the G7/8 to include a wider group of industrialised states and emerging economic powers. The stated objective of the G20 when it was founded was for it to be:

> an informal forum that promotes open and constructive discussion between industrial and emerging-market countries on key issues related to global economic stability

Like the G7/8, the G20 began principally as a meeting of the states' finance ministers. By the time of the 2008 global financial crisis, it had become the key annual forum for world leaders to meet and discuss global economic policy.

Role and membership

Whereas the G7/8 can be criticised as being a narrow alliance of the oldest and most established economic powers, the G20 includes many emerging economic powers and a more geographically diverse range of states.

China, for example, is a key member of the G20 but is not a member of the G7/8, despite many economists predicting that its economy will overtake the USA's as the largest in the world by around 2020. The so-called BRIC countries (Brazil, Russia, India and China), which have been experiencing rapid economic growth since the early 2000s, are included in the G20. A mixture of rising and established economies from South America (Argentina), southeast Asia (Indonesia), the middle east (Saudi Arabia) and Africa (South Africa) are included.

Key features of the G20 include the following:

- Its membership represents both established and emerging economies which, together, account for almost two-thirds of the world population, more than four-fifths of gross world product and three-quarters of world trade.
- The G20 also has the key economic IGOs attend all of its meetings (see Table 4.6). All of the Bretton Woods Institutions attend, along with the UN and the EU. This is very different to the G7/8, where only the EU is a regular additional member in attendance.
- Meetings usually take place annually, with a rotating presidency, as is the case for the G7/8. The presidency state has considerable power over which additional states or other international organisations it invites and the agenda for that year's summit.

Table 4.6 Attendance at the 2016 G20 summit in Hangzhou, China

G20 member states	G20 IGO members	Additionally invited to this summit
Argentina	EU, represented by the ECB and the European Commission	African Union president
Australia		Egypt
Brazil		Kazakhstan
Canada	Financial Stability Board	Laos
China	IMF	Senegal
EU (see next column)	OECD	Singapore
France	UN	Spain
Germany	World Bank	Thailand
India	WTO	
Indonesia		
Italy		
Japan		
Mexico		
Russia		
Saudi Arabia		
South Africa		
South Korea		
Turkey		
UK		
USA		

- The agenda for G20 meetings has become increasingly broad, extending beyond purely economic matters. Climate change and global terrorism, for example, have featured on recent agendas.

Changing role

Some see the G20 as becoming a more influential actor in economic global governance than the G7/8. During the global financial crisis of 2008 it was the G20, rather than the G7/8, that led the response to the crisis of the world's most powerful economic states (see Getting you started, page 129).

The following factors have made the G20 the more effective informal forum:

- The G20 is a balance between traditional, historic economic powers (such as France, the UK and the USA), newly emerged economic powers (such as China, Brazil and India) and emerging economic powers (such as Argentina and Indonesia). This makes the G20 more effective, as it is neither too exclusive (a weakness of the G7/8) nor too comprehensive (a weakness of the WTO) to be able to make decisions.

- The membership also includes more states that do not always agree with each other. This enables the G20 to be more of a forum for dispute resolution and problem solving than the G7/8, whose members broadly agree with each other on most matters and has expelled a member (Russia, in 2014) with whom the majority did not agree. Thus, the G20 is a forum for influencing climate change, where newly emerging economies, such as India, have very different views to more established economies. It can be argued that this makes the G20 more useful.

- The G20's inclusion of and partnership with the major Bretton Woods economic IGOs has significant benefits. It provides the most powerful world economies with a dedicated means of influencing these IGOs and coordinating action on economic matters between them and states.

- The widening of the G20 agenda to include non-economic matters provides another international forum for dispute resolution and influencing. It also provides world leaders from a more diverse range of states (than, for example, the UN Security Council) with a dedicated forum in which to build personal relationships and, occasionally, to make joint statements on issues ranging from the plight of refugees to global terrorism, which can set the global agenda.

- The G20 has taken decisive action on both economic and non-economic matters. It played a central role in agreeing that states would inject significant amounts of government money into banks to ensure they did not collapse and could lend to each other again during the global financial crisis. It has also taken action to ensure that the wealthiest states and IGOs work together, in order to prevent and more tightly regulate those bank accounts funding terrorists.

Criticisms

The G20, however, is not without its critics, who state the following:

- It has become a focal point for anti-capitalist protests. These protests were particularly significant in the early 2000s. Protesters regularly targeted summits for large-scale demonstrations, including violent protests in London during the 2009 summit. The grievances protesters raise range from demanding action from heavily industrialised states on climate change to the lack of regulation in the world banking system and the prevention of excessive bonuses.

■ G20 summits conclude with a communiqué (see Box 4.4) agreed by each state in attendance. There is sometimes criticism that G20 outcomes are 'watered down' or 'lowest common denominator' — in other words, they are the best that each state present could agree upon. Furthermore, there is criticism that states cannot be held accountable for the decisions or actions they agree at G20 summits.

Box 4.4

Summary of final communiqué from the 2016 G20 Summit

The summary of the final communiqué from the 2016 G20 Summit, held in Hangzhou, China, included:

■ responding to populist attacks against globalisation
■ reducing tax evasion by working with the OECD to identify tax havens
■ reducing protectionism
■ agreeing action to boost economic growth
■ support for refugees

Distinguish between

The G7/8 and the G20

The G7/8
■ The North American (USA/Canada) and western European nations dominate the G7/8, making it outdated.
■ It is an alliance of like-minded states, which has the power to expel those it disagrees with.

The G20
■ The G20 has wider membership, reflecting a broader range of economic powers, both established and emerging.
■ It is broader geographically, including African, Asian and South American countries.
■ It is better at and more relevant when dealing with major economic crises, such as the 2008 global financial crisis.

Poverty

A key role for economic global governance is addressing the challenge of world poverty and global inequality. Much of the economic global governance examined so far in this chapter has considered how states can develop their economies, put rules in place to bring order to the global financial system and trade with each other more effectively. This section deals with how states and IGOs work at a global level to improve economic fortunes at a more human and individual level.

The focus on human poverty is not a new concept within the field of economic global governance. One of the UN's founding objectives was to reduce poverty and promote economic development. We have seen that the World Bank and the IMF have a key role to play in reducing poverty.

First, it is necessary to understand exactly what poverty is.

What is poverty?

At its simplest, poverty is when human beings lack the things that they need in order to live a secure, stable and fulfilling life. This covers two central issues.

1 **Income poverty:** not earning an income at all or earning an income that is not sufficient for living safely.
2 **Lack of social needs:** for example, access to shelter, healthcare or education.

There is clearly a wide range of differences between the income and living situation of people in poverty across the world — poverty in the UK has very different characteristics to poverty in Sub-Saharan Africa. In the latter, people living in poverty may entirely lack shelter, education and healthcare, and earn considerably less than people living in poverty in the UK.

In order to clarify poverty, the UN provides two definitions.

1 **Absolute poverty:** in which a person earns less than US$1.25 per day. This measure of poverty is exclusively economic, rather than social. It measures poverty in terms of that person's ability to meet their basic needs, including clothing, food, drinking water and shelter. It does not take into account social factors such as education. India has the largest population of those in the world living in absolute poverty, more than are living in absolute poverty in the whole of Sub-Saharan Africa.
2 **Relative poverty:** this puts the poverty that people are experiencing into context by comparing it with other people who live in the same society or state. Rather than having a global figure, such as US$1.25 per day, as is measured in absolute poverty, it compares people's income against the average income in that country. It judges whether people have the minimum income needed to maintain the average standard of living that people in that country enjoy. This is frequently based around those who live in households that earn below 60% of the middle or median income typical in that state. A recent report from the UK House of Commons estimated that 10 million people were living in relative poverty in the UK and that this figure was increasing.

Reducing world poverty was the first and main objective of the UN's MDGs. The UN reported that 1 billion people had been lifted out of absolute poverty since 1990. It also estimated that, in 1990, nearly half of the population in developing regions lived on less than US$1.25 per day and that by 2015 this had dropped to 14%.

Absolute and relative poverty

Absolute poverty
- Absolute poverty measures poverty against a global standard of US$1.25 per day.
- It does not include the lack of social needs, such as education. Rather it is purely a measure of income.
- It focuses on meeting basic needs required for survival, such as shelter, food and water.

Relative poverty
- Relative poverty measures poverty by comparing it with the average household income in the same state or society.
- What is considered 'relative poverty' in a developed state will differ greatly from the equivalent in a developing state.
- It is based on standard of living, not just income.

What is development?

At its simplest, development is the combination of activities by which a variety of actors in global politics attempt to reduce poverty, and improve the economic and social development for a defined group of people.

There is no single agreed definition of development. There are different views because people disagree on which priorities within development are the most important. Development can therefore include the following:

- Some see it purely in terms of advancing economic growth, with an economy that is productive and generates revenue. Critics of this definition suggest that it fails to take into account the whole of society. For example, the richest may be getting even richer and the economy can be booming, but large sections of the population remain in poverty.
- Others see development as focusing on human development. If human beings are free, they will be able to develop most effectively. Indian economist Amartya Sen outlined this view in in his 1999 book *Development as Freedom*. Sen argued that people are most likely to lift themselves out of poverty when they are empowered to do so. Democracy and human rights are a key part of this.
- There is an increasing focus on sustainable development and an awareness that the development needs of today cannot put at risk the development needs of tomorrow, for example degrading the environment to the extent that it can no longer provide for the next generation. This cautions against economic growth and development that flourishes, but pollutes and causes harm to the natural environment.
- Sociopolitical development focuses on issues such as reducing inequality between men and women, and improving education.

When thinking about the different types of development, it is useful to consider Maslow's hierarchy of needs, which summarises how human beings prioritise their basic needs. Maslow believed that human beings' first priority is to protect their physiological health (for example, by having sufficient food and water) and that once this is achieved, they move on to secure other needs, such

Table 4.7 Maslow's hierarchy of needs

Maslow's hierarchy of needs	Type of development
Self-actualisation	Economic empowerment, such as helping and allowing people to set up their own businesses
Esteem	Reducing inequality of income and opportunity between any groups, e.g. women or ethnic groups
Love/Belonging	Democracy and human rights provide the basis for an inclusive and respectful society
Safety	Protection from dangers such as natural disasters and conflict
Physiological	Access to food and clean drinking water, shelter to avoid physical harm from excessive cold or heat

as the need to belong and be loved. According to Maslow, human development is fundamentally limited and incomplete if humans are not able to successfully progress through and meet each of these needs (see Table 4.7).

In terms of development, Maslow's hierarchy of needs helps us to identify which types of development are the most crucial to human survival. Some would argue that the most basic development needs should be met and invested in first. Others consider that all of the different types of development should be addressed at the same time.

Measuring poverty

Given that development has many different interpretations and priorities, there are also many different ways of measuring development.

Distinguish between

Realism and liberalism: economic development

Realism

- States should focus on their own economic development first and spend government money on the needs of their own populations.
- States only help other states to develop if this helps to protect or advance their own interests (for example, the USA invests most aid assistance in Afghanistan).
- Aid is likely to make the recipient nations dependent on funds and skills from other states.
- Debt relief encourages states to continue to mismanage their economic resources.

Liberalism

- Developed states have a responsibility to help less-developed states. It is in the global interest for less-developed states to be helped.
- IGOs have a key role to play in coordinating the efforts of the international community, for example through the MDGs.
- Aid can be used to empower developing states, for example through microfinance initiatives.
- Debt relief gives states the opportunity to invest in their own development, rather than repaying loans.

Research and discuss in pairs how effectively you think Maslow's hierarchy of needs is met in:
1 the UK
2 a Sub-Saharan African state of your choice
Are there differences between how well Maslow's hierarchy of needs is met for different sectors of society in these states? What are the reasons for this?

Economic growth

This is often considered to be the most *quantitative* measure of development, in the sense that it is based on data that examine how well a state's economy is performing and how much revenue it is producing. For example, if a state has many private companies that are producing and selling products such as cars or natural resources such as oil and gas, this will be factored into various measures of that state's economic development.

The key measures of economic growth are gross domestic product (GDP) and gross national product (GNP).

- **GDP:** a measure of the economic activity that takes place within a state. The UK's GDP takes into account economic activity from both UK and, for example, Japanese companies such as Nissan, which produce and sell in the UK.
- **GNP:** a measure of all economic activity, wherever it takes place in the world, by companies and individuals from a particular state. For example, Japan's GNP takes into account all economic activity from Japanese companies, such as Samsung and Nissan, wherever that activity takes place in the world, including in Japan.

The most basic indicator of positive or negative economic development is whether a state's economy is growing or shrinking. This is measured through its GDP. If a state's GDP decreases in two successive 3-month periods (or 'quarters' of a year), that state is said to be in *recession*. The contrast is that if GDP is increasing, the state is growing. Both are normally measured by a percentage. In early 2017, Venezuela's economy was suffering one of the worst recessions, its economy decreasing in output by 13%. By contrast, the economies of China and India were growing by between 6% and 7%.

It is possible, therefore, to compare a state's economic growth with those of other states. It is also useful to measure a state's economic growth against its recent economic history. While China's and India's economic growth in 2017 looks successful, it has actually decreased from highs in the mid-teens before the global financial crisis.

Critics of economic growth, and of GDP and GNP as measures of development, state the following.

- It is a poor measure of poverty and does not take into account the fact that a state may have high economic growth but the economic benefits of this growth are not shared fairly among the entire population. India, for example, has strong economic growth but has the largest number of people living in absolute poverty anywhere in the world.
- Just as serious problems with poverty may be hidden in seemingly positive GDP figures, inequality of income, where many in a state earn significantly less than the richest, is also hidden.

- It does not take into account political development, such as human rights and democracy. For example, China has high economic growth but a poor record on democracy and human rights.
- Economic growth can be misleading. For example, Pakistan had GDP growth of 7% but required an IMF bailout in 2008 and it still faces chronic human development problems, with lack of access to education and healthcare, and an energy and water resource crisis.

A better measure of economic development that exposes how well income and wealth is spread throughout society is the Gini coefficient (see page 53). This model measures the inequality of income between the richest and the poorest, in other words the gap between the income of the poorest households and that of the wealthiest households. A Gini score of 0 indicates perfect equality, while a score of 100 indicates extreme inequality. The deeper the graph descends towards the richest in society, the more unequal the society. The more level the graph, the more equal the society.

Activity

Answer the following questions.
1   What would a state with high GDP and low GNP look like? Can you think of any examples?
2   What would a state with low GDP and high GNP look like? Can you think of any examples?

Synoptic links

In Component 1, socialist thinkers also grapple with the meaning of development. Should it be measured in terms of economic growth and efficiency, as economist and social reformer Beatrice Webb argued, or must development be viewed much more broadly in terms of emotional fulfilment, as former Labour politician Anthony Crosland suggested?

The Human Development Index and the Multi-dimensional Poverty Index

Human development was a key focus of the MDGs and has become a major priority for the assistance the World Bank provides (see page 139). The Human Development Index (HDI) and the Multi-dimensional Poverty Index (MPI) are measures of poverty that focus on the human development priorities of human wellbeing and empowerment.

The HDI is a composite indicator of poverty, meaning that it takes into account a range of different indicators rather than just a single indictator. The scores for each indicator are put together and converted into a total score out of 100. The index covers 188 countries, making it extremely comprehensive both globally and in terms of the poverty indicators it covers (see Box 4.5). Indian Nobel Prize-winning economist Amartya Sen was one of the key drivers behind this new measure of poverty. It links to Sen's argument that it is essential to measure and address deficiencies of human capabilities.

The HDI covers the following indicators of poverty.

- **Life expectancy at birth:** how long, on average, someone is likely to live.
- **Education:** based on the expected number of years that someone, on average, would be likely to spend attending school.
- **Income:** based on the GNP (sometimes known as gross national income (GNI)) of the state per capita.

Box 4.5

UN Human Development Index rankings for selected countries (2015)

1	Norway (highest) — life expectancy of 81 years, 17.5 years of average schooling, GNI per capita US$64,992
8	USA
14	UK
22	France
39	Saudi Arabia
50	Russia
90	China
121	Iraq
171	Afghanistan
188	Niger (lowest) — life expectancy of 61 years, 5.4 years of average schooling, GNI per capita US$908

A key gap in the HDI is, again, inequality. In 2010, an additional measure was introduced, called the Inequality-Adjusted Human Development Indicator. However, data on inequality were not available for all HDI-covered states. Consequently, it is difficult to effectively compare states and their levels of inequality.

An even more detailed measure of poverty is the MPI, which the UN Development Programme uses. It extends the HDI into ten indicators and is therefore even more comprehensive. Crucially, it includes indicators of standards of living, such as access to drinking water, sanitation and electricity, as well as the health and education indicators of child mortality, nutrition, years of schooling and school attendance. This makes the MPI the most comprehensive measure of poverty.

Difficulties in measuring poverty

While there are a number of different measures of poverty, gathering the data reliably and accurately is not always possible — by definition, the poorest states often face the greatest challenges in gathering these data.

- A census is a government's official count of its population. Censuses are usually carried out every 10 years — the last UK census was held in 2011, with the next in 2021. Much of the world's census data is unreliable. A total of 17 out of 35 Sub-Saharan African countries have not held a census in the last 20 years. Census data is essential for establishing a reliable baseline for other statistical research. For example, a state's Gini coefficient cannot be accurately measured without an accurate figure for the state's population, or without comprehensive data on the number of households and their wealth.
- Accessing remote communities in order to gather data can be difficult in states that are suffering from conflict, have poor infrastructure or are

otherwise inaccessible due to natural disaster or difficult geography (for example, mountainous or jungle regions).

■ Populations that are moving, such as in refugee crises, create difficulties in gathering data. These populations are often those in greatest need. The circumstances in which these individuals find themselves can also change rapidly, meaning that data may quickly become inaccurate or outdated.

■ In some cases, states either manipulate or withhold information on poverty. This may be due to corruption or a desire to hide the extent of a poverty problem that the government is either unwilling or unable to resolve.

Debate

Can poverty be measured?

Yes

■ Measures exist for different types of poverty, including human development.
■ The MDGs are a powerful demonstration that measurable and time-bound goals are possible.
■ The absolute poverty line of US$1.25 per day is a fair level below which human beings anywhere in the world would find it difficult to survive.
■ Relative poverty allows effective comparison within a state, comparing household incomes against the average income in that state.
■ Taken together, absolute and relative poverty provide a balanced means of assessing poverty at both national and global level.

No

■ Inaccuracies exist in the data, making the measures flawed.
■ Poverty and development can be interpreted in different ways, so that one single measure of development is impossible — something will be left out. GDP, for example, purely measures economic growth.
■ Some countries do not report data, or report it in patches.
■ Data are likely to be weakest where development is weakest, for example census material.
■ Very little is spent on improving statistical development (0.16% of all aid).

Causes of poverty

Key term

North/South divide Term coined in the Brandt Report on overseas development in 1980. It is a political rather than a geographical term and contrasts the developed, industrialised world (Global North) with the developing, agricultural world (Global South).

In a globalised world, there are many theories about which factors are the most significant in both causing and reducing poverty. These include the following ideas:

■ There is a **North–South divide** in which the states in the North of the world are richer and more developed than those in the South.
■ Richer, more developed states exploit poorer, less developed states and trap them in a cycle of poverty and underdevelopment. This dependency theory suggests that poorer states cannot catch up with richer states.
■ Colonialism has had a lasting impact on the development of the colonised states, holding back their development and making them dependent on their former colonial powers.
■ Globalisation has brought with it large inequality of income both within states and, more importantly, between states. The rich states have become richer while the poor states have remained poor.

Equally, there are many strategies that global economic governance has developed to try to reduce global poverty. These include the following.

■ **MDGs:** the UN initiated the MDGs in 2000 to bring a united, global focus to reducing world poverty by agreeing targets that all states and IGOs would work towards in partnership.

- **SDGs:** replaced the MDGs in 2015, when the MDGs reached the end of their agreed lifetime. The SDGs redefined and continued the global effort to reduce poverty and introduced a new focus on sustainable development.
- **Debt relief and cancellation:** at the turn of the millennium, there was considerable debate about whether poorer states should have their debts either cancelled or significantly reduced. This would enable poorer states to spend money on reducing poverty, rather than repaying expensive loans.

All of these strategies and theories need careful examination. Theories about what prevents states developing can be disproved if there are states that buck the trends. Theories about which strategies most advance development can equally be tried and tested with real-life examples.

The North–South divide

This theory divides the world into the 'Global North' and the 'Global South'. The idea gained prominence after the former chancellor of West Germany Willy Brandt published a report in 1980. In it, he devised the Brandt Line, which divides predominantly North America, Europe, Russia and Australasia into a developed 'Global North', with Africa, South America and South Asia the less developed 'Global South'. The result is a rough approximation of the North and the South, not a geographically straight line.

The key differences between the Global North and Global South include the following:
- Industrialisation and manufacturing in the North was creating sustained wealth for the North.
- The North was a leading player in shaping global free-trade agreements and its key export industries were making the most of these agreements.
- A lack of industrialisation and reliance on agriculture exports was not creating wealth for the South.
- Many Global South countries and their exports were not yet part of global free-trade agreements, such as the WTO. This meant there was not a level playing field for the countries in the South.
- MNCs based in the Global North were seen to be exploiting states in the Global South for natural resources and cheap labour. The profits were returned to and benefited the North, rather than being shared with the South.
- The South had become dependent on the North for foreign direct investment, manufactured goods, skills and technology.
- States in the North created the Bretton Woods Institutions for their own benefit and they continue to dominate the decision making of, for example, the WTO.

Many of these differences remain valid more than 30 years later. By the time the MDGs concluded in 2015, Sub-Saharan Africa lagged significantly behind the rest of the world on most measures of development (see page 117). Dependency theory (see page 55) supports the view that the industrialised North continues to exploit the South for natural resources.

Most of the world's largest MNCs continue to be based in the Global North, not the South. States in the Global South that look to have rapidly industrialised and grown their economies still suffer from considerable poverty, with India the most notable example. Some states in the Global South continue to suffer worsening poverty, such as Bangladesh and Pakistan. The WTO is currently in gridlock and has so far failed to finalise another free-trade agreement that would widen free trade to more developing states and reduce protectionist measures, such as subsidies on agriculture (see page 144).

However, there is increasing evidence that some (by no means all) states in the Global South are managing to close the gap with the Global North:

- Many states in the Global South have successfully industrialised. These include the so-called newly industrialising countries (NICs), particularly those in the Pacific Rim such as Brazil, Malaysia and the Philippines.
- China, officially in the Global South according to the Brandt Line, has seen a dramatic increase in its economic growth and is set to become the world's largest economy by around 2020. Far from being a continuing member of the Global South, it has itself become an investor in states in the South (predominantly in Sub-Saharan Africa), extracting natural resources to cater for its rapidly expanding industry and population.
- Sustainable development is a huge challenge as states in the Global South attempt to catch up with the North. The World Bank estimated that high-income states in the Global North had been responsible for two-thirds of the carbon dioxide released into the atmosphere since 1850. However, in 2005, China became the world's largest emitter of greenhouse gases. Brazil and India were respectively in fifth and eighth place.
- There is some evidence of more inclusion of states in the Global South in economic global governance. The increasing power and influence of the G20, which includes several newly industrialising economies from the Global South, confirms this.

World systems theory

Key term

Dependency theory The idea that resources flow from a 'periphery' of poor and underdeveloped states to a 'core' of wealthy states, enriching the latter at the expense of the former.

This theory is known by several names: world systems theory, dependency theory and sometimes the core-periphery model. The key thinker behind this theory is the US sociologist and economist Immanuel Wallerstein, who proposed the idea in his 1974 book *The Modern World System*.

Wallerstein advances the principle of dependency in this theory. According to him, global capitalism maintains the developing world in a state of neocolonial dependency. This is because core states in the Global North exploit the labour and raw materials of the Global South, thereby keeping them in a peripheral state and dependent upon the North for capital and investment.

The key aspect of this theory is that it does not consider states in isolation from each other, but analyses how the entire world economic system works and the impact that richer states have on poorer states. It is essentially a model that explains how capitalism has come to dominate the world economic system through three types of nation-states.

1 **Core states:** these wealthy states mirror many of the features of those in the Global North. They are highly industrialised economies, in which MNCs are based, and dominate both domestically and globally, paying high wages and producing a wide range of manufactured, often hi-tech, goods. These countries' populations are internationally mobile, well educated and highly skilled.

2 **Periphery states:** these states are poor and underdeveloped. They mirror many of the features of the Global South. They are yet to industrialise, but typically possess natural resources that the core countries need. Because they lack well-developed industries or manufacturing of their own, they have a surplus of, for example, natural resources that they have little capacity to use but which, by contrast, the core countries often need more and more of.

3   **Semi-peripheral states:** these states fall somewhere between the previous two definitions.

In the model, Wallerstein argued that the 'core' of wealthy states enriches and preserves the economic status of the wealthy states at the expense of the poorer, periphery states. It is a central idea of dependency theory that poor states are impoverished and rich states are enriched by the way poor states are integrated into the 'world system'.

For example:

■ the Democratic Republic of Congo (DRC) is one of the poorest countries in the world. It ranks 176th out of 188 countries in the HDI. The mineral coltan is extracted using cheap labour (paying a minimum wage in some cases of just US$3.00 per day) from mines in the DRC and exported to core countries, where it is used as a key component in making smartphones, an industry which has seen MNCs, including Apple and Samsung, become some of the world's richest companies. At the same time, the DRC remains stuck in a low-wage, low-technology economy that is reliant on the poorly paid investment of foreign MNCs.

■ Angola, a periphery country, is heavily dependent on producing oil for developed countries in the core. As much as 97% of Angola's total exports come from oil. When the global price of oil falls, consumers in the wealthy core countries enjoy cheaper prices. In Angola, however, falling oil prices mean less income, which, with such dependency, has led to the government having to ask international lenders such as Goldman Sachs (also based in the core countries) for emergency loans.

Synoptic links

Component 1 explores socialism as a core political ideology. Karl Marx and Friedrich Engels provide the intellectual foundations for dependency theory by arguing that capitalism is rooted in the desire to perpetuate economic inequality.

The mining industry is the DRC's largest source of export income, but the DRC remains the 176th poorest country in the world

Case study

China, Africa and dependency theory

China needs natural resources, principally oil, in order to keep its rapidly expanding industries operating successfully. Africa has the natural resources that China lacks.

According to Chinese government figures, Chinese foreign direct investment in Africa rose from US$74 million in 2005 to US$5.5 billion in 2009. The scale of the investment and the rapidity of its growth are breathtaking. But when the Chinese economy slowed after the 2008 global financial crisis, Chinese investment in Africa fell rapidly — in 2015, estimates suggested that investment fell by as much as 84%.

A Chinese construction project in Sudan

Africa is increasingly dependent on Chinese investment for infrastructure projects ranging from the building of roads and rail to dams and bridges. As China becomes Africa's biggest trading partner, Africa is increasingly exposed and linked to China's economic fortunes, since when China's economy slows, it needs less of the natural resources that Africa provides.

The impact of globalisation

Connected to world systems theory is the question of whether economic globalisation has benefited merely the richest countries while the poorest have been left behind. This argument is frequently referred to as 'winners and losers', since it claims that, ultimately, it is the poorest states that are the losers in the globalised economic model.

To understand whether globalisation has been positive or negative in reducing world poverty, it is first necessary to distinguish between the different types of globalisation.

- **Economic globalisation:** as the world has become more interconnected, economic activity has become more globalised. Goods, services, money and technology are moved across borders more easily and extensively than ever before. States are increasingly vulnerable to economic downturns that occur outside their borders.
- **Political globalisation:** refers to an increase in attempts to bring order to global politics through global governance. Since the Bretton Woods Conference in 1944, there have been extensive efforts to bring order to the world economic and financial system through global governance. Economic IGOs, such as the IMF and the World Bank, together with UN-led efforts

such as the MDGs and SDGs, are all part of attempts to advance global economic development and reduce poverty.

Evaluating the impact of globalisation on world poverty is complex. Some key international indicators certainly suggest that the benefits of globalisation have not been widely shared. For example, both global and national inequality have worsened in recent decades:

- Oxfam has reported that the wealthiest 85 people in the world are worth more than the poorest 3.5 billion.
- Seven out of ten people live in a country that has seen inequality rise in the last 30 years.
- Income inequality has risen in states that have seen the highest economic growth (for example, China and India).

Debate

Has globalisation helped to reduce global poverty?

Yes

- Globalisation has seen increased foreign direct investment in developing states, which, if taxed efficiently, can create tax revenue that can then be spent on development.
- MNCs bring experience, skills, modernisation and better wages to poorer countries.
- Economic freedom promotes other freedoms, and with freedom comes human development (Amartya Sen). The emergence of an empowered middle class is linked to democratisation, which can be a powerful lever for breaking down inequality and widening equality of opportunity.

No

- Developing countries are exploited for natural resources and minerals.
- Skills that will enable industrialisation are not developed in developing countries. MNCs use too many of their own skilled employees from developed countries and do too little to develop skills and capacity within these countries.
- Wealthy states pay low wages, keeping the poor locked in a low-wage economy.

The impact of colonialism

The earliest demonstration of economic globalisation came with European states empire-building in the eighteenth and nineteenth centuries. Nation-states including France, Great Britain, the Netherlands, Portugal and Spain used military power to occupy territories around the world, installed governments of their own and began a process of building up both the infrastructure and governance of these territories for the purpose of gaining control of their economic resources.

During the post-Second World War period, there was a process of decolonisation, during which most colonised states became independent nation-states in their own right. For Great Britain, this resulted in the partition of British India into the modern-day states of Pakistan and India in 1947. In 1960, Prime Minister Harold Macmillan famously declared in a speech in South Africa that 'the wind of change was blowing through this continent', heralding another wave of decolonisation of British colonies, including Ghana, Kenya and Nigeria. Decolonisation was not always carried out peacefully, with, for example, both the British and French guilty of war crimes in Kenya and Algeria respectively as they initially fought back against popular uprisings fighting for independence.

Synoptic links

In Component 2, the nationalism option explores various forms of nationalist identity. Jamaican political leader Marcus Garvey provides an early condemnation of colonialism as being based on racist exploitation. In its place, 'Pan Africanism' should replace colonial domination with continent-wide black empowerment.

There are several arguments suggesting that the colonial period contributed to modern global poverty, including the following:

■ During the colonial period, the capacity of the local population was sometimes not fully developed. When states gained independence, some had little experience of self-government and found it difficult to develop on their own.

■ During the decolonisation process, borders were often drawn up with little regard for ethnic unity but rather political expediency. This has been a factor in some conflicts since, for example the conflict between India and Pakistan over the disputed region of Kashmir.

■ The dependency theory is highly relevant to colonialism in the sense that colonialism represents the most deliberate attempt by core countries to maximise their own economic growth and keep poorer states in a state of dependency and underdevelopment. The difference with colonialism was that the core colonising states had both political and economic power over the colonised periphery states (whose internal sovereignty was minimal to non-existent), enabling the core states to have a much greater impact than is possible for non-colonising core states today.

Arguments against the colonial period contributing to modern global poverty include the following:

■ Infrastructure was built that continues to be used in the modern era, for example roads, railways, bridges and dams.

■ The newly independent states still use the industry infrastructure that was developed during the colonial period.

■ The rule of law was introduced in some colonial states, which remains in place today and provides the basis for a stable society and one which is attractive to foreign investment.

Modernisation theory

The orthodox model of development is essentially the story of how the first industrialised states developed. US economist Walt Whitman Rostow proposed the idea in 1960, and it is sometimes referred to as the Rostow model of economic growth, or 'modernisation theory'.

Rostow suggested that for states to develop they had to work their way through several stages of growth.

1 **Traditional society:** at this stage, the society is reliant on subsistence farming, little technology, and there is little organised economic activity, such as currency.

2 **Preconditions for take-off:** wealth or savings now exist, which can be invested in vital economic sectors such as transportation, communications and natural resource exploitation. Entrepreneurs may emerge.

3 **Take-off:** the society is focused on economic growth and develops strategies to maximise its economic growth.

4 **Drive to maturity:** the economy begins to diversify. Poverty is likely to be decreasing.

5 **Age of high mass consumption:** the society has developed a strong middle class, which is able to buy goods and services, creating a consumer-based economy.

The Rostow model has been criticised for being a purely Western-focused interpretation of how states both can develop and can reduce poverty. Essentially, the model is the story of the economic development of the West and of the stages of the Industrial Revolution in the nineteenth century.

However, in many ways the connection to how Western capitalist states developed was intentional. Rostow's theory came at a time when governments and many economists in the West wanted to caution developing states away from pursuing a communist model of development, in favour of free-market capitalism. The hope was that the soft-power attractiveness of capitalism would prove persuasive and states would choose to mirror these stages of capitalist economic growth.

The theory strongly contradicts that of world systems theory, in that the orthodox view assumes that all states can progress through the various stages of growth. Critics say that this is unrealistic because the Rostow model does not take into account the fact that states which need to catch up are competing in a global model in which wealthier states can hold them back.

In defence of Rostow's model, there is plenty of evidence that many of today's newly industrialised states have paid attention to the stages. They have invested in heavily diversifying their industries, rather than being overly reliant on one sector. They have carefully invested in developing key industries along the way through subsidies, for example the so-called Asian Tiger economies in southeast Asia invested in high-tech industries, which spurred rapid economic growth.

Distinguish between

World systems and modernisation theories

World systems theory

- A model of economic growth that challenges the idea that less developed states can catch up with developed, industrialised states.
- The developed states exploit less developed states, keeping them dependent on the developed states and trapped in a state of under-development.

Modernisation theory

- A model of economic growth that suggests that less developed states can industrialise following the same steps as Western industrialised states.
- This model does not consider the impact of the wider global financial system on states' ability to develop and industrialise.

Neoliberalism and the Washington Consensus

Economist John Williamson developed the Washington Consensus policy in 1989 to reflect the consensus on the preferred economic reform package in the eyes of the World Bank, IMF and WTO (all based in Washington, DC). The theory is also known as neoliberalism, due to its liberal approach to letting the market respond naturally to the forces of supply and demand. So-called laissez-faire economics suggests minimal government intervention or protectionism.

The key elements of the Washington Consensus include:

- cutting public spending
- tax reform (cutting personal and corporate taxes)
- deregulation of financial markets (setting the market free to innovate and take risks)
- privatisation (selling of state-owned industries, such as electricity, gas, airlines)
- openness to foreign direct investment
- free trade

Associated with President Ronald Reagan and Prime Minister Margaret Thatcher in the 1980s, these elements became a key part of many IMF SAPs (see page 136).

In the aftermath of the 2008 global financial crisis, there was debate as to whether or not the neoliberal approach of the Washington Consensus had failed and if this represented a wider failure of global capitalism. Arguments included the following points:

- Some judged lack of regulation in the banking sector to have been a major cause of the global financial crisis. Banks, it is argued, were able to lend money recklessly to individuals who were unlikely to be able to pay back their loans or mortgages. The laissez-faire approach allowed financial institutions to regulate themselves. Instead, some argued that financial institutions should have been subject to tougher rules on the risks that they could and could not take.
- Excessive greed in the financial sector is often cited as having led to bankers trying to generate more and more profit, rewarded by large bonuses, and being willing to take increasingly large risks.
- State intervention was needed to resolve the global financial crisis, with governments taking banks into public ownership to ensure that they did not collapse. The argument was that banks were 'too big to fail', but this intervention arguably abandoned the Washington Consensus principle of minimal state ownership and the state avoiding intervention to correct market weaknesses. In reality, the banking sector was so central to states' economic stability that states had little choice but to intervene. As of 2016, the UK government still had considerable ownership over several banks that it took into public ownership in 2009.

The Millennium Development Goals

Introduced in 2000 at the UN Millennium Summit, the MDGs were the first internationally agreed set of collective goals on development (see Box 3.4, page 116). Previously, nation-states and IGOs had pursued their own development goals independently.

The MDGs helped states to coordinate their efforts, ensuring that duplication of effort was kept to a minimum. They also provided a useful set of guidance to developing states themselves on how they should prioritise development activities.

MDG successes

The MDGs achieved a number of significant successes:
- Extreme poverty was reduced by half, falling from 1.9 billion people in 1990 to 836 million in 2015. The UN reported that most progress had been made since 2000.
- There was an increase in primary school enrolment, from 83% in 2000 to 91% in 2015. The proportion of girls in school also increased.
- Child mortality was reduced by more than half, from 90 to 43 deaths per 1,000 live births between 1990 and 2015.
- Maternal health improved, with mortality declining by 45% worldwide since 1990. A particularly dramatic decrease of 64% was seen in southern Asia.

There have been several notes of caution alongside the apparent success of the MDGs:
- Economic development and rapid growth in China have been responsible for most of the success in eradicating extreme poverty. Progress elsewhere has been less marked.
- The target of halving the number of people suffering from hunger was missed.
- UN Secretary-General Ban Ki-moon acknowledged that global inequality remained a significant issue.
- The private sector was not given enough of a role in the implementation of the MDGs. This is a gap that has been addressed in the SDGs.

The Sustainable Development Goals

The UN introduced the SDGs in 2015 to replace the MDGs. The key aim of sustainable development is that the development needs of today must not risk the development needs of tomorrow. The SDGs have the same lifespan as the MDGs (a 15-year period lasting until 2030).

The SDGs cover new goals on the environment, including action on climate change, clean water and more sustainable management of ecosystems. Furthermore, there is reference to political freedom as a key goal for the first

The MDGs were successful in producing an increase in the number of children attending primary schools

time, through the inclusion of peace, justice and strong institutions. This responds to one criticism of the MDGs, that it did not refer to conflict, and makes developing peace and security one of the major factors to tackle in reducing underdevelopment and poverty (SDG 16).

Synoptic links

In Component 2, the ecologism option further explores the relationship between mankind's desire for material wellbeing and the importance of respecting the planet as our source of life. According to US author and ecologist Aldo Leopold, humans have no special status on the planet and must sustain it out of duty and reverence.

The SDGs retained many of the MDGs where progress had been made but where there was still more to do. For example, the SDGs retain the commitment to end poverty.

With 17 SDGs, some have criticised the new goals for being too complicated and too extensive (see Box 4.6).

The Sustainable Development Goals

1   **No poverty:** end poverty in all its forms everywhere. A particular focus on a wider definition of poverty to include lack of basic services and hunger.
2   **Zero hunger:** end hunger, achieve food security and improved nutrition, and promote sustainable agriculture.
3   **Good health and wellbeing:** ensure healthy lives and promote wellbeing for all at all ages.
4   **Quality education:** ensure inclusive and equitable quality education and promote lifelong learning opportunities for all.
5   **Gender equality:** achieve gender equality and empower all women and girls.
6   **Clean water and sanitation:** ensure availability and sustainable management of water and sanitation for all.
7   **Affordable and clean energy:** ensure access to affordable, reliable, sustainable and modern energy for all.
8   **Decent work and economic growth:** promote sustained, inclusive and sustainable economic growth, full and productive employment, and decent work for all.
9   **Industry, innovation and infrastructure:** build resilient infrastructure, promote inclusive and sustainable industrialisation, and foster innovation.
10 **Reduced inequalities:** reduce income inequality within and among countries.
11 **Sustainable cities and communities:** make cities and human settlements inclusive, safe, resilient and sustainable.
12 **Responsible consumption and production:** ensure sustainable consumption and production patterns.
13 **Climate action:** take urgent action to combat climate change and its impacts by regulating emissions and promoting developments in renewable energy.
14 **Life below water:** conserve and sustainably use the oceans, seas and marine resources for sustainable development.
15 **Life on land:** protect, restore and promote sustainable use of terrestrial ecosystems, sustainably manage forests, combat desertification, and halt and reverse land degradation and biodiversity loss.
16 Peace, justice and strong institutions.
17 Partnerships for the goals.

The Millennium and Sustainable Development Goals

The MDGs

■ The first global attempt to agree and implement a coordinated set of world development targets.
■ Eight goals, focused primarily on human development.

The SDGs

■ Agreed by the UN in 2015 to replace the MDGs.
■ The 17 SDGs took the MDGs forward, keeping some of the MDGs but adding new goals including tackling climate change and a focus on political development, with the inclusion of goals to promote peace, justice and strong institutions.

What you should know

Having read this chapter, you should have knowledge and understanding of the following:

- Global economic governance efforts began with the Bretton Woods Conference in 1944. Since then, the International Monetary Fund (IMF), World Bank and World Trade Organization (WTO) have been the principal means of coordinating efforts to bring about global economic development, promote free trade and reduce poverty.
- The WTO at one time worked effectively to reduce trade barriers and protectionism. As it has grown larger, it has become more difficult to find global agreement on further extending global free trade.
- The IMF provides an essential safety net for states when they get into economic difficulty. States are working together to ensure that they limit the wider negative impact of states' economic difficulties. The IMF has sometimes been criticised for demanding that states comply with its recommendations in return for loans, creating a clash with state sovereignty.
- There is still a divide between the richest and the poorest states. Global inequality between states and within states is rising. World systems theory argues that the richest states are trapping the poorer states in a cycle of dependency, which prevents poorer states from catching up.

Further reading

Collier, P. (2008) *The Bottom Billion*. Oxford University Press.
Easterly, W. (2007) *White Man's Burden*. Oxford University Press.
Moyo, D. (2010) *Dead Aid*. Penguin.
Sachs, J. (2005) *The End of Poverty*. Penguin.

Exam focus

Section A

1 Examine the strengths and weaknesses of the International Monetary Fund. *[12 marks]*

2 Examine the extent to which the World Trade Organization is no longer fit for purpose. *[12 marks]*

3 Examine the claim that the G7/8 and G20 are more effective than formal international governmental organisations. *[12 marks]*

Section C

1 Evaluate the extent to which economic global governance is failing when it is needed most. *[30 marks]*

2 Evaluate the claim that there is a link between globalisation and poverty. *[30 marks]*

3 Evaluate the extent to which nation-states are better able than other actors in global politics to solve the challenges of economic globalisation. *[30 marks]*

Global governance: human rights

Getting you started

Death by firing squad

In December 2012, an Indonesian court convicted Lindsay Sandiford (56) of drug smuggling. She had arrived at Bali airport with 4.8 kg of cocaine in her suitcase. She had subsequently cooperated with the police and during the trial expressed remorse for what she had done. Her defence lawyers argued that she had been pressured into carrying the drugs because of threats to her family. In January 2013, however, a panel of judges sentenced her to death by firing squad.

The verdict caused widespread shock and disbelief. Sandiford's local MP, Martin Horwood, expressed outrage: 'The days of the death penalty ought to be past. This is not the way that a country that now values democracy and human rights should really be behaving'. UK newspapers were similarly indignant, reminding their readers that Sandiford was both a mother and a grandmother, and a pawn in the hands of more experienced drugs dealers and traffickers. The Foreign Office made representations to the Indonesian government, as did former UK prime minister David Cameron. The anti-death penalty pressure group Reprieve took up Sandiford's case, arguing that, as a vulnerable individual, the case demonstrates the barbarity of the death penalty.

On 25 June 2016, Sandiford celebrated her sixtieth birthday in prison with the threat of the firing squad still looming over her, since the Indonesian Supreme Court had rejected all appeals for mercy. A month later, three Nigerians and an Indonesian were taken from death row and shot for drug smuggling at the Nusankambangan prison island.

However, the outrage was mainly restricted to the UK. Indonesian judges presiding over Sandiford's case have so far rejected appeals for clemency, arguing that her actions deliberately undermined the country's war against drugs. It is impossible to estimate just how many people would have suffered as a result of one person's actions, but such a large amount of cocaine would have had a devastating impact on society. In such circumstances, the severity of the crime may fully justify the use of capital punishment. The imposition of the death penalty may also, hopefully, deter others from smuggling, potentially saving many more lives. Indeed, the Indonesian president, Joko Widodo, has publicly stated that executions of drug smugglers are 'positive' and that other countries must respect how he is dealing with a problem estimated to kill 18,000 young Indonesians a year. Polls suggest that most Indonesians agree with their president on this principle.

The sad case of Lindsay Sandiford, therefore, demonstrates how complicated the issue of human rights is. It is all too easy to be glib and simplistic when talking about 'human rights'. Whose rights are we talking about anyway? Are they the rights of the individual or of society? Are these **universal human rights** or do specific states and cultures determine them? Should religion play any role in determining human rights or is this a secular concern? Is it possible to have an international standard of human rights and, if so, could this ever be enforced? Or are human rights best determined according to Westphalian principles of state sovereignty?

Superficially, then, human rights might seem to be self-evident. In reality the nature, definition, extent and enforceability of human rights are all contested. This chapter will demonstrate that the theory of **international law** raises fundamental issues of sovereignty and identity that are among the most controversial in international relations.

Key terms

Universal human rights Rights to which people are entitled because they are human, regardless of race, nationality, sex or religion. They are fundamental, universal, indivisible and non-negotiable, since they define the fundamental freedoms which lie at the core of humanity.

International law The rules that govern relations between states. States generally accept the binding authority of international law, since it provides a framework for cooperation between states and guards against the dangers of global anarchy. However, there is no supranational authority that can force obedience.

Human rights and international law

The origins and development of international law

International law has helped govern international relations since the rise of the nation-state from the seventeenth century onwards. For most of modern history, international law has been based upon the way in which states react to each other. Adherence to international law has been based upon the principle of reciprocity. In other words, if you obey an international agreement, it is more likely that another state will see a reciprocal interest in obeying it as well. This is why during the Second World War the European powers did not use poison gas against each other. Pragmatic considerations of self-interest governed this decision — moral considerations did not enter into it at all.

Today, most countries abide by the terms of the Treaty on the Non-Proliferation of Nuclear Weapons (1968) and so do not seek to acquire nuclear weapons. Their reasoning generally derives not from any moral revulsion towards nuclear weapons, but from the belief that if they disobey the treaty, others will follow suit, making the world much more dangerous and so undermining global security.

The Nuremberg Trials, 1945–46

Westphalian principles of state sovereignty have traditionally enshrined the concept that human rights are relative. This means that the government under which one lives determines the nature and extent of one's rights. However, following the Second World War the Nuremberg Trials, in which leading Nazis were tried as war criminals for 'crimes against humanity' and 'waging aggressive warfare', demonstrated what could happen if a government acted in defiance of all moral principles. In such circumstances, the realist defence that the actions of a national government were outside the prerogative of the international community seemed inadequate. The way in which the Nazi state had persecuted many of its own citizens, waged war and committed acts of mass genocide suggested that nation-states could not be allowed to act with impunity. If the international community did not learn lessons from these horrors, they would be repeated. As the US chief prosecutor Robert Jackson put it in his opening address at the trial:

> The wrongs which we seek to condemn and punish have been so calculated, so malignant, and so devastating, that civilization cannot tolerate their being ignored, because it cannot survive their being repeated.

The crimes exposed at Nuremberg made the development of a human rights-based approach to international law an urgent concern. No longer was international law simply a way in which states achieved just enough global stability to survive. Instead, it would have to take into account human rights as well as states' self-interest. In order to achieve this, nation-states would need

The crimes exposed at Nuremberg made the development of a human rights-based approach to international law an urgent concern

to come together to establish international institutions of justice and global standards of moral behaviour. Only by doing this could they create a world of peace and justice, and contain the aggressive impulses of nation-states. According to the Spanish-American philosopher George Santayana, 'Those who cannot remember the past are condemned to repeat it'. This dictum had particular meaning for those who met at San Francisco in 1945 to establish the United Nations (UN).

The Charter of the United Nations, 1945

The Charter of the United Nations was drafted in San Francisco, USA during the closing months of the Second World War and in October 1945 the UN was formally established. Given that the two world wars had caused suffering on a global scale, the charter sought to 'banish the scourge of war, which twice in our lifetime had brought untold sorrow to mankind'. It would do this by establishing the UN as the international forum in which disputes would be settled, development encouraged and human rights affirmed. As President Harry Truman put it, when he addressed delegates at the closing session of the UN conference:

> If we had had this charter a few years ago and, above all, the will to use it millions now dead would be alive. If we should falter in the future in our will to use it, millions now living will surely die.

Case study

The Four Freedoms

On 6 January 1941, US president Franklin D. Roosevelt defined the principles by which democracies should live in his 'Four Freedoms' — Freedom of Speech, Freedom of Religion, Freedom from Want and Freedom from Fear. According to Roosevelt, these Freedoms represented:

> No vision of a distant millennium. It is a definite basis for a kind of world attainable in our own time and generation. That kind of world is the very antithesis of the so-called new order of tyranny, which the dictators seek to create with the crash of a bomb.

When the USA entered the Second World War following the Japanese bombing of Pearl Harbor on 7 December 1941, the Four Freedoms became a defining war aim of the Western democracies. In 1948, when the president's widow, Eleanor Roosevelt, chaired the committee that drew up the Universal Declaration of Human Rights, the Four Freedoms were given concrete expression. Today, these values remain at the heart of attempts to create a global standard of rights and justice.

The Universal Declaration of Human Rights, 1948

In 1948, the UN drew up the Universal Declaration of Human Rights (UDHR), which established the absolute civil, political and social freedoms that all humans enjoy. The UDHR is based upon 'the inherent dignity' and 'the equal and inalienable rights of all members of the human family'. According to Eleanor Roosevelt, who chaired the committee that drew up the document, 'the declaration may well become the international Magna Carta for all men everywhere'. Indeed, it is often regarded as one of the most influential political statements of all time. The radical Labour MP Tony Benn was inspired by the UDHR's vision of humanity dedicated to peace and united against aggression on a troop-ship home at the end of the Second World War. Fifty years after its establishment, Pope John Paul II stated to the UN General Assembly (UNGA) that the UDHR, 'reminds us that we do not live in an irrational or meaningless world' and that 'there is a moral logic which is built into human life'.

The UDHR has also provided the basis for the International Covenant on Civil and Political Rights (1966) and the International Covenant on Economic, Social and Cultural Rights (1966), both of which entered into force in 1976 and codified the rights of the UDHR. Taken together, these three documents comprise the International Bill of Human Rights and act as a constant reminder that there are international standards of moral behaviour that states should aspire to and to which they can be held accountable.

United Nations High Commissioner for Human Rights, 1993

The end of the Cold War provided human rights with a new centrality in international relations. In 1993, at the World Conference on Human Rights, the position of UN High Commissioner for Human Rights was established. The commissioner's responsibility is to promote adherence to human rights and expose their violation.

Although lacking in coercive power, the position is important since it carries great moral authority. Since 2014, Jordanian Zeid Ra'ad al-Hussein has acted in the role. In 2016, he gave an especially evocative global update on human rights in which he reminded us all that:

> Hate is becoming mainstreamed. Walls, which tormented previous generations, and have never yielded any sustainable solution to any problem, are returning... Human rights are not costly — they are priceless.

The role of non-governmental organisations

Growing numbers of non-governmental organisations (NGOs) have also highlighted human rights abuses. These include:
- Amnesty International
- Human Rights Watch
- Red Cross
- Save the Children

These global pressure groups use the internet to its full potential, ensuring instantaneous coverage of humanitarian crises. This puts new pressure on the international community to pay attention to abuses. Human Rights Watch, for example, publishes its annual *World Report*, which catalogues nation-states' records on human rights. In 2017, it accused Syrian president Bashar al-Assad of deploying 'a war crimes strategy' in his country, while it has also been highly critical of the growing authoritarianism of China, Russia and Turkey, in which the rule of law is being undermined. In 2016, it also accused President Trump of 'a campaign fomenting hatred' and focused on the way in which European populism is undermining respect for human rights.

How successfully do judicial institutions enforce human rights?

The International Court of Justice

Sometimes known as the World Court, the International Court of Justice (ICJ) is the judicial agency of the UN and permanently sits in The Hague, the Netherlands. It was established by the Charter of the United Nations in 1945 and began operation in 1946.

Key term

International Court of Justice (ICJ) The UN's primary judicial branch established by the UN Charter in 1945 (but started operations in 1946). Sometimes known as the World Court.

The scales of justice: the ICJ is the primary judicial branch of the UN

What is the purpose of the International Court of Justice?

The ICJ's 15 judges represent the 'main forms of civilization and the principal legal systems of the world'. It settles legal disputes submitted to it by states and provides advisory opinions on legal questions submitted to it by international branches, agencies and the UN General Assembly. The ICJ therefore attempts to enforce the rule of law in international disputes in order to create a more stable and peaceful world.

Article 94 of the UN Charter lays down that all members of the UN should, 'comply with the decision of the Court in any case to which it is a party'. If a state does not comply with an ICJ judgment, the other party may approach the UN Security Council (UNSC) to enforce the judgment.

In what ways has the International Court of Justice been successful?

Liberals regard the ICJ as a vital way of establishing a more rules-based approach to international affairs. Rather than resorting to war, cases can be submitted to the ICJ for arbitration. The ICJ possesses great moral authority and nation-states can be unwilling to question its ruling. It has been successful in resolving a number of disputes:

- In 1986, it resolved a border clash between Burkina Faso and Mali.
- In 1992, it settled a complicated border dispute between El Salvador and Honduras.
- In 2002, it settled a dispute between Nigeria and Cameroon over the ownership of an oil-rich peninsula.

Why has the International Court of Justice not been more successful?

Although the ICJ is supposed to operate as a World Court, resolving issues between states before they become armed struggles, its effectiveness is severely limited. Realism still influences the behaviour of states — as 'power-maximisers', states will often put their sovereign interest above that of international law, so challenging the authority of the court.

ICJ influence is therefore undermined because:

- its liberal principles conflict with realist state egoism
- it cannot initiate cases and can only try cases that are presented to it
- states are able to choose whether or not to be subject to the decisions of the court by signing an optional clause, which accepts in advance that they will be subject to the court's ruling (in February 2017, only 72 of the 193 members of the ICJ had signed this optional clause)
- although the UNSC is supposed to enforce ICJ rulings, the veto-wielding permanent five members would be unlikely to do this — this is because the only effective way of ensuring compliance would be coercive action but, according to Chapter 7 of the UN Charter, this can only be undertaken when international peace and security are threatened

As a result of these limitations there have been a number of cases when the ICJ has delivered judgments that the corresponding state has ignored. In such circumstances, it has been almost impossible to hold that state accountable for its actions:

- In 1980, Iran refused to acknowledge ICJ sovereignty when the USA brought a case against it for seizing the US embassy in Tehran in 1979.
- In 1984, the Sandinista government of Nicaragua brought a case against the USA for aiding the Contra rebels by mining Nicaraguan harbours. Although the ICJ found in favour of Nicaragua, the USA refused to accept the judgment, arguing that its actions were helping states like El Salvador that were 'threatened' by Nicaraguan-backed Communist rebels and were therefore 'entirely consistent with international law'.
- In 2012, Colombia announced that it no longer recognised ICJ jurisdiction after it decided a maritime border case in favour of Nicaragua. According to Colombia's president, Juan Mantel Santos, 'the borders between nations cannot be in the hands of a court of law... They must be drawn by agreement between the countries involved'.
- In 2014, Australia brought a case against Japan, condemning its 'scientific' whaling programme in the Antarctic. The ICJ decided in favour of Australia and Japan accepted the decision. However, in 2015, Japan resumed whaling, albeit on a more limited scale, in defiance of the ban.
- Advisory opinions are even more difficult to put into action and depend upon the willing compliance of a state. For example, when the UNGA asked for advice on the wall that Israel was building to separate it from the Palestinian territories, the ICJ declared the structure 'illegal'. The then-Israeli prime minister, Ariel Sharon, condemned the ruling as 'one-sided and politically motivated' and made clear that 'the state of Israel absolutely rejects the ruling [of the court]'.
- In 2010, the ICJ delivered the advisory opinion that Kosovo was legitimately able to declare independence from Serbia in 2008. The decision was welcomed by those states that recognise Kosovo's independence, but ignored by Russia as a key supporter of Serbia.

United Nations special tribunals

In the 1990s, there was growing concern about the way in which the international community should react to genocide, war crimes and crimes against humanity occurring in Rwanda, Sierra Leone and the former Yugoslavia. The UN also worked with the Cambodian government to try the surviving perpetrators of the country's 1970s genocide.

As a result, the UNSC authorised the establishment of four UN war crimes tribunals. These represented a major advance in the development of international law, since an international panel of judges would judge crimes that had happened within states. The tribunals would also have the authority to try heads of state for crimes against humanity and set a precedent for the establishment of the International Criminal Court (ICC) in 2002.

The aims of the UN tribunals were to:

- punish and bring to justice those guilty of human rights abuses (retribution)
- develop the liberal principle of a global community that will no longer tolerate nation-states deliberately abusing the rights of its citizens
- establish the legal principle that the international community can try heads of government for crimes committed within their country
- make public the extent and horror of crimes of genocide, war and crimes against humanity so that they not be repeated

Former Yugoslavia

The International Criminal Tribunal for the Former Yugoslavia was instituted in 1993. It was the first international court set up since the Nuremberg Trials (1945–46) to try individuals accused of war crimes. Its aim was to 'spear-head the shift from impunity to accountability', since without the influence of the tribunal it is very unlikely that the Balkan states would have been willing or able to prosecute those accused of human rights violations. Its supporters noted a number of successes:

- The court claims to have 'brought justice for thousands of victims and given them a voice', and so advanced the cause of a rules-based standard of international justice.
- Like Nuremberg, the cases before the tribunal have made public the atrocities committed so it is now much more difficult to deny them. The trial, for example, of the Bosnian Serb leaders Ratko Mladić and Radovan Karadžić uncovered vast amounts of evidence relating to the 1995 Srebrenica Massacre.
- By 2017, the court had convicted and sentenced 83 war criminals, ranging from low-ranking soldiers to political leaders and senior figures in the military. Radovan Karadžić was sentenced to 40 years in prison for the Srebrenica Massacre. Paramilitary leaders, such as Milan Lukić, also received lengthy prison sentences, while the Bosnian Serb commander Drago Nikolić was sentenced to 35 years. The last case the court tried was that of the Bosnian Serb general Ratko Mladić, who was accused of genocide and war crimes.

Case study

Slobodan Milošević

Slobodan Milošević was Serbia's president from 1989 until mass protests overthrew him in 2000. During the Balkan Wars (1991–95) he backed Serb military forces in Bosnia and Croatia. However, in 1995 he used his influence to help broker the Dayton Peace Accords, which briefly gained him Western goodwill.

In 1998–99, Albanians in Kosovo stepped up their attempts to break free from the Serb Federation. In response, Milošević was accused of instigating ethnic cleansing, provoking the North Atlantic Treaty Organization's (NATO) air war against Serbia. Following his overthrow, Milošević was arrested and then deported to The Hague, where he was put on trial before the UN Tribunal for the Former Yugoslavia.

Milošević never accepted the court's legitimacy and died in 2006 of a heart attack while the case against him was being heard. His trial for war crimes was the first for a former head of state and set an important precedent in the development of international law.

Cambodia

The Cambodia Tribunal is a national court that was established in conjunction with the UN in 1997. It has both Cambodian and international judges, and has tried the surviving members of the murderous Khmer Rouge government (1975–79), which was responsible for the deaths of 2 million people. The court has handed out three life imprisonment sentences, to:

■ Nuon Chea, Khmer Rouge chief political ideologist
■ Kaing Guek Eav, head of the S21 mass killing centre
■ Khieu Samphan, the former head of state

As well as punishing the guilty, the tribunal has engaged many young Cambodians in a better understanding of what happened in their country during the 1970s — in the first trial involving multiple Khmer Rouge leaders, almost 100,000 people attended the hearings in the capital Phnom Penh. The court also offers internships to Cambodian and international lawyers so that they can develop their understanding of international law and genocide.

Rwanda

The International Criminal Tribunal for Rwanda investigating the Rwandan genocide, in which 800,000 Tutsis were murdered, opened its first case in 1997. The tribunal convicted 61 individuals of complicity in the genocide, including former prime minister Jean Kambanda, who became the first head of government to be convicted on charges of genocide. Significantly, the tribunal has developed international law by establishing the precedent that rape could be used as a way of perpetrating genocide.

Sierra Leone

In 2002, the UN established the Special Court for Sierra Leone to try those who had committed atrocities during the country's 10-year civil war. During the 1990s, Liberian president Charles Taylor had supported opposition groups in their attempts to gain control of the country's diamond mines. In the resulting carnage, the Revolutionary United Front and allied criminal gangs, such as the

The International Criminal Tribunal into the Rwandan genocide led to former prime minister Jean Kambanda being the first head of government to be convicted on charges of genocide

West Side Boys, murdered or hacked off the limbs of their victims. By 1999, when the British intervened to end the violence, 50,000 had already died. In 2012, the tribunal sentenced Taylor to 50 years' imprisonment for complicity in the civil war's atrocities, the first head of state to be convicted of war crimes. According to prosecutor Brenda J. Hollis, the conviction of Taylor was so important because it 'reinforces the new reality, that Heads of State will be held to account for war crimes and other international crimes' and that 'No person, no matter how powerful, is above the law'. The tribunal has also imprisoned 15 others, including Augustine Gbao, a leading commander of Sierra Leone's Revolutionary United Front, who was sentenced to 25 years in prison.

Chapter 5 Global governance: human rights

Key terms

International tribunals
UN-mandated international criminal tribunals established to prosecute those responsible for crimes against humanity, war crimes and acts of genocide.

Humanitarian intervention
Based upon the liberal principle that as members of a global community, all states should strive to protect human life through intervention in another sovereign state, if that state is unwilling to resolve a conflict or unable to cope with a natural catastrophe.

The limitations of international tribunals

At the end of the Second World War, the Nuremberg and Tokyo **international tribunals**, which tried those accused of war crimes, were accused by some of delivering 'victors' justice'. The USA, for example, sat in judgment on Japanese war criminals and yet the Americans could themselves have been accused of war crimes for the fire-bombing of Japanese cities and the destruction of Hiroshima and Nagasaki with nuclear bombs. At Nuremberg, Soviet judges represented a regime that was responsible for mass murder, while the British destruction of Dresden, Germany in March 1945, which led to the deaths of thousands of civilian refugees, may well have been a war crime.

The same criticism has been made of more recent tribunals.

- Serbia has criticised the Tribunal for the Former Yugoslavia for unfairly focusing on crimes committed by Serbs and not investigating the war crimes they themselves endured. Former Russian permanent representative at the UN Vitaly Churkin criticised the acquittal on appeal of Ante Gotovina, a lieutenant-general in the Croatian army, and the court's dismissal of the case against Ramush Haradinaj, head of the Kosovo Liberation Army. Decisions such as this, he argued, demonstrated the court's inbuilt bias and have inflamed, rather than reduced, ethnic tensions in the region.

- Mary Robinson, then-UN High Commissioner for Human Rights, criticised NATO air bombing of Serbia during the Kosovo War in 1999. According to Robinson, the civilian loss of life invalidated claims that this was a **humanitarian intervention**. NATO might even be held responsible for claims that it had inflicted war crimes. Both Human Rights Watch and Amnesty International, in particular, condemned as a war crime the deliberate bombing of the headquarters of Serb Radio/Television, which killed 16 civilian workers. However, NATO has never been held responsible for the military actions it carried out in Serbia. This may suggest that there are some grounds for allegations of 'victors' justice'.

- The UN tribunal investigating the Rwandan genocide has also been criticised for only having convicted Hutus. The Tutsi Rwandan Patriotic Front, which now forms the country's government, also committed atrocities during this period. The court never investigated these crimes, leading to accusations that the tribunal has endorsed the official 'narrative' of the war.

- The trial of Charles Taylor of Liberia was held in The Hague and he has been subsequently imprisoned in the UK. Western powers also funded the tribunal's operation, and so critics claim that the court has helped to reinforce neocolonial stereotypes that Africa cannot deliver justice itself.

The effectiveness of international tribunals has also been undermined by the circumstances in which they are established and the extent to which nation-states are prepared to cooperate in their establishment:

- Unlike other heads of state, former Iraqi leader Saddam Hussein was not tried by an international court. Instead, the USA declared that his countrymen could try him in Iraq. Critics of the trial's legitimacy claim that this demonstrates how powerful countries can manipulate international law — by being tried in Iraq, Saddam would be eligible for the death penalty, which international UN tribunals cannot deliver. In addition to this, the requirements for a guilty verdict in Iraq were simply that the tribunal be 'satisfied' of guilt rather than proving guilt 'beyond a reasonable doubt'. Such a partisan approach to global justice challenges the whole rationale of criminal tribunals. If they are only set up in certain circumstances, maybe they do simply represent victors' justice?

- In 2015, Russia vetoed the establishment of a UN tribunal into the shooting down of Malaysian Flight 17 over Ukraine. Russia was widely condemned for being the only member of the UNSC to exercise the veto. The former US envoy to the UN Samantha Power criticised Russia for 'callously disregarding the public outcry in the grieving nations'. However, Russia felt that the court would not serve in its interests and so was able to resist its establishment.

- In a case brought by the Philippines in 2016, an international maritime tribunal in The Hague found that China was illegally claiming Scarborough Shoal and the Spratly Islands as territory. According to the Philippines, China's 'nine-dash line', which it uses to demarcate its territorial claims, is unlawful under the UN Convention on the Law of the Sea, to which both countries are signatories. However, China boycotted the proceedings, arguing that the court had no jurisdiction to try the case and that it would not accept its verdict.

The International Criminal Court

What is the purpose of the International Criminal Court?

During the 1990s, the euphoria that greeted the end of the Cold War soon gave way to horror and disbelief that mass murder, ethnic cleansing and even genocide could claim so many lives in nationalist, ethnic and tribal conflicts. Determined UN secretaries-general Boutros Boutros-Ghali and Kofi Annan put their moral weight behind the creation of an international criminal court. UN special tribunals had set a precedent for the development of human rights-based international law. However, an international criminal court would sit in permanent session as a constant reminder to the global community of the permanence, impartiality and reach of international justice.

In 1998, the Rome Statute established the **International Criminal Court (ICC)** as 'a court of last resort'. It would try individuals, including heads of state, accused of genocide, crimes against humanity and war crimes when national governments were unprepared or unable to do this themselves. In 2002, the ICC was established at The Hague to try 'the most serious crimes of concern to the international community'. A total of 124 states (2017) have ratified the Rome Statute and so accept the ICC's jurisdiction.

In what ways has the International Criminal Court been successful?

The ICC has had two determined chief prosecutors: Luis Moreno-Ocampo (2003–12) and Fatou Bensouda (2012–). By 2017, the ICC had secured three convictions.

1 **2012:** Thomas Lubanga Dyilo, a Congolese warlord, was sentenced to 14 years in prison for human rights abuses, including recruiting child soldiers.
2 **2014:** Germain Katanga, another Congolese warlord, was sentenced to 12 years for atrocities committed during Congo's civil war.
3 **2016:** Jean-Pierre Bemba, former vice-president of the Democratic Republic of the Congo, was sentenced to 18 years for deploying sexual violence as a weapon of war.

In a landmark case, the former president of Côte d'Ivoire, Laurent Gbagbo, is currently appearing before the ICC on charges of 'orchestrating a campaign of violence' in order to illegally hang on to power.

Why has the International Criminal Court not been more successful?

Although the ICC was supposed to initiate a new approach to global justice based upon the centrality of human rights, it soon became obvious that sovereign state self-interest would undermine its liberal intentions:

■ When the Rome Statute was voted upon in 1998, worryingly only 120 states voted in its favour, while 21 abstained and seven voted against it. Right from the start its 'international scope' was significantly in doubt.

■ China, Russia and the USA (the three most powerful members of the UNSC) do not accept the ICC's jurisdiction over their internal sovereign affairs. The USA has signed a number of bilateral agreements with other states in which they are required not to cooperate with the court in handing over US citizens to its jurisdiction. India also does not recognise the ICC's authority, meaning that 70% of the world's population is outside the jurisdiction of the court.

■ The unwillingness of powerful, opinion-forming states to accept limits on their sovereignty significantly undermines the ICC's scope and authority. In 2017, just 124 states fully accepted the Rome Statute, demonstrating that the ICC has failed to develop influence in the way its founders hoped.

■ The ICC undertakes to investigate cases presented to it by nation-states or by the UNSC, although the ICC's chief prosecutor can also take the initiative in launching investigations. However, the court has no coercive power of its own and if nation-states are unprepared to cooperate with it, there is little it can do.

■ Although the ICC indicted Sudanese president Omar al-Bashir for war crimes in Darfur, he continued to travel widely in Africa without arrest. The ICC eventually dropped its investigations into alleged war crimes in Darfur due to the UNSC's lack of cooperation and Sudan's unwillingness to accept the authority of what al-Bashir called 'a colonial court'.

■ The ICC indicted Kenyan president Uhuru Kenyatta for the killing of over 1,000 people following the country's disputed 2007 election. Although Kenya, unlike Sudan, accepted the jurisdiction of the court, the Kenyan government refused to hand over the necessary evidence for the case to be prosecuted. As a result, Chief Prosecutor Fatou Bensouda decided to drop the case. In response, President Kenyatta claimed that the ICC's attempt to prosecute him had been 'blatantly biased' and that the court was simply the 'toy of declining imperialist powers'.

■ Since its establishment, the ICC has only indicted and convicted Africans. This has raised complaints that it is institutionally biased. Consequently, the African Union (AU) has urged its members not to cooperate with the ICC and in 2016 Burundi, Namibia and, most significantly, South Africa declared that they were severing their ties with the ICC, as membership conflicted with their national interests.

- A further blow to the ICC's authority came in 2016 when President Putin withdrew his signature from the Rome Statute over the court's criticism of the Russian annexation of Crimea. Russia had not ratified the Rome Statute and so was not subject to ICC authority but the decision nonetheless further undermined the Court's authority. The Russian Foreign Ministry's criticism of the ICC for being 'one-sided and inefficient' is therefore another sign that the goodwill it needs to flourish is in increasingly short supply.

The ICC's authority has been undermined by the continued importance of state sovereignty and claims that it has a neocolonial agenda based on outdated western European ideals of cultural superiority. Its influence is likely to be further damaged if states follow the lead of President Trump and even more fiercely prioritise their national interests over those of the global community. In his inaugural speech, President Trump declared that, 'it is the right of all nations to put their own interests first'. Such an assertion of state realism over global liberalism could prove fatal to the ICC.

Synoptic links

The problems that international judicial institutions face in seeking to establish a global standard of accountability are associated with all the key elements of global politics: the importance of state sovereignty, the tension between realism and liberalism, and the importance of power in determining outcomes.

Case study

Law not war: Benjamin Ferencz

Benjamin B. Ferencz was born in 1920 in Hungary. A year later his parents immigrated with him to the USA. He won a scholarship to Harvard Law School and during the Second World War fought his way across Europe as a sergeant in the US army. In 1947, he stood as US chief prosecutor at the trial of Nazi Einsatzgruppen (task force) leaders, who were held responsible for the deaths of over a million people. Associated Press called it 'the biggest murder trial in history', and Ferencz opened his prosecution by reminding the court of 'man's right to live in peace and dignity' as he made 'his plea of humanity to law'.

Since then, Ferencz, as both a lawyer and peace activist, has devoted his life to the cause of international law, arguing that the rule of law must replace the rule of force. As a leading advocate of international justice, his ideas played a significant role in the establishment of the ICC in 2002, and in 2011 the prosecution invited him to speak at the conclusion of the

trial of Congolese warlord Thomas Lubanga, the first case to be heard by the ICC. Sixty-four years after leading the prosecution at Nuremberg, Ferencz once again made his 'plea of humanity to law', as he called for international standards of justice to be used to ensure that 'human beings behave in a humane and lawful manner'.

Dismayed by the withdrawal of South Africa from the ICC, he regards British prime minister Theresa May's criticisms of the European Convention on Human Rights as 'short-sighted'. At 97, he admits that he is still busy 'trying to save the world'. You can learn more at **benferencz.org**.

Lawyer and peace activist Benjamin Ferencz

Case study

Mike Campbell (Pvt) Ltd vs Zimbabwe

Following independence in 1979, the Zimbabwe government sought to create a fairer distribution of land between white and blacks since, historically, the white minority had owned a hugely excessive share of the land. During the early 2000s, Robert Mugabe's government accelerated the takeover of white land by tacitly encouraging 'war veterans' to invade and claim it for themselves, even though they had no legal claim to it. In 2006, a law was passed, which gave the Zimbabwean government the authority to compulsorily acquire selected land. The existing 'owners' would have to leave it or face eviction.

Facing the loss of his land, a white farmer, Mike Campbell, applied to the tribunal of the Southern African Development Community (SADC) for a judgment in the case. As a member of SADC, Zimbabwe was bound by the court's authority to settle issues involving 'human rights, democracy and the rule of law'. In the resulting 2008 case, the tribunal declared that the Zimbabwe government had acted illegally in nationalising the land, since Campbell, and others, had been discriminated against on the grounds of race.

However, in 2009, Zimbabwe announced that the tribunal did not have authority in its internal affairs. According to President Mugabe:

> Land distribution will continue. It will not stop. The few remaining white farmers should quickly vacate their farms as they have no place there... Our land issues are not subject to the SADC tribunal.

Mike Campbell was subsequently beaten and tortured, and then evicted from his farm. He died in 2011. In the same year, the SADC suspended the tribunal as a result of criticism from the member states that it had no legitimacy to intervene in their domestic affairs.

Debate

Is the International Criminal Court effective?

Yes
- Since the ICC is in permanent session, unlike ad hoc tribunals, it provides a constant standard of international justice to which governments should aspire.
- By convicting human rights abusers before an international court, it establishes precedents for the development of international human rights-based law.
- By delivering retribution and punishment within countries, future human rights abuses may be deterred, as war criminals realise they cannot hide from justice behind borders.
- Its prosecution of Laurent Gbagbo has reinforced the principle that heads of state are morally responsible for their actions.
- It has recorded and made public evidence of atrocities, so making subsequent 'denial' more difficult.
- It is able to provide justice in cases where nation-states might not be able to, either because of prejudice or lack of governance.

No
- The ICC interferes with state sovereignty. Nation-states have the responsibility to protect their citizens. The international community has no mandate to intervene within states and the court therefore lacks legitimacy.
- Article 2 of the UN Charter lays down the principle of 'sovereign equality' of all member states and 'that nothing contained in the present Charter shall authorize the United Nations to intervene in matters which are essentially in the domestic jurisdiction of any state'.
- It challenges the legitimacy of states to try cases within their own borders.
- Its authority is undermined by the refusal of three members of the UNSC (China, Russia and the USA) to accept its jurisdiction. With so many powerful countries absent, the ICC only provides 'partial' justice and cannot claim to provide international justice.
- By 2017, the ICC had only successfully prosecuted three individuals — it is costly and very slow moving and has achieved little.
- So far, the only people to have been indicted by the court are Africans. Given the global extent of human rights abuses, this indicates an inbuilt bias against Africa. This is why South Africa has withdrawn its signature from the court.

The International Court of Justice and the International Criminal Court

The International Court of Justice

- The ICJ was established in 1946 and is the judicial body of the UN.
- Its 15 judges sit in The Hague.
- All 193 countries that are UN members are party to the court.
- It settles disputes between states and can provide advisory opinions when approached by a UN agency.
- Its decisions are enforceable by the UNSC, although this has never occurred.
- If states refuse to accept ICJ rulings, it is very unlikely that they will be forced to comply.

The International Criminal Court

- The ICC opened in 2002 and is independent of the UN. The UNSC can refer cases to it or it can initiate cases itself.
- Its 18 judges all come from states that accept the ICC's jurisdiction. It sits in The Hague.
- 124 states have ratified the Rome Statute and so accept the ICC's jurisdiction.
- The ICC is independent of the UN.
- It prosecutes individuals who are charged with war crimes, genocide or crimes against humanity.
- Its decisions are binding on the individuals concerned.

The European Court of Human Rights

What is the purpose of the European Court of Human Rights?

In 1949, the Council of Europe (not to be confused with the EU) was established. It is responsible for promoting human rights and the rule of law in Europe, and in 1950 it introduced the European Convention on Human Rights (ECHR). In the wake of the devastation of the Second World War, the ECHR sought to define those rights that all European citizens could claim. This would protect the rights of individuals from possible persecution and so help to contribute to peace in Europe.

The European Court of Human Rights (ECtHR) was established in 1959. The court sits in Strasbourg, France and has 47 judges, one for each member of the European Council. European states and individuals can apply to the court in cases where they feel that human rights have been abused.

In what ways has the European Court of Human Rights been successful?

The ECtHR possesses great moral authority and its decisions, therefore, carry great weight. Compliance with its judgments is estimated to be 90%. The number of cases on which the ECtHR is asked to deliver verdicts has dramatically increased in recent years and in high-profile cases it has:

- condemned human-rights abuses by Russia in Chechnya (2005)
- ruled that the Bosnian constitution discriminates against Jews and Roma (2009)
- blocked the deportation of the radical cleric Abu Qatada from the UK to Jordan (2012)

Its supporters argue that it provides all European states with a moral code to emulate and, by its judgments, is continually holding European nation-states accountable for their observance of human rights.

Why has the European Court of Human Rights not been more successful?

As with other international courts, state sovereignty weakens the ECtHR's authority. If sovereign states ignore the rulings of the court, it has no coercive power. Therefore states may be prepared to risk criticism of the court if it means that they can still act according to their perceived national interest:

- The UK has acted in defiance of the ECtHR by not accepting rulings that UK prisoners should be allowed to vote and by authorising life imprisonment, which Strasbourg regards as 'inhumane'.

- In 2016, the ECtHR ruled that the UK government's Investigatory Powers Act was illegal. This is likely to cause another clash between the UK Parliament and Strasbourg. If parliament, as the supreme law-making body, decides to ignore the ruling, there is nothing practical that Strasbourg can do to enforce compliance.
- In 2015, Russia passed a law enshrining the principle that, in cases of conflict, Russian national law takes precedence over the rulings of the ECtHR.

Conclusion

Although they have achieved some successes and have also developed the principle that the international community can try crimes committed within states, international courts and tribunals do still find it difficult to enforce a universal standard of human rights due to a lack of:

- universal human rights hard law (anarchic world order)
- global jurisdiction to which all states are equally accountable
- enforcement tools

Human rights and state sovereignty

The clash between human rights and state sovereignty neatly illustrates the conflict between the realist and liberal approaches to international relations. For realists, the state determines the extent of the human rights that one may claim. Conversely, for liberals, human rights are universal and derive from our shared humanity rather than from the nation-state in which we are born or choose to live.

Why is it so difficult to enforce an international standard of human rights?

State sovereignty

The cosmopolitan values of universal human rights conflict with the theory of state sovereignty. According to the principle of external sovereignty, states are independent and autonomous, and so determine the legality of everything that happens within their borders. Article 2 of the UN Charter confirms the 'sovereign equality' of all nation-states, and UNGA Resolution 2131 (1965) acknowledges that, 'no state has the right to intervene, directly or indirectly, for any reason whatsoever, in the internal or external affairs of another state'.

As a result, the claims of international law, such as the UDHR, merely represent soft law. This is because nation-states remain sovereign over their internal affairs and can choose whether or not to accept outside jurisdiction in cases affecting their citizens. The lack of a supranational authority to which all states are equally accountable therefore undermines the potential for enforcing an international standard of human rights:

- The UK government is not only in defiance of the ECtHR by not allowing prisoners the vote and retaining life imprisonment for certain crimes, but from 2001 to 2005 the Blair government also 'derogated' from Article 5 when it held foreign terrorist suspects in prison without trial.
- Such is the USA's opposition to the ICC that during the George W. Bush administration, the country passed the American Service Members' Protection Act. This allows the president to take 'all necessary means' to release US soldiers held by the court.

- A UNSC resolution censured Israel in December 2016 for its policy of building settlements in the occupied territories. However, Israel's prime minister, Benjamin Netanyahu, immediately responded that, as a sovereign state, his country would continue constructing settlements.
- Saudi Arabia has also been criticised for flagrant human rights violations. In 2015, the blogger Raif Badawi was sentenced to 1,000 lashes and 10 years in jail for 'insulting Islam'. Saudi Arabia also legally equates terrorism with atheism, while abandoning Islam for another religion is a capital offence (apostasy).

Activity

Article 18 of the UDHR states that:

> Everyone has the right to freedom of thought, conscience and religion; this right includes freedom to change his religion or belief, and freedom, either alone or in community with others and in public or private, to manifest his religion or belief in teaching, practice, worship and observance

In Saudi Arabia, those who abandon Islam are deemed to have committed the crime of apostasy. According to Saudi Arabia's penal code, this is punishable by death. In China, Protestant House Churches are banned and a spiritual movement known as Falun Gong has been illegal since 1999. The ECHR provides for freedom of thought, conscience and religion (Article 9) and yet the *niqab* (Islamic full veil) is banned in France, Belgium and the Netherlands.

1   Should all states act according to the principles of Article 18 of the UDHR?
2   If states act in defiance of these principles, what should the international community do?

Different cultural traditions

In spite of the UDHR, there is no one standard of international human rights. Western powers have generally been influenced by the principles of the Enlightenment, which emphasised the importance of the individual's right to self-expression. It is therefore claimed that the concept of human rights is too eurocentric and does not take into account the competing claims of very different cultural traditions.

Cultural relativists argue that each culture determines the rights that its people enjoy, and that the concept of a universal standard of human rights is an example of Western cultural imperialism. The West may no longer possess territorial empires, but it still seeks moral empire through the transmission of its values via the UDHR and the ICC. As Edward W. Said put it in his 1978 book *Orientalism*:

> What is right for one society may not be right for other societies, a position that suggests that the outside world should respect the choices made by individual nation-states.

The following are examples of competing claims of different cultural traditions:

- The 1993 Bangkok Declaration of Asian governments rejects the West's focus on the rights of individuals and instead focuses on communal rights that we all owe to society. It is this emphasis on the community that many states, such as China, use to justify the death penalty.

- In the West, for most people gay rights are self-evident and yet these 'rights' should not be taken for granted. In large parts of the developing world, which is generally more socially conservative, homosexuality is a crime. In 72 countries, primarily in Africa and Asia, homosexuality is illegal and in ten countries it is punishable by death. When President Museveni of Uganda was, for example, criticised in the West for signing anti-gay legislation, which included the threat of life imprisonment, he responded that homosexuality is 'disgusting' and the outside world should 'respect African society and values … if we are wrong we shall find out in our own way'.

- In Russia, the conservative principles of the Orthodox Church are reflected in the government's unwillingness to treat homosexuality and heterosexuality as equally legitimate. Furthermore, the members of the pop group Pussy Riot were prosecuted for 'offending public morals by their sexually explicit actions' within an Orthodox Church. President Putin has said that individualism and moral relativity lead to decadence and depravity, and deplores the deteriorating 'moral values and ethical norms' of the West. For Putin, Russia now stands as a bastion of 'family values' against a West that, as a result of the decline of Christianity, accepts 'the equality of good and evil'.

- In many Muslim countries, standards of human rights are determined by the 'higher law' of Islam. Iran, for example, is an Islamic theocracy in which the Qu'ran is the ultimate authority in determining the meaning of the law. Saudi Arabia bases its legal system on a literalist Wahhabi interpretation of the Qu'ran, which sets it at odds with many of the UDHR's Enlightenment principles. On issues such as freedom of belief and gender equality, the West has been highly critical of Saudi Arabia's legal position. In response its leaders state its values are superior to those of the West, since they are divinely ordained.

In large parts of the developing world, which is generally more socially conservative, homosexuality is a crime

Powerful states are unaccountable for their actions

If an international standard of human rights law is going to exist, all states would need to be held equally accountable before that law. If international law, like domestic law, is to be legitimate, it must treat all states in the same way. This principle is undermined because powerful states often ignore international law if it is against their national interests:

- Russia has refused to cooperate with the UN in the establishment of an international criminal court to investigate the shooting down of Flight MH17 over Ukraine. The USA has continually resisted calls from the UN to close down its Guantánamo Bay prison.
- The War on Terror also demonstrates how the USA is prepared to infringe human rights in order to achieve its goals of defeating terrorism. In 2014, a US senate enquiry stated that the CIA utilised 'abhorrent techniques' in the War on Terror following the 9/11 terror attacks. However, former vice-president Dick Cheney dismissed the report, asserting that, 'I think what needed to be done was done. I think we were perfectly justified in doing it. And I'd do it again in a minute.'
- Water-boarding, the indefinite internment of terror suspects at Guantánamo Bay and the USA moving terrorist suspects to states such as Pakistan, where they can be more discreetly tortured, also highlight the way in which powerful states undermine the principle that human rights can be universally applied. President Trump has said that in order to defeat terrorism, 'we have to fight with fire' and, if he is assured that torture works, admits that he will be prepared to use it in order to protect the lives of US citizens.
- The way in which the USA's drone strikes have killed many innocent bystanders during its War on Terror further shows how human rights can be undermined in times of war, and that powerful states will not be held accountable for their actions. Even the White House accepted that from 2009 to 2016 drone strikes might have killed 116 civilians, although human rights groups put the figure in the thousands.
- China executes more people per year than the rest of the world combined. It discriminates against the rights of Mongolians, Tibetans and Uighurs and tightly controls religion. The human rights activist Liu Xiaobo, who was awarded the Nobel Peace Prize in 2010, has been imprisoned for 11 years for the crime of subversion. Despite international calls for his release, China has responded that foreign critics should 'respect China's judicial sovereignty and . . . not do things that will interfere in China's internal affairs'. The whole concept of human rights is, according to the Chinese government, an excuse for 'foreign infiltration'.
- States with powerful backers are often judged less harshly than others. Islam Karimov, who died in 2016, was the ruthless dictator of Uzbekistan where, according to the UN, torture was 'systematic' and two of his opponents were boiled to death. However, given his massive oil and gas reserves and useful geostrategic position during the War on Terror, the West rarely criticised him.

These examples demonstrate that the censures of the international community do not concern powerful and influential states. Since leaders are unlikely to be held accountable for their actions, they are able to act with impunity. For human rights to be effectively protected, all states would have to be equally accountable before the law. The way in which powerful states can put their own interests before those of international standards of human rights therefore creates the sort of double standards that undermine the potential for global human rights. As the philosopher and political activist Noam Chomsky once put it, 'For the powerful, crimes are those that others commit'.

Debate

Are human rights effectively protected in the modern world?

Yes

- The establishment of international courts, such as the ECtHR and the ICC, shows willingness to protect human rights through legal methods.
- UN criminal tribunals (Cambodia, former Yugoslavia, Rwanda and Sierra Leone) have been set up to bring to justice those who have committed crimes against humanity.
- Leading war criminals, such as Radovan Karadžić and Charles Taylor, have been tried and convicted in these courts.
- These courts have developed the principle that heads of government may be held accountable for war crimes, and have set new precedents in an international setting, such as including rape as a way of perpetrating genocide.
- The 2005 UN Responsibility to Protect (R2P) and the establishment of the principle that state sovereignty is 'provisional' present the message that states that abuse their own citizens forfeit their sovereignty, giving the UN a 'responsibility' to intervene.
- The internet has made human rights abuses more globally known. States, as well as transnational corporations (TNCs), are now more likely to be held accountable for their actions.
- NGOs, such as Amnesty International and Human Rights Watch, work to highlight abuses. TNCs are increasingly concerned to demonstrate corporate social responsibility.

No

- International human rights law is soft law. Westphalian principles of state sovereignty undermine liberal principles of human rights observance.
- Nation-states are unprepared to sacrifice their realist self-interest to liberal cosmopolitanism.
- Powerful states, including China, Russia and the USA, do not accept the ICC's authority, while state sovereignty limits ECtHR jurisdiction.
- The ICC is accused of neocolonial bias against Africa, undermining its potential. Cases against Omar al-Bashir (Sudan) and Uhuru Kenyatta (Kenya) were dropped due to the lack of cooperation.
- Different cultural traditions challenge the principle of a universal standard of human rights.
- The principles of the UDHR are based upon a Western interpretation of human rights, which is significantly different to African, Asian and Russian interpretations of communal over individual rights. The Muslim interpretation of human rights places divine law above secular law.

Activity

Robert Jackson, US chief prosecutor at the opening of the Nuremberg Trials, stated on 10 November 1945:

> If certain acts of violation of treaties are crimes, they are crimes whether the United States does them or whether Germany does them, and we are not prepared to lay down a rule of criminal conduct against others which we would not be willing to have invoked against us.

On 21 December 2003, President George W. Bush responded to criticism that his policy in Iraq was contrary to international law:

> International law? I better call my lawyer. He didn't bring that up to me.

Using these two quotations and your background knowledge, to what extent do you think that international law is an impossible dream?

Human intervention is based upon the liberal principle that as members of a global community, all states should strive to protect human life. If sovereign states cannot do this, either because they are deliberately perpetrating mass murder or are unable to cope with the enormity of a natural catastrophe, the international community should intervene to restore order and save lives. Therefore, humanitarian intervention is instigated by the altruistic principle of 'saving strangers' rather than geostrategic considerations of self-interest.

The end of the Cold War

The end of the Cold War was greeted with such optimism that it generated huge international support for liberal principles of global governance and international justice. 'People power' played an important role in the collapse of communism in eastern Europe and the Soviet Union, placing people at the centre of political debate in a way not seen during the Cold War.

In the early 1990s, the future therefore appeared to be one of greater global cooperation, as states increasingly embraced common values. This led President George H. W. Bush to speak of a 'New World Order' based on a global community working together to resolve the problems it jointly faced.

The First Gulf War (1991)

This new, more positive world order was illustrated in 1991 when states cooperated to expel Iraqi forces from Kuwait. This seemed to suggest that the global community was prepared to live up to UN ideals and punish what George H. W. Bush termed the 'naked aggression' of Saddam Hussein. However, Bush was not prepared to intervene within Iraq itself, despite some of his advisers suggesting that, having liberated Kuwait, the USA should go on to topple Saddam.

However, when Saddam went on to brutally suppress Kurdish uprisings in northern Iraq, this was too much for the UNSC. Its speedy passage of UN Resolution 688, condemning Saddam Hussein's retribution against Kurdish rebels, provided France, the UK and the USA with the authority to establish 'no-fly zones' within Iraqi borders. This signalled that the state would no longer be all-powerful if it sought to persecute its own people. Significantly, the intervention was code-named 'Operation Provide Comfort', indicating the way in which morality, rather than strategic self-interest, was used to justify action.

Somalia (1992–93)

Operation Provide Comfort was not a one-off. In December 1992, in one of his last acts as president, George H. W. Bush committed 28,000 US troops to Somalia, a state that had disintegrated into anarchy and in which over a million were threatened with starvation. When General Colin Powell, then Chairman of the Joint Chiefs of Staff, asked Bush what the USA's mission was in aid of, he stated it was 'to end the starvation'. Then, in his broadcast to the nation, he declared that the USA would 'answer the call' and 'get the food through'.

Such humanitarianism was easier to achieve in the 1990s since, following the collapse of the Soviet Union, the USA was the sole global superpower. If the USA was prepared to act according to moral principles in the development of a New World Order, it appeared that a more liberal world order could be established.

Synoptic links

The moral justification for humanitarian intervention is explored further under liberalism in Component 1. John Locke and John Stuart Mill both focused on the extent to which the state can demand the loyalty of its citizens. Working within this tradition, philosopher John Rawls coined the term 'outlaw states' for those states that wantonly exist outside reasonable principles of justice.

Case study

The Battle of Mogadishu, 3–4 October 1993

President George H. W. Bush made his decision to commit US troops to Somalia during the final weeks of his presidency with the best possible intentions. The USA had little strategic interest in the region and the US military was tasked with restoring the conditions necessary for the delivery of aid to the starving population. However, this was easier said than done, and US forces found themselves pulled into relentless bitter clan fighting.

In October, Operation Gothic Serpent aimed to capture rebel leaders loyal to self-proclaimed president Mohamed Farrah Aidid. Early on in the engagement, Somali militiamen shot down two US Black Hawk helicopters and the offensive operation suddenly became a rescue mission, as US ground troops fought their way to the two crash sites. Eighteen US soldiers were killed and television footage showed jubilant Somali mobs dragging the bodies through the streets of Mogadishu, provoking revulsion across the USA and sparking debate over US involvement in a conflict that was of no concern to the USA and, anyway, was quite likely unsolvable. As the radical Texas congressman Ron Paul put it on 15 October, 'Somalia is just one more reason why we should mind our own business and not stir the flames of hatred there or anywhere else in the world'.

As a result of the events, Bush's successor to the White House, Bill Clinton, decided that the risks to US servicemen and women were not worth it. Four days later, he pulled US troops out of combat and, by March 1994, all US forces left Somalia. A year later, the UN also abandoned operations and to this day, Somalia remains a failed state and a haven for pirates and Islamist terrorists.

Somalia demonstrates many of the problems connected with humanitarian interventionism. Realists question whether it is justifiable to risk the lives of servicemen in conflicts that do not directly affect national interests. There is also the danger that involvement in a complicated conflict can become open-ended, with no easy exit strategy. Furthermore, does intervention in an alien culture really achieve its humanitarian objectives or might it even exacerbate conflict as resentment grows for the 'foreign imperialist interlopers'? After the First Gulf War, one of George H. W. Bush's advisers allegedly stated that 'now was the time to solve the problems of the middle east', to which another aide responded, 'Mr President, we can't even solve the traffic problem in DC, let alone the middle east'. No wonder realists question both the justification and the practicality of humanitarian intervention.

The lessons of Bosnia and Rwanda

The civil war that erupted upon the break-up of the Yugoslav Federation severely tested the principle of humanitarian intervention. President Bill Clinton was wary of involving the USA in such a complicated and bloody conflict. The EU was similarly paralysed by indecision and unwilling to take sides. The UN sent peacekeepers into the warzone but, as the UN Secretary-General Boutros Boutros-Ghali put it, they were being expected to keep the peace 'when there was no peace to keep'.

As a result of this lack of resolve, the killings multiplied. In the biggest mass murder in Europe since the end of the Second World War, Bosnian Serbs murdered 7,000 Bosnian Muslim men and boys when they overran the UN safe haven of Srebrenica. This coincided with developments in satellite broadcasting, which made the killings 'instantaneous news', further highlighting the moral consequences of the reticence to intervene.

The Rwandan genocide took place from April to June 1994. As many as 800,000 Rwandans may have been killed in the bloodbath, representing 20% of the population. The tiny UN force in Rwanda did not have either the manpower or the mandate to take decisive action. When, at last, the UNSC did agree to send reinforcements, the killing was mostly over. As the scale of this tragedy became known, so the failure of the international community to intervene was widely condemned.

Clearly, if humanitarian intervention were to work in the future, it would require full military involvement, acceptance that there would be risks and casualties, and an absolute commitment to success.

NATO's intervention in Bosnia (1995)

By 1995, the extent of suffering in Bosnia at last persuaded NATO to intervene in the civil war. Bosnian Serb artillery attacks on Sarajevo, including a particularly bloody attack on a busy civilian marketplace, together with the Srebrenica Massacre, proved to be the final straw.

Since its establishment in 1949, NATO's purpose had been to deter Soviet aggression. However, with the Cold War over and a humanitarian disaster occurring on the EU border, NATO leaders agreed to deploy troops and air power to its 'near abroad'. It launched Operation Deliberate Force against the Bosnian Serbs, who were soon pushed back by the overwhelming military power that NATO could deploy. In December 1995, all sides agreed to the Dayton Peace Accords. To ensure compliance, NATO deployed 60,000 troops in Bosnia, with a robust mandate to disarm rival military factions, rebuild Bosnia and try to restore trust between the rival ethnic and religious groups in the region.

Nation-building in Bosnia

The commitment NATO made to rebuilding Bosnia after the civil war demonstrated that, if it was to work, humanitarian intervention would have to involve nation-building. It was not enough to stop the fighting — peacekeeping forces would need to step in to create the conditions necessary for lasting peace. In 2002–6, former Liberal Democrat leader Paddy Ashdown served as International High Representative for Bosnia and Herzegovina. He had many practical successes during his time as High Representative, but some criticised the intervention as neocolonialism. However, if it *was* imperialism, it was a very benign form, designed to establish the conditions necessary for the rebuilding of Bosnia.

Activity

During 1876, a nationalist revolt broke out in Bulgaria (then part of the Ottoman Empire). Turkish forces crushed the rebels with extreme severity — poorly disciplined irregular forces were responsible for atrocities against the civilian population and, in Philippopolis alone, it is estimated that 15,000 people were murdered. The Conservative government of Benjamin Disraeli ignored these atrocities. Its main foreign policy objective was to prevent the expansion of the Russian Empire, and that meant bolstering the Turkish Empire as a counterweight. Issues of morality simply did not play a part in the British government's grand diplomatic strategy.

Disraeli's great political opponent and leader of the Liberal Party, William Gladstone, was at that time contemplating retiring from politics. But the events in Bulgaria galvanised him into action. For Gladstone, politics was inseparable from moral considerations, and Britain could not stand idly by in the knowledge that such atrocities were taking place. In 1876, he swiftly wrote *The Bulgarian Horrors and the Question of the East*, in which he reminded the public of the moral responsibility of government to place human life above self-interest. The pamphlet quickly sold 200,000 copies and established Gladstone as the moral voice of Victorian Britain.

The battle-lines were therefore drawn between the realist pragmatism of Disraeli, who quipped that of all the Bulgarian atrocities Gladstone's prose style was the worst, and the liberal idealism of Gladstone, who demanded that 'the Turks now carry away their abuses in the only possible manner, namely by carrying off themselves'. Eventually, at the Congress of Berlin in 1878, Disraeli helped negotiate a settlement that prevented a general European war. It did little to protect the rights of Bulgarians, but it did allow him to proclaim 'peace with honour'. However, Gladstone's moral legacy has arguably had even greater impact. A silver wreath still hangs in the Gladstone Library, which was laid on his tomb 'from the grateful Bulgarian nation', and his dictum that 'nothing that is morally wrong can be politically right' has influenced politicians from Woodrow Wilson to Tony Blair.

1 To what extent do you think that foreign policy should be based upon moral considerations?

2 Or do you agree with the Catholic writer G. K. Chesterton, that the greatest threat to peace and stability is when 'virtue runs amok'?

Use as many examples of modern humanitarian intervention as you can to justify your arguments.

Tony Blair and the principle of the international community

In 1997, Labour leader Tony Blair became UK prime minister. The most devoutly Christian prime minister since Gladstone, Blair shared his predecessor's conviction that politics and morality are inseparable. Foreign policy must, as his first foreign secretary Robin Cook put it, be 'ethical'.

During his Lord Mayor's banquet speech in 1997, Blair announced that 'human rights may sometimes seem an abstraction in the comfort of the West, but when they are ignored, human misery and political instability all too easily follow'. For Blair these were not empty words and, in the years to come, he would use his international stature to encourage the international community to live up to the idealism of a more liberal global cosmopolitanism. Under Blair's government, respect for human rights would inform British foreign policy just as much as geostrategic self-interest.

Synoptic links

Component 1 explores the way in which socialism developed as a universalist creed based upon a sense of global fraternity. The principle of an 'obligation to save strangers', therefore, has roots within the socialist tradition of a common indivisible humanity.

Kosovo (1999)

In 1999, conflict in the Balkans once again gained international attention. This time the violence was within Serbia. Kosovar Albanians wanted to separate from Serbia and establish an independent state. In response, the Serbian president, Slobodan Milošević, launched a major military offensive in order to crush the separatist movement. To many in the West this seemed to herald yet more 'ethnic cleansing' in the region and Tony Blair, remembering how long it had taken to end the war in Bosnia, was among those most eager to push for military intervention. In March, NATO began an aerial bombardment against Serbia. In April, Blair flew to Washington, DC to persuade President Clinton that NATO might need to prepare for a full-scale land invasion.

Eventually, the threat of a NATO ground offensive forced Milošević to hand over Kosovo to NATO administration, although it would legally remain a part of Serbia. Subsequently, Kosovo Force (KFOR) took over the responsibilities of re-establishing the infrastructure, disarming rival groups, resettling refugees and preventing acts of revenge.

In some ways, Kosovo represents the high point of humanitarian intervention. During the conflict, Blair was unequivocal on his assertion that NATO had intervened to protect our 'fellow human beings' and that it was 'simply the right thing to do'. In his Chicago speech in April 1999, he reinforced these commitments in what later became known as the 'Blair Doctrine', in which he stated that 'acts of genocide can never be a purely internal matter'. At the dawn of the new millennium it really did seem as though a new empire of the good was under creation: if nation-states chose to make war against their own people, they would have to face the consequences.

Activity

On 22 April 1999, Prime Minister Tony Blair made a speech in Chicago, offering the international community a set of criteria for deciding when and how to intervene militarily in the affairs of another country where the threat was not to the outside world, but to a domestic population. These proposals came to be known as the 'Blair Doctrine':

> In the end, values and interests merge. If we can establish and spread the values of liberty, the rule of law, human rights and an open society then that is in our national interests. The spread of our values makes us safer. As John Kennedy put it, 'Freedom is indivisible and when one man is enslaved who is free?' Non-interference has long been considered an important principle of international order. And it is not one we would want to jettison too readily ... But the principle of non-interference must be qualified in important respects. Acts of genocide can never be a purely internal matter. When oppression produces massive flows of refugees which unsettle neighbouring countries then they can properly be described as 'threats to international peace and security'.

1   In what circumstances does Tony Blair claim that it can be right to intervene within the affairs of a sovereign state?
2   To what extent is his justification idealistic or pragmatic?
3   How convincing do you find his arguments? Support your arguments with examples of intervention and non-intervention.

The Clinton Doctrine (1999)

When President Clinton announced that where American values and interests met, the USA should be prepared to intervene, liberals were further emboldened to believe that the new millennium would usher in a more humanitarian approach to foreign policy. Like Tony Blair, Clinton further accepted that 'Genocide is in and of itself a national interest where we should act' and that the USA had a responsibility to promote human rights and democracy. This was not only morally right, but a world governed according to these principles would be safer and more secure for US interests. Possibly, too, his assertions were fuelled by guilt: in the early years of his presidency, Clinton had ignored the Rwandan genocide. His foreign policy legacy would therefore be to challenge Westphalian principles of state sovereignty by emphasising the universality of human rights.

The United Nations Responsibility to Protect (2005)

As UN secretary-general, Kofi Annan was keen to refine the extent to which a state could act in defiance of the moral precepts of the international community. In the wake of the Kosovo intervention in 1999, Annan argued, like Blair and Clinton, that states could now no longer claim absolute authority over their citizens. Instead, a state's sovereignty was 'conditional' upon its ability to protect its citizens' human rights. This represented a dramatic assault on Westphalian principles, since it suggested that state sovereignty involved *responsibilities* as well as rights.

The International Commission on Intervention and State Sovereignty was established in 2000, and coined the term 'responsibility to protect'. According to this principle, the state has a 'responsibility' to protect its citizens from harm. If it fails in this duty, that 'responsibility' passes to the international community. In a global political commitment, all UN members voted to endorse the Responsibility to Protect (R2P) at the UN World Summit in 2005, in order to prevent genocide, war crimes, ethnic cleansing and crimes against humanity. Where such atrocities occur, the UNSC should be prepared to authorise humanitarian intervention.

The concept of 'responsible sovereignty' established a new onus on both nation-states and the global community to ensure that people could live without fear of violent persecution within their own countries.

Activity

The UN R2P states that:

> The right to protect gives the world community the right to intervene in the case of national authorities manifestly failing to protect their populations from genocide, war crimes, ethnic cleansing and crimes against humanity.

The liberal cosmopolitan principles of the UN R2P therefore present the international community with the right to intervene in states to protect the human rights of their citizens.

1 What is the justification for this principle?
2 Since its publication in 2005 there have been a number of occasions when the R2P would have mandated action within states, and yet nothing has happened. Why do you think this has been the case?

Why have some humanitarian interventions been more successful than others?

Successful interventions

The Balkans (1992–1995)

The fact that UN peacekeepers were not mandated to take offensive military action undermined initial UN involvement in the conflict in former Yugoslavia. Peacekeepers were operating in a war zone, but without the means even to defend themselves. For example, Srebrenica fell when lightly armed UN Dutch peacekeepers handed over control of the enclave to superior Bosnian Serb forces.

However, when NATO launched Operation Deliberate Force in 1995, it established conditions for a lasting peace. Subdued by air power, the Bosnian Serbs agreed to a peace deal at Dayton, Ohio. As part of the settlement, NATO forces were deployed to rebuild Bosnia. The operation's success was due to the fact that, at its peak, 60,000 troops were deployed, often in a policing role. Furthermore, a UN mandate confirmed NATO's operational legitimacy when it established and assigned a UN High Representative to ensure good and impartial governance in the region. The commitment to nation-building demonstrated in Bosnia established a model for rebuilding the foundations of a civil society.

This model of active nation-building was followed in Kosovo. When Serb forces evacuated, NATO troops quickly replaced them. Once again, a new civilian administration was established and as many as 50,000 troops were deployed in order to provide the necessary conditions for the restoration of

---

Activity

During the 1990s, partly in response to the Balkans conflict, the political scientist Mary Kaldor developed her 'New War' thesis. According to Kaldor, wars between states were becoming less likely. However, wars within failed or failing states would become more prevalent, with civilians finding themselves increasingly on the front line as armed militias and paramilitaries struggled for control.

In this sort of new environment, the traditional role of the military would have to change — no longer would military forces primarily be deployed to win battles, but troops should also be trained for police work in unstable political environments. In order to achieve successful nation-building, soldiers would have to deploy great sensitivity and restraint in highly charged environments — the excessive use of force, xenophobia, cultural arrogance or partisanship could be as devastating as losing a battle. Military intervention could no longer solely be used to defeat an adversary and secure a peace treaty. Instead, initial military engagements would become the precursor to a potentially long, drawn-out occupation based on achieving an inclusive settlement.

The USA has, however, been slow to adapt to these principles. In the aftermath of the Iraq War, former US defense secretary Donald Rumsfeld cautioned that 'we don't do nation-building'. The subsequent rounding up of suspects in Iraq, while failing to distinguish between combatants and civilians, and deploying soldiers in full combat gear seemed to confirm this. This has consequently created huge resentment, which has contributed to the rise of the militant group Islamic State. Similarly, in Afghanistan, so great is the gap in cultural understanding between the occupying Western forces and the Afghans that it has been difficult to establish a meaningful dialogue between the two. The difficulty, too, in providing security in such a massive country with limited military forces and no knowledge of tribal and ethnic loyalties has further undermined the potential for success.

To what extent do you think that failures of intervention have primarily been due to a misunderstanding of the role of the military in modern-day warfare? In your answer, you could refer to a variety of conflicts including Afghanistan, Bosnia, East Timor, Iraq, Kosovo, Libya and Sierra Leone.

peace and stability. As in Bosnia, NATO troops were actively involved in a wide variety of military and non-military roles, ranging from disarming militias to safely accompanying children to school. This demonstrated that active participation in a nation's reconstruction is vital if it is to be successful.

East Timor (1999–2001)

Indonesia annexed East Timor, a former Portuguese colony, in 1975. The cultural heritage of East Timor was very distinct from Indonesia and large parts of the mostly Catholic population demanded independence. Following years of separatist resistance, in 1999 the Indonesian government reluctantly agreed to allow East Timor an independence referendum. Those in favour of independence won 78% of the vote. This provoked a violent backlash by pro-Indonesian militias backed by the government in Jakarta.

During the resulting violence, half a million East Timorese were driven from their homes, threatening a refugee crisis. Australian prime minister John Howard swiftly declared that, as the largest regional power and the one most likely to be affected by a refugee catastrophe, Australia would lead any UN force deployed to keep the peace. Meanwhile, President Clinton put significant economic pressure on Indonesia to allow a UN peacemaking force into the country. As a result of such concerted international pressure, UN Resolution 1264 authorised a multinational force, led by Australia, to enter East Timor, with a robust mandate to defeat and disarm militias. Once stability had been restored, in 2001, elections were held for East Timor's constituent assembly, which approved a constitution. On 20 May 2003, East Timor formally gained independence.

In 1999, the Indonesian government reluctantly agreed to an independence referendum in East Timor

Sierra Leone (2000)

During the 1990s, Sierra Leone endured a particularly brutal civil war. The Revolutionary United Front (RUF), led by Foday Sankoh, was responsible for numerous atrocities, including mutilation, and was backed by Charles Taylor, President of Liberia, in return for 'blood diamonds'. In May 2000, as the RUF advanced on the capital, Freetown, the Blair government sent a military force to help evacuate foreign nationals. Having quickly achieved this, elite British troops began to engage in highly mobile operations against the RUF and allied militia, such as the West Side Boys. What were, in effect, criminal gangs were no match for British troops' superior training and equipment. Consequently, the Sierra Leone government was able to successfully crush the rebels.

Having turned the tide, British troops remained to train and advise Sierra Leone's armed forces and, in 2001, the RUF agreed to disarm. In 2003, as a result of international pressure and condemnation, Taylor stood down as president and went into exile. In 2006, the UN's Special Court for Sierra Leone charged Taylor with 11 counts of war crimes and he was sentenced to 50 years in prison.

Côte d'Ivoire (2011)

In 2011, President Laurent Gbagbo of Côte d'Ivoire refused to accept defeat in the general election. This provoked a political crisis, which pushed the country towards civil war. The UNSC mandated the destruction of Gbagbo's military capability and France, the former colonial power, militarily intervened with both air and ground forces.

The legitimacy of the intervention was never in doubt, especially since UN observers were unequivocal that Gbagbo had lost the election. Furthermore, as with Sierra Leone, Côte d'Ivoire is relatively compact and, being on the west coast of Africa, was readily accessible to French intervention. Gbagbo's remaining supporters were mostly armed gangs whose only loyalty was to the president. When Gbagbo was arrested and the legitimate government took office, favourable conditions for peace and stability were created.

Unsuccessful interventions

Somalia (1992–93)

President George H. W. Bush deployed US troops in Somalia with the best-possible humanitarian intentions. However, troops soon found themselves in a quagmire, unable to distinguish between rival clans, militias and civilians. Lacking a legitimate government to defend, the US military was unable to successfully cooperate with forces within Somalia. US troops were quickly seen as an alien occupying force.

The US people also quickly forgot the initial humanitarian justification for intervention, especially after grisly footage of the aftermath of the Battle of Mogadishu was broadcast on national television. Lacking public support for continued US involvement and with no end in sight to the fighting, President Clinton withdrew all US forces from Somalia by 1994. To achieve its objectives, a humanitarian intervention therefore needs to have both a realistic chance of success and the political will to be carried through to completion. In Somalia, neither proved to be the case.

Darfur (2003–)

Darfur, western Sudan, has a black Muslim population that claims independence from Sudan. As separatist demands grew, the government sent in Arab militia, known as Janjaweed, who pillaged and murdered throughout the region. As early as 2004, US Secretary of State Colin Powell told the Senate Foreign Relations Committee that this systematic policy of violence against Darfuris amounted to 'genocide', amid reports that as many as 300,000 people may have died and 5 million were displaced from their homes.

Demonstrating that it had yet to learn lessons from the Rwandan genocide, the UNSC dithered over whether the atrocities amounted to 'genocide' or 'war crimes'. China, in particular, was wary of condemning Sudan for genocide, since it had significant economic interest in the country.

Eventually, in 2007, when most of the killing had already taken place, Sudan's president, Omar al-Bashir, agreed to allow a UN/AU peacekeeping mission (UNAMID) into Darfur. At its peak, UNAMID had 23,000 personnel in the field, but Darfur's size, remoteness and lack of basic infrastructure made its work extremely difficult. The government's lack of cooperation further hampered its success and, in 2011, the Sudan government condemned 'all attempts to interfere in the internal affairs of Sudan and tarnish the image of the country'. The UN has therefore had to continually balance the 'sovereignty, unity, independence and territorial integrity of Sudan' with the protection of the Darfuris. There is no clear agreement as to the future status of Darfur, which has continually undermined any chance of conflict resolution.

Afghanistan (2001–2014)

Although Western intervention in Afghanistan after 9/11 was primarily launched to eliminate the terrorist threat from al-Qaeda, it also had a humanitarian dimension. Even before 9/11, there had been widespread international condemnation of the Taliban's brutal rule, which involved extensive human rights abuses. By establishing the conditions for a liberal democracy in Afghanistan, foreign intervention would make the world safer from terrorism, end the violation of female rights and create a more tolerant and inclusive society.

However, such high-minded idealism was unsuited to a country as culturally remote from the West as Afghanistan. Even though NATO made a huge military commitment, as the USA had found in Vietnam, it was one thing establishing a temporary presence in a village or town, but quite another ensuring its long-term security. Fundamental Islamism, especially in the majority Pashtun areas of southern and eastern Afghanistan, was also far more resonant in local conditions than liberal attempts to encourage gender equality and human rights. Equally, it was extremely difficult for Western forces to understand the significance of ethnic, tribal and family alliances and tensions. This undermined attempts to build trust within communities.

In October 1963, when he handed office to Alec Douglas-Home, former UK prime minister Harold Macmillan is alleged to have advised him, 'My dear boy, as long as you don't invade Afghanistan you'll be absolutely fine'. Unfortunately, post-9/11 intervention in Afghanistan was simply too ambitious in its aims. John Reid, Tony Blair's defence secretary, had optimistically said that he would be happy for British forces to leave Helmand province without firing a shot. Like Blair, he had fatally ignored the master of realpolitik Otto Von Bismarck's guiding dictum that 'politics is the art of the possible'.

Iraq (2003–2011)

Iraq, like Afghanistan, was a post-9/11 liberal intervention designed to stabilise the region and reduce threats to the international community. By overthrowing Saddam Hussein and replacing his brutal dictatorship with a liberal democracy, regional and global stability would be encouraged and the Iraqis' human rights would be protected.

Unfortunately, although Saddam Hussein was quickly overthrown, almost no attention was paid to post-war reconstruction. The Bush administration had an optimistic faith that, once Saddam was removed, Iraq would move towards democracy with minimum outside interference. Indeed, the US secretary of defense, Donald Rumsfeld, was determined that the USA should only have a 'light footprint' in post-war Iraq. This would not only save money, lives and resources but would prevent accusations of American imperialism. President George W. Bush himself told his National Security Council that, 'we don't do police work'.

As a consequence, chaos quickly ensued. By disbanding the Iraqi army and dismissing the government and civil service, the USA encouraged the disintegration of law and order. Sunni Muslims, whose interests had been most closely associated with Saddam, launched an insurgency. This, in turn, provoked widespread killing and brutal arrest and interrogation by occupying forces, who were too few to provide real security and yet numerous enough to exacerbate anti-Western hatred. The subsequent development of so-called Islamic State is a direct result of this failure to achieve nation-building in post-war Iraq.

Libya (2011)

In 2011, an uprising against the regime of President Gaddafi broke out in Libya. Civil war quickly ensued and, as government troops moved on the rebel stronghold of Benghazi, Gaddafi announced on radio: 'We are coming tonight. There won't be any mercy.'

As the bloodshed increased, UN Security Resolutions 1970 and 1973 authorised that 'all necessary measures' be taken to protect Libyan civilians. NATO took on responsibility for enforcing these resolutions and focused on destroying Gaddafi's air force and artillery. Deprived of air support and heavy weapons, Libyan government forces were pushed back. Gaddafi was captured and killed, and the Libyan National Transitional Council took control of the country. NATO Secretary-General Anders Fogh Rasmussen called the operation 'one of the most successful in NATO history' when he announced that the organisation was withdrawing its forces from Libya 'because our military job is now done'.

However, lessons learned in Iraq were not transferred to Libya. Although Rasmussen expressed confidence that Libyans could now control their own destiny without any further outside involvement, in reality the country was a mess of competing ethnic and clan rivalries, previously held together by Gaddafi's brute force. Lacking any history of liberal democracy, centralised government broke down, as armed gangs seized control of large parts of the country and so-called Islamic State extended its influence in the power vacuum. In 2012, the US ambassador to Libya, J. Christopher Stevens, was murdered in Benghazi during an attack on the consulate. In 2016, conditions had got so bad that the top US general in Africa, David Rodriguez, referred to Libya as a 'failed state'.

What factors determine whether or not a humanitarian intervention is successful?

Feasibility

Although humanitarian interventions are motivated by the principle of 'saving strangers', they also need to have achievable objectives. Some crises may be so intractable and open-ended that, as Henry Kissinger put it, you 'may with a bleeding heart have to let it go':

- By the time the USA intervened in Somalia, it was already a failed state and US forces were quickly dragged into clan fighting, which they did not understand.
- Tribal warfare in the Democratic Republic of the Congo (DRC) may have caused the deaths of 6 million people since the late 1990s. However, the DRC is the size of western Europe, and the intricacies of tribal conflict are difficult for outsiders to comprehend. To try to resolve such conflicts may require a level of military commitment and nuanced local understanding that is realistically impossible to achieve.
- The logistical difficulties of imposing a Western-influenced democracy on a country as vast, inaccessible and culturally conservative as Afghanistan were never fully appreciated. In the nineteenth century, the British were bloodily expelled from Kabul in 1842 and in 1880 British forces suffered one of their greatest-ever military disasters at Maiwand. A young Winston Churchill saw first-hand the ferocity of Pashtun fighters, remarking that:

  > The Pashtun tribes are always engaged in private or public war. Every man is a warrior, a politician and a theologian. Every large house is a real feudal fortress... Every family cultivates its vendetta; every clan, its feud.

- The attempt by Russian forces to occupy such an alien country as Afghanistan in 1979 also ended in complete disaster. In these circumstances, nation-building in the country was never very likely to be successful.
- The intervention in Kosovo had a much stronger chance of success. NATO commanders estimated that Serb resistance against overwhelming air power could not last long, especially because, in 1999, Serbia could not rely upon support from a still-weakened Russia. Once Serbia agreed to withdraw its forces from Kosovo, NATO troops were ready to be deployed in a nation-building operation under the authority of the UN.
- The British intervention in Sierra Leone also stood a good chance of success. Sierra Leone is easily accessible by both air and sea and is relatively small. The main threat to stability was from armed gangs, and there was a legitimate government to protect. In such circumstances, a targeted British response was able to quickly achieve its objectives.
- Côte d'Ivoire represented a similar scenario. Like Sierra Leone, it lies on the west African coast and so was easily accessible to the French military. Gbagbo's power basis was declining, the illegitimacy of his government was widely acknowledged and there was a rival government in waiting.

It is therefore very important that outsiders do not rush into interventions on the principle that 'something must be done'. Instead, there must be a cool and calm analysis of 'cost–benefit'. How likely is it that an intervention will achieve its objectives? How long will it take? What will the likely loss of life be? This may seem harsh, but ill-thought-out interventions have proven to stir up yet more violence by bringing another player to the field. Furthermore, new military and humanitarian equipment is introduced into conflict, which can too easily fall into the wrong hands, financing yet more fighting (this represented a serious problem during initial UN involvement in Bosnia). Governments therefore seriously need to consider a number of factors before taking action, or intervention can lead to catastrophic consequences.

A robust mandate and commitment to success

If an intervention is not mandated to exercise sufficient force, this will undermine its potential for success. If a military solution to a problem is going to be attempted, it is therefore vital that no half measures are taken and that the intervening powers are fully committed to success.

In 1957, Winston Churchill reflected that if he had been Anthony Eden he would never have intervened in Egypt to take over the Suez Canal. But if he had, he would not have left until he had secured total victory. It is this sort of mindset that is necessary if military success is to be achieved.

Other examples include the following:

- UN peacekeeping operations in Bosnia in the early 1990s were hampered by restrictions on the offensive military action they were able to take. Unable to act proactively, forces could not repel aggression. Too often they seemed passive in the face of aggression, such as when UN peacekeepers surrendered the 'safe haven' of Srebrenica to Bosnian Serb forces.
- In Rwanda, UN peacekeepers were only mandated to 'monitor' the situation. As a result, the tiny force was able to protect only a small number of Tutsis within the capital city, Kigali. Elsewhere, Hutu killing squads were able to act with absolute impunity.
- In Darfur, the Sudanese government's lack of cooperation has weakened the UNAMID mission. China, as a major investor in Sudan, has also helped to ensure that the UN mandate infringes Sudanese sovereignty as little as possible. AU leaders, often concerned about separatist movements in their own countries, have also proved more willing to support Sudanese sovereignty over the human rights of Darfuris.
- In both Afghanistan and Iraq the escalating loss of life for such little obvious progress led to massive military disengagement. During the Obama administration, the NATO commitment to Afghanistan was scaled down from 130,000 personnel to just 10,000 by 2017. In Iraq in 2017, there were just 5,000 US troops working in a military advisory capacity.
- However, in East Timor an Australian-led UN force was able to operate under much more robust terms of engagement. Trained in counter-insurgency and prepared to engage in aggressive police actions against criminal gangs, it was able to establish the conditions necessary for free elections.
- In Bosnia in 1995, NATO was able to take offensive military action, which led to the signing of the Dayton Peace Accords. In 1999, NATO bombed Serbia when it was accused of ethnic cleansing in Kosovo. Initially, it seemed as though Serbia would not back down, but Tony Blair took the lead in unequivocally stating that NATO would do all that was necessary to achieve its humanitarian objectives.

A commitment to nation-building

If a humanitarian intervention is launched without a commitment to nation-building, it is unlikely to be successful. States that have been under the control of brutal dictators or those that have descended into anarchy will not possess

By 2017, there were just 5,000 US troops based in Afghanistan

the necessary political heritage or viable organs of government to ensure stability and the rule of law. If intervention takes place, it must be done with the proviso that without a subsequent commitment to nation-building, it may do more harm than good.

For example:

■ In Bosnia and Kosovo, UN protectorates were established, which encouraged a return to political stability. The way in which NATO troops then took on a policing role in the Balkans further enabled normal life to resume — in Kosovo, there was one peacekeeper for every 48 people. However, in Afghanistan, there was one peacekeeper for every 5,000. Since large parts of the country were so inaccessible to patrols, it was impossible for them to engage in meaningful reconstruction.

■ In East Timor, UN forces adopted an assertive policing role, which crushed the criminal gangs and militias that had threatened anarchy once Indonesian troops had withdrawn.

■ The absence of NATO nation-building in Libya allowed the country to descend into anarchy. Western leaders like David Cameron and former French president Nicolas Sarkozy were too ready to take the credit for overthrowing President Gaddafi and saving Benghazi, without giving sufficient thought to what happened next. This was a massive mistake. Gaddafi had ruled Libya since 1969 and the country lacked any history of pluralist democracy. Freed from his ruthless dictatorship, Libyans lacked the necessary democratic traditions and tools to craft their own future.

■ In Somalia, US troops, who had not been trained in principles of police work, were soon engulfed by the anarchic conditions they encountered. Unable to distinguish between rival clans and lacking a legitimate government to work with, there was no formal strategy for success and so, in 1994, President Clinton ordered their withdrawal.

■ In Iraq, US forces only gradually appreciated the importance of attempting to nation-build and in the early stages of the occupation their lack of appreciation of Iraqi culture made it easy for them to be portrayed as an alien influence, so fuelling the insurgency.

At the time of the 2003 invasion of Iraq, the US secretary of state, Colin Powell, referred to the 'Pottery Barn' analogy. In this analogy, if you are driving along a US highway you may occasionally see a Pottery Barn (a US upscale home furnishings store) selling wares. The sign on the door may say 'If you break it, you own it'. This, according to Powell, is also true of interventions in another state. Once you do it, you 'own' that state. You can only properly withdraw once you have given it a newer and brighter future.

A legitimate government

The existence of a legitimate government can be vital to the success of interventionism. In the 1960s and 1970s the US-supported government of South Vietnam was brutal and corrupt. Its lack of moral legitimacy, therefore, significantly undermined US attempts to prop it up and in 1975, Communists achieved the reunification of Vietnam.

In the 1950s, the British in Malaya were far better able to repel Communist insurgency. The Malayan government was generally popular and the Communist insurgents were mostly Chinese and therefore 'outsiders'.

The relative legitimacy of the government you seek to support can, therefore, help to define the success or failure of an intervention:

■ In Libya, NATO forces withdrew before a new government was established, encouraging the slide into anarchy.
■ Afghanistan and Iraq both had elected governments, but many questioned their legitimacy and their influence was often confined to loyalist areas.
■ However, when the British intervened in Sierra Leone and the French in Côte d'Ivoire, these were not failing states. Instead, the British intervened on behalf of a popular and legitimate government and the French on behalf of Alassane Ouattara, who was both nationally and internationally recognised as the victor in the 2010 presidential election (see Table 5.1).

Table 5.1 Humanitarian interventions: successes and failures

Successes	Failures
Safe havens in Iraq (1991): limited objectives, international mandate, sufficient air power	**Somalia (1992–93):** no legitimate government to support, anarchic conditions, US troops not trained in nation-building
Bosnia (1995): international legitimacy, commitment to nation-building, sufficient military forces engaged	**Rwanda (1994):** very limited and slow intervention — by the time the French sent adequate forces most of the killing was already over
Kosovo (1999): coherent objectives, NATO mandate, commitment to nation-building, large-scale military commitment	**Democratic Republic of the Congo (1999–):** immense country size, limited forces, complicated tribal rivalries
East Timor (1999–2001): UN endorsement, commitment to nation-building/police work by Australian-led international force	**Afghanistan (2001–):** immense territory to control, alien culture, porous border with Pakistan across which Taliban and al-Qaeda can cross
Sierra Leone (2000): achievable objectives, support to legitimate government, criminal gangs no match for British Special Forces	**Iraq (2003–):** US/UK intervention not UN-mandated, disbanding of Iraqi state apparatus encouraged anarchic conditions, limited US troop deployment ('light footprint') undermined nation-building
Côte d'Ivoire (2011): UN-endorsed French intervention, limited geographical area, easily accessible	**Darfur (2003–):** limited AU/UN mandate, inaccessible territory
Mali (2013): French intervention on behalf of legitimate government, AU-endorsed, jihadist intervention within Mali unpopular, so providing French involvement with popular legitimacy	**Libya (2011):** no commitment to nation-building in a state with no tradition of pluralist democracy

In 1859, as calls were being made for Great Britain to support Italian patriots in the unification of Italy, the liberal English philosopher John Stuart Mill wrote a pamphlet entitled 'A Few Words on Non-Intervention'. According to Mill:

> No people ever was or remained free, but because it was determined to be so ... If a people ... does not value [freedom] sufficiently to fight for it, and maintain it against any force which can be mustered within the country ... it is only a question of how few years or months that people will be enslaved.

1 What considerations is Mill suggesting should be taken into account when deciding whether or not to intervene within a nation's internal affairs?
2 How might Mill's arguments be used when deciding whether or not modern-day interventions have a good enough chance of success to be launched?

Conclusion

The circumstances of every humanitarian intervention are different and there is, unfortunately, no golden rule for success. In Afghanistan, NATO troops did try to engage in nation-building and police work. However, the huge difference in cultural traditions, and the inaccessibility and remoteness of so much of the country, made success impossible. In Somalia, there was a large troop commitment, but conditions were so anarchic that it could not stabilise the country. Rwanda was small enough for a speedy military intervention to have stopped the gangs that were killing their neighbours. However, the UNSC lacked the political will to take action in such a remote and little-known part of central Africa.

There are, however, certain questions that should be asked to determine whether or not a humanitarian intervention is likely to succeed. If all of these questions can be answered with a 'yes', intervention may be justified. However, if any produces a 'no', the likelihood of success may be too limited to merit action.

1 Are the objectives likely to be achievable?
2 Is there international, or at least regional, support for the intervention?
3 Will the likely number of casualties be acceptable?
4 Can sufficient military force be deployed to achieve success?
5 Is there a long-term commitment to subsequent nation-building?

Why has humanitarian intervention been selective?

Legitimacy

Those who launch interventions in the affairs of other states are acutely aware of the importance of being able to claim legitimacy for their actions. This is vital if international and regional support is going to be forthcoming, and will be especially important if the intervention is likely to be costly in terms of lives.

- In 1995, NATO mandated the military intervention in Bosnia. The legitimacy of the action was vital in forcing the Bosnian Serbs to accept defeat and agree to peace negotiations at Dayton, Ohio. In 1999, the bombing campaign in Serbia was also a legitimate action and so helped to persuade President Milošević to withdraw his forces from Kosovo.
- In 1999, the UN oversaw the referendum over East Timor's independence from Indonesia. When violence continued, the UNSC unanimously authorised

an Australian-led multinational force to intervene, using 'all necessary measures' to restore order.

■ In 2011, the NATO intervention against President Gaddafi could claim legitimacy, since UN Resolution 1973 had demanded 'an immediate ceasefire in Libya, including an end to the current attacks against civilians, which it said might constitute crimes against humanity'. NATO could thus claim that it was fulfilling the terms of the resolution by intervening on the side of the rebels.

■ In 2013, the AU endorsed the French intervention in Mali, providing it with legitimacy. Subsequently, AU forces have cooperated with the French in trying to stabilise the country and defeat terrorism.

If, however, there is doubt over the legality of action, the case for intervention is dramatically undermined. The support of other countries will be less forthcoming and the public less likely to endure losses if the action is legally uncertain. It may even be possible that illegitimacy would provoke military and economic counter-measures:

■ President Mugabe's Zimbabwe government has committed significant human rights abuses. However, the government can claim legitimacy and so any attempt by the West to intervene in Zimbabwean affairs would have disastrous consequences. The AU, China and Russia would all condemn action as colonial aggression, and so the safest policy thus far has been one of inaction.

■ In Syria, President Assad claims legitimacy. In 2012, a Syrian referendum on a new constitution gave him, he claimed, 90% support. In 2014, he won the presidential election with close to 90% support. Although such figures are

President Assad's portrait in the capital Damascus, Syria

unlikely to be a true reflection of Syrian attitudes, there is no doubt that Assad does have widespread support in parts of his country, and both Russia and China recognise the legitimacy of his government. In such circumstances, the legal, practical and long-term implications of intervention are so uncertain that they make Western intervention highly unlikely.

Leadership

The leadership of powerful opinion-forming states is vital in determining whether or not intervention occurs. If a world leader is prepared to take the initiative, it is more likely that an international consensus for action can be established. Failing that, regional or individual action may still be taken if the government is convinced that there is an overwhelming moral or strategic case for intervention:

- In 1991, overwhelming evidence that Saddam Hussein was committing war crimes against the Kurds provoked the British, French and Americans to establish safe havens within northern Iraq. The UK prime minister, John Major, put forward the proposal to the UNSC, stating, with characteristic understatement, that, 'I think Saddam Hussein would be very ill-advised to attack a safe haven under United Nations protection'.

- In 1992, George H. W. Bush used his presidential authority to intervene in Somalia in response to harrowing images of starvation. Having already lost the 1992 election to Bill Clinton, Bush was determined to use his remaining time in office to 'save thousands of innocents'. He was conscious, too, that as the world's last remaining superpower, the USA would have to take a lead 'as a catalyst for broader involvement of the community of nations'.

- In 1999, Tony Blair deployed his popularity and charisma to persuade NATO and EU leaders that they should intervene in Kosovo. When he received the Charlemagne Prize for European Achievement for his work in Northern Ireland, he utilised the moral authority with which this endowed him to make the case for war. Commenting on President Milošević's actions in Kosovo, Blair told his audience, 'He was determined to wipe a people from the face of his country. We are determined to stop him — and we will'.

- In 2013, President François Hollande sent French troops to Mali to stop 'an assault by terrorist elements coming from the north whose brutality and fanaticism is known across the world'. As a former French colony, Mail has a strong connection with France and the government of Mail welcomed the intervention. In such circumstances, Hollande felt that the strategic and humanitarian objectives involved in defeating the jihadists were achievable.

However, if there is a lack of global leadership, it will be difficult to mobilise either national or international support for intervention. The good intentions of some leaders can be thwarted by the intransigence of others on the UNSC, and if powerful states are not prepared to take action, humanitarian disasters can be quickly sidelined:

- In 1994, President Clinton, having withdrawn US forces from the quagmire of Somalia, was unprepared to take a leadership role when mass killing began in Rwanda. French president François Mitterrand was also slow to take action. For 20 years French diplomacy in central Africa had been to provide support to the pro-French Hutu government against the Tutsi Rwandan Patriotic Front, which they perceived as being pro-British. Even as the genocide was occurring, it was difficult to change this mindset.

- In 2013, before Russia militarily engaged in Syria, it did seem as though the West might launch air strikes against the Assad regime after it was accused of using chemical weapons, which are banned by international law. However, UK prime minister David Cameron could not persuade parliament to support military strikes on Assad. MPs, too, well remembered Tony Blair's moral and strategic case for intervening in Iraq and what had then subsequently occurred in the region. They therefore voted 285/272 against air strikes on the Syrian government. The consequences of this vote were far-reaching. President Obama's foreign policy was very much based on pragmatic considerations of national self-interest — knowing that the UK would not take action, he was wary of acting unilaterally and so delayed a decision until after consulting Congress. The momentum was lost and the West did not take action.

In 2016, the election of Donald Trump as President of the United States suggests that for the immediate future the cause of humanitarian intervention will lack US support. President Trump has stated that the USA should not seek to impose its values on other countries. Prime Minister Theresa May, on her first meeting with Trump, endorsed this position. Since the two countries most associated with a morally based foreign policy have backed away from this position, the future for humanitarian intervention looks bleak.

Public interest: the 'CNN factor'

If the media succeeds in sufficiently shocking the public, it may create the irresistible impulse that 'something must be done'. Equally, if the media pays insufficient attention to a crisis, politicians may lack the public impulse to get involved. However, media influence can be a double-edged sword. It was shocking images of starvation that provoked President George H. W. Bush to intervene in Somalia, but within a year, horrifying images of dead US servicemen being dragged naked through the streets of Mogadishu persuaded President Bill Clinton to withdraw US troops.

In what has become known as 'the CNN factor', the media has influenced other outcomes:

- In 1999, ethnic cleansing in Kosovo generated a great deal of media coverage, especially in the EU — the events were worryingly reminiscent of the conditions that had allowed the Srebrenica Massacre to take place. There was, therefore, significant public pressure for action.
- On the other hand, the media has widely ignored the atrocities occurring in the DRC and Darfur, and so politicians have not faced the same pressure to take action.

National self-interest

Strategic considerations can determine whether or not a nation is prepared to take the initiative in pressing for action. A humanitarian disaster that impacts a state's own security will be especially pressing. If, however, the emergency is in a distant land and outside a state's sphere of influence, it may be safer to ignore it, especially if intervention could upset the regional, or even global, balance of power. As Henry Kissinger pointed out, a purely altruistic approach to international diplomacy would be disastrous, since at what point would you stop acting on behalf of oppressed minorities? As he stated in a *Washington Post* opinion piece in 2012, 'Is, for example, Saudi Arabia an ally only until public demonstrations develop on its territory?'

Strategic considerations have played a significant role in several recent crises:

■ During the Kosovo crisis, one of the most powerful arguments that politicians, like Tony Blair, could use was that if the West did not intervene, the conflict might spread throughout the Balkans, potentially threatening the peace and stability of the EU itself.

■ In 2000, Australian prime minister John Howard committed Australian troops to leading the UN intervention in East Timor because the developing refugee crisis would have soon threatened northern Australia.

■ Neoconservatives (those politicians with an aggressively liberal interventionist approach to global affairs) within the George W. Bush administration, such as Donald Rumsfeld and Dick Cheney, regarded the 9/11 terror attacks as an opportunity to advance US interests in the middle east by making Iraq part of an 'Axis of Evil', which had to be defeated as part of the War on Terror.

If, on the other hand, the conflict — however bloody — does not directly affect the interests of the great powers, it is much more likely to be ignored by the international community:

■ Mass killing in Darfur and civil war in the DRC pose no threat to global stability, and so there is much less incentive to take action.

■ In Syria, the West has been unwilling to challenge President Assad. Attempts to overthrow him could provoke conflict with Russia and, were Assad to be removed, there is no certainty that the terrorist threat to the West would be reduced. It might even be increased. In such circumstances, the most sensible policy has thus far been to steer clear of unnecessary risks.

Likelihood of success

Before intervening in the internal affairs of another state, any government will have to weigh up the likely consequences of action or inaction. One may want to intervene in a crisis but how likely is it that an intervention will save lives? Governments need to make tough decisions based upon a realistic assessment of numbers of troops required to get the job done, the international, or at least regional, support base for intervention and the risk of potentially widening the conflict. Based upon these considerations, one can see why action was taken in:

■ East Timor (1999)
■ Sierra Leone (2000)
■ Côte d'Ivoire (2011)
■ Libya (2011)
■ Mali (2013)

Equally, one can appreciate why, scarred by Afghanistan and Iraq, Western powers have been much less prepared to involve themselves in other protracted conflicts, where the chance of achieving realistic success is much less. Such failures to intervene effectively include:

■ Darfur
■ DRC
■ Syria
■ Zimbabwe

It could be argued that all possess equal moral grounds for intervention, but the likelihood that intervening states will fail in their objectives and, in the case of Syria, risk global conflict have contributed to inaction.

Does the responsibility to protect outweigh state sovereignty?

Yes

- Liberals argue that there is a 'moral responsibility' to 'save strangers'. If nation-states commit atrocities against their own people, the international community should intervene to save lives.

- State sovereignty is 'conditional' — it brings with it rights but also responsibilities. A state that engages in widespread killing of its own citizens has, therefore, forfeited its sovereignty. The acknowledgement of this principle will, therefore, encourage 'responsible' sovereignty.

- If nation-states are free to abuse their own people, this encourages other would-be despots to act with impunity, leading to further violence.

- Failures to intervene have allowed appalling, but also avoidable, losses of life to occur (e.g. Darfur, Libya, Rwanda, Syria).

- Regional and global stability are threatened if mass murder and human rights abuses are not punished. The migrant crisis caused by the Syrian civil war has threatened European stability. By not intervening in Libya and by withdrawing forces from Iraq, we have created the conditions for the rise of Islamist terrorism.

No

- Westphalian principles of state sovereignty provide the foundations for global stability. Realists argue that the only justification for military action against another state is self-defence.

- According to offensive realists, states are 'power-maximisers' and, therefore, humanitarian intervention can be used as an excuse to advance strategic self-interest.

- Interventions in Afghanistan, Bosnia, Iraq, Kosovo and Libya were used to advance liberal Western agendas. Russia justified its war with Georgia on the grounds that it was abusing the rights of people in the province of South Ossetia. Claims that the ethnic Russians' rights are being 'abused' could subsequently give Russia the 'justification' to intervene.

- The way in which humanitarian intervention can be used as a pretext for strategic self-interest could risk regional and even global war. Western intervention against President Assad would risk provoking war with his ally, Russia.

The migrant crisis has threatened European stability

- Enlightened self-interest can, therefore, inform humanitarian intervention. By not punishing evildoers, wickedness is legitimised and crises may then spill over, threatening the peace of other regions.
- The destabilising potential of 'zones of conflict' can only be reduced if military action is promptly taken to stop humanitarian crises spiralling out of control, engulfing a region and threatening further conflict. The French intervention in Mali is designed to protect human rights, but also to stop Islamist terrorism from spreading through north Africa, so threatening Europe.

- States do not have the 'right' to risk the lives of their own citizens in conflicts that do not concern themselves.
- Humanitarian missions can raise false expectations and make the situation worse. In Somalia and Bosnia, warring factions often hijacked UN aid convoys, and post-Gaddafi Libya is ungovernable. Western intervention in Iraq has increased the terrorist threat in the middle east.
- The principle of humanitarian intervention is undermined by being selective. The justification for interventions in Bosnia and Kosovo is therefore undermined by failures to act in Rwanda, Tibet or Zimbabwe.

Synoptic links

The R2P raises significant issues concerning whether one's loyalty should be to the state in which one lives or to a wider community that is more resonant with individual identity. This is further covered in Component 2, under the competing claims of nationalism, anarchism, ecologism, feminism and multiculturalism.

Activity

On 19 February 2013, during a heated Prime Minister's Questions session, Respect MP George Galloway criticised David Cameron for wanting parliament to agree to the use of force against President Assad. According to Galloway, seeking to overthrow Assad would further destabilise the region and encourage the spread of jihadism and terrorism. Galloway ended by asking 'Has the prime minister read *Frankenstein*, and did he read it to the end?'

In February 2017, Amnesty International estimated that 13,000 inmates have been executed at the Syrian government's Sednaya prison. According to the NGO, this has amounted to a 'policy of extermination'. Another investigation, which the UN launched in 2016, accused the Syrian government of a policy of 'extermination' in its jails. By 2017, it was estimated that 400,000 had died in the Syrian civil war since it began in 2011.

Using this example, and your wider understanding, can it ever be justifiable to seek to overthrow cruel dictators?

Does Western hypocrisy undermine the principle of humanitarian intervention?

The USA promotes its commitment to being a 'beacon' of human rights in a world in which ruthless rulers can too often trample upon the rights of their people.

During the Cold War, President Ronald Reagan brilliantly articulated this concept of 'American exceptionalism', contrasting the liberties of Americans with the repression that existed under communism. So effective was Reagan that he helped to undermine the alternative 'narrative' of communism, which contributed to the collapse of communism in eastern Europe.

However, in his *The Clash of Civilizations*, Samuel Huntington noted that 'hypocrisy and double standards are the price of universalist pretensions'. Therefore, although powerful countries like the USA claim the moral high ground, the decisions that their governments take are much more pragmatic. Thus, human rights abuses are condemned in some parts of the world but not in others. President Franklin D. Roosevelt was once asked how the USA could condone the abuses being carried out by Nicaraguan president Anastasio Somoza Garcia, to which he, allegedly, replied: 'He's a bitch, but he's our son of a bitch.'

Double standards

Accusations of double standards can be made about liberal interventionism. Too often when a humanitarian intervention takes place, it masks self-interest. Critics of interventionism argue that Western democracies have carefully selected those interventions that are most likely to be to their strategic and economic advantage:

- During the 1990s, interventions in Bosnia and Kosovo undermined Serbia, which is a long-time Slavic and Orthodox ally of Russia. By challenging Serbian influence in the region, it could be replaced with the economic and political influence of the EU.
- By intervening in Afghanistan in 2001, the USA was primarily concerned with destroying al-Qaeda. If 9/11 had not occurred, it is highly unlikely that Western powers would have intervened in Afghanistan, even though the Taliban's human rights abuses were already widely known.
- Geostrategic interests motivated the 2003 invasion of Iraq. Following his invasion of Kuwait in August 1990, Saddam Hussein was perceived to be a threat to regional stability and so it was to the US and its allies' advantage to replace him with a government that was more conducive to Western economic and political interests. In the 1980s, during the Iran/Iraq War, however, the USA had economically supported Saddam because he was then perceived to be a bulwark against the greater threat of Iran. Indeed, one of the worst atrocities the Saddam regime committed occurred in 1988, when his forces launched a chemical gas attack on the Kurdish town of Halabja, killing up to 5,000 people. At this point Saddam still enjoyed US support. He only irrevocably lost it when he invaded Kuwait in 1990, fatally misjudging the US reaction.

Elsewhere in the world, many other governments have been free to commit war crimes, ethnic cleansing, mass killings and possibly even genocide without being held accountable for their actions. Critics of humanitarian intervention argue that by ignoring such crimes, the moral basis of humanitarian intervention is fatally undermined:

- In Zimbabwe, President Mugabe is alleged to have deliberately starved those areas that voted for his political opponents, as well as violently taking over white-run farms. However, China has significant business interests in Zimbabwe, and Western powers, especially the UK, are fearful of being accused of acting in an imperialist fashion in the region. As a result, Mugabe has escaped censure and his crimes have gone unpunished.

■ China has major economic interests in Sudan, and it was one of the many countries President Omar al-Bashir continued to visit, even though he was under indictment for war crimes. In 2015, China even paid for the opening of a new presidential palace for al-Bashir, as it tightened its economic and diplomatic links within the country.

■ As a member of the UNSC and the world's largest nuclear weapons power, Russia has, unsurprisingly, not been held accountable for its actions. For example, Russia's repression of Chechen separatism in the 1990s may have caused the deaths of thousands of civilians. Prior to its assault on the Chechen capital, Grozny, in 1999–2000, the Russian military announced that 'persons who stay in the city will be considered terrorists and bandits and will be destroyed by artillery and aviation. There will be no further negotiations'. The city was then razed, making it, according to the UN, the most destroyed city on Earth. In 2016, UN High Commissioner for Human Rights Zeid Ra'ad al-Hussein announced that the Russian/Syrian bombing of East Aleppo was a war crime of 'historic' proportions. Save the Children has also condemned the Syrian government's use of cluster bombs, which are banned by international law. However, given Russia's global influence, it is hard to see under what circumstances the West will hold either Russia or its ally Syria fully accountable for their actions.

It would thus be naïve to suggest that geostrategic interests do not influence intervention. Equally, it would be cynical to suggest that they are simply a cover for the self-interest of powerful states. US intervention in Somalia, although flawed, was carried out with the best of intentions. Intervention in Sierra Leone did nothing to advance UK interests, and appalling human rights violations *were* taking place in the Balkans during the 1990s.

Of course, there have also been many occasions when appalling crimes have been ignored. The Rwandan genocide, mass killing in Darfur, the brutal land nationalisation programme in Zimbabwe and ongoing tribal warfare in the DRC have all attracted too little global condemnation. Human rights abuses by Russia in Chechnya and, according to Human Rights Watch, now in Syria have also gone unpunished. There is considerable concern over how China treats its ethnic and religious minorities.

However, international politics is the study of the world as it is, rather than how we would like it to be. The West may not always like what China and Russia do, but there is no way that military action is going to make them change their ways. Indeed, a US intervention against Russian and Syrian forces during the bombing of Eastern Aleppo could have had incalculable consequences for world peace. The USA itself is hardly blameless — as Guantánamo Bay and water-boarding prove — when it comes to human rights violations. Terrible things occur in countries across the world, but if the government claims legitimacy would a Western intervention really make things better? Might it actually make things considerably worse and, given recent failures, would there be the necessary public support for a costly and bloody intervention with no obvious end in sight? In other words, if you don't have a dog in a particular fight, do you really want to get involved?

It would be glib to suggest that double standards wholly compromise humanitarian intervention — politicians are rarely either totally selfish or fully altruistic. This means that some horrendous crimes will be ignored, but that is not to say that others will go unpunished. As former UK foreign secretary Douglas Hurd put it, 'We should do good where we can, but not pretend that we can do good everywhere'. In other words, an ethical foreign policy will always be open to the charge of hypocrisy. That, however, is hardly a sufficient reason to totally abandon the principle.

What you should know

Having read this chapter you should have knowledge and understanding of the following:

- Diverse cultural traditions possess very different approaches to the nature of human rights. We therefore need to be careful not to refer to 'human rights' as though everyone shares the same understanding of what we mean.
- Asian and Muslim interpretations of human rights differ considerably from Western interpretations, and it is important not to presuppose that one standard of human rights is necessarily superior to another.
- There are certain basic standards of human rights that all cultures can accept, for example the Four Freedoms, to which the Universal Declaration of Human Rights (UDHR) gives formal expression. However, for most of the Cold War, superpower rivalry curtailed their influence.
- The concept of 'human rights' as a guide to foreign policy became more significant at the end of the Cold War. Liberals hoped this new period of calm would, at last, enable the United Nations (UN) to live up to the idealistic claims of its charter.
- Adherence to the guiding principles of the UDHR, it was hoped, would achieve a new centrality in global affairs. George H. W. Bush's declaration of a 'New World Order' seemed to herald a brighter future. Tony Blair, Bill Clinton and Kofi Annan all imagined a world in which global standards of justice would outlaw crimes against humanity, genocide and ethnic cleansing.
- Interventions in the Balkans, East Timor and Sierra Leone seemed to provide a template for a more stable and morally focused world order. The establishment of UN tribunals, the opening of the International Criminal Court (ICC) and the publication of the Responsibility to Protect indicated that if governments chose to act in defiance of international moral standards, they would now be held accountable for their actions.
- History, however, has not turned out as we expected. The bold hope of liberals, that there is such a thing as a global community, motivated by the same respect for human rights, soon proved to be hopelessly optimistic.
- Even during the optimism of the 1990s, the USA pulled out of Somalia and stood by as Rwanda slid into the abyss, and in the early 2000s provided little leadership over Darfur. Failures to achieve US objectives in Afghanistan and Iraq further discredited interventionism in the White House.
- Russia's regaining of international self-confidence and China's growing assertiveness on the UN Security Council have further challenged the liberal dream of shared values and international cooperation. The disastrous failure to rebuild Libya after Gaddafi's downfall and the West's impotence in the face of the mounting Syrian death toll further demonstrate that the liberal impulse that Tony Blair had so memorably voiced is being challenged in this new, more realist world order.
- By 2017, the ICC had achieved only three convictions. Rather than expanding its remit, its future looks bleak, as South Africa signalled its intention of abandoning the jurisdiction of the court. This is not to say that human rights and humanitarian intervention are now only of historical interest. Interventionism has saved many lives and punished the perpetrators of wicked crimes.
- The work of the ICC and the European Court of Human Rights will continue and states will keep on weighing up the consequences of intervention in humanitarian disasters.
- We can be certain that the questions raised in this chapter will remain fundamental to our understanding of global politics, and that the way in which they are answered will continue to surprise us.

Further reading

Ashdown, P. (2008) *Swords and Ploughshares: Building Peace in the Twenty-first Century*. Phoenix.

Hehir, A. (2012) *The Responsibility to Protect: Rhetoric, Reality and the Future of Humanitarian Intervention*. Palgrave Macmillan.

Hurd, D. & Young, E. (2011) *Choose Your Weapons*. Weidenfeld & Nicolson.

Power, S. (2009) *Chasing the Flame*. Penguin.

Power, S. (2010) *A Problem from Hell: America and the Age of Genocide*. Flamingo.

Human Rights Watch: www.hrw.org

Exam focus

Section A

1 Examine why the idea of an international standard of human rights is so controversial. *[12 marks]*

2 Examine the tension between human rights and state sovereignty. *[12 marks]*

3 Examine how effective international courts are in upholding global standards of justice. *[12 marks]*

4 Examine why humanitarian intervention occurs in some cases but not in others. *[12 marks]*

5 Examine the circumstances in which humanitarian intervention might be regarded as justifiable. *[12 marks]*

Section C

1 Evaluate the extent to which universal human rights have become more important in global politics. *[30 marks]*

2 Evaluate the extent to which humanitarian intervention is an abandoned project. *[30 marks]*

3 Evaluate the validity of the view that 'International law will always be undermined by state sovereignty'. *[30 marks]*

4 Evaluate why some humanitarian interventions are more successful than others. *[30 marks]*

5 Evaluate the view that 'The concept of human rights is a form of Western cultural imperialism'. *[30 marks]*

Chapter 6

Global governance: environmental

> ## Learning outcomes
>
> By the end of this chapter you should be able to:
> - understand the environmental challenges facing the global commons, including the threat and potential impact of climate change
> - evaluate the effectiveness of environmental global governance in attempting to protect the global commons (through the United Nations Framework Convention on Climate Change and the Intergovernmental Panel on Climate Change)
> - understand and evaluate different views on how to tackle environmental issues, and the obstacles to international cooperation and agreement
> - evaluate the strengths and weaknesses of major international agreements on climate change, including the obstacles to international cooperation and agreement
> - understand the role and significance of global civil society and non-state actors in addressing and resolving global environmental challenges

Getting you started

Climate change: a mortal threat?

In 2009, the president of the Maldives, Mohamed Nasheed, dived 15 m below sea level to chair his country's first underwater cabinet meeting. His ministers were unable to discuss much through their oxygen masks, but the meeting made a clear point to the international community: rising sea levels, brought about by climate change, are threatening to make the Maldives completely uninhabitable within a century. The very existence of this island nation-state is under threat. It is a threat caused by global climate change and one that the Maldives is unable to solve alone.

By 2017, scientists estimated that Antarctic sea ice had reached its smallest annual extent on record. In a decade, the Arctic ice pack has reduced in size by 10,000 km^2. One scientist even proposed a solution to re-freeze the Arctic, pumping in billions of gallons of water during the winter from 10 million wind-powered pumps.

In 2016, world average temperatures reached a record high, rising for the third successive year. The World Bank has stated that the rise in temperatures would most likely affect poorer countries. Experts predict an increase in extreme weather events including drought, floods and heat waves. Coastal cities are at risk and food and water supplies are threatened.

This was the context in which world leaders met at a conference in Paris at the end of 2015, with the aim to reach a new international agreement on tackling climate change. Paris joined a long list of cities in hosting climate

During the Maldives', underwater cabinet meeting, President Mohamed Nasheed signed a declaration calling for concerted global action on climate change

change talks, including Rio de Janeiro (1992), Kyoto (1997) and Copenhagen (2009). Previous summits had failed to produce binding targets on reducing emissions. Each had seen some states agree to take action, only to later renege on those commitments. At each summit, some powerful or developing states, such as India and the USA, had said that they were unfairly targeted and refused to agree to certain commitments.

Eventually, over 2 weeks, and with 196 parties involved, a deal was struck. The member states attending the Paris Summit agreed the first climate change deal, in which all countries were committed to taking action to cut emissions.

The Paris Agreement is the latest chapter in decades of efforts to tackle the ultimate collective action problem: climate change. Climate change is not caused by one state alone, it does not impact one state alone and it cannot be solved by one state alone. This chapter explains the international attempts to tackle climate change at a global level, first to agree the extent and existence of a problem, and second to tackle it fairly and effectively.

Why is there a need for environmental global governance?

Global governance is the process by which nation-states cooperate with each other and with non-state actors in order to try to resolve collective dilemmas. As with any area of global governance, it is necessary to understand why a global governance response to climate change is required. What environmental challenges does the world face that impact on many states and cannot be solved by one state alone?

Climate change is perhaps unique as a collective action problem, in that:

- every state contributes in some way, small or large, to its causes
- every state is affected in some way, small or large, by its effects
- every state can have an impact, small or large, in solving the problem

This is different to other collective action problems, such as global terrorism or the international drug trade, which may pose a large threat to some states but little or no threat to others. All states are affected in some way by environmental challenges. The widespread impact of industrialisation has seen to this, with all developed and most developing states contributing to global pollution.

To tackle environmental challenges effectively, states need to agree to international standards and laws that govern how they develop and limit their impact on the environment. If no attempts were made to make international laws to protect the environment, states would be left to their own good or bad intentions. Why would one state decide to take action to protect the environment, potentially at an economic cost, if it were not reassured that many other states were also doing so, and doing so with similar seriousness?

Just as universal human rights are of little value internationally if states do not agree to international law, so international efforts to protect the environment are likely to be fruitless without effective environmental global governance. In an essentially anarchical society (see page 11), the same difficulties of forcing states to take action come into play:

- States need a *framework* within which they can agree that there is a problem and how serious that problem is. With respect to the environment, this has been especially important in terms of agreeing that climate change *does* exist, in the face of temptation to some states to deny its existence (see page 229). It requires independent scientific advice, which provides a collective view that all states can equally trust.

- States need *forums* to discuss the solutions that could make a difference, to reject some solutions and to seek agreement on areas of common ground. States will not accept a higher authority forcing decisions or laws upon them, so discussion and negotiation is essential. Dedicated forums and summits, such as the 2015 Paris Summit, are required to enable states to focus on environmental issues in sufficient detail.

- States need *international laws and treaties* to be agreed so that they can be confident that other states (and non-state actors) are taking action and are held accountable for the promises they have made. This enables states to legitimise their actions and for this to be, potentially, meaningful.

Protecting the global commons

Clearly, if one state chooses to pollute the environment, this will have an impact both within and beyond its borders. Pollutants will most affect a state's immediate neighbours, but they may also have a global impact, certainly when combined with the pollution of other states. For example, China and the USA combined account for 40% of the world's carbon emissions. Some scientists have attributed pollution in China as the cause of intensifying storms over the Pacific Ocean, which have impacted weather systems in North America.

This principle of a shared global environment that can be both harmed and protected by states' individual and collective actions is known as the **global commons**. It refers to the natural environment that is shared between nation-states. The UN defines the global commons as 'resources or areas that lie outside the political reach of any one nation-state'. This includes the following.

- **The high seas:** the world's oceans are increasingly vulnerable to the impact of waste and chemical pollution from both state and non-state actors. British Petroleum's (BP) Deepwater Horizon oil spill in 2010 was the world's worst oil disaster and caused widespread environmental damage to the Gulf of Mexico, affecting 176,000 square kilometres of ocean. An estimated 8 million tonnes of plastic waste reach the world's oceans each year. Some estimates suggest that by 2050, the plastic in the ocean could weigh more than the fish that reside there.

■ **The atmosphere:** environmental global governance has focused on the atmosphere since the early 1990s, when the impact of greenhouse gases on accelerating climate change gained prominence. Former UN secretary-general Ban Ki-moon called climate change the 'major, over-riding environmental issue of our time'. Industrial pollution from the burning of fossil fuels remains the major cause of air pollution, but emissions from car exhausts and household fuel cooking also make a significant contribution. The UN Environment Programme (UNEP) highlights both the short-term impact (with 3.5 million deaths each year from air pollution) and long-term impact (changing weather patterns threatening food production and rising sea levels) of this issue.

■ **The polar regions:** both the Arctic and Antarctic have huge economic potential in terms of minerals and gas resources. Both are also key indicators for scientists of the effects of climate change. In 1959, 12 states signed the Antarctic Treaty, which protects Antarctica as a region for scientific research only, and bans military activity or resource extraction. Protection of the Arctic regions is less clear, however, and they have been subject to Russian territorial claims. In 2007, two Russian explorers planted a Russian flag on the sea bed below the North Pole in a sign of increasing competition over ownership of the Arctic Ocean. The US Department of Energy estimates that 13% of the world's undiscovered oil reserves are under the Arctic.

■ **Outer space:** with many international actors now owning active space stations and satellites, outer space has become increasingly crowded. In 2013, the US space agency NASA estimated that there were as many as 500,000 pieces of human-generated space debris orbiting the Earth.

Certain Arctic sea regions and passages are under dispute

There are several international laws designed to protect the global commons.

- **The UN Convention on the Laws of the Sea (UNCLOS):** includes laws that prevent the pollution of seas, as well as setting out the limits of states' territorial waters. UNCLOS makes it clear that states have a responsibility to prevent pollution of their own territorial waters that would, in turn, pollute international waters.
- **The Antarctic Treaty System:** sets out various environmental protections for the region, including dedicating Antarctica solely to scientific research.
- **The UN Framework Convention on Climate Change (UNFCCC):** established a process through which international treaties have been agreed to protect the atmosphere (see page 232).

The tragedy of the commons

It is easy to agree on and identify examples of pollution of, for example, the atmosphere or the oceans, which have a harmful impact on our shared environment. It is also easy, in principle, to identify that resources such as the oceans, atmosphere, polar regions and space are beyond the authority of any single nation-state and therefore are shared between states. What is harder, in global politics, is for states to avoid competing over these supposedly shared resources, or to prevent states from harming these shared resources in the pursuit of their own national interest.

The challenge of protecting the global commons is known as the **tragedy of the commons**. At the most pessimistic analysis, the global commons is doomed to remain something that states harm and compete for through their own self-interest, rather than protect and nurture as shared goals. This is down to several factors:

- States act with realist motivations in efforts to seek to protect their own national interest. This might mean that a state will refuse to sign up to international emissions targets if it believes that doing so will be expensive or make its national economic output uncompetitive.
- States are competing for economic power and resources, and this extends to natural resources. States are not acting in isolation from each other. A realist state will not want to slow its economic development by switching from easily exploited fossil fuels to more complicated and underdeveloped renewable energy.

The tragedy of the commons suggests that states' national interests and international environmental interests rarely align with one another. There are, however, increasing signs that things are changing, since sometimes what is harmful at an international level is also harmful at a national level:

- The impacts of high levels of pollution are felt most significantly at the local and national level. Extremely high levels of pollution in Chinese cities (so-called air-pocalypse) were a key factor in the country agreeing to international climate change agreements, notably the Paris Agreement. Air pollution in China accounts for around 500,000 deaths per year. In some cities, the World Health Organization (WHO) found pollution levels 56 times more than that deemed safe, and visibility in cities is sometimes reduced to less than 100m. The immediate impacts of air pollution have become a national and local issue.
- In recent climate change agreements, there have been efforts to ensure that states at different levels of development take equal steps on the road to

Key term

Tragedy of the commons
The challenge that, in a system of global politics dominated by selfish national interest and competition for economic power and natural resources, states will be motivated to use and even harm the global commons to advance their own interests, rather than working together to protect these shared resources and environments.

Extremely high levels of pollution in Chinese cities were a key factor in the country agreeing to international climate change agreements

change. For example, the 2015 Paris climate change agreement agreed that poorer states would receive financial assistance to help them move towards using cleaner sources of energy.

■ There is increasing acceptance that climate change brings with it a risk of natural disasters, such as flooding or drought, which have an immediate impact on human security and food production. India is particularly vulnerable to the impacts of climate change and, in 2016, it agreed to ratify the Paris Agreement.

What is climate change?

Environmental global governance has focused in recent decades on reducing the harmful impact of human activity and pollution in the Earth's atmosphere. In the 1980s, scientists established that the Earth's greenhouse gases (the natural gases that keep the Earth warm to enable it to sustain life) were increasing rapidly to harmful levels, and by as much as 35%. This increase in greenhouse gases would see a dangerous rise in global temperatures, warming the planet excessively. This is known as climate change or global warming.

Scientists have gradually concluded with increasingly convincing evidence that human activity has caused the increase in greenhouse gases. The key changes have been growing emissions of carbon dioxide (responsible for approximately 63% of global warming) and methane (responsible for approximately 19% of global warming). This is caused by increased burning of fossil fuels, such as oil and coal, as well as deforestation leading to fewer trees absorbing carbon dioxide from the atmosphere.

> ### Synoptic links
>
> In Component 1 there is an exploration of the global consequences of 'socialism'. For Karl Marx, Friedrich Engels and Rosa Luxemburg, socialism must be an international movement challenging nationalist self-interest. Socialists have, therefore, often endorsed global action on climate change as a way of confronting the human and environmental degradations of global capitalism.

Since 1990, it is estimated that global temperatures have risen by 0.7°C. Experts now believe that, if we don't take action to reduce greenhouse gases, global temperatures could rise by as much as 6°C by the end of this century.

There has been growing agreement among world leaders as to the existence of climate change, and that it poses a threat to human society at both national and global levels. By 2016, the world's top three 'super-polluters' (China, India and the USA) had all signed the Paris Agreement, even if they had not yet ratified it (see page 246). However, early in his presidency Donald Trump confirmed that the USA would withdraw from the Paris Agreement, which had been signed by President Obama. Now that Trump has been elected as president, many analysts predict that China will become the most powerful world leader on the issue of climate change.

The harmful effects of climate change include the following.

- Some scientists suggest that human existence itself could be threatened if temperatures rise by more than 6°C, as some forecasts suggest they might by the end of this century.
- Rising sea levels could see some nation-states disappear entirely (which has led to small island states in the Atlantic, Indian and Pacific oceans forming their own intergovernmental organisation (IGO) — the Alliance of Small Island States — to make their case), and states and cities with vulnerable coastlines come under threat.
- There could be an increase in global poverty and a decrease in global food security, caused by drought and lack of predictability of agricultural production. There is also an increased risk of natural disasters occurring with greater frequency and impact. Analysts point to the devastating 2011 floods in Pakistan and 2013's Typhoon Haiyan in the Philippines as evidence of change in weather patterns. The impact of natural disasters in poor countries has been estimated as 20–30 times larger than in industrialised countries.
- Ban Ki-moon identified climate change as 'a threat to international peace and security'. Possible causes include increased poverty and conflict over scarce resources such as food and water. The scope for heightened tensions between India and Pakistan over Himalayan water supplies for their rapidly expanding populations is a particularly worrying potential flashpoint.

What can be done to reduce climate change?

The solutions to climate change are focused on three related areas.

1   Reducing harmful emissions, mainly from fossil fuels.
2   Moving from harmful emissions to cleaner energy.
3   Developing cleaner and economically efficient clean energy.

It is important to consider that actors other than nation-states are also a part of the solution and have a role to play in tackling climate change.

- **Industry and corporations:** the key polluters are not so much states as the industries and corporations that operate within them. Of course, national governments encourage and often direct these industries (usually privately owned) to increase a state's economic power and international competitiveness. However, as climate change is a global problem, the role of multinational corporations (MNCs) is particularly important as both a cause and potential solution. Powerful MNCs can sometimes be an obstacle to state action against climate change, particularly in poorer or developing states, which are reluctant to turn down foreign direct investment to uphold strict emissions targets.

- **National laws and taxes:** states can act alone in deciding to tackle climate change, particularly the harmful effects on their immediate home environment. They can create their own national laws, which require companies to reduce their emissions (the UK's Clean Air Act was passed in 1956, decades before any international attempts to clean up the environment were seriously entertained). Alternatively, states may punish companies or citizens that pollute through higher taxes (again, UK taxes on petrol introduced in the early 1990s were aimed at taxing and punishing environmentally harmful behaviours). States can also try to encourage good behaviour or investment in cleaner technologies.

- **Non-governmental organisations (NGOs):** those NGOs dedicated to environmental campaigning, such as Greenpeace and the Worldwide Fund for Nature, can be a vital source of pressure on governments. These international pressure groups can play a similar role to global human rights advocacy groups, highlighting issues that governments or others might miss.

- **IGOs:** these play a vital role in providing states (and all other global actors listed here) with a forum in which joint action to tackle environmental challenges can be discussed, negotiated and agreed fairly. IGO-chaired talks can often appear more neutral and inclusive, as the IGO has to serve the interests of all the member states. The UNFCCC (see page 232) has provided the international basis for discussions on climate change since 1992. Increasingly, other IGOs discuss and take action on environmental matters. The European Union (EU) has been particularly active in this area, introducing EU-wide regulations on air and water quality, for example.

- **City administration:** given that it is people living in cities who suffer most from pollution, many city administrators (such as mayors with limited powers to govern a city) have taken decisions and implemented policies to reduce emissions or adopt cleaner energy. For example, London's Congestion Charge (see page 247), introduced in 2003, charges all vehicles entering central London and has subsequently reduced traffic volume in the region by 10%. The Indian city of Bangalore has converted 6,000 buses to use compressed natural gas.

- **The international science community:** a key part of environmental global governance. The UN created the Intergovernmental Panel on Climate Change (IPCC, see page 233) as a means of both pooling international expertise and also ensuring that the given scientific advice was seen to be legitimate and neutral, rather than influenced by any one state.

China: a world leader on climate change?

With climate change sceptic President Donald Trump elected to the White House, following former president Obama's more climate change-conscious presidency, there are signs that China may now take over as the most vocal international supporter of climate change action.

There are a variety of reasons why China might become a world leader on climate change:

- China's leaders' public statements are increasingly recognising the importance of protecting the environment, even referring to the need to conserve the global commons. In 2016, President Xi Jinping referred to the Paris climate change agreement as:

    a milestone in the history of climate governance. We must ensure this endeavour is not derailed. There is only one Earth in the universe and we, mankind, have only one homeland.

- The seriousness of its own pollution problems at home. Even if the USA becomes less committed to collective action, the need in China for decisive action at national level will remain compelling. The growing cost of serious health problems may become a major economic, as well as human, concern — as many as 1.6 million people are estimated to die in China each year from pollution-related causes.
- There are signs that the clean energy industry in China is becoming extremely profitable. Rather than arguing that moving from fossil fuels to cleaner energy will be costly to economic growth, China is seeing an opportunity to dominate the global market for renewable energy technology in a world that will become increasingly reliant on this energy. In 2016, China was investing twice as much as the USA in the renewable energy market.
- Chinese foreign investment abroad means that its own climate change action is not just limited to China. It is estimated to have spent US$32 billion on renewable energy projects in other countries in 2016 alone. With investment and partnerships in Africa far exceeding those of any other state, the opportunities for China to have an impact in helping poorer states move to cleaner energy sources are real.

Different viewpoints on tackling climate change

Deep and shallow ecology

Ecologism is a political ideology that places considerable importance on states' and other actors' impact on the natural environment. Ecologists believe that actors in global politics should take steps to protect the natural environment. They also believe that protecting the environment is a moral responsibility, and they criticise human behaviours that selfishly do not take into account environmental concerns.

Politicians, as opposed to scientists alone, became more concerned with environmental issues between the late 1960s and early 1970s. During this period, some politicians began to champion environmental concerns, regarding them as something only individual and collective action could solve.

Deep ecology

The Norwegian philosopher Arne Naess introduced the idea of deep green ecology as a way of thinking about humans and the environment. It is both a scientific and philosophical, and even a religious, argument. Its aim is to preserve and protect the natural environment for the benefit of the natural environment itself, regardless of the positive impact on humans. Deep ecology rejects the notion that there are only state interests and argues that protecting the natural environment and the global commons itself are essential political objectives in their own right.

Many actors in global politics do not express the views of deep ecology. Even the most committed NGOs and environmental campaign groups follow the ideas of shallow ecology, and try to persuade governments and others of the need to protect the environment for the sake of human security and wellbeing.

Shallow ecology

US philosopher Anthony Weston put forward the idea of shallow green ecology. Its aim is to preserve the natural environment so that human beings can continue to benefit from it, rather than because protecting the environment is itself a noble objective. For example, natural resources that are useful to human beings, such as oil and gas, should be used carefully and efficiently so that future generations can also make use of these resources. Shallow green ecology is more pragmatic than deep ecology and is more rooted in politics than in religion or spiritualism.

> **Synoptic links**
>
> In Component 2, ecologism explores the development of radical or deep ecology. This sort of ecology is founded on reverence for the planet rather than practical self-interest, and is associated with the groundbreaking work of Aldo Leopold and Rachel Carson.

The idea of green politics emerged in the late 1970s, and with it the first references to 'green' political thinking and political parties. The first 'green' political parties were founded in Belgium and Germany. In the UK, the Ecology Party became the Green Party in 1990.

Green parties have generally struggled to gain enough electoral support to form governments, though in some European states (for example, Germany and Latvia) they have governed as junior partners in a coalition government.

The differences between developing and developed states

As the international community has tried to find solutions to climate change and ways of reducing its impact, at various points developing states have argued that the pressure put on them to take steps to reduce climate change is not fair. The differences of opinion between developed and developing states have reduced considerably in recent years. Nevertheless, we will see that during key international environmental negotiations, developing states have raised grievances, including the following.

- Developed states did not have to consider protecting the environment when they were industrialising. They did so unrestricted by environmental regulations. Now that developing states are industrialising and aiming to catch up with developed states, they are having to do so while under international pressure to agree to rules, for example that limit the types of energy they are able to use. Developing states argue that they are being held accountable to a higher standard than was required of developed states when they were developing.

- Environmental restrictions may impact on the speed and success of developing states' progress. Such restrictions were not part of the modernisation theory that currently developed states followed.
- Developing states still have large populations living in poverty. Industrialisation is one way of reducing poverty, with expanding industry providing jobs and energy production to enable more people to enter employment, develop skills and earn better wages. Developing states argue that their development journey is just beginning. India's government estimates that 'more than half of the India of 2030 is yet to be built'. For some states, development through carbon energy is seen to be a cheaper alternative to investment in more expensive, cleaner sources of energy.
- Developed states caused much of the impact of pollution and climate change during their period of industrialisation. In its submission to the Paris climate change conference, India estimated that it was responsible for only 3% of historic cumulative emissions, whereas the USA and EU were responsible for 16% and 15% respectively. China, the EU, Japan, Russia and the USA together have been responsible for two-thirds of the world's historic carbon dioxide emissions. The argument goes that current restrictions on developing states are a result of the historical emissions and damaged caused by developed states.

On the other hand, it is argued that developing states should play a significant role in tackling climate change:
- Emissions in developed states are stable, while those in developing states are rapidly increasing. Scientists estimate that if India's economic growth continues at the rate of 8.5% per year, its emissions will soon reach one-fifth of the total world emissions that scientists believe the world can cope with before exceeding a harmful 2°C temperate increase.

Global population is expected to keep growing — some estimates have put the total population at 9.6 billion by 2050

- It is the poorest states that are the most vulnerable to the impact of climate change, such as through natural disasters or food production difficulties. Natural disasters, such as devastating floods, have a short-term impact on human security and safety, but a longer-term impact on economic development when crucial infrastructure is destroyed.
- Large population growth makes the potential challenge more pressing in developing states. Emissions are currently increasing and, if no action were taken, would increase dramatically as populations rise.

In recent years, however, developing states have come increasingly to accept the need to take action on climate change. The largest developing countries responsible for global emissions, Brazil and India, and the African Union (AU) have all made clear commitments:

- India signed and ratified the Paris Agreement in 2016. It has promised to generate 40% of energy from non-fossil fuels by 2030, although it will need help from the international community to achieve this. It estimated that the cost of meeting its commitments to reduce climate change would be over US$2.9 trillion. India's population is likely to grow from 1.2 billion to 1.5 billion by 2030, making its future energy needs very high — in 2012, nearly 20% of the existing population did not have access to electricity.
- Brazil has both signed and ratified the Paris Agreement, making it the third-largest country responsible for global emissions, after China and the USA, to ratify the deal. It has said that it will increase renewable energy sources to 45% of all energy consumption by 2030. Brazil's contribution to climate change is somewhat different to other states, in that deforestation in the Amazon basin is the main cause of its emissions, rather than the burning of fossil fuels. Brazil has reduced deforestation by 80% since 2004, although small rises in deforestation in 2013 and 2015 confirm the continuing challenges of managing this reduction. Brazil ratified the climate change deal in the face of a slowing economy.
- The AU has been supportive of the most recent climate change negotiations in Paris. The majority of African states have at least signed the Paris Agreement. Climate change is frequently on the agenda of AU summits. The World Bank is an example of an IGO that supports African states in meeting their climate change commitments, for example by funding US$16 billion of investment through the Africa Climate Business Plan. The World Bank estimated in 2015 that Africa would need US$5–10 billion per year to meet the Paris climate change targets, and that these costs would only rise by the middle of the century.

Equally, there has been increasing agreement that developed states should help developing states to take action on climate change, and that they will not be able to fund meaningful action on their own. The first commitment came in the first international summit on the environment, the 1972 Stockholm Declaration on the Environment. Here, it was agreed that developing states needed financial assistance to safeguard the environment. This has been a continuing theme, amounting to more specific help in the Paris Agreement in 2016, where it was agreed to provide US$100 billion a year in climate finance to developing countries by 2020, with a commitment to further finance in the future.

Is it fair to ask developing states to do more to tackle climate change?

Yes

- Pollution from developing states is increasing. This will eventually overtake the pollution from developed states, so now is the time to act to reduce future emissions.
- Protecting the environment is essential, rather than an impediment, to states' development. Former Indian prime minister Indira Gandhi put forward this idea as early as 1972.
- Developing states are most likely to be affected by the negative impact of climate change, in terms of natural disasters.
- The right to develop need not be incompatible with developing in a way that does not harm the global commons.
- Developed countries that went through their own periods of industrialisation in the nineteenth and twentieth centuries didn't have access to the same technology and clean energy currently available to developing countries. It is not unreasonable to ask developing states to use this technology now that it is accessible.

No

- Pollution from developed states is not increasing, but currently developed states do pollute more than developing states. Developed states should therefore concentrate on reducing their emissions. They are also in a better position to do so, as they remain economically powerful.
- Economic growth is more stable and industrialisation is well established in developed states, making them better able to fund and innovate ways of tackling climate change. The benefits of this innovation could then be transferred to developing states.
- Developing states have a right to develop. Dependency theory (see page 159) and the unequal spread of globalisation benefits both already mean that developing states face huge challenges in catching up to developed states. Asking developing states to take action on climate change while they develop merely makes their catching up harder to achieve.
- Historically, developed states have contributed hugely to the emissions that have caused harm to the planet. It is unfair for developing states now to be asked to contribute to a problem largely caused by developed states.

Research the actions that both developed and developing states have taken to reduce climate change, before comparing and contrasting these actions. You can use the following examples.
- **Emerging economic powers:** China, Brazil, India
- **Established economic powers:** Germany, the UK, the USA
- **Less developed and less powerful states:** Ghana, Nigeria, Sudan

Do you think that all of these states are doing enough to combat climate change?

Sustainable development
A form of development that seeks to conserve the natural environment so that the requirements of the present do not compromise the needs of the future.

Sustainability

Then-US secretary of state John Kerry highlighted the impact of climate change on future generations and the need for **sustainable development** when he signed the Paris Agreement in 2016 alongside his granddaughter.

Sustainable development is important for reducing poverty (see page 115) and has become a major focus with the Sustainable Development Goals (SDGs) agreed in 2015, replacing the largely successful Millennium Development Goals (MDGs), which did not given the same importance to climate change. Furthermore, clearly sustainable development plays an important role in tackling climate change — SDG 13 focuses on 'taking urgent action to tackle climate change and its harmful impacts'.

SDG 13 does not attempt to replace any of the UN's existing agreements or forums on climate change, such as the UNFCCC (see page 232), but the SDGs as a whole do offer the UN a means by which it can support nation-states in tackling climate change. States and MNCs can, of course, take the most meaningful action, but the SDG programme provides a framework of meaningful assistance for them to achieve their goals.

The UN states that it provides 'enabling support' to those countries that otherwise might find it difficult to take action alone. There are several key areas of support.

- **Science for decision making:** in addition to the scientific support the IPCC provides (see page 233), the UN provides funding and training for research within states, particularly developing states. Developing this expertise helps to build a knowledge base of information and science on the extent of climate change and how it impacts specific regions and communities.
- **Low carbon technologies:** shifting from a reliance on fossil fuels to cleaner energy can be expensive for developing states. The UN works to bring together different stakeholders, such as renewable energy companies, governments and scientists, to help link the needs of governments and societies with a private sector that is developing cleaner energy technology, so that both are better able to understand these needs and challenges.
- **Education and training:** the UN has funded education in schools and universities as a way of driving economic and social change. Training has also focused on helping people develop professional skills, such as carrying out accurate assessments of the environmental or the health impact of pollution or other economic activity. The UN has also provided technical advice when governments are developing national climate change plans.
- **Data and information:** tackling climate change effectively relies on accurate data, to allow for accurate measurement of future impacts. The UN has helped by advising states on how they can use population surveys (census) to measure the impact and potential risk of climate change. Studies have also been carried out to analyse the impact of climate change on migration, where families and communities have been forced to move for climate-related reasons.

Climate change scepticism and denial

Of course, there is still not universal agreement that climate change exists or that it is having a serious impact. There are three main groups that oppose scientific opinion on climate change:

1 Those who do not believe that climate change is happening at all and believe that the Earth is not warming.
2 Those who believe that the Earth may be warming, but that this is happening naturally and is not caused by human activity. Some climate change deniers believe the sun should be blamed for global warming, with scientific research from 2014 stating that solar activity is a leading cause of rising temperatures.
3 Those who accept that the Earth is warming, but question the speed at which this is happening and the impact it is likely to have.

Given that climate change denial and scepticism still exists, and that some states have historically used it to avoid taking action, many early climate change summits focused on the need to get states to agree that the science is correct and that climate change does, indeed, exist. This was a necessary first step before later summits could agree upon exactly what action states could and should take.

Debate

How do realists and liberals view climate change?

Realists

- It is important to address climate change, but not before other states also address it. All states should move forward at a similar pace and at a similar level of seriousness — one state must not take more action than another.
- Any action must take into account the economic impact — actions must not harm the economy and allow other, rival states to take economic advantage.
- National interest drives all thinking on appropriate state action. If a measure is likely to be harmful to a state's economy and development, that state may not be persuaded to take action. If inaction is likely to be harmful, for example through increased risk of natural disasters, a state may be persuaded to take action.

Liberals

- Climate change is a collective action problem and global governance is required to fix it. The global commons is a resource from which all states benefit and all should protect, and individual states must not harm it through their own self-interest.
- IGOs provide a useful forum for states to discuss climate change and to agree international law, to hold states accountable for their promises on climate change.
- Developed states should help developing states to take action on climate change, since their contribution to climate change will be most dramatic. If unchecked, climate change will also have the most serious impact on poorer, developing states, so they must receive assistance to act.

Case study

Is the Trump administration in denial of climate change?

In 2012, Donald Trump argued that China had invented the notion of climate change in order to make US manufacturing non-competitive. Around 20 years earlier, similar claims were made in China that climate change was designed to hold back China's economic development.

The Chinese government strongly rejected Trump's accusation. Vice-Foreign Minister Liu Zhenmin said in 2016 that:

> if you look at the history of climate change negotiations, these were initiated by the IPCC with the support of the Republican presidents during the Reagan and senior Bush administration during the late 1980s.

Foreign affairs warned that the reversal of climate change policies (under President Trump) could bring about a global knock-on effect, pushing the world towards harsh nationalism and reducing international cooperation. Upon election, President Trump published an America First Energy Plan, indicating that he would overturn President Obama's Climate Action Plan and stating that his administration would 'take advantage of the estimated US$50 trillion in untapped shale, oil and natural gas reserves' on US soil, in an effort to reduce the USA's energy dependency.

He has also stated that he is committed to clean coal technology and to reviving the US coal industry. In his first weeks in office, Trump was criticised by environmentalists for approving the construction of a new oil pipeline from Canada to Texas. The policy highlighted a continuing thirst for using oil and threatened damage to sensitive environments along the pipeline's path.

During his election campaign, Trump was inconsistent about his views on the Paris Agreement. He also modified his position on the extent of climate change, from being a 'hoax' to stating that 'there was some connectivity, some' between human activity and climate change. In June 2017, Trump officially withdrew the USA from the Paris Agreement, stating that the USA would, 'begin negotiations to re-enter either the Paris Accord or an entirely new transaction on terms that are fair to the United States, its businesses, its workers, its people, its taxpayers'.

Global governance efforts

The first global governance efforts to protect the environment began in the 1970s. Since those early days, states have agreed upon a whole range of new agreements, institutions and laws by working together in international bodies (see Box 6.1). It is important to assess the impact these global governance efforts have had. Where has progress been made? What has delayed progress?

Global governance of environmental matters has been focused on the following key areas.

- **Agreement on the need to protect the global commons:** without this, states would not agree on or wish to become involved with global efforts to protect the global commons. They would either do nothing or be discouraged from acting if other states didn't also play their part.

- **Agreement on the scientific evidence for environmental threats affecting the global commons:** crucially, this involves agreeing on the causes of harm to the environment in order to take action against them. If states were to disagree on the causes, they would either avoid action or target the wrong issues, thereby reducing their impact. The IPCC is the main international body responsible for providing the UN and states with rigorous and impartial scientific evidence, in response to which states can make the most suitable decisions.

- **Providing a negotiating framework for states and non-state actors to take action:** the idea of a negotiating framework may sound like a vague concept. However, states have signed up to the UNFCCC, in which they agree to be part of ongoing negotiations and discussions to tackle climate change. Without this guiding process and commitment to continual efforts to reach ever better and more comprehensive agreements, global environmental governance efforts would be rudderless. Within this framework, more specific agreements can be made (such as the Paris Agreement).

- **International summits to agree specific principles and action to be taken:** gatherings of world leaders and other actors, such as NGOs, MNCs and scientists, are required to give focus to — and sometimes to revive — international efforts.

Key international meetings on climate change

There have been several key international meetings in relation to climate change.

- **Stockholm UN Conference on the Human Environment (1972):** members agreed on the principle of the need to protect the global commons. There was an emphasis on states taking individual, rather than collective, action.
- **Rio Earth Summit (1992):** the UNFCCC was agreed as part of three so-called Rio Declarations. The convention requires that states agree to work together to reach more specific international agreements on future climate change.
- **Kyoto Summit (1997):** set internationally binding targets to reduce carbon emissions. The targets apply only to industrialised states. Over 100 industrialising states, including Brazil, China, India and South Africa, are exempt from emissions targets. The USA signed but did not ratify the Kyoto Protocol. The protocol came into full legal force nearly a decade later, in 2005.
- **Copenhagen Climate Change Confererence (2009):** included the 15th Conference of the Parties (COP 15), but did not agree legally binding commitments. A key challenge in the negotiations was the problem of fairness between targets for developed and developing states. Unlike Kyoto, it agreed that developing states would do more to combat climate change and that developed states would also help raise US$100 billion by 2020 for developing states to invest in tackling climate change.
- **UN Climate Change Conference/Paris COP 21 Summit (2016):** the agreement was the first to achieve commitment from all states to cut carbon emissions. Fewer differences were allowed between developed and developing states. The agreement was partly legally binding and partly voluntary. States agreed to an ambitious pledge to prevent global temperature from rising above 2°C this century. There was more funding to help developing states play their part in tackling climate change.

The UN Framework Convention on Climate Change

The **United Nations Framework Convention on Climate Change (UNFCCC)** was agreed in 1992 at the Rio Earth Summit and provides a pathway for international cooperation. The UN Secretariat manages and organises summits and convention negotiations (see page 235). States who signed the UNFCCC committed to beginning a journey together where they, under UN guidance and encouragement, would work towards international agreements and ever more detailed and ambitious commitments. The UNFCCC's overall focus has been to work to limit global average temperature rises.

A total of 197 states have signed the UNFCCC. As of early 2017, 127 parties had both signed and ratified the convention.

As a direct result of the UNFCCC, there have been two major further agreements.

- **The Kyoto Protocol (see page 239):** set legally binding targets for reducing emissions.
- **The Paris Agreement (see page 244):** strengthened the global response to climate change and states pledged to keep global temperature rises this century below 2°C and to aim to limit global temperature rises to 1.5°C.

The UNFCCC commits member states to the following principles, through which they can take more specific action in the future.

- It requires member states to agree to act in the interests of human safety, even in the face of scientific uncertainty.
- It identified reducing dangerous greenhouse gases as the primary focus. It pledges to keep greenhouse gases at a level that prevents human-caused harm to the climate and to ensure that food production 'is not threatened, and to enable economic development to proceed in a sustainable manner'.

- It specifically asks developed countries to do the most to reduce climate change, since 'they are the source of most past and current greenhouse gas emissions' and 'are expected to do the most to cut emissions on home ground'.
- It requires developed states to commit to helping developing states to tackle climate change through financial support.
- It asks developed states to report their progress on climate change policies annually and to publish figures on their greenhouse gas emissions. These country statements began to provide a useful means by which the UN could monitor the promises and progress individual states were making. These state reports could then be independently monitored, praised or criticised. This was the first step towards states being more accountable for the actions they take to reduce climate change.

From the beginning, the UNFCCC recognised the need to treat developed and developing states differently. It does not state that developing states should do nothing to tackle climate change, but recognises that they should have financial help from more industrialised states. The UNFCCC also acknowledges that economic development is vital to developing states, and that achieving this is difficult, even without the requirements to take steps to reduce climate change. However, it does not let developing states off the hook, but instead promises to help them reduce their emissions in a way that prevents any adverse effects on their economic development.

The UNFCCC's strengths are that it has extremely wide membership, with 197 states signed and 127 ratifying the treaty. Before the UNFCCC, international meetings on environmental matters were infrequent and unfocused, and there was no way of ensuring that states would continue to participate in regular climate change discussion. The UNFCCC therefore provides its principles as a roadmap for negotiations between all of the world's current major polluters and future polluters, all of which have participated consistently and annually since 1992. No state has subsequently decided to leave the UNFCCC. It has continued to act as the international driving force behind future agreements. However imperfect they may be, future agreements in Kyoto and Paris would have been much harder to achieve without the negotiating structures and agreements on principle set out in the convention.

When the government of a state signs and ratifies an international treaty, such as the UNFCCC, future governments of that state are bound by that treaty unless they decide to withdraw from it. Withdrawing from an international treaty, particularly one with such international legitimacy and recognition as the UNFCCC, is politically controversial and places more pressure on new governments to stick with commitments made by their predecessors. The UNFCCC has, therefore, encouraged successive governments to continue with international discussion and negotiations, some of which have been highly successful (for example, when legally binding emissions targets were agreed at Kyoto).

The Intergovernmental Panel on Climate Change

In the 1970s and 1980s, the scientific evidence for climate change was at a very early stage of development. It was clear that greenhouse gases were having a harmful impact on the environment and that human activity was the most probable cause. Just as action to combat environmental harm existed only at national level (and in some cases not at all), scientific research and investigation was similarly uncoordinated. Scientific investigations required international funding and knowledge needed to be pooled and maximised.

A further problem was that scientific advice and research risked becoming associated with individual states and their governments, or at the very least with the economic world view of a particular state. There was a need for the scientific advice to be seen as impartial and neutral, rather than advancing the interests of any one state and its economy.

By the late 1980s, the Stockholm Declaration had agreed much on the principles of collective action to prevent global environmental harm. The declaration had, in many ways, been achieved based on very little scientific evidence. In order to achieve more meaningful global action, it was clear that states required scientific advice of the highest quality and credibility.

The **Intergovernmental Panel on Climate Change (IPCC)** was created in 1988 to address these difficulties. Its aim is to provide governments and other decision-makers with expert advice through the following principles.

- **Regular assessments of the impact and extent of climate change:** this has been especially important since states have begun, individually and collectively, to take steps to reduce climate change. Regular tracking of global and national progress, including emissions levels, is essential for progress in the right areas.
- **Regular assessments of the causes and risks of climate change:** with each international conference on climate change, the evidence base improves. A reliable and well-researched evidence base is essential in order to persuade states to make commitments and prove the link between human activity and climate change. A weak evidence base would fail to persuade nations to act and leave them unaware of the potential risks and dangers.
- **Possible solutions to reduce the impact or manage the effects of climate change:** for some states, investing in renewable energy sources will be costly. International research into new technologies is more efficient than states conducting their own research. In this way, the IPCC has helped to propose clear and viable solutions for actions and initiatives that can reduce climate change.

Just as the responsibility for addressing climate change is a collective action problem, so too is the scientific assessment of the issues. Furthermore, pooling the expertise of scientists from across the world ensures that evidence for climate change is not seen to come from any one state.

The IPCC operates in the following ways.

- It advises governments but does not, and cannot, force them into upholding its advice.
- It aims to provide both balanced and rigorous advice and assessments.
- Hundreds of scientists from many countries are involved in developing IPCC assessments and advice. This allows for many different views on climate change to be fed through to the IPCC in an open and transparent manner. For example, 86 experts from 39 states will carry out the next assessment of global temperature rises. These experts have been selected through 560 nominations from states and designated observer organisations (including agencies such as the UN Development Programme and NGOs such as Greenpeace and the Worldwide Fund for Nature). A total of 38% of the experts are women, and 51% are from what the IPCC refers to as 'developing states' and 'economies in transition'.
- It has produced regular reports since its founding (see Box 6.2). These assessment reports are major pieces of scientific research, which help to inform international meetings under the UNFCCC.

Box 6.2

Key IPCC reports

The IPCC has produced a number of key climate change reports.

- **First Assessment Report (1990):** confirmed that increased greenhouse gases were causing climate change and that human activity had caused an increase in greenhouse gases. It predicted global temperature rises of 0.3°C per decade.
- **Second Assessment Report (1995):** showed that greenhouse gases were continuing to rise, with global temperature rises per decade remaining as predicted in 1990.
- **Third Assessment Report (2001):** some ecosystems and species would be irretrievably lost if action to reduce climate change was not taken. Some counter-measures were recommended, for example flood defences, which may reduce the impact of climate change, but these measures cannot be guaranteed.
- **Fourth Assessment Report (2007):** many of the impacts of climate change can be reduced, delayed or avoided through mitigation. The report was 90% certain that global warming is caused by human activity. Unmitigated climate change would, in the long term, be likely to 'exceed the capacity of natural, managed and human systems to adapt'.
- **Fifth Assessment Report (2015):** produced using the expertise of over 800 experts. It was likely that the period between 1983 and 2013 was the warmest 30-year period for 1,400 years. It confirmed the loss of ice sheets in Antarctica and Greenland, concluding that it was 95–100% certain that human activity had caused global warming. The projection for global mean temperature rises by 2100 was more than 1.5°C in each of the modelled scenarios.

The IPCC has largely been very successful at establishing a credible, trusted and neutral evidence base. It has been highly inclusive, with scientists from both developed and developing states participating in its research. In doing so, it has helped to build the capacity and skills of scientists in developing states so that they can better assess the impact of climate change, not just internationally but at a national level.

The pooling of such a wide range of expertise has also been a form of academic compromise. When states negotiate with each other on matters of policy, they put their views across, debate them and reach a compromise that is not just one state's view but one on which they can all agree. Similarly, the IPCC takes into account a wide variety of scientific research and ensures that a compromise is reached in its advice and assessments. This reduces the risk that the scientific advice provided to states is unbalanced, or too sceptical or extreme in its views. Consulting a group of scientists numbered in the hundreds ensures that all theories and research are taken into account.

International summits

International summits bring together states and other actors, ranging from MNCs to NGOs and scientists, to agree steps they can jointly take to protect the environment. The first summit — the Stockholm Conference on the Human Environment — was held in 1972.

The aims of international summits can be broadly summarised as follows.

- **Identifying and agreeing the problem and the need for collective action:** the Stockholm Conference on the Human Environment (1972) and the Rio Earth Summit (1992). These summits clarified the idea that humans had a right to a healthy and clean environment, linked with the idea of third generation human rights.
- **Agreeing specific action to be taken and making collective action a reality:** Kyoto (1997), Copenhagen (2009) and Paris (2015). These summits began to hold states accountable for binding commitments to reduce the causes and impact of climate change.

The United Nations Conference on the Human Environment (1972)

This summit, held in Stockholm, Sweden (and hence sometimes referred to as the Stockholm Conference) agreed 26 key principles, at a very early stage both in the development of scientific evidence for and international responses to climate change. However, it did not amount to international law or any binding commitments — the only requirement at this stage was for a majority of states to agree that there *was* a problem and that the problem could only be solved through international cooperation (see Box 6.3).

The conference came about after the UN Economic and Social Council (ECOSOC, see page 107) and the UN General Assembly (see page 105) voted in favour of a UN-led international conference on the human impact on the environment.

Some of the key principles of the Stockholm Declaration included:

- natural resources must be safeguarded
- non-renewable resources must be shared and safeguarded
- pollution must not exceed the environment's capacity to clean itself
- development is needed to improve the environment
- developing countries need financial assistance to develop environmental safeguards
- science and technology must be used to protect the environment
- each nation must establish its own standards

Box 6.3

Indira Gandhi

India's prime minister Indira Gandhi gave an important speech at the 1972 Stockholm Conference. For the first time, the leader of a developing state made an explicit link between successful development and the need to protect the environment. Gandhi argued that both were needed for states to develop properly:

> There are grave misgivings that the discussion on ecology may be designed to distract attention from the problems of war and poverty... We have to prove to the disinherited majority of the world that ecology and conservation will not work against their interest but will bring an improvement in their lives.

> The environmental problems of developing countries are not the side effects of excessive industrialisation but reflect the inadequacy of development.

Former Indian prime minister Indira Gandhi

Unlike the climate conferences of today, impartial and comprehensive scientific research, such as that conducted by the IPCC, was not yet readily available for assessment in Stockholm. There was plenty of scientific research highlighting the negative impact of humans on the environment, and increasing political agitation for ecological causes (seen through the increasing prominence of shallow and deep ecology (see page 225)), but scientific evidence and the political process were still acting in isolation from each other and had not yet been fully joined up.

Furthermore, there was still the sense at this stage that nation-states should develop their own policies to react to climate change, rather than agreeing to international standards — in fact, one of the declaration's principles was that 'each nation should develop its own standards'. This is very different to the idea today that states should adopt common standards. In many ways, this is unsurprising. At the time, states were taking little or insufficient action of their own. Stockholm's key objective was to ensure that states began acting independently to protect the environment. It was a leap too far to expect collective action at this point — that would come later.

The Montreal Protocol (1989)

The Montreal Protocol (full name the Montreal Protocol on Substances that Deplete the Ozone Layer) has been celebrated as one of the earliest successes of environmental global governance. Its achievements are all the more impressive given that both the scientific and the political institutions supporting environmental global governance were not yet fully developed — there was certainly no support structure as well developed as the UNFCCC, within which states could make agreements.

The protocol aimed to protect the ozone layer (the layer in the Earth's atmosphere that absorbs much of the sun's radiation, reducing excessive warming of the planet). Key measures included the banning of chlorofluorocarbons (CFCs) and other chemicals, whose emissions harmed the ozone layer and exposed the Earth to the risk of significant temperature rises.

It is a testament to the success of the Montreal Protocol that later climate change negotiations and agreements have mostly been focused on reducing carbon dioxide emissions, based on the hugely successful steps made in Montreal to reduce harmful non-carbon dioxide emissions. Recent research reveals that, had it not been for the Montreal Protocol, non-carbon dioxide emissions would have become more serious and harmful than carbon dioxide emissions in terms of their contribution to global warming. For that reason alone, scientists estimate that the Montreal Protocol had five to six times greater impact on reducing climate change than the Kyoto Protocol (see page 239). Other studies predict that the ozone layer will return to its 1980 condition by 2050 or 2070 as a result of the measures taken in Montreal.

A total of 197 states have now ratified the Montreal Protocol. Other Montreal successes include the following.

■ It was the first example of an environmental global governance treaty where a certain number of states were required to sign and ratify the treaty before it would come into force. This principle, designed to encourage collective action, would later be used to full effect in the Kyoto Protocol and the Paris Agreement.

■ The Montreal Protocol saw the first use of the *precautionary principle*. This is an agreement to take action as a precaution even if the science underpinning the need for action is not yet fully proven. The burden lies in proving that there are *not* harmful effects, rather than proving that there are.

■ The protocol recognised the need for states to take different types of action, with some states needing to do more than others. This was another key principle to which later summits would adhere, sometimes to their cost (in the case of the Kyoto Protocol) and sometimes to their benefit (in the case of the Paris Agreement).

The success of the Montreal Protocol perhaps lies in the fact that states did not feel that their economic interests would be harmed through ratifying and implementing the treaty. Unlike later requirements to reduce carbon emissions and move to cleaner energy, moving away from CFCs was far less costly and did not have any wider impact on economies as a whole, unlike in the case of moving a fossil fuel-reliant economy to cleaner energy.

Another Montreal success was the widespread feeling among states that they were sharing the burden of action equally, something that was missing at the notably less successful Kyoto Summit.

The Rio Earth Summit (1992)

The UN Rio Earth Summit was the second major meeting of nation-states working in a forum to discuss global protection of the environment.

There had been a gap of 20 years since the Stockholm Conference and Declaration. In the interim period, states had mostly been left to their own devices in terms of their response to dealing with climate change. The Stockholm Declaration had agreed the principles of protecting the global environment but had not set out a pathway for future, more detailed discussion and agreement. There was a need to give fresh international impetus and revive environmental global governance efforts. Above all, there was a need to establish a process by which states and the UN could continue to work together.

The summit met for 2 weeks and 172 governments were in attendance, including 112 heads of state. This gave the summit considerable legitimacy and made the negotiations more impactful. NGOs were also represented in their thousands. Alongside meetings between world leaders, there was a people's summit, with 17,000 ordinary citizens from across the world in attendance. It was the most comprehensive global environment conference that had ever taken place.

Unlike more recent summits, which have focused on precise actions that can be taken to reduce climate change, the key goal at Rio was to get states to agree to a framework for future action. In this way, it was continuing the work of the Stockholm Declaration. The major success of the Rio Earth Summit was agreeing to the UNFCCC (see page 232).

Alongside the UNFCCC, the Rio Declaration set out some very important key agreements on the principles at stake in protecting the global commons:

■ Economic progress is only ensured if it is linked with the protection of the environment. Economic progress would, ultimately, be harmed if the environment were not protected.

■ The international community should aim to develop further international agreements in order to protect the global environment and ensure responsible development.

■ People are entitled to a healthy and productive life. This, for the first time, introduced a strong link between human rights and the environment. Human rights had long protected the rights to, for example, food and shelter, but not clean air.

- The future basis of sustainable development — development today should not threaten the needs of present and future generations.
- States have the right to exploit their own resources, but not by causing damage to the environment beyond their borders.
- Environmental issues are best managed by the participation of all citizens. This confirmed environmental issues as a collective action problem.
- Scientific knowledge of the problem needed to be improved. States agreed to share knowledge and technologies to manage climate change.

How successful was the Rio Earth Summit? The UNFCCC is undoubtedly the major success of the summit, as it locked in signatory states to a process of annual negotiations and, ultimately, legally binding agreements.

In terms of specific actions to tackle climate change, there was little achieved. But, arguably, the Rio Summit and Declaration represented a major success, because it led to the international community agreeing that there was indeed a problem and that the problem needed to be solved through collective action and continued commitment. These agreements did not exist before the Rio Summit, and future action would not be possible without states coming together on these two basic principles.

Kyoto COP Summit and Protocol (1997)

The next major international conference on climate change was held in 1997 in Kyoto, Japan. The UNFCCC showed that the Rio Summit had been a major step forward, but legally binding emissions targets were now required to hold states accountable for their actions. Therefore, the Kyoto meetings marked a shift in environmental global governance, from agreeing the existence of the problem, to identifying *specific actions* that states could take in order to reduce climate change. It was also the first attempt to hold states accountable for their actions via legally binding commitments.

During the Kyoto Summit, industrialised states made a commitment to reduce global greenhouse gas emissions

The Kyoto Protocol endorsed the following principles.

- There would be legally binding targets to reduce emissions (known as quantified emissions limitation and reduction objectives). These would only be required of 37 industrialised states and the EU. Coverage was not comprehensive and not all states agreed to these legally binding targets.
- Industrialised states were committed to reducing emissions of greenhouse gases by around 5% over the next decade.
- The principle of collective action was reinforced, as the Kyoto Protocol would not legally come into force until enough countries (who were together responsible for at least 55% of the world's carbon emissions) had ratified it. Additionally, a total of 55 states were required to ratify the treaty before it came into force. This principle of collective action would reassure states that others were also taking action, they would not be acting alone and meaningful global action through many states acting together would have the greatest impact, making any national sacrifices (for example, to economic development) easier to justify.
- Brazil, China, India and South Africa were granted exemption from emissions targets. In total, 100 developing states were exempt from the treaty.
- States that did not keep to their targets should face legally binding consequences.
- The Kyoto Protocol was also time-limited, with an expiry date set in 2012. This meant that a further climate change conference would be required to take the deal further and to review Kyoto's success.
- Individual states agreed to their own targets for emissions reductions. Some states with low emissions, such as Iceland and Portugal, were allowed to increase their emissions.
- The treaty set up an international trading system, by which states could earn 'carbon credits' towards meeting their emissions targets by investing in reducing emissions in other states.

While the Kyoto Protocol was a major step forward in terms of agreeing specific global steps to combat climate change and legally binding targets, these stringent targets were beset with problems.

- The protocol did not come into force until 2005, nearly a decade after the Kyoto Summit and nearly halfway through the lifetime of the treaty (the original time period for meeting targets being 1997–2012).
- While states deliberated, emissions increased by as much as 40–50% between 1990 and 2009.
- The agreement was not comprehensive, with Brazil, China, India and South Africa entirely exempt. This was a key factor in the USA deciding to reject the treaty (see Case study), which in turn led to Canada revoking its consent. The protocol's inconsistencies created too many grievances, with states questioning whether others were being asked to do enough. It would take a more comprehensive and universal approach to reassure states that a majority were making a broadly equal and fair contribution. Both China and Russia were also not covered by legally binding targets. Russia did later ratify the treaty, but only 7 years after the summit. China did not sign the treaty, and it is estimated that its emissions have increased by nearly 300% during the treaty's lifetime.

The USA rejects Kyoto

President Bill Clinton (Democrat) signed the Kyoto Protocol, but it was never submitted to the Senate for ratification. It was clear that the Senate would not ratify Kyoto, and in 2001 the incoming president, George W. Bush (Republican), formally renounced the protocol, stating that it would harm the economy and that the USA would never sign it. President Bush's key objection was that developing states were not being asked to do enough to combat climate change.

Ultimately, the Kyoto Protocol never included the world's major polluter, the USA being responsible for around 36% of global emissions at that point. This demonstrated that securing world leaders' signatures on climate change treaties is one thing, but getting states to ratify those treaties into national law to ensure said treaties have legal effect is quite another.

When the world's largest polluting state decided not to ratify the Kyoto Protocol, it was dealt a significant blow. If the biggest polluter had not signed up, why should other, less-polluting states do so?

Synoptic links

Component 1 explores the importance of small government in the development of modern-day conservatism. According to conservative thinkers, such as Ayn Rand and Robert Nozick, the influence of the state should be kept to a minimum. Conservative thinkers have often, therefore, regarded demands for action on climate change as a veiled attempt to increase the power of the state over the individual.

In spite of the obvious failures of the Kyoto Protocol, there were some successes. Some regions and states did indeed stick to their commitments to successfully reduce emissions. The EU reduced its emissions by around 8% during its compliance with the protocol. The EU's success perhaps reflects its ability to create regulations that apply to a group of states (see page 299) while reassuring European countries that they are all acting together, rather than bearing the burden alone. The USA did actually reduce its carbon emissions during this period, with pollution decreasing to levels previously seen in 1992. In all, 30 countries pledged to continue to meet Kyoto's targets, even once the treaty had officially expired in 2012.

Copenhagen COP 15 Summit (2009)

By 2009, it was widely agreed that the Kyoto Protocol had failed. The most significant polluting states had either been exempt or had withdrawn from the protocol. A new round of climate change negotiations was required. The Kyoto deal was also set to expire in 2012 and a new deal was needed to replace it.

The key challenge was the need for collective action and a comprehensive agreement. Kyoto had failed, in part, because there were legally binding targets for some, but not all, states, with some entirely exempt. Yet others were allowed to increase their emissions targets. Therefore, a key objective of the Copenhagen Summit was to get the largest polluters, especially the USA, to agree on collective action. It also needed to address the question of those contributions expected of developing states, in order for developed states to agree to the deal. Developing states required help, but not exemptions.

Politically, the Copenhagen Summit was timely. There had been a change of US president that same year, and Barack Obama came to office pledging that the USA would commit to international collective action in order to tackle climate change. In fact, President Obama committed considerable personal effort to the talks, directly leading negotiations with representatives from Brazil, China, India and South Africa. Obama recognised that at the heart of Kyoto's failure was a perceived lack of equality, which needed resolution in this fresh round of negotiations.

The key principles to come out of the Copenhagen Accord included:

■ an agreement that there was a need to limit global temperature rises to less than 2°C
■ a method for verifying industrialised nations' reductions in emissions, resulting in greater transparency — China, in particular, had been opposed to this
■ the promise of new resources for developing states, with an annual total of US$100 billion provided by 2020
■ the introduction of the Green Climate Fund, to help with climate change-related projects in developing states
■ a requirement that states would make public their plans for reducing carbon emissions by 2020
■ the requirement that the implementation of the Copenhagen Accord would be reviewed in 2015 (this eventually took place at the Paris Summit)

Crucially, the Copenhagen Accord did not include:

■ any legally binding targets, either for developed or developing states
■ any plan for the agreements made in the Copenhagen Accord to become legally binding in the future
■ approval by member states — rather states 'recognised' the principles of the Accord. Unanimous support for the deal was also not achieved — it was not clear whether or not the Accord represented a formal UN agreement in international law
■ a promise to take action to ensure global temperature rises remained below 2°C — there was merely agreement on the scientific evidence and the need to limit global temperature rise
■ penalties for states that did not meet their commitments, even in the case of less ambitious requirements, such as publishing plans for cutting carbon emissions by 2020

Therefore, the key weaknesses of the Copenhagen Accord were that it did not include any legally binding targets, nor was it clear whether the accord itself carried the weight of international law. There was therefore very little scope for holding states accountable for the pledges they had made. The UN secretary-general Ban Ki-moon criticised the deal for these oversights and urged parties to make the deal legally binding at future meetings.

Synoptic links

In Component 2, the 'nationalism' option explores the way in which exclusive/chauvinistic nationalism is founded upon a sense of cultural superiority. The rise of this sort of nationalism in recent years is likely to undermine the mutual trust and respect between nation-states necessary to achieve global progress on climate change.

Furthermore, another key obstacle was once again the challenge of turning signatures into ratification. However much enthusiasm President Obama showed, he needed the US legislature to ratify the Copenhagen deal. But Congress proved unwilling to do so, even without the presence of the legally binding targets that had proved so unpalatable to the previous Bush administration. In many ways, the Copenhagen Accord was of lesser consequence than the Kyoto Protocol, given that the USA was required to make fewer clear commitments. President Obama himself was muted in his praise for the Copenhagen Accord, stating that it was 'not enough' and the discussions were 'extraordinarily complex and difficult ... laying the foundations for international action in the years to come'.

There was also strong criticism for the USA and Chinese delegations, which disagreed strongly with each other during the summit. The so-called BASIC group (comprising Brazil, South Africa, India and China) and the USA negotiated with each other almost entirely behind the scenes, as the most significant polluting states tried to hammer out a deal. In many ways, the Copenhagen Summit was a forum in which these powerful, polluting states needed to make a deal with each other to enable the whole process to move forward. President Obama announced that the five states had reached an initial agreement, including on the 2°C temperature rise limit. Other states complained that they hadn't even seen the deal the USA and BASIC group had negotiated.

The so-called G77 also presented another, separate negotiating group of 77 of the world's developing states. At one stage during the conference, negotiations were suspended when the G77 refused to cooperate and accused the Danish organisers of conducting talks on the sidelines that excluded developing states. The situation was later resolved, but it reflected both the sense that developing states felt marginalised at the conference and the increasing frustration that developed states were not doing enough to combat climate change, something that would most harm developing states.

Consequently, the negotiations were hardly inclusive or comprehensive. Arguably, states were not yet ready to negotiate in a group of 190. Rather, they still needed to achieve agreements within powerful blocs of states. As Kyoto had proven, without the commitment of these states, any overarching agreement would be worthless. The lack of agreement on legally binding targets further suggests that the most powerful states remained unwilling to accept legal targets and preferred, instead, less formal commitments.

In defence of the Copenhagen Accord, world leaders said that any deal was better than no deal — China and India had, after all, agreed to reduce carbon emissions for the first time (even if the targets were not legally binding).

Overall, the Copenhagen Summit was a failure. The accords lacked legal force. The challenge of unifying states into collective action remained elusive. The negotiations had been fractious and highlighted divisions between developed and developing states, and between powerful developing states (the BASIC group) and less powerful developing states (the G77). The head of the G77 stated that, for Africa, the deal was 'a suicide pact, in order to maintain the economic dominance of a few countries'.

Greenpeace's closing statement labelled Copenhagen:

a crime scene tonight, with guilty men and women fleeing to the airport. There are no targets for carbon cuts and no agreement on a legally binding treaty. Too few politicians are capable of looking beyond the horizon of their narrow self-interest, let alone caring much for the millions of people who are facing down the threat of climate change.

Paris Summit (COP 21, 2015)

COP 21 was hosted amid high security after the 2015 terrorist attacks in Paris. Once again, attendees were conscious of the need to put right the failures of previous summits, including the lack of:

- legally binding targets, where both Kyoto and Copenhagen had failed — this time, attendees needed to agree comprehensive, legally binding targets with no exemptions to major polluters in the developing world
- a comprehensive and unified approach, both to the negotiations themselves and the solutions proposed — no more behind-the-scenes deals and developing states could not be sidelined

The result was the first international climate change deal that committed all states to cut emissions. The key parts of the Paris Agreement were:

- an agreement to keep global temperature increase 'well below' 2°C and to pursue efforts to limit it to 1.5°C
- to peak greenhouse gas emissions as soon as possible, and achieve a balance between sources and sinks of greenhouse gases in the second half of this century
- to review progress every 5 years

Distinguish between

The Copenhagen Accord and the Paris Agreement

The Copenhagen Accord (2009)
- No legally binding targets of any kind, either collective or at state level.
- The agreement itself never took legal effect.
- There was no agreement on collective action. Developed and developing states did not agree to any specific actions to reduce global temperature rises to less than 2°C.

The Paris Agreement (2015)
- Nationally determined contributions — states make their own plans for reducing carbon emissions.
- The agreement took legal effect in 2016.
- There is a legally binding commitment to collective action. Individual states do not face penalties if they fail to meet targets.

Box 6.4

US presidents on climate change

Ronald Reagan (1981–89): Reagan was president during the early period of global environmental governance, during which time the world was still waking up to the challenge and was only beginning to organise itself to tackle this collective action problem. Reagan did champion the Montreal Protocol in 1988, calling it 'a monumental effort of science and diplomacy', and the US Senate unanimously ratified the protocol. Within the USA, critics say that the Reagan administration was weak in its enforcement of anti-pollution regulations and was too keen to allow private industry to exploit land for mining and other resource extraction.

George H. W. Bush (1989–93): President Bush's speech at the Rio Earth Summit in 1992 set a far more positive tone towards global environmental action than we would hear during the later presidency of his son, George W. Bush. Bush Snr directly challenged the notion that environmental protection put economic growth at risk, stating that 'those who say that economic growth and environmental protection cannot be compatible [should] come to the USA, where in the 20 years since Stockholm, our economy has grown by 57% and yet we've cut the lead going into the air by 97%, the carbon monoxide by 41%'. However, Bush Snr's presidency lasted only one term and, while the USA signed and ratified the Rio Declaration and joined the UNFCCC during this time, little more was asked of the USA beyond agreeing to the declaration's principles.

Bill Clinton (1993–2001): the first Democratic president in the modern era of environmental governance signed, but did not ratify, the Kyoto Protocol, as US Congress would not approve it. Despite this failure, Clinton voiced his strong support for the Kyoto Protocol. This is an example of a US president negotiating at an international summit with his hands tied — Clinton still negotiated in support of the protocol, knowing that Congress would be unlikely to give its support and ratify the treaty. He voiced concern that developing states 'must participate in a meaningful way if we are to truly tackle this problem', and defended the protocol against claims in Congress that it would hurt the US economy.

George W. Bush (2001–9): Bush Jnr withdrew support for the Kyoto Protocol, stating that it was unfair that developing states were not required to commit to emissions targets. However, while withdrawing from the protocol, President Bush did implement a national plan to reduce carbon emissions by 18%, and the pace of US emissions did slow during the Bush Jnr administration. During this period, the Kyoto Protocol was the subject of frequent efforts to revive it, but the USA's position on the protocol did not change.

Barack Obama (2009–17): Obama negotiated the Copenhagen Accord in 2009, early in his presidency. He was criticised for negotiating with the BASIC countries (Brazil, South Africa, India, China) 'behind closed doors', although by that stage no agreement would have been possible without key states hammering one out. Obama also campaigned to reverse the Bush administration's rejection of the Kyoto Protocol. At national level, Obama was much more successful — highlights include the Clean Power Plan, which set the USA's first national limit on carbon pollution.

Donald Trump (2017–): during his election campaign, Trump pledged to withdraw US funding from UN climate change projects and 'cancel' the Paris Agreement. During transition in 2016/17, Trump changed his position, stating that he had an 'open mind' to the Paris Agreement. In June 2017, Trump confirmed that the USA would withdraw from the Paris Agreement and that he would try to seek a new agreement on climate change that would better protect US economic interests.

- a fund of US$100 billion a year to 2020 in climate finance for developing countries, with a pledge to increase this over time
- once the deal came into force, countries that ratified it would have to wait a minimum of 3 years before exit
- an agreement to cut emissions according to national plans, which would remain voluntary — so-called Intended Nationally Determined Contributions (INDCs) would require states to set out their plans for cutting their post-2020 emissions

INDCs were the Paris Agreement's method for resolving the disagreement between developed and developing states that had seen previous summits fail in their objectives. States themselves would outline contributions, which the UN would then review, rather than any other authority imposing them. This signalled a change from the Kyoto proposals, where industrialised states were subject to enforced emissions targets imposed by a higher authority, and where industrialising states would need to take 'nationally appropriate mitigation actions'. With INDCs, both developed and developing states would be required to cut emissions and produce their own national plans for how they would achieve this.

Of course, one weakness of states agreeing their own national targets is that their planned actions may not be sufficient. There were also delays in states submitting their INDCs to the UN for approval. Furthermore, in 2016, scientists estimated that the emissions pledges would limit global temperature rises only to as much as 3°C, rather than the intended 2°C.

Within this framework, however, the world's major polluters agreed to ambitious targets, and there is no evidence to suggest that the freedom to set targets resulted in states being less ambitious:

- The USA set out plans to cut carbon emissions by 28% by 2025 (although has since withdrawn from the agreement altogether).
- The EU promised to cut carbon emissions by 40% by 2030. Once again, the EU was highly efficient at being able to agree its emissions targets, within existing institutions for negotiation and implementation.
- China proposed to cut its emissions by 60–65% by 2030.
- India put forward a plan to cut emissions by up to 35% by 2030.

However, the UN concluded that, overall, more would need to be done in future national plans to meet the 2°C limit — emissions growth would slow down, but this was not enough to meet the Paris target.

There was some evidence to suggest that less-developed states found the process of completing their INDCs difficult, due to lack of expertise. The timetable to produce INDCs was also very short — just 1 year — which was a challenging time limit for resolving political disagreements within states on a highly important aspect of economic and environmental policy.

However, ratification of the Paris Agreement was far smoother and had fewer difficulties than ratification of the Kyoto Protocol. China, India, Russia and the USA all ratified the Paris Agreement. These states now have a collective legal obligation to work together to limit global temperature rises to less than 2°C. That collective legal obligation is quite different to the individual legal obligations on states that were proposed, and failed, under the Kyoto Protocol. The difficulty with the Paris Agreement's ratification came when President Trump confirmed that the USA would withdraw from the agreement. Trump promised to negotiate a new agreement, but the initially promising agreement once again seems under threat.

World leaders, scientists and campaigners agree that the Paris Agreement has been the most successful international agreement so far, but that it is currently insufficient and unlikely to meet its target. Greenpeace has said that 'far tougher action is needed to rapidly slash emissions'. In the context of global environmental governance, it is a considerable achievement for all states to have finally agreed to limit carbon emissions. While increasing individual states' action is likely to be on the agenda at future summits, it is unlikely that global environmental governance will repeat the mistakes of the Kyoto process in trying to force states to comply.

Is the Paris Agreement the best deal yet on climate change?

Yes

- Allowing states to make their own commitments, rather than forcing states to take legally binding steps, has encouraged them to cooperate.
- States such as China and India no longer need to be persuaded of the need to take action. They have set themselves stretching targets because they are acutely aware of the dangers climate change poses.
- Both developed and developing states agree that they need to take action. There are no exemptions, and states have the freedom to decide what action is most appropriate — but they do not have the choice of whether or not to cut their emissions.

No

- The pledges that states have made, and have been allowed to set themselves, are insufficient in limiting global temperature rises to below 2°C.
- Giving states the power to set their own targets enables them to make decisions where they may prioritise their economic interest above environmental interests.
- Too much trust is placed on states taking action, without any means of punishing or holding them accountable if they do not keep their promises.
- There is too little power within the treaty to even question whether states are proposing sufficient action in their INDCs. Once again, a major polluter and world power has failed to remain committed to the agreement, with President Trump withdrawing the USA from the agreement in June 2017.

Activity

Imagine that you are producing the agenda for the next international summit on climate change.
1   What actions do states need to take next?
2   Should states be encouraged or, as Greenpeace recommends, forced to take more action?
3   What do you think could be the biggest obstacle to making progress on climate change at the next summit?

Non-state actors and efforts to resolve climate change

There are many non-state actors working to resolve climate change.

Cities

Frequently, where national governments or international agreements are slow to take action, city governments can react far quicker.

- **London Congestion Charge:** London's first mayor, Ken Livingstone, introduced the congestion charge in 2003 after decades of discussion about how to manage London's increasingly congested roads and reduce pollution. Livingstone proposed an £8 charge for all vehicles entering central London. The result was a 13% reduction in greenhouse gases in the city in the first year alone. Public transport use rose, especially on buses, which saw a 37% increase. Milan, Singapore and Stockholm have all now introduced similar congestion charge schemes.
- **Supertree Grove:** Singapore has developed many projects to reduce pollution in the city-state. Supertree Grove is an area of man-made, tree-like vertical gardens. Each column is between 25 m and 50 m tall, has planting panels for the 'living skin' and is topped with solar panels.
- **Bosco Verticale:** Milan has recently built the Bosco Verticale ('Vertical Forest') residential towers, which support more than 800 trees. The project has won international awards and has been lauded as the future of urban housing construction.

247

Singapore's Supertree Grove: the man-made structures are fitted with environmental technologies that mimic the ecological function of trees

Multinational corporations

While national government action is important and can be successful in forcing MNCs to take action on climate change, MNCs themselves are beginning to offer more solutions to climate change:

- MNCs provide a valuable source of renewable energy technology. There is a rapidly expanding renewable energy industry. With this industry in private ownership, there is competition for ideas, efficiency and price. There are signs that the industry is becoming more competitive and innovative.
- Through corporate social responsibility funding, companies devise projects for charitable or social purposes. For example, the US multinational company Unilever has set up a Sustainable Living Plan project, which aims to reduce the company's own carbon footprint (the impact of its activities on carbon emissions).

National governments

Just as with effective human rights protection, the most meaningful actions to combat global climate change will take place at nation-state level. Consistent with the principle of there being no higher authority in global politics than nation-states (see page 252), what really matters in the fight to tackle climate change are the national regulations that states put into place.

In many cases, national action to combat pollution came many decades before international action. The UK's Clean Air Act, passed in 1956 (see page 223), was the first example of environmental regulation in the country. What follows are some further examples.

- The UK Department of Energy & Climate Change (DECC) was created in 2008, the first specific UK government department tasked with energy and climate change policy. In 2016, when Theresa May became prime minister, the DECC was merged with the Department for Business, Innovation & Skills to form the new Department for Business, Energy and Industrial Strategy (BEIS). Alongside the creation of the DECC, the UK Parliament passed the

The London Congestion Charge, introduced in 2003, resulted in a 13% reduction in greenhouse gases in the city in the first year alone

Climate Change Act 2008, which ratified into UK law, with broad consensus, the promises the Labour government had made as part of the Kyoto Protocol. This made it a legal requirement for both current and future UK governments to take steps to cut UK carbon emissions by 80% by 2050.

■ In 2003, Brazil passed the Native Vegetation Protection Act, which aims to recover 20 million hectares of vegetation in the Amazon rainforest by 2036.

■ Carbon or green taxes are another way in which national governments can pass legislation to force private companies to consider and reduce their impact on the environment. The EU utilises a member-wide tax on carbon. Governments can also provide tax breaks or reductions for citizens when they buy products that are less harmful to the environment, such as wind turbines, solar panels or electric cars. The UK government provides a grant of up to 35% of the value of an electric car.

What you should know

Having read this chapter you should have knowledge and understanding of the following:

■ Global environmental governance efforts have taken place under the United Nations Framework Convention on Climate Change, which has allowed for a succession of international summits and agreements to be reached. The United Nations has played a key leadership role.

■ Protecting the global commons is a key part of global governance. It is impossible for the international community to take meaningful action if states do not discuss and negotiate the collective action they can take together. States are unlikely to be persuaded to act alone and the actions of lone states will not solve serious problems such as climate change.

■ Developed and developing states have disagreed about how to tackle climate change. Developing states feel most at risk, particularly from natural disasters, and have felt that developed states have been the primary cause of global warming and should do the most to reduce its impact.

■ Environmental global governance efforts have tended to fail when states have been forced to act or when states have felt that contributions are not fair.

■ In recent years, there has been more agreement between developed and developing states, with both consenting at the Paris Summit (2015) to take steps at a national level to cut emissions.

Gore, A. (2006). *An Inconvenient Truth*. Bloomsbury. Also the documentary film
    by the former US vice-president of the same name.
Hansen, J. (2011) *Storms of My Grandchildren*. Bloomsbury Paperbacks.
Klein, N. (2014) *This Changes Everything: Capitalism vs the Climate*. Penguin.
Lynas, M. (2008) *Six Degrees: Our Future on a Hotter Planet*. Harper Perennial.

Exam focus

Section A

1 Examine the main factors that prevent states from cooperating over climate change.   *[12 marks]*

2 Examine why 'shallow' ecology strategies have been adopted more often than 'deep'
   ecology strategies.   *[12 marks]*

3 Examine the implications of the idea of 'sustainable development'.   *[12 marks]*

Section C

1 Evaluate the view that 'It is fair and legitimate for developed states to bear the greatest
   burden in tackling climate change'.   *[30 marks]*

2 Evaluate the view that 'Climate change will never be reduced without state and non-state
   actors being forced to take action'.   *[30 marks]*

3 Evaluate the extent to which international action on climate change has been blocked
   by conflict between developed and developing states.   *[30 marks]*

4 Evaluate the extent to which the environment remains a prominent global issue.   *[30 marks]*

5 Evaluate the view that 'International conferences on climate change are doomed to disappoint'.   *[30 marks]*

Chapter 7

Power and developments

Learning outcomes

By the end of this chapter you should be able to:

- explain the meanings of hard, soft and smart power, and how they can be used in global politics
- define and explain different forms of state power, including superpowers, great powers and emerging powers, with examples
- identify and explain different types of polarity, including unipolar, bipolar, and multipolar, with examples, and be able to discuss these in relation to each other and global stability
- identify different systems of government, including democratic, semi-democratic, autocratic, failed states and rogue states, and be able to explain their characteristics and consequences for the global order
- discuss different 'spreads and developments' in global politics, including trends like the spread of liberal economies and democracies, and developments in the rule of law
- discuss how developments in global power have impacted on different global issues, including conflict, poverty, human rights and the environment, allowing you to make synoptic links across topics

Getting you started

The early 1980s represented a particularly dangerous period in the history of the Cold War. Ronald Reagan, who had been elected president in 1980, was vehemently anti-communist and in March 1983 referred to the Soviet Union as an 'Evil Empire'. Later that year, in August, the Russians shot down a South Korean airliner when it strayed into Soviet airspace. Flight 007 had been travelling from New York to Seoul and among the 269 fatalities was US congressman Larry McDonald. The reaction in the USA was one of shock and outrage, which dramatically increased tension between it and the Soviet Union.

Then in November, Soviet High Command mistook a NATO exercise, Operation Able Archer, for a genuine military strike against the Warsaw Pact. The Soviet Union readied itself for a nuclear strike on the West and only stepped back from the brink when one of its spies, Oleg Gordievsky, who had secretly gone over to the West, persuaded them that Able Archer was indeed just an exercise.

Even some of the most popular rock music of the period illustrates the fear that confrontation between East and West was imminent. Listen to the German rock group Nena's '99 Red Balloons' (1983) and Frankie Goes to Hollywood's 'Two Tribes' (1984) for an insight into the tense and even apocalyptic atmosphere of the period.

It might, therefore, seem surprising that a number of realist scholars of international relations, such as Kenneth Waltz, now look back on the Cold War as a period of bipolar stability, and contrast it with the dangers inherent in the more fluid and uncertain world of contemporary global politics. They argue that during the Cold War, each side was so evenly matched that it created an

The BRICS countries: Brazil, Russia, India, China, South Africa

equilibrium for peace (this is known as a balance of power). Now, however, everything is much less stable, with more powers jockeying for global influence, and there is the fear that conflict could break out as the USA seeks to maintain global dominance against emerging powers, such as the BRICS countries (Brazil, Russia, India, China and South Africa). Are the uncertainties of today therefore more dangerous and destabilising than the certainties of the Cold War?

In this chapter we will consider what represents power in global politics, the extent to which the balance of power is changing and also the political realities between then and now.

Different types of global power

'Power' is a frequently used term in global relations. However, it can be hard to define. At its essence, power means the ability to exert influence through various means over others. In the case of global politics, this relates to the methods nation-states use to exercise control and achieve the outcomes they want.

Realists suggest that nation-states exist in a global 'self-help' environment and therefore their focus is on survival in an anarchic world order in which there is no supranational authority capable of enforcing global standards of behaviour. Dalton's Billiard Ball Model (see page 11) provides us with a good illustration, because states are constantly colliding with each other as they seek to protect their own interests. As a result, conflict is inevitable. This also demonstrates another way that realists often see states as accumulating power through the structural dynamics of a system of international anarchy.

For liberals, power in the international system is interwoven and interconnected — especially now, with the advance of globalisation — so they see the global order in terms of the Cobweb Model (see page 21), whereby the interests of states are so closely intertwined that they gain more from cooperation than from competition. These two models help us begin to establish how the balance of power affects the global political system.

One way to consider the power of a nation-state is in terms of its key capabilities. A state's strength can be measured based on several fundamental capabilities.

Activity

Jim O'Neill, the former chairman of Goldman Sachs Asset Management, coined the term 'BRICS' as shorthand for the five major emerging economies of Brazil, Russia, India, China and South Africa. The BRICS have met annually since 2009, taking turns to host the event in a different location in the same 5-year cycle, starting with Russia and ending with South Africa. The latter first attended in 2010 as a guest, and first hosted as a full member in 2013.

The initial BRIC country grouping was controversial, with some of the countries in the group more developed than others, particularly economically. It was also controversial that the group did not initially include any African countries, especially considering that it was supposed to represent newly emerging global powers, and therefore intended to contest the traditional global power hierarchies. This is one of the main reasons behind South Africa's admission. Nigeria, another African country with dramatic potential for growth, has since been added to the MINT countries, also a term O'Neill coined. The MINT countries represent a similar but more recent grouping to the BRICS, and comprise Mexico, Indonesia, Nigeria and Turkey.

The rise of the BRICS and MINT countries demonstrates the way in which the landscape of international politics is changing. In recent history, the Global North has dominated economic development. However, the twenty-first century may see economic and with it political influence shifting from West to East. The Group of Twenty (G20), unlike the Group of Seven (G7), represents developing as well as developed nations and is increasing in global influence. In 2015, China established the Asian Infrastructure Investment Bank (AIIB), providing a rival centre of economic structural power to the Western-dominated World Bank and International Monetary Fund (IMF). By around 2020, China is expected to have the largest economy in the world.

1 Research the economic power of the BRICS and the MINT countries in terms of gross domestic product (GDP), foreign direct investment, and influence in global and regional organisations (economic structural power).
2 Make a table showing which of these countries is the most/least economically impressive.
3 Do you agree that Jim O'Neill included appropriate emerging countries in his acronyms?
4 To what extentd do you think economic influence always brings with it political influence?

■ **Economic capability:** often measured in gross domestic product (GDP), or GDP per capita, but it may also include factors such as trade balances, levels of debt, stability of economic growth, influence over trade rules and contributions to international programmes and organisations, including non-governmental organisations (NGOs), international aid, and research and development (R&D — see below).

■ **Military strength:** this not only includes the size of a nation's standing army, but crucially its global reach (a criterion for being a superpower) — that is to say, a state's ability to deploy anywhere at any time. This includes naval strength, air force capacity and, importantly, technological capacities, including nuclear weapons, drones, intelligence and increasingly cyber technology.

■ **Cultural appeal:** this represents a state's global cultural outreach, for example through television, film, food, fashion, celebrities and brand names. This is a more controversial and complex characteristic, which is harder to measure. Some argue that the world is becoming increasingly homogenised (see Chapter 2), while others argue that the world has become a 'melting pot', with many different cultures competing for global influence. Whichever approach you agree with, there is no doubt that a nation-state's cultural appeal can provide it with important soft-power influence in international relations. Globalisation has, for example, traditionally been seen as a way in which the USA has been able to globally expand its influence through the appeal of its political values and culture. This is often referred to as Americanization or, more negatively, 'McDonaldization' or 'Coca-Colonization'.

■ **Diplomatic strength:** this includes a number of features, including elements of structural power, the reach of its foreign policy, and the global impression a state makes, together with its ability to utilise its power of influence. For a state to exert diplomatic strength it should be prepared to provide global leadership on issues such as conflict resolution, the environment, the global economy, poverty and development.

■ **Population:** although on face value this is a relatively straightforward measure, it does have underlying complexities. A large population can give a state significant power and influence, but it can also create problems. This is because if a state has a large population, many of whom live below the poverty level, it may be preoccupied with the internal social and economic problems this creates. It is also important to note whether or not the population of a state is ageing and how fertile its population is. Russia has very poor fertility levels and has a declining population. Japan has also suffered from its resistance to immigration, which, some critics argue, has reduced its capacity for innovation. In contrast, the USA has an expanding and youthful population — by 2050, it is estimated that the US population will be 438 million. If present trends continue, the Russian population could sink to 80 million by then.

■ **Structural power:** this represents a state's capacity to influence intergovernmental organs such as the United Nations (UN), the Bretton Woods Institutions (the IMF, World Bank and World Trade Organization (WTO)), the Asian Infrastructure Investment Bank (AIIB), and the G7 and G20. The USA, for example, provides the largest share of funding for the World Bank and IMF, while China financially dominates the AIIB.

■ **Regional power:** some states have significant influence in their respective regions. They may pool sovereignty to enhance their influence, which may give them a greater level of structural and diplomatic pressure, especially in terms of their influence over IGOs and NGOs. The USA, for example, is the dominant force on the Organization of American States and Russia is by far the most important member of the Eurasian Customs Union. Indeed, some critics have suggested that Russia is using the Eurasian Customs Union (Armenia, Belarus, Kazakhstan, Kyrgyzstan and Russia) to reassert influence within its immediate zone of influence.

■ **Research and development (R&D):** refers to the amount that a state spends on R&D. This serves as a status symbol and can provide a state with strategic advantage, especially in terms of new technology.

■ **Natural resources:** states that are resource-rich can possess significant bargaining power. They can also be harder to sanction due to other states' reliance on their resources. Furthermore, a resource-rich state may be able to act more independently, since it does not need to rely as heavily on other states. However, being resource-rich is a hindrance to some states, particularly those in Sub-Saharan Africa. This has been described as the 'resource curse', since it can encourage powerful states to try to economically dominate poorer countries, thus relegating them to a state of neocolonial dependency.

Activity

Think of an example and provide evidence for a country that is powerful in each of the key areas of global power. You should find that different countries are powerful in different ways.

Hard and soft power

According to liberal theorist Joseph Nye, the two main types of power in global politics are **hard power** and **soft power**. Often realists will give more weight

Key terms

Hard power A state's military and economic power.
Soft power A state's diplomatic or cultural power.

to hard power, while liberals will argue that soft power is just as significant, especially in a more globalised world.

Hard power

Hard power fits into the realist idea of the Billiard Ball Model, in which states fight, and often collide, with each other in their attempts to maximise their influence. It is defined by the more physical elements of military and economic power. For example, a powerful state is more likely to have the military strength to both physically defend itself, or to attack or intervene in another state. A state with a strong economy will also be able to place sanctions on another state. Both military and economic actions are considered to be a form of command power, through which a state can change the actions of a rival state. Hard power therefore focuses on those ways in which a nation state can compel obedience to its will.

Soft power

Soft power is best understood as the way in which a nation-state achieves its objectives through the attractiveness of its culture and political system. Soft power therefore focuses on those non-military and non-economic ways in which a state can persuade other states to emulate its world view. Given the massive expansion of the internet and the spread of globalisation, the opportunity for states to advance their cultural and political values has never been greater, and so soft power provides a cheaper, less risky and potentially more effective way by which a state can seek to achieve its political objectives by winning friends and achieving positive global recognition.

As Joseph Nye puts it, the important thing in global relations is 'whose story wins'. The USA's cultural appeal therefore played a significant role in the ending of the Cold War, since totalitarianism could not compete with the materialistic/consumer appeal of free-market capitalism. As the US journalist and satirist P. J. O'Rourke puts it, communism collapsed 'because nobody wanted to wear Bulgarian shoes'. Instead, the world turned towards US brands.

Smart power

Joseph Nye also coined the term 'smart power', which refers to a state using both hard- and soft-power methods to achieve its aims. For example, smart power was a key feature of President Obama's administration, and further popularised by former US secretary of state Hillary Clinton.

Obama's use of smart power was most clearly demonstrated in his approach to the middle east. In his 2009 Cairo speech, early in his first presidential term, he focused on the benefits of Islamic culture and emphasised the need for cooperation and co-existence. This marked a significant break from the rhetoric of the previous Bush administration, which had emphasised the neoconservative approach of hard power through the 'War on Terror'. Through Obama's acknowledgement that the West had been antagonistic to the Arabic world in the past, and his demonstration of cultural understanding, he was presenting a softer approach.

However, during his first term, and certainly his second, Obama also demonstrated a clear willingness to use hard power where necessary. Even during the Cairo speech Obama stated that the USA would not tolerate extremist threats to its national security. Furthermore, his rhetoric towards terrorism changed over time, in light of events such as the beheading of US hostages by so-called Islamic State, and his administration increasingly focused on drone strikes against militant targets. Therefore, the Obama administration exhibited the use of both hard and soft power.

Millions have protested President Obama's 'hard power' use of drone strikes in regions such as Pakistan and Syria

'Carrots and sticks'

Often realists illustrate the concept of power within the international system with reference to 'carrots and sticks'. The carrot is a reward or an incentive (most often in the form of financial and military aid), while the stick represents punishment (usually expressed through the withdrawing of aid, the imposition of sanctions and possible military strikes). Both are considered to be types of hard power. For example, in the past the USA has offered North Korea the 'carrot' of aid money and the 'stick' of economic sanctions in relation to its testing of nuclear weapons — North Korea can have its 'carrot' if it stops testing but will face the 'stick' (in the form of economic sanctions as well as the US offering military and economic support to its neighbour, South Korea, in order to temper North Korea's aggression) if it continues with its nuclear programme. President Theodore Roosevelt put this principle succinctly when he said, in regard to US foreign policy, 'Speak softly and carry a big stick'.

Table 7.1 summarises the types of power, along with examples.

Table 7.1 Types of global power and theoretical links

Types of power	Theoretical links	Examples
Hard: economic and military strength	**Realist:** the idea of 'carrots and sticks'. For realists, hard power is by far the dominant form of power and is most significant in defining a state's strength. They argue that without sufficient hard power a state's sovereignty is weakened. Hard power is crucial in an anarchic system in which every state is competing and conflict is inevitable. Hard power is seen as a coercive force and is generally used unilaterally.	Bush's neoconservative approach during the War on Terror. The USA used its military power to lead a coalition of forces in Afghanistan and Iraq. Obama ordered drone strikes in various countries, including Afghanistan, Iraq and Syria. Russia's invasion of Crimea in 2014 (and ongoing presence in various parts of Ukraine) has been a clear challenge to Ukraine's sovereignty through the use of hard power. The economic sanctions placed on Russia by various countrie as a result of its actions in Crimea, including Australia, Canada and the USA, and regional blocs and organisations such as the European Union (EU) and the North Atlantic Treaty Organization (NATO). In April 2017 President Trump launched 59 Tomahawk cruise missies against the Assad regime to deter further chemical attacks.
Soft: cultural, economic and diplomatic strength	**Liberal:** soft power is the way in which a nation-state achieves influence through persuasion. This can be manifested through its cultural and diplomatic appeal.	Obama's Cairo speech marked a move towards the increased use of soft power in US foreign policy, especially in relation to the Arabic world. States may use foreign aid as a means of soft power to attract, persuade and influence.

Types of power	Theoretical links	Examples
	For liberals this is an increasingly important form of power in an increasingly globalised world, where interconnectedness is a common feature and systems of global governance are a necessity. Soft power is generally used multilaterally and liberals see it as a way to promote stability.	Arguably the formation of the BRICS was a move to increase their soft power by bolstering their diplomatic influence, especially within IGOs (the G20, the IMF, the World Bank). The USA has often been said to have a significant global cultural influence, with globalisation even sometimes called 'Americanization', seen in its influence over popular culture, fashion, music, fast food etc. Germany has arguably exerted its soft power during the 2015/16 migrant crisis in Europe, taking a leading role on the issue and accepting large numbers of refugees.
Smart: hard and soft power used in combination	**Liberal/softer realist:** mostly a liberal idea, although some softer realists may also see the merits of using soft power to reinforce hard power (although they ultimately give hard power precedence). Joseph Nye coined the term.	The Obama administration's approach to the middle east used soft power (e.g. in the Cairo speech) in combination with hard power (e.g. drone strikes). The UN can also be seen to use smart power, e.g. it offers large amounts of aid and humanitarian relief (forms of soft power), but it also enforces sanctions and military intervention in certain instances.

Activity

President Ronald Reagan was a former Hollywood actor and radio presenter who was elected US president in 1980 at the age of 69. He served two full terms and, as the Soviet Union began to reform under Mikhail Gorbachev, Reagan enjoyed contrasting the economic hardship and lack of freedom under communism with the 'American Dream'. He often did this in the form of televised jokes:

> Two Russians were walking down the street, one asked the other, 'Have we really achieved full communism?'
>
> The other said, 'Oh no. Things are about to get worse.'

And another example:

> Two men, an American and a Russian, were arguing. One said, 'In my country, I can go to the White House, walk to the president's office and pound the desk and say "Mr President! I don't like how you're running things in this country!"'
>
> The Russian said, 'I can do that too!'
>
> 'Really?' asked the American.
>
> 'Yes! I can go to the Kremlin, walk into the general secretary's office and pound the desk and say "Mr Secretary, I don't like how President Reagan is running his country!"'

And another:

> It's hard to buy a car in the Soviet Union. They are owned mainly by elite bureaucrats. It takes an average of ten years to get a car. Just one out of seven families own a car. You have to go through a major process and put the money out in advance. So this man did this and the dealer said 'Okay, in ten years come get your car.'
>
> 'Morning or afternoon?' the man replied.
>
> 'Well, what difference does it make?' said the dealer.
>
> 'The plumber is coming in the morning.'

The jokes Reagan told show that he understood the value of 'whose story wins'. This is also reflected in the way in which the Moscow Peace Festival, 12–13 August 1989, featured many British and US pop groups, including the glam-rock band The Scorpions whose inspiring song 'Wind of Change' became emblematic of the way in which many Russians craved reform. As the Soviet leadership lost control of the narrative of events, so its political influence waned. In November 1989, the Berlin Wall came down and in August 1991 uprisings within Russia itself destroyed Communist rule from the inside. Although President Trump in many ways models himself on President Reagan, he is less concerned with how the rest of the world views the USA. He is, therefore, not interested in whether his 'story' wins. When Fox News' Bill O'Reilly pointed out to Trump that President Putin has people killed, Trump responded, 'What do you think? Our country's so innocent?' Trump's unwillingness to put American values on a global pedestal for the rest of the world to admire represents, for some, refreshing candour. For others it is a sorry end to the 'American Dream', which has encouraged people not only in the USA but also globally to live up to their highest aspirations.

President Reagan believed that the USA's soft and hard power were inseparable. President Trump is primarily focused on US hard power as a means of achieving his objectives. Who do you think is right? Explain your answer fully.

The changing balance of global power

Key terms

Great power A state that wields significant global influence militarily and economically and through its leading role in IGOs such as the UN, G7/8, G20 and the Bretton Woods Institutions. It therefore has a forward foreign policy and plays an influential role in global issues.

Superpower A state that possesses all the characteristics of a great power, but will be able to make its influence felt anywhere in the world through advanced nuclear and cyber technology (and the means of delivering a devastating military response anywhere in the world at any time), diplomacy and influence over its allies, who share its ideological beliefs.

As well as understanding the different types of power, one must consider how states are viewed as powers within the international system, and their varying significance to global affairs. It is important to understand how and why this power is classified. This means considering how we might describe the most powerful states — or states where the power is spread across several significant but not ultimate powers — or those states that have only recently become more powerful. We will describe power in relation to the types of power we have explored above.

In global politics, this is often seen within the changing historical context. Prior to the First World War there were several **great powers**, including Great Britain, France and the Austro-Hungarian Empire. The emergence of new powers during the interwar period, such as Fascist Italy, Japan, Nazi Germany, the Communist Soviet Union and the USA, meant that global power was now shared more equally. But after the Second World War, power shifted again to the war's successors, the dominant Allied powers (China, Great Britain, France, the Soviet Union and the USA). This is reflected in the many international institutions that were formed by and contained representatives of these powers, for example the UN Security Council (UNSC).

The balance shifted again in the Cold War era, during which time there were two clear superpowers: the Soviet Union and the USA, who were engaging in a **superpower** rivalry based around ideology. These two superpowers were unrivalled by any other state, and both had their own clear ideological and regional spheres, with the USA dominating the Western world with capitalism and the Soviet Union dominating the Eastern world with communism. Virtually every other world state was aligned to either the USA or the Soviet Union and their respective ideologies during this period.

Distinguish between

Great powers and superpowers

Great powers
- Great powers must have significant regional influence within their 'near abroad'.
- They should have the capacity for significant military outreach.
- They should possess a major role in international organisations, providing them with significant structural power.
- They will have some of the strongest economies in the world.

Superpowers
- A superpower must have significant global power and 'global reach'. This is particularly true in the case of military power.
- It must have nuclear weapons, although recent developments in cyber technology may reduce nuclear importance.
- It should exert dominant structural power within important institutions of regional and global governance.
- It should be able to assert its global influence anywhere in the world at any time.
- It will possess a world view and the willingness to proactively enforce that world view in international relations.
- As US foreign policy professor W. T. R. Fox put it in 1944, a superpower will possess 'great power plus great mobility of power'.

When communism collapsed in eastern Europe, leading to the fall of the Soviet Union in 1991, the USA, as the sole remaining superpower, possessed global hegemonic status. No other power came close to matching its influence, and leading US political commentator Charles Krauthammer coined the phrase America's 'unipolar moment'. However, especially since the bloody aftermath of the Iraq War and the global financial crisis, emerging powers, such as China and Russia, have begun to challenge US hegemony. This has led to some political philosophers, like John Mearsheimer, predicting that we are once again entering a period of power transition, which is likely to lead to a more multipolar balance of power.

Table 7.2 The BRICS powers

	Brazil	Russia	India	China	South Africa
2015 GDP ranking (World Bank)	9	13	7	2	32
2015 population ranking (World Bank)	5	9	2	1	24
Nuclear weapons	No — Brazil has the technology but has signed the Treaty on the Non-Proliferation of Nuclear Weapons (NPT)	Yes	Yes	Yes	No — it has done in the past but dismantled them when it signed the NPT
2015 military spend (Stockholm International Peace Institute)	11	4	6	2	Significantly lower, not in the top 30
Natural resources and trade	Brazil has many natural resources, including gold, iron, uranium and petroleum, among many others. It also has a significant amount of hydropower. It trades heavily in agriculture (especially coffee, beef, soya, and sugar). Brazil is also a big supplier of timber and oil. It has significant textiles and electronics industries.	Russia has significant natural resources, including oil, gas and coal (especially in the Ural mountains). It also has uranium. Natural resources dominate Russia's exports. It also has a significant proportion of the globe's fossil fuels.	India has lots of major mineral resources, including coal, iron ore and bauxite, as well as natural gas, diamonds and limestone. It also has nuclear reserves in uranium and thorium. India has been famous for its telecommunications industry, with lots of MNCs outsourcing to India.	China is behind only the USA and Russia in terms of the proportion of natural resources it holds. It has significant resources of coal, iron, tin, copper and zinc, among various others. China is renowned for its electronics exports.	South Africa has many natural resources, including diamonds, gold and silver. It also has salt, iron, cobalt, copper, uranium and bauxite, among others. Its main exports are tropical fruit, sugar, wool, gold and diamonds. South Africa is yet to unlock the full extent of its natural resources.
IGO membership	Member of the G20. Member of the sub-regional bloc Mercosur.	Member of the G20. Permanent member of the UNSC. Was a G7/8 member until suspension for its invasion of Ukraine.	Member of the G20. India is not a UNSC permanent member but has been a key contender whenever there are talks to expand the permanent membership base.	Member of the G20. Permanent member on the UNSC.	Member of the G20. Member of the African Union (AU).

Polarity The way in which power is distributed in the international system, into unipolarity, bipolarity and multipolarity.

Unipolarity A single pole of power, meaning one state dominates all others. To be hegemonic, a state must therefore possess ultimate power in all of its capabilities and be able to engage in unilateral action anywhere in the world at any time.

Bipolarity Two competing poles of power. This is best characterised with the superpower rivalry between the USA and Soviet Union during the Cold War. For true bipolarity, the two powers are evenly matched and there is a clear balance of power.

Activity

A good way to learn the types of power each state has and how they compare with each other is to make Top Trumps cards. You could do this with classmates, or ask your teacher to do it in a lesson so you don't have to make all the cards yourself. If you don't know how to play Top Trumps, use the following instructions:

1 Make your cards using the criteria in Table 7.2, or applying the criteria to another group, such as the G20. Cut them out so that you have a deck. (Note: for categories that don't have a clear 'value' you might need to rank them based on which country you think is the best and worst in that particular field.)

2 To start, shuffle and deal all the cards evenly between all players, face down. Each player should shield his or her cards from opponents.

3 The player to the dealer's left begins. S/he chooses a category (e.g. GDP ranking) from his/her card and reads out the value. Each player then reads his/her value for the category. The player with the highest value wins and takes all the other players' top/front cards and puts these cards to the bottom of his/her pile. It is then his/her turn to choose a category from the next card.

4 If the cards share the same value or there are no data for that category, all the 'in play' cards are placed in the middle and the same player chooses from the next card in his/her deck. The winner of this next hand also wins the cards in the middle.

5 The person holding all the cards at the end wins.

Polarity

Key term

Multipolarity Multiple poles of power, in which several states compete with each other. They may have different strengths and weaknesses in terms of their power, but each wields relatively equal influence on the international stage.

Polarity refers to 'poles of power'. There are three main forms of polarity: **unipolarity** (a single pole of power), **bipolarity** (two poles of power) and **multipolarity** (multiple poles of power).

Bipolarity: the Cold War era

One of the key questions polarity raises is to do with how stable the international system is/was during a certain power dynamic.

The Cold War provides a classic example of a bipolar system, in which there were two key and equally matched superpowers competing for global influence. During this period, the UN became largely redundant, since the Soviet Union and USA, as permanent members of the UNSC, would veto any perceived threats to their own interests (see Box 7.1). Each superpower also had its own military alliances and client states whose support it could rely upon. The USA was the leading member of NATO and the Soviet Union dominated the Warsaw Pact. In addition, Israel had close ties with the USA and Cuba with the Soviet Union, while both superpowers continually sought to reduce the other's influence in non-aligned states, such as Egypt, India and Indonesia.

Box 7.1

Key events of the Cold War

1946	Winston Churchill delivers his 'Iron Curtain' speech at Fulton, Missouri, USA, in which he warns that an Iron Curtain is beginning to separate eastern from western Europe.
1947	The Truman Doctrine offers military support to nations resisting Communist infiltration and the Marshall Plan offers financial support to countries devastated by the Second World War in order to lessen the appeal of communism. Tensions with the Soviet Union dramatically increase.
1948–49	The Soviet Union blockades the Western-controlled sector of Berlin.
1948	The Soviet Union explodes its first nuclear weapon.
1949	NATO is established. It is based on the principle of collective security (Article 5). This means that an attack on one member will provoke a military response by all. NATO claims this is defensive, while the Soviet Union responds that it is an offensive act of aggression.
1950–53	The Korean War breaks out when Communist North Korea invades South Korea: the Western allies send military support to South Korea to repel Communist aggression.
1952	The USA develops the hydrogen bomb.
1953	The Soviet Union also develops the hydrogen bomb.
1955	The Warsaw Pact is established, dividing Europe into two armed camps.
1956	Soviet intervention crushes the Hungarian Uprising.
1957	The Soviet Union launches Sputnik: the beginning of the Space Race. The USA begins to fear a 'missile gap'.
1960	An American U2 spy plane is shot down over the Soviet Union. Soviet Secretary-General Nikita Khrushchev calls the flight 'an act of war'. East/West tensions rise.
1961	Construction of the Berlin Wall physically divided East Berlin (now under Soviet control) from West Berlin (now under the control of the Western Allies).
1962	The Soviet Union places nuclear missiles in Cuba, provoking the Cuban Missile Crisis. President Kennedy responds with a 'quarantine' of Cuba, which takes the superpowers to the brink of nuclear war.
c.1963–75	The USA sends military support to South Vietnam in its struggle against Communist North Vietnam. In 1975, North Vietnam achieves the reunification of Vietnam.
1972	President Richard Nixon becomes the first US president to visit China, establishing diplomatic relations between the two powers. Nixon also signs the Strategic Arms Limitation Treaty (SALT) with Soviet Secretary-General Leonid Brezhnev, leading to détente (a loosening of tension) between the two sides.
1975	President Gerald Ford and Soviet leader Leonid Brezhnev agree to the Helsinki Accords, which guarantee the borders of Europe. This is often seen as being the high point of détente.
1979–89	Russian intervention in Afghanistan: the West condemns this as Soviet imperialism.
1980	Election of President Ronald Reagan. The first Reagan administration (1981–85) dramatically increases Cold War tensions — cruise missiles are placed in western Europe and plans are developed for the Strategic Defence Initiative ('Star Wars') to protect the USA from Soviet missile attack.
1985	Mikhail Gorbachev becomes Soviet leader. Gorbachev initiates reform of the Soviet Union (*perestroika* — a restructuring of the economy away from state control) and *glasnost* (greater political freedom).
1986	The Reykjavik Summit between Gorbachev and Reagan significantly reduces Cold War tensions.
1987	Reagan and Gorbachev sign the Intermediate Nuclear Forces Treaty.
1989	Fall of the Berlin Wall: Communist regimes are subsequently overthrown in eastern Europe.
1990	Germany is reunited.
1991	The Soviet Union collapses.

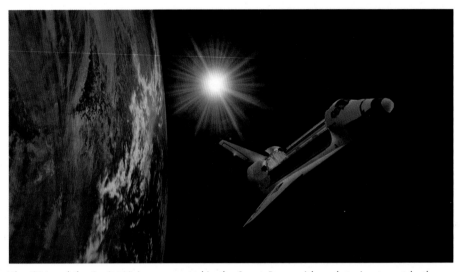

The USA and the Soviet Union competed in the Space Race, with each trying to outdo the other's scientific and technological capabilities

1 Why do you think the world came so close to nuclear catastrophe during the Cuban Missile Crisis?
2 Are there any other crises during the Cold War that you think might have provoked direct conflict between the Soviet Union and the USA?
3 Why did these crises not lead to war?
4 Using your research, to what extent do you think the nuclear bipolarity of the Cold War made direct military confrontation between the superpowers more or less likely?
5 Do you agree with the realist political philosopher Kenneth Waltz that the Cold War was a period of stability? Explain your answer fully. Note: this question is subtly different to the previous question. Consider whether peace is simply the absence of war.

What are the implications of bipolarity for global stability?

Liberals and realists have very different opinions on whether or not this system of Cold War bipolarity created global stability.

According to realists such as Kenneth Waltz, the Cold War promoted peace, since the existence of two evenly balanced powers meant that neither side was capable of eliminating the other. As a result, both sides appreciated the limits of what they could achieve and so a balance of power was established, which it was not in the interests of either side to try to undermine. If one side had risked war, the results for both would have been catastrophic.

This therefore created an equilibrium that neither side was prepared to break, since by destabilising the equilibrium it would have created conflict due to the threat of mutually assured destruction (MAD). Indeed, some political commentators have even argued that Cold War bipolarity actually encouraged understanding and conflict resolution, since both sides understood that often the best way of advancing their own interests was by working with the other. For example, following the death of Joseph Stalin in 1953, diplomatic relations briefly improved between the secretary-general of the Soviet Union, Nikita Khrushchev, and President Dwight Eisenhower. In 1959 in Moscow, for example, Khrushchev and Vice-President Richard Nixon engaged in an informal and jocular exchange about the relative merits of their two world views. Soon after, Khrushchev visited Eisenhower in Washington, DC to further try to develop trust between the two sides.

During the 1970s, President Richard Nixon and Secretary-General Leonid Brezhnev established a period of détente between the USA and the Soviet Union. One consequence of this was the Strategic Arms Limitations Treaty (1972), which slowed the arms build-up between the two powers. The 1975, Helsinki Accords, which were signed between Nixon's successor, Gerald Ford, and Leonid Brezhnev, provide the best example of the sort of cooperation that can be achieved in a bipolar world. Not only did Helsinki involve each side, guaranteeing the borders of the other, it even included commitments to increase economic, technical and cultural relations between them.

However, according to liberals, bipolarity is destabilising and dangerous. This is because both sides will continually be advancing their military, diplomatic and economic interests at the expense of the other, so creating fear, suspicion and latent hostility. It, therefore, does not provide the conditions for a lasting or meaningful peace. According to the Ancient Greek historian Thucydides, it was actually the inherent dangers of bipolarity that led to the Peloponnesian War between Athens and Sparta (431 BCE–404 BCE), since 'what made the war inevitable was the growth of Athenian power and the fear which this caused Sparta'.

Therefore, liberals claim that the Cold War was much more defined by very long periods of mutual distrust and antagonism, as illustrated by US paranoia about a 'missile gap' in the 1950s or the ease with which the Cuban Missile Crisis could have provoked nuclear war as the Soviet Union sought to pull ahead in the arms race by placing nuclear missiles in Cuba.

The early 1980s were also profoundly unstable as President Ronald Reagan dramatically increased spending on nuclear weapons in order to prove US superiority over the Soviet Union. In 1983, as we have seen, the Soviet Union shot down a South Korean airliner, which could have provoked a military response from the USA. In the same year, the Soviets came close to a military strike on the West when they made the mistake of thinking that the NATO military exercise Operation Able Archer was the real thing. The way in which both events came very close to provoking direct military confrontation was, of course, due to the profound distrust between the two adversaries. Indeed, according to Robert S. McNamara, who served as US defense secretary from 1961 to 1968, 'Cold War: hell it was a hot war!'

Proxy and peripheral wars

During the Cold War, both sides also tried to extend their global influence at the expense of the other through 'hot wars'. In the Vietnam War (c.1963–75), the Soviet Union and the USA were not in direct combat, but they took opposing sides and backed these sides (North Vietnam and South Vietnam respectively) to win. Each saw a victory as furthering their position in the superpower rivalry.

Alternatively, peripheral wars were fought between one superpower and another country (but the superpower's opposition would be allied to their

Mutually assured destruction acted as a disincentive for conflict between the two superpower nations (the Soviet Union and the USA) during the Cold War

Was the Cold War system a stable system?

Yes

- Realists mostly hold this view. The balance of power between the Soviet Union and the USA created a stable equilibrium, which meant that neither side would gain from waging all-out war against the other.
- In his 1987 book *The Long Peace*, key realist proponent John Lewis Gaddis argued that the Cold War was a time of relative stability because although there were lesser conflicts, there was no direct conflict between the two main powers. Conflicts between other powers were also ultimately less likely because all states revolved around the two main ideologies (communism and capitalism).
- The principle of mutually assured destruction (MAD) meant that neither power would launch a military or nuclear attack on the other. Both sides therefore had an incentive to avoid war.

No

- Liberals generally hold this view, since they see the Cold War as a dangerous and turbulent time.
- Although avoiding direct conflict throughout the entire period, both sides tested the resolve of the other through global proxy wars.
- MAD was far from stable — it nearly ended in nuclear war during the Cuban Missile Crisis in 1962. According to Robert S. McNamara, who was John F. Kennedy's defense secretary at the time, 'We lucked out. It was luck that saved us.'
- There were no stabilising checks and balances on the superpowers, given the UN's ineffectiveness at this time.

superpower rival). For example, during the Korean War (1950–53) the USA fought alongside South Korea to restrict Communist advance in the Korean peninsula.

Activity

Decide whether or not you agree with the liberal or realist viewpoint as to whether the Cold War era characterised a time of stability. Write a short paragraph justifying your answer.

The end of the Cold War and the rise of US hegemony

During Ronald Reagan's presidency (1981–89) the USA achieved a commanding lead in the Cold War. The economic pressures of competing with the USA undermined the Soviet economy and under Secretary-General Mikhail Gorbachev, economic and political reforms were introduced. According to the nineteenth-century French historian and political theorist Alexis de Tocqueville, the most dangerous time for a dictatorship is when it begins to reform, since that reform is likely to be too slow to please its restive population. This was certainly the case with Gorbachev's reforms. As the momentum behind reform gathered pace, he gave more and more power to the constituent parts of the Soviet Union, the biggest of which, by far, was Russia led by Boris Yeltsin. When Communist hardliners tried to overthrow Gorbachev in 1991, it was Yeltsin who rallied the nationalist opposition, defeated the coup and then, by declaring Russia independent, led to the dismantling of the Soviet Union. The union was formally dissolved on 26 December 1991.

The break-up of the Soviet Union established 15 new independent states. Russia was, of course, the biggest, but many of the others were extremely weak economically and left politically fragile from years of oppressive communism. They also faced struggle in terms of divided ethnic identities, particularly as state borders were being redefined.

Georgia

- Georgia has had a tumultuous history with Russia. It was part of the Soviet Union and became independent in 1991.
- There is still tension between the USA and Russia over Georgia, since Russia still regards it as within her sphere of influence.
- After the break-up of the Soviet Union, Georgia went through a period of sharp economic decline.
- Georgia has expressed its desire to be part of both the EU and NATO, which is a source of tension for Russia. The 2003 Rose Revolution, which marked the end of pro-Russian leadership in Georgia, was a clear demonstration of pro-Western feeling.
- Georgia regards South Ossetia and Abkhazia as rightfully hers. However, in 1993, Abkhazia declared itself an independent state. In 2008, as a result of war between Georgia and Russia, South Ossetia also declared itself independent. Both now look towards Russia for protection.

Ukraine

- Ukraine has had a similar experience to Georgia since the break-up of the Soviet Union. It also became independent in 1991.
- It was left in economic ruin after the break-up of the Soviet Union.
- It is also internally divided. Many Ukrainians are pro-West, while others are fiercely loyal to Russia.
- The 2004 Orange Revolution saw mass demonstrations in the capital, Kiev, against corruption.
- Ukraine's government has close ties with the EU and would like eventual membership.
- The annexation of Crimea in 2014 saw tensions flare up once more between Russia and the West. Russia's actions resulted in international economic sanctions, as well as Russia's suspension from the G7/8. Tensions are ongoing.

Russia after the break-up of the Soviet Union

After the break-up of the Soviet Union in 1991, Russia was left politically and economically unstable. The sudden shift from a command economy to a free-market economy encouraged huge levels of corruption, mass unemployment and hyperinflation. Poverty and HIV/AIDS rates dramatically increased and Russia's global influence sharply deteriorated. Large-scale ethnic division further exacerbated the problems. In Chechnya, for example, the government fought two bloody wars to defeat the separatist movement.

Boris Yeltsin, who served as Russian president from 1991 to 1999, was unable to provide the leadership necessary to restore stability and on 31 December 1999 he handed over the office to his prime minister, Vladimir Putin, admitting to the Russian people that he had failed as their leader:

> I want to ask for your forgiveness, that many of our dreams didn't come true. That what seemed to us to be simple turned out painfully difficult.

Since 2000, Vladimir Putin and Dmitry Medvedev have led Russia as president (Medvedev won the 2008 election, but did not run for a second term in 2012, leading to Putin's re-election). Opposition to the government has been severely weakened and Russia is now, at most, a semi-democratic state. The government has been accused of tolerating corruption in high places, undermining a free media and encouraging nationalist hatred of the West. However, Putin has also succeeded in restoring Russian self-confidence in global affairs by his annexation of Crimea, which was hugely popular in Russia, as well as militarily intervening in Syria, while the West dithered. Under Putin, Russia's military has also been reformed and the Eurasian Customs Union established as a counterweight to the EU in Russia's 'near abroad'.

Whether Russia can once again claim equal global influence with the USA is far from certain. Russia has almost no soft power global influence and, like a developing country, is hugely dependent on the export of raw materials. Indeed, Senator John McCain has ridiculed Russia for being 'a gas station masquerading as a country'. Russia also has just ten military bases overseas (compared with the USA's 800) and just one operational aircraft carrier (compared with the USA's 13 (2017)). Suspended from the G8 in 2014 for its annexation of Crimea, Russia may be seen as primarily the 'cheer leader' for disaffected powers and a spoiler of US influence, rather than a proactive influence on the world stage.

What are the implications of unipolarity for global stability?

When the Soviet Union collapsed in 1991, the USA achieved hegemonic status, since there was now no other state that could globally compete with it. The resulting world order that characterised the ending of the Cold War was therefore unipolar. According to Joseph Nye, 'not since Rome has one nation loomed so large above the others'. Charles Krauthammer has referred to this period as representing the USA's 'unipolar moment'. One aide of George W. Bush is even alleged to have gone so far as to claim that 'we're an empire now, and when we act, we create our own reality'.

According to the hegemonic stability theory, a hegemon that is perceived by most other global players as being benign can act as a global policeman, and this will therefore encourage and promote global stability. The awesome and unchallengeable power of Rome provided stability in the ancient world for centuries, since no other power could challenge its authority. This long period of peace therefore became known as the Pax Romana. In the second half of the nineteenth century, the naval outreach of Great Britain also provided international stability, as British ships patrolled global sea lanes and no other power was prepared to seek to displace Great Britain as global hegemon.

At the end of the Cold War, a similar Pax Americana was also achieved. American ideals of free-market liberal democracy, as Francis Fukuyama pointed out in *The End of History*, were triumphant and the global popularity of the USA's economic, political and cultural identity was assured. Other powers 'bandwagoned' behind the USA in order to secure their protection, share its ideals and avoid its wrath.

Case study

The First Gulf War

The First Gulf War (in 1991) provides an excellent example of the benign hegemon theory in operation. When Saddam Hussein invaded Kuwait in August 1990, President George H. W. Bush used the USA's unrivalled global prestige to build a truly global coalition to liberate Kuwait from Iraqi forces under a UN mandate. Under President Clinton, the USA also provided leadership during the NATO bombing of the Bosnian Serbs in 1995 and Serbia in 1999 during the Kosovo War. In the middle east, President Clinton used US influence to encourage the acceptance of the Oslo Accords between the Palestine Liberation Organization chairman Yasser Arafat and Israel's prime minister, Yitzhak Rabin. Significantly, the Accords, which provided the Palestinians with limited self-government, were endorsed by both men on the White House lawns under the benevolent gaze of Clinton in 1993. Clinton also played a key role in encouraging the Northern Ireland peace process in the late 1990s. In March 2017, Clinton attended the funeral of former Deputy First Minister of Ireland Martin McGuinness, using the occasion to further encourage both unionists and republicans to seek peace in the province.

In all these military and diplomatic interventions the USA was perceived as being a legitimate global leader while, in the immediate aftermath of the Cold War, it was not in the interests or capability of any other power to challenge its hegemonic status. The USA's unrivalled military outreach has also deterred lesser powers from seeking to increase their regional influence. For example, the USA's significant military presence in the Pacific has deterred China's ambitions in the region. The US Fifth Fleet also patrols the Straits of Hormuz, which lies between the Persian Gulf and the Gulf of Oman and through which 20% of the world's supply of oil passes, so deterring Iran from seeking to alter the regional balance of power in its favour.

In addition, the global triumph of the Washington Consensus, based upon the free-market capitalism associated with the USA, has also led to greater trade between nations than ever before, further encouraging trust and cooperation. As a result, it has not been in the interests of other powers to seek to challenge the economic principles upon which the USA has succeeded in establishing a more globally interconnected economy.

It can therefore be to the advantage of countries to be part of a world under the protection of a global hegemon. This is because that hegemon's military, political and economic influence can guarantee the sort of international stability that is necessary for the free flow of goods and capital. Disputes between states are also more likely to be resolved, since the unchallengeable military power of the hegemon can both deter aggression and enforce obedience in the world order. States with no ideological aversion to a hegemon can therefore successfully 'freeload' off the back of a benign hegemon. This has provided the basis to the post-Cold War Pax Americana.

The dangers of unipolarity

However, according to realists like Kenneth Waltz, a unipolar world can also be highly unstable. This is because the hegemonic status of one state can encourage dangerous resentment among emerging powers. Waltz argues that because states are security-maximisers, in their attempts to protect themselves, they will feel constrained by another power's claims to global hegemony. This will be particularly dangerous and destabilising when a hegemon is declining in power and influence. Such a state of affairs has been referred to as power transition and can make international relations extremely volatile.

It has been argued that this provoked the First World War, since a rapidly growing Germany, emboldened by British failures in the Boer War, decided to challenge what had been the hegemonic status of Great Britain. According to this principle, US hegemony encouraged stability, so long as her position was unrivalled. However, the USA's failure to achieve its objectives in either Afghanistan or Iraq, followed by the collapse of the US bank Lehman Brothers, has more recently highlighted US military and economic weakness, so undermining the USA's claims to global leadership.

The attitude of emerging powers towards the existing hegemon is therefore vital. If the hegemon is resented and emerging states decide that they can achieve more by challenging it, this can create the environment for destabilising power transition. Until recently, for example, China has been prepared to accept US hegemony. However, its increasing assertiveness in its 'near abroad', represented by its building of reefs in the South China Sea in defiance of US-led regional condemnation, suggests that it feels able to challenge US dominance. Equally, the Russian annexation of Crimea from Ukraine in 2014 in defiance of an onslaught of Western criticism indicates that Russia may also begin to probe US weakness. The way in which President Barack Obama also refused to provide global leadership during the Arab Uprisings and then stood by as Russia militarily intervened in Syria on behalf of President Assad further suggests the limitations of US power.

The radical political philosopher Noam Chomsky has also argued that the possession by one state of hegemonic power is very dangerous, since a lack of constraints on what it is able to do can encourage it to act in defiance of international norms of behaviour. This can therefore create the potential for malign hegemony, in which one state becomes so powerful that it no longer takes into account the views of other states. Chomsky argues that a unipolar world can encourage a hegemon to become a 'rogue superpower', pursuing its own interests at the expanse of international law. The way, for example, in which the USA invaded Iraq in 2003 without a UN mandate demonstrates the danger of one power having such pre-eminent power that it can ignore the wishes of other states and international organs of global governance.

Case study

Inauguration addresses

Compare these extracts from the inaugural addresses of President John F. Kennedy in 1961 and President Donald Trump in 2017.

> Let every nation know, whether it wishes us well or ill, that we shall pay any price, bear any burden, meet any hardship, support any friend, oppose any foe to assure the survival and the success of liberty. This much we pledge — and more.
>
> President John F. Kennedy, 20 January 1961
>
> We will seek friendship and goodwill with the nations of the world but we do so with the understanding that it is the right of all nations to put their own interests first. We do not seek to impose our life on anyone.
>
> President Donald Trump, 20 January 2017

1 In what ways are they different?
2 What do they suggest about the USA's changing attitude towards global leadership?
3 Why might these differences be significant in terms of the maintenance of global stability?

Debate

Is the USA still the global hegemon?

Yes

Economic

- The USA remains the largest economy in the world. US GDP in 2016 was US$18.56 trillion.
- The US dollar is the main form of international currency.
- Wall Street is the world's central global trading hub.
- The USA has huge amounts of structural power in important organs of global economic governance, such as the World Bank, IMF and WTO.
- The USA has an expanding population that is estimated to reach 439 million by 2050.

No

Economic

- China is expected to overtake the USA in terms of its GDP and foreign direct investment by around 2020.
- US debt to China in January 2017 amounted to US$1.051 trillion.
- The collapse of Lehman Brothers, which helped to precipitate the 2008 global financial crisis, has undermined faith in the Washington Consensus.
- China has overtaken the USA as the biggest investor in Africa and South America.
- The AIIB is based in Beijing and is designed to challenge the World Bank as a major lender in the developing world.
- Only three of the top ten wealthiest companies in the world in 2017 are American (Walmart, Exxon Mobil and Apple). Three of them are now Chinese (State Grid, China National Petroleum and Sinopec).

Yes

Cultural

- The USA is pre-eminent in terms of soft-power influence. It is world-renowned in television and film, and has globally leading fashion and corporate brands. The ten highest-grossing films in history have all been American.
- In 2015, according to *Forbes*, eight of the ten most successful brands in the world were American (Apple, Microsoft, Google, Coca-Cola, IBM, McDonald's, General Electric and Facebook).
- The dominance of American cultural values has encouraged some political commentators to argue that 'globalisation' is another word for 'Americanization'.

Political

- The USA possesses important structural power in many IGOs. It is the most proactive permanent member of the UNSC and plays the dominant role in IGOs such as the IMF, World Bank, G7 and NATO.

Military

- The USA has the world's largest military budget. In 2015, it spent US$610 billion on defence, which is more than the rest of the world's spending on defence put together (US$601 billion). The USA's nearest rival, China, spent US$216 billion.
- The USA has 800 military bases in more than 70 countries across the globe and so can deploy troops anywhere in the world at any time.
- The aggregate tonnage of the US navy, which forms the basis of US outreach, is greater in size than that of the next 17 navies combined. The USA has 13 operational aircraft carriers compared with China (one) and Russia (one).

No

Cultural

- Other cultures are becoming more influential on a global scale. Bollywood is in direct competition with Hollywood. Association Football is the most popular sport in the world and the most popular sports teams in the world are Manchester United and Real Madrid.
- The USA's global soft-power influence has been dramatically undermined by controversies such as the Iraq War, water-boarding and Guantánamo Bay. Meanwhile, China has been expanding its global cultural influence by opening Confucius Institutes across the world, which spread Chinese values.

Chinatown in New York: due to immigration, there are a number of 'melting pots' in Western countries

Political

- There are rivals to the USA's structural power, with many of the emerging powers taking on increasingly significant roles. China and Russia are also permanent five members. India is fast becoming a significant actor for the Global South. Many of these emerging powers hold significant regional power. Furthermore, the Bretton Woods Institutions have increasingly come under criticism for their Western (and, in particular, US) dominance. This has been a key feature of the anti-globalisation movement.
- President Donald Trump's 'America First' rhetoric may alienate other countries, therefore undermining the USA's soft-power global influence. His withdrawal of the USA from the Paris climate change agreement in June 2017 has also provided China with the opportunity to seize global leadership in combatting climate change.

Military

- Russia and China are both beginning to challenge US military might both in terms of the global reach of their forces and the sophistication of their weaponry.
- China is developing short- and medium-range missiles, and Jin and Shang nuclear-powered submarines, in order to have the dominant military force in the South China Sea.
- In 2016, Russia announced that it had constructed the world's most lethal nuclear weapon: the RS: 28 Sarmat, which can dodge radar, travel up to 10,000 km and carry up to 12 warheads.

One of the most important foreign policy decisions of the Obama administration was the 'Pivot to Asia'. Born in Hawaii, Obama saw himself as the first Pacific-American president and he strongly believed that the USA must ensure that China does not achieve regional hegemony across Asia. US military resources and diplomatic initiatives were, therefore, increasingly focused on countering the growth of Chinese influence. As a result, Obama provided no global leadership when the Arab Uprisings broke out: during the Libyan Rising, for example, he urged the European leaders Prime Minister David Cameron and President Nicolas Sarkozy to provide the military lead. In 2013, when President Assad used chemical weapons against his opponents in Syria, Obama again chose not to act, encouraging an emboldened Putin to then intervene on behalf of Assad. Obama was similarly unfocused on Europe, and when Russia annexed Crimea from Ukraine in 2014, many accused his administration of providing insufficient leadership.

1   Using the evidence above and your own research, what have been the consequences of President Obama's 'Pivot to Asia'?

2   To what extent does President Obama's 'Pivot to Asia' suggest that the USA's claim to global hegemony is coming to an end?

In March 1999, NATO launched a bombing campaign against Serbia in order to stop the violence that was taking place in Kosovo. Serbia is a Slavic/Orthodox nation-state with close cultural, ethnic and nationalist associations with Russia. Indeed, one of the key reasons why the First World War broke out in 1914 was because Russia militarily supported Serbia when Austria-Hungary declared war on Serbia, following the murder of Archduke Franz Ferdinand in Sarajevo by a Bosnian Serb nationalist.

A sustained NATO attack on Serbia, which involved intensive bombing of Belgrade, was therefore likely to outrage Moscow, and Russian president Boris Yeltsin declared that he was 'deeply upset' by this 'open aggression' against Serbia. Vladimir Lukin, Russia's former ambassador to the USA, complained that 'The USA and its European allies … have wiped their feet on us' and Yeltsin threatened a military response. However, nothing came of this, and NATO achieved its objectives. Russian pride was assuaged when NATO agreed to Russian troops also entering Kosovo as part of an international peacekeeping force.

During the NATO bombing campaign on 8 May 1999, US missiles hit the Chinese embassy in Belgrade, killing three Chinese journalists. The Chinese government condemned the attacks as 'barbaric' and a gross violation of Chinese sovereignty. The Clinton administration admitted that the strikes had been a mistake, enabling a gradual rapprochement between the two countries to take place.

1   Suppose the events above happened in 2019 rather than 1999. What do you think the consequences for international peace might be?

2   What does this suggest about the changing balance of global power?

In what ways is the world becoming more multipolar?

Multipolarity is a system of global power in which there are a number of relatively evenly matched powers. This means that no one power can claim hegemonic influence over the others. As a result of the changing balance of economic and military global power, the consequences of globalisation and advances in military technology, it has been claimed that the contemporary world is increasingly multipolar. This is because no one power can dominate all others, as was the case during the Roman Empire and was, briefly, the case at the end of the Cold War when the USA was the unchallenged hegemon. Today, power is much more evenly distributed between states, IGOs and NGOs, and there are so many more constraints on a state's freedom of action that even the USA cannot make its presence felt everywhere in the world.

Economic and cultural dominance

Although the USA is still the world's pre-eminent power, its economic dominance is being challenged not only by China, but also by the rise of other emerging powers, such as Brazil, India, Russia and, perhaps most notably, the EU, which is now the most lucrative single market in the world. Global brands are challenging US brands and China has become the world's greatest neocolonial power, investing massively in Africa and South America — regions that were traditionally within the USA's economic zone of influence. The fact, too, that China controls so much of the USA's debt further illustrates how the economic balance of power has shifted eastwards, while the Washington Consensus of free-market liberalism is increasingly being challenged by the Beijing Consensus of state-orientated capitalism, which weathered the 2008 financial crisis surprisingly unscathed. The establishment in 2015 of the Asian Infrastructure Investment Bank (AIIB) as a rival to the World Bank in influencing the developing world provides a further example of the way in which economic power is moving eastwards.

The election of Donald Trump has demonstrated extraordinary class and racial divisions within the USA, which contrasts with the burgeoning nationalist self-confidence of Putin's Russia, Recep Erdogan's Turkey and Xi Jinping's China. The way in which global news networks such as Al Jazeera and RT (formerly Russia Today) increasingly challenge the USA's traditional dominance of global news has also fostered this greater sense of empowerment among emerging powers. Germany and the UK also regularly compete with the USA for pre-eminence in global soft-power influence. Widespread coverage of human rights abuses, such as water-boarding, has also eroded the USA's global cultural influence. President Trump has even admitted that the USA is no better than any other country in terms of human rights violations. This has therefore undermined the USA's traditional claim of moral exclusivity, indicating that the USA may now see itself more on a par with other powers.

Military and cyber technology dominance

Militarily, the rise of China is also challenging the USA. China is investing heavily in long-range bombers, nuclear submarines and medium-range missiles in order to stake its claim as the pre-eminent power in the Pacific. President Obama's tactical decision to militarily focus on the Pacific rather than the Atlantic has been seen by some political commentators as a tacit admission that the USA is no longer prepared to fight on both these fronts. The ability to fight such a two-front war has traditionally been seen as defining hegemonic status.

Humiliations in Afghanistan and Iraq also demonstrate that there are severe limitations on what the USA is militarily able to achieve. President Obama's unwillingness to provide either a diplomatic or military lead during the Arab Uprisings, as well as his failure to intervene in the Syrian civil war, has enabled both Russia and Turkey to take the initiative in developing the peace process. Russia has also been emboldened by its success in regaining Crimea from Ukraine and so is now flexing its military muscles outside its 'near abroad' for the first time since the end of the Cold War.

In addition, the growing significance of cyber technology further illustrates that any power with a sophisticated computer cadre (easily achieved with the globalisation of human ingenuity and free passage of computer scientists across borders) could make the USA's hegemonic status as the world's most powerful nuclear state redundant. This is because a cyber attack could enable a relatively weak state to bring a significantly more powerful one to its knees.

Therefore, as the USA progressively finds its military, economic, diplomatic and cultural influence challenged by emerging powers, it is likely that the world

Case study

Is the USA a declining power?

The United States no longer carries the same image of a vital society on the move with its brightest days ahead.

Political commentators have been keen to argue that the USA is now a declining hegemon and that the world is moving from unipolarity to multipolarity, with all the associated dangers associated with power transition. It is therefore interesting that the above quotation is from Senator John F. Kennedy during his presidential debate with Vice-President Richard Nixon on 21 October 1960.

We should therefore be careful about making too many assumptions regarding what may or may not happen in global politics. In the late 1950s, the Soviet Union was generally seen as being ahead of the USA in terms of missile and space technology. In 1968, as the USA became more closely embroiled in Vietnam and the assassinations of Martin Luther King and Senator Robert Kennedy tore the country apart, Henry Kissinger commented that the rise of 'political multipolarity … makes it impossible to impose an American design'. Then, in the 1970s, the resignation of President Nixon over the Watergate scandal in 1974 and the humiliating fall of Saigon in 1975, which signalled the end of the Vietnam War, and the Soviet invasion of Afghanistan in 1979, persuaded many critics that the USA was in terminal decline.

The election of Donald Trump in 2016 is not, therefore, sufficient evidence alone to suggest that the USA is a declining superpower. In his inaugural speech on 20 January 2017, Trump's language suggested that he was keen to abdicate the USA's global leadership role:

We've defended other nations' borders while refusing to defend our own and spent trillions of dollars overseas while America's infrastructure has fallen into disrepair and decay.

However, on 7 April 2017, Trump ordered the launch of 59 Tomahawk cruise missiles against a Syrian chemical weapons store following the chemical attack on Khan Sheikhoun. According to Trump, the Syrian government had 'launched a horrible chemical weapons attack on innocent civilians'. Disregarding Russian condemnation, he then called 'on all civilised nations to join us in seeking to end this slaughter and bloodshed in Syria and also to end terrorism of all kinds and all types'. On the same day, as Trump was meeting Chinese president Xi Jinping, the US secretary of state, Rex Tillerson, announced that regarding North Korea's nuclear ambitions the USA would, 'chart our own course if this is something China is just unable to coordinate with us'.

In 1992, when most pundits had written off his campaign, Bill Clinton came second in the New Hampshire primary. Calling himself 'the Comeback Kid', Clinton went on to win the Democrat nomination and beat George H. W. Bush to the presidency. Perhaps we should not make the same mistake about the USA? So often written off, it may, like Clinton, still prove to be 'the Comeback Kid'.

Activity

Make a table that is headed 'Is the USA in decline?', and include a Yes and No column.

1   Using the Case study on the previous page, what arguments can you find on both sides of this debate?

2   Can you add anything else from what you have read elsewhere in the chapter?

will become increasingly multipolar. This dispersal of power to the BRICS, MINT and regional power blocs, such as the EU, will prove difficult to reverse, while on the UNSC, the USA increasingly finds itself confronted by a more assertive Russia and China. Some have also suggested that globalisation has more widely dispersed power to non-state actors, such as global pressure groups, powerful transnational corporations and IGOs. This means that, as the centrality of the state in global relations is challenged, so this will make it progressively harder for one state to dominate the rest of the global community.

What are the implications of multipolarity for global stability?

A multipolar system is likely to have five or six centres of power, which are not grouped into tight alliances. Each state therefore follows its own perceived best interests and so the distribution of power continually shifts between them.

The realist viewpoint

Realists, like John Mearsheimer, argue that multipolarity represents the most unstable distribution of global power. This is because the system is much more fluid than bipolarity and unipolarity, since there is a constantly shifting balance of power as a number of relatively evenly matched states seek to maximise their influence at the expense of others. This creates fear and uncertainty among the states involved and, since there are so many players, the risk of possible conflicts is increased.

According to this theory, in a bipolar world two evenly matched superpowers will not want to risk open conflict and, when politics is unipolar, the global hegemon can deter the aggressive impulses of lesser powers. However, a multipolar world encourages risk-taking by states, so undermining the potential for a long-lasting balance of power. It could be argued that the Second World War broke out because global politics had become multipolar in the 1930s and so the Axis Powers (Germany, Italy and Japan) were prepared to take the risk of rebalancing global relations in their favour. Should the USA become just one among a number of relatively equal states, then the great power rivalries of the mid-twentieth century could well be replayed in the twenty-first century (see Figure 7.1).

The liberal viewpoint

However, liberals are more optimistic about the consequences of multipolarity for global peace and stability. They argue that, in the absence of a global hegemon or a superpower rivalry, states are more likely to cooperate in multilateral organs of global governance. The existence of more evenly matched states therefore provides greater opportunities for cooperation than either bipolarity or unipolarity.

Therefore, it could be argued that the relative security of a multipolar world depends upon whether the leading players are prepared to work through international agencies of government, or whether they prefer to compete within alliance structures. The latter is, of course, much more dangerous for peace than the former, and characterised the period of the two world wars. Liberals therefore argue that for multipolarity to provide peace, nation-states must set aside state egoism and be prepared to cooperate through organisations such as the G7, G20, UN and WTO.

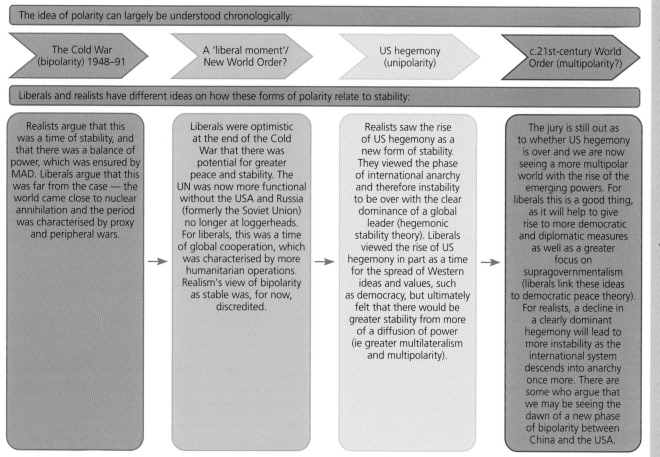

The idea of polarity can largely be understood chronologically:

The Cold War (bipolarity) 1948–91 → A 'liberal moment'/ New World Order? → US hegemony (unipolarity) → c.21st-century World Order (multipolarity?)

Liberals and realists have different ideas on how these forms of polarity relate to stability:

Realists argue that this was a time of stability, and that there was a balance of power, which was ensured by MAD. Liberals argue that this was far from the case — the world came close to nuclear annihilation and the period was characterised by proxy and peripheral wars.

Liberals were optimistic at the end of the Cold War that there was potential for greater peace and stability. The UN was now more functional without the USA and Russia (formerly the Soviet Union) no longer at loggerheads. For liberals, this was a time of global cooperation, which was characterised by more humanitarian operations. Realism's view of bipolarity as stable was, for now, discredited.

Realists saw the rise of US hegemony as a new form of stability. They viewed the phase of international anarchy and therefore instability to be over with the clear dominance of a global leader (hegemonic stability theory). Liberals viewed the rise of US hegemony in part as a time for the spread of Western ideas and values, such as democracy, but ultimately felt that there would be greater stability from more of a diffusion of power (ie greater multilateralism and multipolarity).

The jury is still out as to whether US hegemony is over and we are now seeing a more multipolar world with the rise of the emerging powers. For liberals this is a good thing, as it will help to give rise to more democratic and diplomatic measures as well as a greater focus on supragovernmentalism (liberals link these ideas to democratic peace theory). For realists, a decline in a clearly dominant hegemony will lead to more instability as the international system descends into anarchy once more. There are some who argue that we may be seeing the dawn of a new phase of bipolarity between China and the USA.

Figure 7.1 Polarity

Debate

Is there multipolarity in today's system?

Yes

- There are new emerging powers, such as the BRICS nations, which are becoming increasingly powerful on the global stage, challenging the idea that there is one clear hegemon. This suggests that that USA's economic hegemony is in decline.
- China has a dramatically expanding economy and is now more prepared to assert itself in diplomatic relations.
- Russia is more self-confident following its interventions in Crimea (2014) and Syria (2015).
- The world is now a global civil society through increased cosmopolitanism — globalisation is no longer limited to 'Americanization'.
- There is increasing competition from violent non-state actors to states, representing a diffusion of power. So-called Islamic State and al-Qaeda are examples of this new power challenge.

No

- The USA remains a hegemonic power in terms of its economic strength and military outreach.
- China's military outreach is only regional compared with the USA's global military outreach.
- Russia lacks allies, and socially and economically it has many of the characteristics of a developing state. Its military outreach is insignificant compared with that of the USA.
- Arguably, Americanization remains more pervasive than cosmopolitanism, with US culture still incredibly influential.

Key term

Failed state A state whose government is no longer able to provide its citizens with protection. Law, order and central government have collapsed, the economy no longer functions and there is a descent into anarchy. It is no longer a viable political unit and therefore will not be able to engage in diplomatic relations with other states.

Activity

In 1999, Mary Kaldor published *New and Old Wars: Organized Violence in a Global Era*. According to Kaldor, the increasing number of **failed states** would lead to new sorts of wars in which outside powers would be forced to intervene in order to stop the failed states becoming a magnet for violent extremism and terrorism. These wars would be different to traditional wars in which nation-states battled each other. The advance of military technology, together with the interconnectedness of globalisation, made this type of war less likely, since neither side would be likely to benefit. Both sides would suffer economically (see Thomas Friedman and the Dell Theory of Conflict Resolution, page 56). Militarily they would also be irrational. Either one side would be so militarily dominant as to quickly crush the other, as happened when the UK and the USA invaded Iraq in 2003, or they would be so equally matched that the destruction wrought by both sides would ensure there could be no winner.

The characteristics of 'new wars' include the following:

- Warfare will be within a failed or failing state.
- The fighting will involve irregular forces rather than the armies of nation-states fighting each other.
- The fighting will generally be classed as an insurgency, in which irregular forces often linked to criminal gangs and terrorists will seek to take over control of what is left of the state.
- New wars can be termed 'asymmetrical', since regular forces (often from outside powers) will be likely to have superior military equipment, but will not be able to deploy it effectively against the insurgents.
- Civilian casualties will be very high. This is because the insurgents may use terror tactics and regular troops will find it difficult to distinguish between insurgents and civilians.
- There will be no set-piece battles — fighting is much closer to guerrilla warfare.
- Old wars have a clear beginning and end. In new wars, the descent into anarchy is gradual and, as there is no defined rival army or government to surrender, new wars are likely to be prolonged indefinitely without an obvious end point.
- Historians will appreciate that such wars are not entirely new. Similar insurgencies occurred with Spanish partisans against French occupation during the Peninsula War (1808–13), the Irish War of Independence (1919–21) and the Vietnam War.

1 Provide as many examples as you can of modern-day insurgencies. Why do they share the characteristics of new wars?

2 Explain why insurgencies are so difficult to defeat.

Systems of government: characteristics

Key term

Democratic state Characterised by free, fair and regular elections in which governments are elected that are accountable to the public. They value liberal rights and freedoms and place a higher emphasis on the empowerment of individuals. A democratic state derives its legitimacy from the popular consent of the public.

There are a wide variety of ways in which states are governed (see Table 7.3). **Democratic states** have elected leaders and regular elections, which a variety of political parties contest. This provides the electorate with genuine choice so that the government that is elected has a genuine mandate from the people and therefore enjoys democratic legitimacy. In liberal democracies, the rule of law means that the rights of all citizens are equally protected. The separation of powers between the executive/legislature and the judiciary ensures this. As a result, the government is expected to act within the law and the judiciary can hold it accountable for legal breaches.

Table 7.3 Countries and their systems of government

Country	System of government
China	Communist, authoritarian (one-party state), military dictatorship (Peoples' Liberation Army)
India	World's largest democracy
Russia	In practice an authoritarian state, but claims to be a multiparty state
South Africa	Democratic, but with a level of corruption, arguably semi-democratic
UK and USA	Liberal democracies

Semi-democratic states superficially possess democratic characteristics, but on closer examination also contain authoritarian tendencies. The government is not constrained by the rule of law and so can put its own interests before those of its citizens. This is often achieved through amending the constitution in favour of the government, discouraging dissent, only allowing certain political parties to contest elections and limiting the freedom of the media. Electoral fraud and the intimidation of opposition parties are characteristic of elections and so the transfer of power is unlikely to be smooth. Semi-democratic states can also be referred to as 'majoritarian' (rather than liberal) democracies. This is because the interests of the majority are placed above those of the minority.

The governments of **non-democratic states** lack any democratic legitimacy. Since a non-democratic government is not accountable to its citizenry, it therefore lacks a popular mandate. These sorts of governments are classed as authoritarian. This means that those in government have sole authority for the running of the country. They are permanent and do not, therefore, need to seek the electoral endorsement of their citizens.

Authoritarian states place power with one individual or one ruling party. They rule in an autocratic fashion, since political dissent is not tolerated. The government controls the media and the judiciary acts according to the government's wishes, so threatening human rights. Alternative political parties are banned and state control is total. Authoritarian leaders do not willingly relinquish power and so the government perpetuates itself without ever seeking legitimisation from its citizens. The most repressive of authoritarian states are generally referred to as totalitarian states. For example, North Korea is best termed a totalitarian state.

Key terms

Semi-democratic state A state that superficially possesses the features of a democracy, but has underlying authoritarian features, ensuring the government won't willingly relinquish power. The rule of law is limited, since the government is not fully committed to democratic principles of justice, fairness and tolerance.

Non-democratic state An autocratic or authoritarian state, in which power is concentrated either in the hands of an individual or a select few. They vary in the despotic tendencies of their governments, with totalitarian states the most ruthless in their crushing of internal dissent.

Authoritarian state A state in which power is concentrated solely in the hands of a single, usually unelected, person or party. Power is hereditary and sometimes seized, and is unlimited, given the lack of accountability.

> **Distinguish between**
>
> ## Autocratic and democratic states
>
> ### Autocratic states
>
> - In autocratic states, power is centralised in the hands of a single, dominant party or individual.
> - There are no elections. Referendums (plebiscites) may be allowed but they are not fair and are a way of providing the government with popular acclamation.
> - The judiciary lacks independence from the government, so undermining the principle of the rule of law.
> - There is heavy state control over political institutions and the populace at large.
>
> ### Democratic states
>
> - In a democracy, power is distributed across society, with various checks and balances.
> - There are free and fair elections, so providing the government with democratic legitimacy.
> - The government is regularly made accountable to the public and can so claim a popular mandate.
> - There is a greater emphasis on individualism.
> - The rule of law ensures that there are limits on what the government can do, so protecting citizens' rights.

Failed and rogue states

Democratic Republic of the Congo: a failed state

A good example of a failed state is the Democratic Republic of the Congo (DRC).

- The country is characterised by civil war, which bought about the end of President Mobutu Sese Seko's brutal dictatorship in 1996.
- It suffers from significant ethnic and provincial divides (see Figure 7.2), which were arguably exacerbated by particularly oppressive Belgian colonial rule, the legacy of which perpetuates to this day.
- It has had a tumultuous relationship with some of its neighbours in what has historically been an unstable region (the DRC borders both Rwanda and Uganda, both of which also have recent histories of appalling human rights abuses).
- There is deep-seated corruption, both at the highest levels of authority and in the lower echelons, with militias being prominent in the country's history.

Figure 7.2 Provincial boundaries, the DRC

- Rape has been used as a widespread weapon of war and there is massive recruitment of child soldiers.
- It has suffered from the 'resource curse', whereby its being very rich in many natural resources has actually left the country in a dire position. Colonial powers first exploited these resources, followed by brutal dictatorships. The country is also rife with civil war, corruption and militia groups using the black market for their own gains. Given the DRC's lack of infrastructure and development, it has lacked the amenities it needs to benefit from harnessing these resources itself.
- It has arguably been a victim of the West in terms of colonialism, the exploitation of its resources through black markets and Western interference (or lack thereof) in this part of Africa.

Continued

Democratic People's Republic of Korea: a rogue state

The Democratic People's Republic of Korea (DPRK), or North Korea, is a good example of a **rogue state**.

North Korea's significant nuclear arsenal is a key feature of its 'rogue' status. Its readiness to both test and threaten the use of nuclear weapons poses a threat to international stability and directly threatens other nation-states.

North Korea and its neighbour, South Korea, have had a long-standing, hostile history (see Figure 7.3). This was perpetuated by the Cold War, during which Korea was drawn into a lengthy and

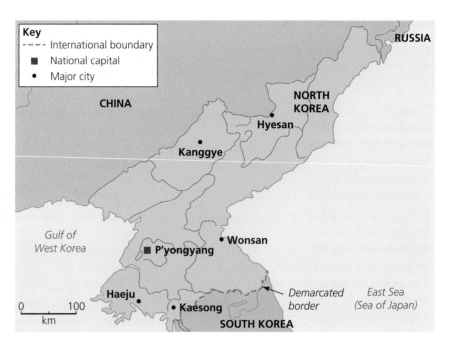

Figure 7.3 The DPRK (North Korea)

costly peripheral war, in which the USA supported the more liberal South and the Soviet Union the Communist North.

The USA continues to have a tense relationship with North Korea. North Korea does not cooperate in the international system and has frequently flouted international laws. It has one of the worst human rights records, directly contravening the UN Charter, and has failed to uphold international agreements even when it has signed them, for example the Treaty on the Non-Proliferation of Nuclear Weapons (NPT).

North Korea's population is deliberately isolated from the rest of world and its government pursues a deeply isolationist foreign policy.

Rogue state A state that acts in defiance of international norms of behaviour by threatening regional and global stability, through the development of weapons of mass destruction in defiance of international agreements and/or its connections with global terrorism.

Democracy

This chapter has already examined the impact of democracy on stability. Liberals generally argue that increased globalisation leads to global governance, multilateralism and cooperation, as well as the spread of liberal democratic values, and that overall this creates stability (democratic peace theory, see page 286). But there are many wider advantages and disadvantages to the democratic system and democratic governments.

Is democracy the best form of government?

Yes

- Democracy is good for political development, as it empowers the populace.
- Democracy goes hand in hand with liberal values and freedoms and liberal democracy is the system that, according to Fukuyama, brings us to 'the end of history' as the ideal form of government.
- Democracy complements capitalism and free trade, meaning it is also a significant factor in economic development.
- Democracies bring peace and stability to the international system. They are better at multilateral cooperation (democratic peace theory).
- Democratic governments are held to account and are, therefore, more transparent, both of which are essential to upholding human rights.

No

- Democracy shouldn't be seen as 'one size fits all' — a benign dictator can benefit a relatively new or underdeveloped country through strong leadership.
- Democracy is unsustainable if implemented too early. Economist and author Dambisa Moyo argues that states first need a strong economy before they can implement a successful democracy.
- Many developing countries benefit from protectionist policies (which require strong leadership and state control) as they are a good way to stabilise economic growth.
- Western liberals assume that democracies always provide the best form of government and that authoritarian governments impede development. However, some authoritarian countries have achieved impressive growth rates and domestic stability, and are able to play a constructive role in global politics. China is based on one-party rule and its government has dramatically reduced Chinese levels of poverty. By around 2020, China is set to overtake the USA as the world's biggest economy. Singapore is a one-party state and so is far from the Western ideal of a liberal democracy, and yet in terms of crime, economic freedom and life expectancy, Singapore is a much better place to live than the USA.

A false spring?

The Arab Spring began in Tunisia in 2010, when the populace mounted protests against President Zine El Abidine Ben Ali's oppressive regime. This sparked a revolutionary wave of support for the installation of democracy across the Arab world, with varying degrees of violence and success. The revolution resulted in extended violence in Egypt, Iraq, Libya, Syria and Yemen.

A key feature of these protests was the use of technology. Globalisation has allowed technology to spread the idea of liberal values and freedoms across the world. People are therefore much more aware than ever before of the freedoms experienced in other nations. Arguably, this was one of the major triggers for the Arab Uprisings. In particular, Facebook and Twitter played a key role in mobilising populations against their governments, so challenging the repressive governments that had often been in power for decades.

During the Arab Uprisings, the populace mounted challenges against sovereign governments throughout the middle east and north Africa

Liberals initially saw the Arab Uprisings as a 're-run' of the fall of communism in eastern Europe in 1988–89. Repressive dictatorships would be replaced with people power,

Continued

so establishing a surge of liberal democracy throughout the Arab world. History, however, does not always progress the way we may want it to. It was not only pro-Western liberals who wanted to see the back of repressive dictators, such as Hosni Mubarak of Egypt and Muammar Gaddafi. Radical Muslims, who fear and resent Western liberalism, also often led the protests against these dictators and so when tyrannies were challenged, the results were much more bloody and anarchic than anticipated. In Libya, for example, anarchy reigns, and the Syrian civil war has led to the deaths of as many as 400,000 (2017). In Egypt, the military has re-imposed a semblance of order with the tacit acknowledgement of the West and in Yemen a brutal civil war has involved both Saudi Arabia and Islamist militants in a struggle for control.

Therefore, the consequence of the Arab Uprisings has not been the rise of new democracies. Instead, there is a greater threat than ever before of failed, rogue and authoritarian states defining the future of the region. According to the British historian A. J. P. Taylor, the liberal revolutions in Germany in 1848 ended up simply reinforcing authoritarianism: 'German history reached its turning point and failed to turn.' The same may, unfortunately, be true of the Arab Uprisings today.

How has the global balance of power changed since the end of the Cold War?

To what extent is China a superpower?

In 1972, President Richard Nixon became the first US president to visit the People's Republic of China. His meeting with Chairman Mao provided the initial foundation for China's decision to develop trade with the rest of the world. The consequences of this for China's seismic economic growth have been profound and it is generally accepted that China's economy will overtake the USA's GDP by around 2020. In 1994, the year he died, Nixon presciently warned that:

> Today, China's economic power makes US lectures about human rights imprudent. Within a decade it will make them irrelevant. Within two decades it will make them laughable.

China's economic outreach is certainly global. For almost 30 years, China's annual growth rates have been between 8% and 10%, and are only now gradually cooling to 6.7% in 2016. China's state-run capitalist model weathered the global financial crisis significantly better than the models of Western powers and, by 2010, the Chinese economy was 90 times greater than it had been in 1978. With the world's largest population (1.35 billion), China has massive reserves of cheap labour, making it the manufacturing and export heart of the world.

Although still considered to be a developing nation (due to the levels of poverty and the lack of development of significant parts of the country, especially in rural areas), China has also become the most successful neocolonial power in the world. It is Africa's biggest trading partner and in 2014 Chinese–African trade amounted to US$200 billion. In defiance of the Monroe Doctrine, which regards South America as firmly within the USA's sphere of influence, China has dramatically increased investment in the region. From 2000 to 2013, trade between China and South America increased 22 times and in just 3 years

(2013–16) President Xi Jinping has made three visits to the continent in order to further develop economic and diplomatic ties.

Chinese investments are also global. Chinese investors own Birmingham City Football Club, House of Fraser, Pizza Express, Volvo and Weetabix. A Chinese investment of £6 billion is financing the proposed Hinkley Point C nuclear reactor in Somerset. Chinese investors are also financing the Nicaragua Canal, which will cost US$50 billion and is designed to challenge the Panama Canal.

China's structural economic power is dramatically increasing, further extending its global outreach. Since 2001, China has been a member of the WTO and, in 2015, Beijing established the AIIB, which provides loans to developing countries in the Asia-Pacific region. China also heavily invests in the USA in the form of foreign direct investment. This demonstrates how China has grown, given that it used to rely on foreign direct investment from the West.

China's militarily influence is also increasing. In 2016, China spent US$131 billion on its defence budget and Jane's Information Group estimates that by 2020 its army will be second only to that of the USA in terms of military efficiency. China has purchased an aircraft carrier from Ukraine and is constructing another. It is also attempting to militarise reefs in the South China Sea and is building up its submarine and missile capability in the region. In 2014, for example, China deployed the Jin-class ballistic missile submarine in the South China Sea. Each submarine is armed with 12 JL-2 nuclear missiles.

Limitations

However, these developments do not confirm that China is close to becoming a superpower. Some critics have likened China at the beginning of the twenty-first century to Prussia at the end of the nineteenth century. In short, China is great and powerful in its 'near abroad'. However, its military and diplomatic outreach does not match its economic outreach. The USA, for example, has almost 800 military bases in 70 countries as well as alliances across the globe. Only in 2016 did China open its first overseas military base, at Djibouti in the Indian Ocean.

China's global influence is also limited by its Communist ideology. American democratic values have, especially since the Second World War, had a global appeal, which China's more authoritarian approach lacks. In its immediate zone of influence, Japan, the Philippines, Singapore, South Korea and Taiwan all look to the USA for both ideology and protection, therefore affecting its soft power on a local and a global scale. ASEAN also provides an alternative model of development. India, as the world's largest democracy, represents a potential barrier to China's global influence. Even Russia, which is increasingly authoritarian and understands the value of courting China, shares a 4,000 km disputed border with China, making its friendship unreliable.

There is also the question of whether China actually wants to be a superpower. In order to be a superpower a nation-state needs to have a clear world mission and be willing to take on a global leadership role. Rome in the ancient world had this sense of mission, as did Great Britain in the nineteenth century, and in recent years so has the USA. However, China has generally viewed world affairs according to Westphalian principles, by not seeking to impose its values on other states and jealously protecting its sovereignty from outside influence. In 2015, President Xi Jinping announced at a military parade commemorating the 70th anniversary of the end of the Second World War that, 'China will remain committed to peaceful development. We Chinese love peace. No matter how much stronger it may become, China will never seek hegemony or expansion.'

This may change. In 2017, in the wake of President Trump's abandonment of the Paris treaty, China quickly positioned itself as the global leader on climate change. However, at least for the moment, China's immediate ambition is to be the dominant power in the Pacific rather than a global hegemon. But even this may be too much for the USA to accept.

To what extent does the rise of China threaten global stability?

According to US historian Robert Kagan in *The Return of History and the End of Dreams*, 'Power changes nations. It expands their wants and desires; increases their sense of entitlement'. According to the offensive realist John Mearsheimer, the rise of China is unlikely to be peaceful. The USA still jealously guards its hegemonic status and, according to power transition theory, will even be prepared to fight to preserve it. As Mearsheimer puts it, 'if China continues to rise you better be very careful, because that will drive the United States stark raving crazy'.

China's expansion of its military influence in the South China Sea could therefore bring it into conflict with other regional powers, such as Japan, South Korea and Taiwan. These powers have strong military and diplomatic support from the USA and so China's attempts to achieve regional hegemony could provoke a showdown with the USA, which also sees itself as a Pacific power and as the guarantor of these states' independence. A particularly contentious issue is North Korea. The USA feels threatened by its nuclear programme and US Secretary of State Rex Tillerson has promised that, should China fail to act, the USA will 'resolve the problem alone'. Such unilateral action in the region could also provoke conflict with China.

However, China and the USA depend on each other for trade and investment, and it is not in the economic interests of either country to provoke a war with the other. Niall Fergusson has even coined the term 'Chimerica' to emphasise the depth of their economic dependency on each other. China has also shown that it can work closely with the USA: for example, their joint climate change deal in 2014, which paved the way for progress at the Paris Climate Conference in 2015. At his first meeting with President Trump, President Xi Jinping noted that, 'We have a thousand reasons to get China–US relations right, and not one reason to spoil the China–US relationship'. However, since then Trump has pulled out of the Paris climate change agreement in a move that has been seen as globally antagonistic and has received large-scale bad press. President Trump has agreed in other areas, stating that both countries had a similar interest in de-escalating tension in Korea by stopping North Korea's nuclear missile programme. As Henry Kissinger has pointed out, viewing China as a threat to peace could simply end up being 'a self-fulfilling prophecy'.

In what ways has the changing balance of global power impacted on contemporary global issues?

Synoptic links are key to this section of the Power and developments component. You need to be able to identify the extent to which changing relationships and state actions relate to various developments in power, and how they impact contemporary global issues. These include conflict, poverty, human rights and the environment. The impact of power and development on these global issues is inextricably linked to globalisation.

How have attitudes towards human rights changed since the end of the Second World War?

The Cold War

At the end of the Second World War, the UN took the moral lead in trying to establish an international community in which the rule of law and respect for human rights would challenge aggressive nationalism and racism. The Charter of the United Nations (1945) laid the foundations for a new world order based upon cooperation between nation-states rather than conflict. In 1948, the Universal Declaration of Human Rights (UDHR) for the first time established an international standard of human rights to which all states should aspire to exist.

Tragically, 1948 also coincided with the Soviet take-over of Czechoslovakia and the Berlin Airlift, so that the beginning of the Cold War soon overshadowed the fine cosmopolitan ideals of the UDHR. The resulting deterioration in relations between the Soviet Union and the USA therefore meant that the UN generally became gridlocked, as each superpower vetoed the resolutions of the other. In addition, it was in the interests of each superpower to advance its tactical interests at the expense of the other. This meant that each state became engaged in proxy wars to advance the interests of its allies, often exacerbating and prolonging military conflicts. The protection of human rights was therefore considerably less important to the leaders of East and West than advancing strategic self-interest and guaranteeing their security.

Case study

Rule of law

The rule of law refers to the principle that the legal system should provide impartial justice for everyone within a nation-state. This means that no individual can claim to be above the law and that the government is itself bound to obey the rule of law. The government (executive) is separate from the judiciary, ensuring that the judiciary is not simply a tool of the government as it is in totalitarian states. The powers of the government are therefore limited, so protecting the civil liberties of the public from arbitrary interference.

A liberal democracy, like the UK, is governed according to the rule of law, in contrast to an authoritarian government in which there are no constraints on how the government acts.

The USA's 'unipolar moment', c.1991–c.2003

When the Soviet Union collapsed in 1991, the USA became the only remaining superpower. US power was unchallengeable and so the USA achieved hegemonic status. President George H. W. Bush referred to a 'New World Order', which would now be defined by free trade, the spread of democracy, greater cooperation between nation-states and a greater commitment to human rights.

When Iraq invaded Kuwait in 1990, Bush succeeded in winning global support for a UN-backed invasion force to expel the forces of Saddam Hussein. For Bush, this was a crime of 'naked aggression' that had to be stopped. In 1992, he sent US troops into Somalia in order to ensure that humanitarian relief efforts reached famine victims. His successor, Bill Clinton, was also keen to associate the USA with the global promotion of human rights.

- In 1995, the USA played the leading role in NATO's bombing of the Bosnian Serbs following the Srebrenica Massacre. At the subsequent Dayton, Ohio Peace Talks, the then-US secretary of state Warren Christopher succeeded in brokering an end to the civil war.
- In 1999, the USA led the NATO bombing of Serbia to stop the ethnic cleansing in Kosovo.
- During the 1990s, the USA played a key role in encouraging the peace process in Northern Ireland and Palestine.

In addition, the end of the Cold War persuaded scholars of international relations, like Francis Fukuyama, that the future now lay with liberal democracies. According to liberals, when there are more democracies there is greater international stability (democratic peace theory). According to this principle, democracies are hesitant to go to war since they are inherently more peaceful than other political systems. In recent history, for example, there are virtually no examples of two liberal democracies in conflict on the battlefield.

Democratic peace theory has its beginnings in the ideas of German philosopher Immanuel Kant, who argued that through democracy and cooperation we can attain perpetual peace. During the 1960s the theory became more cohesive, developing the principle that democracies are more accountable and transparent. Arguably, therefore, democracies are more amenable to multilateral engagement and tend to be less prepared to take destabilising unilateral action in order to achieve more power. These features allow for more effective global governance, which is better for peace and stability in general.

However, we should beware of looking back on the 1990s as a golden period for human rights protection and humanitarian intervention. According to former New York Governor Mario Cuomo, 'You campaign in poetry. You govern in prose'. In other words, even the most liberal democratic leader often has to act according to realist self-interest and accept that there are limits on what he/she can do to advance a human rights agenda.

- In 1993, following the battle of Mogadishu in which 18 US soldiers were killed, President Clinton withdrew US military forces from Somalia, sternly informing the UN General Assembly on 28 September 1993 that, 'If the American people are to say yes to UN peacekeeping, the United Nations must know when to say no'.
- In 1994, as Rwanda was sliding into anarchy, the Clinton administration failed to provide either moral or military leadership. Instead, its priority was to evacuate foreign nationals and UN peacekeepers, allowing the genocide of 800,000 Tutsis and moderate Hutus.

Therefore, even when the USA enjoyed global prestige and unrivalled hard- and soft-power outreach, there were clear limits on what it was prepared to do to advance human rights.

The limits of US power, c.2003–

The War on Terror further undermined the USA's commitment to a human rights-based foreign policy. During his first few months in power, President George W. Bush scribbled on a report of the Clinton administration's failure to intervene to stop the genocide in Rwanda: 'not on my watch'. However, the way in which the USA conducted the War on Terror, often in defiance of international norms of behaviour, severely undermined its reputation as a bastion of human rights.

In addition, the rise of more authoritarian governments, such as those of China and Russia in the early twenty-first century, has further challenged the ongoing importance of human rights in international relations. President Putin has militarily intervened on behalf of President Assad in Syria in order to protect Russian interests in the region and stop the further spread of Islamist terrorism. That the Assad regime has an appalling record on human rights has not deterred Putin's enthusiastic support. China has also continually condemned criticisms of its own record on human rights. In 2017, a Chinese report on human rights even went on the offensive against the USA, claiming that America was too ready to wield 'the baton of human rights' in spite of 'paying no attention to its own terrible human rights problems'.

The dramatic events of 2016 have also made many liberals question the extent to which human rights is under greater threat than at any time since the early Cold War. The 2016 Brexit referendum unleashed significant anti-immigrant feeling and leading European politicians, such as Nigel Farage, Viktor Orban, Geert Wilders and Marine Le Pen, have won considerable acclaim for their denunciation of 'outsiders'. Much of this could be seen as a backlash against the so-called refugee crisis. During his election campaign, President Trump also offended many liberals with his ruthlessly pragmatic campaign, which promised to build a wall on the Mexican border and 'bring a hell of a lot worse than water-boarding'.

The debates surrounding Brexit centred on anti-immigration and British sovereignty

President Clinton

On 26 February 1999, President Bill Clinton gave a speech in which he laid out a number of principles that later became known as the Clinton Doctrine. According to Clinton, genocide could never be purely a domestic affair and the USA should be prepared to intervene within states to stop ethnic cleansing. These principles later on became enshrined in the UN's Responsibility to Protect (2005):

> It's easy … to say that we really have no interests in who lives in this or that valley in Bosnia, or who owns a strip of brush land in the Horn of Africa, or some piece of parched earth by the Jordan River. But the true measure of our interests lies not in how small or distant these places are, or in whether we have trouble pronouncing their names. The question we must ask is, what are the consequences to our security of letting conflicts fester and spread? We cannot, indeed, we should not, do everything or be everywhere. But where our values and our interests are at stake, and where we can make a difference, we must be prepared to do so.

However, critics point out that before developing this doctrine, Clinton had withdrawn US troops from Somalia following the Battle of Mogadishu in 1993, allowing that country to further descend into anarchy. His administration was also resolute for inaction as the Rwandan genocide took place in 1994. In 1999, it was Prime Minister Tony Blair who persuaded a reluctant Clinton that he should be prepared to commit grounds troops in Kosovo if the air bombing campaign did not lead to a withdrawal of the Serbian military.

President Trump

During his presidential campaign in 2016, Donald Trump shocked liberals across the world by abandoning the principle that the USA should act as the world's moral policeman. What mattered to Trump was stability rather than morality — his approach to politics was therefore realist rather than liberal. For example, in his second presidential debate with Hillary Clinton he acknowledged that: 'I don't like Assad at all, but Assad is killing ISIS.' Then, in his inaugural speech on 20 January 2017, he categorically stated that, 'we will seek friendship and good will with the nations of the world but we do so with the understanding that it is the right of all nations to put their own interests first'.

On 7 April 2017, following the chemical attack on Khan Sheikhoun, Syria, President Trump launched 59 Tomahawk missiles against Syrian government military complexes. Russia responded that this was a blatant attack on a sovereign state. However, European leaders were much more supportive of Trump's assertion that what had happened was an 'affront to humanity'. Trump stated:

> On Tuesday, Syrian dictator Bashar al-Assad launched a horrible chemical weapons attack on innocent civilians. Using a deadly nerve agent, Assad choked out the lives of helpless men, women and children. It was a slow and brutal death for so many. Even beautiful babies were cruelly murdered in this very barbaric attack. No child of God should ever suffer such horror.

> Tonight I ordered a targeted military strike on the airfield in Syria from where the chemical attack was launched. We ask for God's wisdom as we face the challenge of our very troubled world. We pray for the lives of the wounded and for the souls of those who have passed and we hope that as long as America stands for justice, that peace and harmony will in the end prevail.

> Good night and God bless America and the entire world. Thank you.

1 Using this evidence and your wider understanding, to what extent do you agree that the 'golden age' of human rights protection is in the past?

However, we should be careful not to argue that human rights were once a global priority and have now become an irrelevance because of the rise of authoritarianism and populism. Arguably the human rights agenda has always been fraught. It took 4 years (from 1991 to 1995) for NATO to intervene in Bosnia to stop the carnage. In 1994, the world community did nothing as genocide engulfed Rwanda. Since the end of the Cold War, appalling human rights abuses have also gone unpunished in Darfur and Zimbabwe. President Obama won the Nobel Peace Prize in 2009, but the drone strikes he launched caused numerous civilian casualties, while he steadfastly refused to intervene in the Syrian civil war since vital US strategic interests were not at stake.

To suggest, therefore, that the protection of human rights has suddenly become an irrelevance to a new breed of authoritarian and nationalist leaders is misleading. After all, it was the alleged arch-realist Donald Trump, rather than the supposed liberal Barack Obama, who launched missile strikes on Syria in April 2017 for its use of chemical weapons on civilians.

How has the changing balance of world power affected conflict?

As we have seen, challenges to US hegemony may encourage greater possibility of conflict. Realists fear that conditions of power transition can lead to conflict as emerging powers, keen to expand their influence, challenge the hegemon's attempts to retain its global standing. Since realists argue that states seek power and security, the uncertainties of power transition are, therefore, highly unstable, as aspiring powers are more likely to take risks in order to achieve greater power and influence.

On the other hand, liberals have argued that a more multipolar world can encourage states to work together if they are prepared to cooperate through organs of global governance. In a more evenly balanced world no one power is able to unilaterally impose its will on the others (the malign hegemony theory) and so countries can more effectively resolve their differences through dialogue.

Neither interpretation is wholly satisfying, since each is based upon a different interpretation of what motivates states. If states are motivated solely by the desire for power, then the first interpretation holds. If, however, states are communitarian in their outlook then the second interpretation will be truest. In reality, states, like people, are neither entirely realist nor entirely liberal in their attitudes and so the best we can predict is that the changing balance of world power will bring with it both dangers and opportunities.

However, what is more certain is that the challenges of failed and rogue states are unlikely to disappear. The extent to which the global community succeeds, or fails, in dealing with failed states like Syria, or rogue states like North Korea, is therefore likely to determine the sort of direction in which global politics progresses in the twenty-first century.

How has the changing balance of world power affected poverty?

Globalisation has led to an increase in free-market capitalism. This has dramatically reduced global poverty, since it has enabled developing countries to take advantage of the opportunities for growth that global trading presents. As a result, there has been a significant convergence between the Global North and the Global South, challenging the utility of the concept of a North/South divide. The share, for example, of the developing world's population living on less than US$1.25 a day (the international definition of poverty) has fallen from 30% in 2000 to below 10% in 2014. One of the main reasons why the Millennium Development Goals (2000–15) achieved the success they did was because globalisation provided greater opportunities for extreme poverty reduction than ever before.

A number of developing countries have achieved remarkable success in lifting their citizens out of poverty. In 2017, South Korea had the 11th biggest economy in the world, beating Russia into 12th place. Among the top ten biggest economies in the world, three are in the developing world — China (2nd), India (7th) and Brazil (9th) (2016). African countries with the most spectacular growth rates are those that have focused on taking advantage of new opportunities in global trade, such as Ethiopia (textiles and coffee) and Côte d'Ivoire (the world's largest exporter of cocoa beans). Across Africa, too, Chinese investment is providing massive opportunities for the development of infrastructure. In 2015, for example, President Xi Jinping pledged a further US$60 billion to African investment.

However, although millions have been lifted out of poverty in emerging economies such as China, India and the East Asian Tigers (Hong Kong, Singapore, South Korea and Taiwan), the changing balance of global power has had much less of an impact on what Paul Collier has called 'the Bottom Billion'. Often located in Sub-Saharan Africa, the billion people living in poor-resourced, land-locked and poorly governed states are more likely to be victims of globalisation, as cheap manufactured products are 'dumped' on them, undermining their potential for achieving initial-stage industrialisation. Neo-Marxists, such as Immanuel Wallerstein in his 'world systems' theory, also argue that even those developing states that seem to be expanding as a result of globalisation are actually being exploited. Neocolonial powers utilise their cheap labour and raw materials so that the profits from globalisation go to the core (colonising) rather than the peripheral (colonised) power. Furthermore, their growth rates can be misleading, given they are starting from a very low baseline.

Amy Chua has also argued in 2002's *World on Fire* that the sudden imposition of free markets can dramatically increase inequality and resentment. Globalisation does have the potential to raise all boats but not equally, and so in increasing numbers of states (both North and South) the gap between rich and poor is becoming worryingly extreme. The election of Donald Trump in 2016 was due, in part, to his victory in the 'rust-belt' states such as Michigan, Pennsylvania and Wisconsin, where manufacturing jobs have steadily been lost to the developing world, so creating a new poverty underclass.

Distinguish between

Free trade and protectionism

Free trade

- Trade is largely left to its own devices, with little government regulation. This means that it is free and is sometimes referred to as 'trade liberalisation'.
- There is little interference from the government in the form of taxes, tariffs or quotas.
- Adam Smith, one of free trade's key proponents, argued that if left to their own devices, economies would self-regulate (the 'invisible hand'). The laws of supply and demand therefore create an equitable share and price for produce.
- Often (but not always), free trade goes hand in hand with democracy, since there is less government authority over the economy.
- Free trade promotes competition and innovation. It therefore boosts profit and, in turn, GDP.

Protectionism

- In a protectionist system, governments more tightly control the operation of the free market.
- There is greater government intervention in markets, for example through subsidies, taxes, tariffs and/or quotas, which boost domestic production at the expense of foreign competition.
- Governments promote domestic trade as far as possible so that there is less reliance on imports.
- Protectionism is sometimes associated with more authoritarian regimes, since these sorts of governments are more likely to be controlling and interventionist.

Protectionist policies can be linked to socialism. This is covered, as a political ideology, in Component 1, whereby the state should intervene to help promote domestic growth. Socialist economics, as exemplified by Karl Marx and Friedrich Engels, sees the state as the key driver of economic success.

Neoliberal economic policy views the state as a hindrance to economic growth rather than its promoter. Key conservative thinkers in Component 1 include Ayn Rand, whose novels, such as *The Fountainhead* (1943) and *Atlas Shrugged* (1957), revere the individual entrepreneur for building success.

How has the changing balance of world power affected the environment?

The changes in the global order have had a mixed impact on the environment. On the one hand, the increased focus on trade, global travel and industrialisation has taken a massive toll on the environment. On the other, the increased cooperation that has come with globalisation, together with greater emphasis on global governance, has led to climate change and environmental protection gaining greater prominence in international debate.

The rapid economic growth of emerging powers has led to significant environmental damage due to heavy industrialisation, deforestation and increasing pollution, all of which have significantly increased carbon emissions. The focus of the developing world on lifting their populations out of poverty has made it difficult to address the problem of climate change. This has meant that the developing world has prioritised economic growth over sustainable development. The way, too, in which the developed world has criticised the developing world for its use of cheap, carbon-emitting fuels, like coal, might also be seen as hypocritical. After all, during the last two centuries, the developed world became rich by polluting the atmosphere and now it could be seen as trying to deny the developing world the opportunity to become wealthy. The difficulty of achieving a consensus between the developed and developing worlds on how best to limit carbon emissions is one of the key reasons why the Copenhagen Conference (2009) was not more successful (see Chapter 6).

The political economist Thomas Malthus pessimistically argued that population growth was unsustainable and that we do not have the global resources to continue to support growth at current rates. In other words, there is a 'limit to this growth'. While we have now passed Malthus' predicted time of crisis, many have adopted the ideas of neo-Malthusianism, arguing that without a significant focus on resource management and sustainable development, we will reach a crisis point characterised by famine, disease and civil war. Arguably, we are already witnessing these effects in certain parts of the world.

However, the Danish economist Ester Boserup argued that the challenges created by population growth necessarily force us to come up with new and better solutions. There will be a growth in the creation of new technologies and this will enable us to better manage resources, so that population growth will once again be sustainable.

In addition, the Paris Climate Change Conference (2015) demonstrated that the developing world is becoming much more aware of the dangers of unrestricted economic growth. Thus, the conference succeeded in getting nearly all of the 200 states represented to agree that temperature rise in the twenty-first century should be kept as close to 1.5°C as possible. Nation-states will also accept regular reviews of their efforts to limit carbon emissions and the developed world will provide 'climate finance' to help the developing world transfer to greener technology.

Furthermore, in 2017 the attitude of the leaders of the developed and developing world to climate change seemed to 'flip'. In January, China reversed plans for 104 new coal plants and President Xi Jinping expressed regret that President Trump had not lived up to the global aspirations of the Paris treaty. In March, the Trump administration reversed the restrictions President Obama had put on the extraction of fossil fuels. It is therefore difficult to predict the way in which the changing balance of world power will continue to impact the environment.

Synoptic links

Environmentalism and conservation are further covered in the ecologism option in Component 2. The British economist E. F. Schumacher, for example, argued that the traditional focus on economic growth as an end in itself needs to be questioned.

What you should know

Having read this chapter you should have knowledge and understanding of the following:
- 'Power' is a frequently used term in global relations. At its essence, power means the ability to exert influence through various means over others. In the case of global politics, this relates to the methods nation-states use to exercise control and achieve the outcomes they want.
- The two main types of power in global politics are hard power and soft power. Often realists give more weight to hard power, in which states fight, and often collide, with each other in their attempts to maximise their influence. Liberals argue that soft power, best understood as the way in which a nation-state achieves its objectives through the attractiveness of its culture and political system, is just as significant, especially in a more globalised world.
- Joseph Nye also coined the term 'smart power', which refers to a state using both hard- and soft-power methods to achieve its aims.
- Since the rise of the nation-state in the nineteenth century the global balance of power has continually shifted between the great powers, superpowers and emerging powers, with important repercussions for peace and global stability.
- Polarity refers to 'poles of power'. There are three main forms of polarity: unipolarity (a single pole of power), bipolarity (two poles of power) and multipolarity (multiple poles of power). The Cold War provides a classic example of a bipolar system, in which there were two key and equally matched superpowers (the Soviet Union and the USA) competing for global influence. When the Soviet Union collapsed in 1991, the USA achieved hegemonic status, since there was now no other state that could globally compete with it. The resulting world order that characterised the ending of the Cold War was therefore unipolar. As a result of the changing balance of economic and military global power, the consequences of globalisation and advances in military technology, it has been claimed that the contemporary world is increasingly multipolar, with some arguing that China is on the verge of claiming superpower status.
- There are a wide variety of ways in which states are governed, including democratic, semi-democratic, non-democratic and authoritarian states. The Democratic Republic of Congo and the Democratic People's Republic of Korea are modern examples of failed and rogue states, respectively.
- Liberals tend to regard democracy as the best form of government, however some authoritarian countries have achieved impressive growth rates and domestic stability, and are able to play a constructive role in global politics (e.g. China, Singapore).
- Changing relationships and state actions relate to various developments in power and have impacted contemporary global issues, including conflict, poverty, human rights and the environment. The impact of power and development on these global issues is inextricably linked to globalisation.

Further reading

Chomsky, N. (2003) *Hegemony or Survival: America's Quest for Global Dominance.* Henry Holt and Company.

Fukuyama, F. (1992) *The End of History and the Last Man.* Free Press.

Kaldor, M. (1999) *New and Old Wars: Organized Violence in a Global Era.* Stanford University Press.

Kissinger, H. (2015) *World Order: Reflections on the Character of Nations and the Course of History.* Penguin.

Marshall, T. (2016) *Prisoners of Geography.* Elliott & Thompson Limited.

Exam focus

Section A

1 Examine the view that unipolarity encourages global stability. *[12 marks]*

2 Examine the main differences between the liberal and realist approaches to global politics. *[12 marks]*

3 Examine the view that hard power represents the main currency of international politics. *[12 marks]*

4 Examine the implications of emerging powers for world politics. *[12 marks]*

Section C

1 Evaluate the extent to which the USA can still claim global hegemonic status. *[30 marks]*

2 Evaluate the extent to which multipolarity encourages peace and stability in the international order. *[30 marks]*

3 Evaluate the extent to which China can now be viewed as a superpower. *[30 marks]*

Regionalism and the European Union

Getting you started

Key term

European Union (EU)
A collection of 28 European nation-states (pre-Brexit), with both intergovernmental and supranational institutions designed to promote cooperation around its shared values, aims and agreements.

Just after 7 a.m. on the morning of Friday 24 June 2016, the UK's Electoral Commission announced that the UK had voted to leave the **European Union (EU)**, the 'Leave' campaign having won the nationwide referendum by 51.89% to 48.11%. On the steps of Downing Street, Prime Minister David Cameron confirmed both his own resignation (Cameron had backed the losing 'Remain' campaign) and that the UK's 43 years of membership would be coming to an end. 'The British people have voted to leave the European Union, and their will must be respected. The will of the British people is an instruction that must be delivered,' he said.

In March 2017, Cameron's successor, Theresa May, formally triggered Article 50 of the Treaty of Lisbon. This gave the EU formal notice of the UK's decision to leave. Under Article 50, a member state that wishes to leave has 2 years to negotiate its exit from the EU. This process set the UK on the path to leaving the EU by April 2019.

The EU flag: the blue represents the sky of the Western world, the 12 stars the peoples of Europe (12 being the symbol for completeness and perfection)

Key term

Regionalism A group of countries in a given geographic region, also known as a bloc, that share common features, aims, incentives or goals. Different regional blocs can differ quite significantly in their powers and functions.

The EU is widely agreed to be the most famous example of **regionalism**, due to the unique level of integration among its member states and its expanding membership. It is a collection of 28 European countries (pre-Brexit) and both intergovernmental and supranational institutions, and is designed to promote cooperation centred on its shared values, aims and agreements.

The UK's decision to leave is the first decision of its kind from an EU member state. During the run-up to the referendum, the 'Leave' campaign argued that membership of a regional organisation like the EU resulted in a loss of power and sovereignty, and made the case for the UK 'taking back control' of its borders and decision-making. The 'Remain' campaign argued that in a globalised and interconnected world, EU membership gave the UK influence and access to free trade with its nearest neighbours on a wide range of shared interests.

The debate over whether membership of regional organisations has a negative or positive impact on a member state's power and sovereignty is one of the central questions when considering the significance of regional organisations. We will explore this debate in this chapter.

The growth of regionalism

The EU is an example of a regional bloc that focuses on economic and political union. Its member states have integrated so widely (in terms of member state numbers) and deeply (in terms of the EU's functions and powers) that it can arguably be seen as an example of **federalism**.

In a federal system, power is shared between a central authority above nation-state level (in this case, where member states have given up power over some decisions to central institutions of the EU, such as the European Commission) and state-level authority (in this case, where states retain power over other decisions in their national governments).

Regionalism grew in significance in the late twentieth century. Just as states have looked for means of global governance at international level, for example through the United Nations (UN), states have also tried to find ways of working

Key term

Federalism Regionalism theory suggests that a centralised federal body exercises power, acting on behalf of the regional bloc. It therefore advocates supranationalism and deeper economic and political integration.

295

together at regional level, for example through the EU, the North American Free Trade Area (NAFTA) and the Association of Southeast Asian Nations (ASEAN). This has had an impact on the world order and reshaped the international stage, making international relations less state-centric. Regional organisations were founded to give states a smaller, more focused and less cumbersome means of working together than is sometimes possible at international level with larger memberships.

Regionalism and power

A key consideration when analysing regionalism and regional organisations is the amount of power these organisations, such as the EU or African Union (AU), have over their member states. These powers are usually decided in the treaties that states signed when the organisations were founded (see Table 8.1). These treaties set out the rules and legal basis for how the organisations work. For example, the Treaty of Lisbon sets out in Article 50 the legal process by which a member state voluntarily leaves the EU.

Table 8.1 Timeline of regional organisations and treaties

Date	Organisation	Purpose
1949	Council of Europe and the European Convention on Human Rights (ECHR)	Created a mechanism for human rights to be agreed and protected above nation-state level, enforced by the European Court of Human Rights (ECtHR). The ECHR and ECtHR were founded as part of the Council of Europe, which now has 47 members, including Russia and Turkey, and is separate to the EU.
1951	Treaty of Paris, founding the European Coal and Steel Community (ECSC)	Created a common market for coal and steel between Belgium, France, Italy, Luxembourg, the Netherlands and West Germany. One of its founders, former French foreign minister Robert Schumann, said that it would 'make war [between its member states] not only unthinkable but materially impossible'.
1957	Treaty of Rome, founding the European Economic Community (EEC)	The six members of the ECSC signed a treaty creating the EEC, which committed its members to making 'ever closer union among the peoples of Europe'. The treaty formed the main institutions of today's EU, the European Commission, the European Court of Justice, the European Parliament and the Council of Ministers.
1963	Founding of the Organisation of African Unity (OAU)	The first attempts to create regional governance in Africa. The OAU was founded as former colonies gained their independence and was designed to strengthen and defend newly independent states' sovereignty.
1967	Founding of the Association of Southeast Asian Nations (ASEAN)	The first members of ASEAN were Indonesia, Malaysia, the Philippines, Singapore and Thailand. ASEAN's aim was to enhance economic cooperation in the region.
1992	Maastricht Treaty — the European Community becomes the EU	By now, the EU had developed into a common market of 12 members (the UK joined in 1973), with free movement of people, goods and services. The treaty began the process for creating a single European currency. The euro came into circulation in 2002 in 13 member states.
1994	North American Free Trade Agreement (NAFTA)	Agreed between Canada, Mexico and the USA in order to eliminate tariff and non-tariff barriers to trade in the North America region.
2001	Organisation of African Unity becomes the African Union (AU)	The AU has seen African states cooperate on both security and development issues. It has sent peacekeepers to Somalia and, as a bloc, has also threatened to withdraw from the International Criminal Court (ICC), stating that the ICC is biased against Africans.
2007	Treaty of Lisbon	Created a constitution for the EU and included moves to make decision making simpler (by reducing the policy areas where unanimous agreement was needed), given that the EU had seen its biggest enlargement in 2005 with ten new members states, including many former Soviet states in eastern Europe. The treaty also created the position of President of the European Council (as of 2017, Donald Tusk) and a High Representative for Foreign Affairs, designed to strengthen the EU's independent voice on the world stage.
2016	Brexit	The UK voted to leave the EU and, in 2017, triggered Article 50, the first member state to do so.

Intergovernmentalism Governments work together to come up with mutually beneficial agreements, but their sovereignty remains intact. There is shallower integration in this form of regionalism.

Supranationalism Certain institutions take decisions above the level of domestic governments, therefore diminishing the sovereignty of those states. Certain forms of regionalism have significant aspects of supranationalism, which is controversial, given the impact it has on state sovereignty.

There are two ways in which power and decision making work within regional organisations.

1 **Intergovernmentalism:** member states make all of the decisions. Decisions are not delegated to separate institutions and no institution can force states to do something that they do not agree with (as is the case with the African Union (AU)). With this type of decision making, states retain more control over decisions and therefore the impact on sovereignty and the sacrifices that states make are lessened. It can also be said that this type of decision making is more democratic, if elected national governments are taking decisions themselves.

2 **Supranationalism:** the regional organisation makes all of the decisions and imposes them on its member states (supranational literally means 'above nation-state level'). In the case of the EU, the European Commission is the only part that can propose new laws, and in many policy areas the law will be agreed if at least 55% of the member states representing at least 65% of the EU population agrees it in the Council of Ministers (this is known as 'qualified majority voting', where each member state's voting power is not equal but is weighted according to the size of its population). This type of decision making is often criticised as resulting in states giving up too much power and sovereignty. It is also argued that supranationalism is undemocratic and, within the EU, this is often referred to as the organisation's 'democratic deficit', meaning that decisions are taken that member-state populations have not voted for.

Why a European Union?

The EU was originally founded to further economic and political cooperation within Europe between states that had fought two world wars only two decades apart.

The EU has had most impact in terms of:

- peace and security (between its member states)
- economic and monetary union
- political union (including social and environmental policy)
- human rights (although the ECtHR and ECHR are separate to the EU)
- police and judicial cooperation
- common foreign and security policy

Peace and security

The EU has been very successful in preventing violent conflict between its member states.

In 1951, France, West Germany and the Benelux countries (Belgium, the Netherlands and Luxembourg) signed the Treaty of Paris, which established the ECSC. The coal- and steel-rich regions between France and Germany, particularly in the Ruhr valley, were key natural resources fought over during both world wars.

The ECSC subsequently became part of the EU, which was formally established with the Maastricht Treaty on 1 November 1993. Therefore, while the initial reasons behind the EU were economic, it came into being at a time when Europe was keen to promote peace and stability, having just emerged from the Second World War. The initial trade agreement was a way to ensure this peace and stability by encouraging cooperation and reducing competition and conflict, particularly between France and Germany. However, it has left the EU with a legacy and clear mission to promote the liberal values of democracy and freedom (the liberal idea of 'democratic peace theory' (see page 286)). Over time, the level of integration has become so deep between EU member states that the idea of war between European nations is now unthinkable. The EU was awarded the Nobel Peace Prize in 2012 in recognition of its 'six decades' contribution to the advancement of peace and reconciliation, democracy and human rights in Europe'.

Economic union

The core of the EU project has been a deepening of economic and monetary union between its member states. In 2002, the first regional shared currency came into operation with the creation of the euro. Before this, the EU in its various preceding forms had created a common market with freedom of movement for people, goods and services. The EU has therefore focused on removing tariff and non-tariff barriers to trade between EU member states.

The 'four freedoms' of movement are a key feature of the European Single Market.

- **People:** under the Schengen Agreement (1985), 26 European states (including non-EU member states) have created a travel zone in which there are no border or passport checks. This allows for free movement of people, while EU member state citizens are free to live and work without restriction in other EU member states. The Schengen Area has been under pressure in recent years, with some states reinstating border controls to deal with the migrant crisis caused by conflict in the middle east (notably Syria) and terrorism threats (in the case of the state of emergency, which France imposed in 2015).
- **Goods:** Single Market member states have removed all customs checks and restrictions within the Single Market region. This allows for free movement of goods between member states.
- **Capital:** large amounts of money used for payments or investments can be moved freely without restriction within the Single Market.
- **Services:** companies within the EU are free to set up companies and provide services (for example, any service from banking to car hire) in other EU countries.

Distinguish between

Tariff and non-tariff barriers

Tarriff barriers
- Taxes and charges that the government of the state receiving imports adds to these imports.

Non-tariff barriers
- Other barriers to free trade, which include a government setting a limit or quota on imports of particular goods or services, or other measures that restrict trade.

Another key element of the EU's economic activities has been the creation of a single European currency, the only regional currency of its kind in the world. States gave up their national currencies, such as the French franc or the

German Deutschmark, for the euro, which was introduced in 1999 (for financial transactions, but not in notes and coins) and fully introduced as notes and coins on 1 January 2002. The Eurozone now has 19 member states using its currency.

Key challenges for the euro have included the following:

■ The creation of new EU institutions for the Eurozone in the form of the European Central Bank (ECB), which has the power to set monetary policy for the Eurozone area (including centrally imposed interest rates).

■ Ensuring that members of the Eurozone all tax and spend responsibly (known as fiscal policy, the amount states tax and spend). The Eurozone sets non-binding guidelines for states to follow. These guidelines came under severe pressure after the 2008 global financial crisis, during which Greece, in particular, experienced a debt crisis and required the ECB and other Eurozone member states to provide financial assistance to 'bail out' its economy. Governments feared that, without this assistance, the Greek economy would collapse, causing considerable damage to all Eurozone member states and the potential collapse of the euro. In 2012, the European Fiscal Compact was signed as a legal intergovernmental treaty requiring states to keep their national budgets in balance or in surplus.

Political and social union

Another key pillar of the EU has been social and political union, which has seen the creation of a huge amount of laws. The EU has also created a forum for its member states to work together in order to agree laws and other measures to tackle the challenges facing all member states.

In terms of social policy, the European Social Fund gives money to projects aiming, for example, to reduce unemployment. Around 10% of the EU budget is spent on the Social Fund. The EU has also harmonised labour laws through individual EU laws, known as 'directives'. These laws harmonise social policy on matters as diverse as working hours and unemployment rights. The European Commission proposes EU directives, and the EU's Council of Ministers and the European Parliament agree them. The European Court of Justice interprets the law and ensures that EU law (including directives) is applied fairly across all EU member states (see page 314).

EU directives are agreed on a wide range of matters, ranging from social policy to trade and the environment. Indeed, a key argument of the UK's 'Leave' campaign was that the EU was creating too many directives and imposing them on member states. Directives have been agreed relating to industrial emissions, regulation of pharmaceuticals, standardising weights and measures of produce into the metric system, and bans on appliances that use too much power. A frequently debated EU directive focuses on the shape of bananas, and states that bananas should be 'free of malformation or abnormal curvature' — although nothing is actually banned under this directive, it does outline different classes of 'curvature'.

Judicial and policing

The EU has also introduced close cooperation on justice and policing matters between member states, including coordination of law and enforcement on matters such as international terrorism and organised crime.

The European Arrest Warrant allows for a police force in one member state to issue an arrest warrant and for a police force in any other member state to arrest the individual wherever they may be in the EU. This removes the need for states to negotiate extradition of a suspect back to his/her home state.

Human rights

The EU has been a persuasive advocate for human rights. The European Convention on Human Rights (ECHR) was created in 1953, therefore coming into existence before the European Community (later the EU). It was one of the earliest elements of the European agenda, aimed at preventing a repeat of human rights abuses committed during the Second World War. The ECHR has a wider membership than the EU, being made up of member states of the Council of Europe (which includes non-EU member states such as Russia and Turkey). The EU has also established its own Charter of Fundamental Rights, which sets out the specific rights (economic, social, political) that should be in place for all European citizens.

The EU has often been criticised for lacking the means and the will to intervene militarily to uphold human rights. For example, it did not play a major role in responding to the genocide that took place in former Yugoslavia in 1995 (see Chapter 5), the biggest European genocide since the Second World War. With little power of its own to conduct a coordinated foreign policy, the EU did not intervene, while the UN and NATO led the military response through a UN Protection Force and NATO air strikes.

Arguably, this prompted the EU to do more in terms of promoting human rights. In 1992 (notably, in the midst of the crisis in the former Yugoslavia), the European Commission established the Directorate-General for European Civil Protection and Humanitarian Aid Operations (ECHO). ECHO provides humanitarian aid money and emergency aid workers, and responds to natural disasters and crises. It also works closely with several non-governmental organisations (NGOs) and currently has a strong presence in Syria, among other regions.

The environment

In the international community, the EU has been at the forefront of global governance efforts to protect the environment. It has managed to introduce environmental laws at regional level that have not been possible to agree at international level, and has done so much earlier than any international climate agreements. These successes are due in large part to the EU's small size (compared with the number of parties involved in international agreements) and the similar levels of economic development among its member states (compared with international agreements needing to balance the demands made of both developed and developing states).

The creation of trade laws as part of the Single Market has allowed the EU to develop laws protecting the environment as part of the same process. Sustainable development, that is to say developing trade and protecting the environment at the same time so as not to put future generations' development at risk, has been a consideration throughout the Single Market's development. For example:

- EU member states have agreed to legally binding targets on reducing emissions and developing renewable energy technology. These go further than the non-binding targets that nation-states agreed at the Paris Summit in 2015. The EU has been committed to these goals, but President Trump's withdrawal of the USA from the agreement in June 2017 seems a blow. However, the EU has set a path to achieving the following by 2020:
  - ☐ a 20% cut in greenhouse gas emissions
  - ☐ finding 20% of EU energy from renewables
  - ☐ a 20% improvement in energy efficiency

- The EU has agreed a wealth of environmental protection directives, harmonised across the EU and enforceable by the European Court of Justice. These include a directive requiring public and private sector organisations to carry out an environmental impact assessment before any new building or infrastructure projects.

One area in which the EU has especially maximised its structural power has been in international environmental talks and governance. For example, the EU has used its observer status in the UN and its role in the Group of Twenty (G20) to promote environmental causes on the international stage. The EU has been integral to the development of various international environmental agreements (for example, the 2009 Copenhagen Agreement on climate change — see page 241) and has been fundamental in promoting and upholding them.

Poverty

The EU has had a significant role in encouraging development outside of its borders and has been a key actor in the global mission to eradicate poverty. It is also the world's largest aid donor — in 2015, it provided US$15.56 billion in development aid. This money has gone to different regions around the globe but, significantly, the largest sum has gone to areas in Europe itself. The aid has not been limited to any one sector, covering everything from service provision and infrastructure development to humanitarian aid.

However, some have criticised the EU's Common Agricultural Policy (CAP) for making it harder for farmers in developing states outside the EU to sell their produce into the EU. This is because the CAP provides subsidies for EU farmers (see page 144), which enable them to keep their prices lower (and therefore more competitive) when they sell their produce to the developing world (the CAP covers approximately half of the EU's budget, costing 30 billion euros per year).

Regionalism

Regionalism refers to the idea that nation-states in a certain geographically defined area are united by common:
- goals
- incentives
- interests
- aims

These geographically defined areas are often referred to as 'regional blocs'. Regionalism has arguably existed since the end of the Second World War and is therefore not necessarily a new phenomenon, but it has grown and intensified in recent years, much the same as globalisation.

The Cold War was a time of distinct bipolarity rather than regionalism — the whole world was divided into two distinct halves around the ideologies of capitalism and communism, meaning there were only two real regional blocs during this period (centred on the USA and western Europe on the one hand, and the Soviet Union and Warsaw Pact states on the other). However, with the increase of social, political, cultural and economic interconnectedness, it has become ever more important for states in a more multipolar world to form alliances and agreements with one another.

Regional alliances are often appealing to states and make practical sense if states within a region have shared interests that they wish to advance or defend

Table 8.2 The differences between economic, political and security regionalism

Economic regionalism	Political regionalism	Security regionalism
Focuses on economic progress, free trade and removing barriers to trade within the region.	Needs longer term strategic aims.	Focuses on defence and security against shared threats.
Must have interdependent economies and economic interests.	Focuses on resolving challenges and maximising opportunities that two or more states face (e.g. climate change or terrorism).	Often there will be shared political ties too.
Does not necessarily need a common cultural interest.	To some extent, relies on shared values and so there need to be cultural similarities.	Territorial borders are especially important and these states have a common interest in protecting this area (e.g. a common threat).
Does not need longer term strategic aims.	Is likely to be more inward looking and acting in the region's self-interest.	This may have some impact on sovereignty because of the emphasis on a common defence policy, but this might be quite specific and so limited to a certain context.
Tends to be more outward looking than political regional blocs, including reaching trade deals as a bloc with other states outside the region.	The emphasis on pooled sovereignty and deeper integration means there is more of an erosion of sovereignty.	
Involves limited erosion of sovereignty, except in the case of a single regional currency like the euro, which involves considerable impact on sovereignty.	Enables states to form common positions and achieve greater influence through pooling sovereignty (particularly in the case of smaller states).	

(for example, advancing free trade in the case of the EU or tackling internal violent conflict in the case of the AU). In this way, regionalism and globalisation are intertwined, but they can also work against each other.

Types of regionalism

There are several different forms of regionalism, most commonly characterised through states wishing to work together on developing their economies, shared political challenges and/or security (see Table 8.2). Regional blocs may follow only one of these types of regionalism or a combination of all these types.

Economic regionalism

States that have shared economic aims and, therefore, incentives to cooperate may form a regional bloc, often based around trade deals (see Box 8.1). An example of an economic bloc based solely on trade is the North American Free Trade Agreement (NAFTA). This agreement between Canada, Mexico and the USA enables these states to trade freely with one another through the reduction of trade barriers.

Box 8.1

Regional trade agreements

There are several major regional trade agreements in existence today, including the following.

- **Trans-Pacific Partnership (TPP):** a regional trade deal agreed in 2016 between the states of the Pacific Rim, but excluding China and the USA. President Barack Obama had championed the trade deal, but his successor President Donald Trump withdrew the USA from the TPP on 28 January 2017.
- **Trans-Atlantic Trade and Investment Partnership (TTIP):** a trade deal between the EU and the USA, which was still under negotiation in 2017. The deal will need to be approved by all EU member states (not including the UK) through a decision in the Council of Ministers.
- **North American Free Trade Area (NAFTA):** agreed between Canada, Mexico and the USA in 1992.

Often states make mutually beneficial trade agreements, which enable them to maximise their own economies. This may be via a free-trade agreement, whereby states liberalise trade by reducing or removing restrictions between the regional states, such as taxes, tariffs, quotas and embargos.

States also use regional protectionist policies to protect domestic trade. For example, they may place limitations on quotas from outside their region, which fortifies their own economies — by restricting imports, domestic populations are encouraged to buy products produced within the region. The EU, for example, is protectionist over its agricultural industry. The CAP offers farmers subsidies, which enable them to produce cheaper goods, thereby encouraging EU citizens to buy these goods over more expensive products from outside the region.

President Barack Obama famously intervened in the 2016 referendum on the UK's membership of the EU by stating that if the UK decided to leave the union, it would be 'at the back of the queue' when it came to negotiating a new trade deal with the USA. At the time, Obama was focusing on agreeing a trade deal — the Trans-Atlantic Trade and Investment Partnership (TTIP) — between the USA and the EU bloc. The 'Remain' and 'Leave' campaigns differed on their views as to whether it was in the UK's interests to negotiate with the USA as part of a united regional bloc, or whether seeking the UK's own bespoke trade deal with the USA would better defend the UK's economic and trading interests.

Political regionalism

Political regionalism tends to focus on tackling collective action problems that two or more states within a particular region are faced with. It can be a deeper form of integration because it requires shared cultural ties and a common value system, both of which give a regional bloc a more distinct identity. Often there will be longer-term strategic aims and a broader political vision. Countries that enter into political regionalism will generally gain an advantage from pooling **sovereignty**, because they are more influential collectively than they are individually (see Box 8.2). Therefore, political regionalism can significantly increase states' structural power within international organisations and informal forums. For example, the EU is a member of the G20 and is an observer state of the UN.

Key term

Sovereignty The principle of absolute and unlimited power that a nation-state exercises over its population and territory, and the defining characteristic of a state. Some forms of regionalism weaken sovereignty due to states handing over some power to international bodies.

Box 8.2

Examples of regional political alliances

There are several major regional political alliances in existence today, including the following.

- **Arab League:** founded in 1945 and comprises 22 member states (as of 2017, Syria's membership was suspended) across the middle east and north Africa region. The Arab League does not have its own institutions that operate in the same way as those of the EU. Rather, it conducts its business primarily through Arab League summits, in which it aims to agree common positions on any policy area of shared interest.
- **Alliance of Small Island States (ASIS):** established in 1990 with no formal constitution, the ASIS was created to give a unified voice to small island states at risk from climate change. It comprises many small states, including the Maldives, Nauru (one of the world's smallest states) and the Seychelles. ASIS allows these states to work together in organisations such as the UN and at major climate change conferences to achieve greater influence than they would alone.

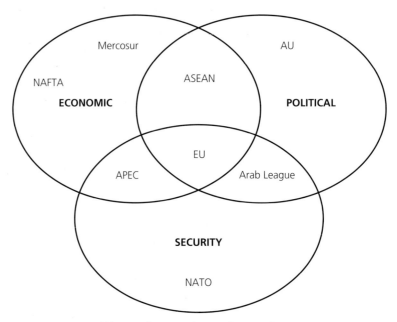

Figure 8.1 Regional blocs and various forms of regionalism

Figure 8.1 depicts how different regional blocs might fit into the various forms of regionalism. In practice, this will not always be clear-cut and some of these definitions are open to debate.

Over time, regionalism has evolved to include both a **widening** and a **deepening** of regional relations. Widening refers to the expansion of regional blocs, a good example being the steady growth of the EU, with many countries still wanting to join the union. Deepening refers to the idea that there is a greater involvement of states in the regional bloc, or that sovereignty is pooled. When integration is deeper, states necessarily see some of their internal sovereignty eroded (but importantly not taken away) in order for it to be pooled.

Regionalism has both intergovernmental and supranational aspects and, depending on the type of regionalism, it may be one or a combination of the two. If there are supranational elements within a regional bloc, we can expect to see deeper integration and pooled sovereignty.

Security regionalism

In the case of security regionalism, states make an alliance to better strengthen their regional borders. Often this involves militaristic alliances or agreements that if an outsider attacks any of the states within the regional bloc, all regional members will react. Therefore, security regionalism directly relates to defence policies, while the alliance of such states may be centred on a common threat. For example, NATO (see page 119) emerged initially as a defence against the spread of communism during the Cold War and it remains a protective buffer against Russia.

The EU has tried to gain more influence over security policy through its Common Foreign and Security Policy (CFSP). The Lisbon Treaty signed in 2007 agreed more powers for the EU to project its own unified foreign and security policy through the appointment of a High Representative of the Union for Foreign Affairs and Security Policy and the President of the European Council. In reality, however, despite the EU gaining more of a unified voice than had previously been the case, NATO remains the most influential security organisation for European states — the majority of the EU's member states are also members of NATO. The EU's CFSP confirms that NATO is the principle organisation responsible for the territorial defence of Europe.

Sometimes security alliances are centred on the movement of people. Some states consider relatively free movement between regional members to be safe, but they maintain a common policy to restrict immigration from further afield or to prevent illegal asylum seekers. This has been significant discussion within the EU throughout the so-called migrant crisis, which has been exacerbated by discussions over immigration in the context of Brexit.

Debates and significance of regionalism

There has been much debate over the extent to which regionalism has been significant and in what ways it has impacted global politics. One of the key debates is the extent to which regionalism is compatible with globalisation. Some argue that the two are integral to one another, while others argue that they are incongruous (in other words, they are not compatible).

Furthermore, there has been much discussion over the impact that regionalism has on sovereignty and governance, at both regional and global levels. Many observers argue that the impact of both globalisation and regionalism has challenged the idea of Westphalian sovereignty to the extent that it is no longer the defining feature of international relations.

Regionalism and globalisation

There is significant debate over whether or not regionalism works with, or against, globalisation. On the one hand it can be argued that regional blocs merely act as a way to better organise global relations — in other words, they are *building blocks*. Since states group together based around common features, it is far easier to conduct international affairs. Arguably, this makes global processes easier to manage and therefore can enhance globalisation, because these processes become more efficient.

Others have argued that regionalism acts as a *stumbling block* to the globalisation process, as regional blocs become more inward looking — they focus their efforts on their own part of the globe and lose interest in the global picture.

Debate

Does regionalism act as a building block or stumbling block to globalisation?

Building block

- Regional blocs enhance globalisation by essentially compartmentalising the globe, making it 'smaller' and more manageable. This has been termed the 'global village argument', meaning the 'global' and 'local' begin to merge.
- Regional blocs organise states into those that have similar goals, making the processes of global governance more efficient.
- Regionalism is compatible with globalisation — it involves similar processes of cooperation, multilateralism and governance, just on a smaller scale.
- Outwardly looking regional blocs want to make the most of global networks and are simply acting as a larger unit than a nation-state.

Stumbling block

- Inwardly looking regional blocs display a 'regional egoism', in that they are only really interested in the concerns of their own region and are therefore fairly isolationist in policy.
- Regional blocs may cut off economically through the implementation of protectionist policies that impinge the free movement of global trade.
- Regionalism is incongruous with globalisation because instead of enhancing a global community and a global civil society, it further divides the world into segments. This leads to the restriction of global cosmopolitanism.
- Regional blocs are all quite different in character, meaning they cannot effectively act together to organise global relations.

Prospects for political regionalism and governance

Political regionalism has clear ramifications for governance at a state, regional and global level. Regionalism has generally progressed from simple and mutually agreeable deals of a mostly economic nature to a much more involved system. In the case of political regionalism, this has also seen the rise of regional governance, to the extent that some blocs now act almost as federal powers. It has even led to the debate of whether, due to this level of integration, we could consider a regional bloc, such as the EU, to be a superpower.

There is also debate over whether or not regional blocs are a help or a hindrance to global governance. This returns to the idea of building blocks and stumbling blocks. On the one hand, regional blocs offer more easily manageable groups of actors, which make for easier negotiations and more probable agreements. Furthermore, they are naturally allied groups with a more unified voice. This can enable smaller, or weaker, states to have a greater influence, both within their region and on the global stage. Arguably, this has gone some way to redressing many of the structural imbalances in international organisations with supranational elements (for example, the UN) — many observers agree that regional blocs have enabled previously sidelined states, such as those from the Global South, to become empowered in a way they never could as lone states.

Impact on state sovereignty

Regionalism has also had a clear impact on sovereignty, but the extent to which this is the case depends on the way regionalism is conducted. If regionalism is predominantly intergovernmental, the impact on sovereignty is minimal — states retain their sovereignty in intergovernmental agreements that are mutually beneficial to all. If regionalism is supranational, then there must be a necessary

Distinguish between

Intergovernmental and supranational sovereignty

Intergovernmental
- Nation-states make mutually beneficial agreements but act independently and in their own self-interest.
- Sovereignty remains fully intact.
- States can still easily opt out of agreements at an intergovernmental level.
- Intergovernmentalism may go beyond decision-making bodies and include scrutinising and steering bodies etc.

Supranational
- Refers to international institutions of law that can act above state level.
- State sovereignty is eroded through supranationalism.
- States are not acting on their own behalf but rather as part of a bigger organisation.
- Usually the erosion of sovereignty is voluntary and related to specific areas, e.g. trade.
- Supranationalism generally refers to decision-making bodies. Interdependence is given institutional recognition.

erosion of sovereignty for it to succeed. However, states can ultimately still choose to leave a supranational agreement (as has been demonstrated by Brexit) or to ignore it. Therefore, it can be said that states ultimately remain as sovereign entities and continue to act predominantly in their own self-interest.

Liberals and realists have different views regarding the impact regionalism has had on sovereignty, and indeed whether or not the implications are of a positive or negative nature. For liberals, cooperation is always good whether on a regional or a global scale, as long as one does not impede the other. States are strengthened through cooperation and liberals argue that governance on a regional and a global scale is the only effective way to deal with a more interconnected world, given that some issues simply cannot be addressed by states acting alone. Issues such as human rights, movement of people, global trade and climate change all increasingly require strong relationships between states if we are to tackle them.

On the other hand, realists argue that ultimately regional and global governance is futile because states will continue to act in their own self-interest, with strong states still able to abuse the system, or even ignore it entirely. Therefore, while strong states can ultimately reclaim their sovereign power, there is little point in the whole exercise.

There are three main regionalism theories in relation to sovereignty.

1 **Federalism:** regionalism can and should be seen as a federal-style system with a central authority. There will be a significant impact on sovereignty, as it is pooled.
2 **Functionalism:** regional blocs develop to fulfil specific functions only, rather than as broader entities. There will be a more limited impact on sovereignty.
3 **Neofunctionalism:** falls somewhere between the two – while there may be initial functions for the regional bloc, these may well 'spill over' into other areas. There will be a mixed impact on sovereignty.

These theories consider how regional blocs are integrated and help us to understand how regionalism emerged in the first instance, and the impact it has since had on sovereignty. They highlight that there is a clear relationship between the level of integration and impact, in that the deeper the regional integration, the greater the supranational element and, therefore, the greater the impact on sovereignty. We will examine these theories in more detail later in the chapter in regard to the EU, arguably the best-known form of regionalism, given that it is the most established and deepest form of regionalism in the world.

Further to the above established theories, there is also the idea of 'new regionalism'. This refers to the substantial increase in regionalism in the 1990s, which saw it have a global, rather than local, effect, much of which was based around economic integration.

The development of regional organisations (excluding the EU)

There are many examples of regional organisations representing different types of regionalism. Regional blocs are the most significant (see Figure 8.2), and they vary in terms of character and type of regionalism (either economic, political or security).

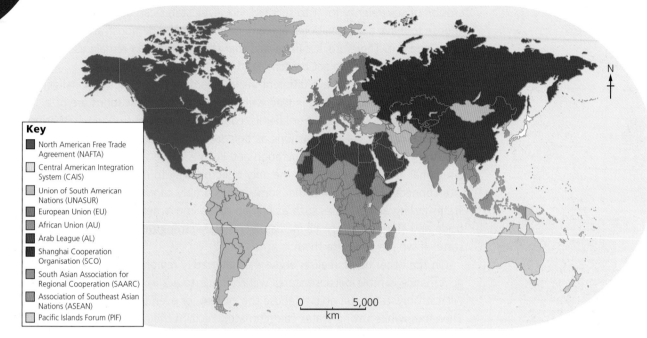

Key

- ■ North American Free Trade Agreement (NAFTA)
- □ Central American Integration System (CAIS)
- ▨ Union of South American Nations (UNASUR)
- ▨ European Union (EU)
- ▨ African Union (AU)
- ■ Arab League (AL)
- ■ Shanghai Cooperation Organisation (SCO)
- ▨ South Asian Association for Regional Cooperation (SAARC)
- ▨ Association of Southeast Asian Nations (ASEAN)
- □ Pacific Islands Forum (PIF)

0 ——— 5,000
km

Figure 8.2 The world's significant regional blocs

Regional blocs

Table 8.3 shows examples of regional organisations outside the EU.

Table 8.3 Regional organisations outside the EU

Regional organisation	North American Free Trade Agreement (NAFTA)	African Union (AU)	Arab League	Association of Southeast Asian Nations (ASEAN)
Members	Canada, Mexico and the USA	All African countries that are not disputed territories	22 members (with Syria currently suspended) from north Africa and the middle east, including Egypt, Iraq, Jordan and Saudi Arabia	6 major members, 10 countries in total, including Indonesia, the Philippines and Thailand, but not China or Japan
Type of regionalism	Economic	Political	Political and security	Economic (and some political)
Key features	An economic agreement based on free trade. Does not extend beyond economic terms, with the three nation-states still retaining quite different goals in other areas. Does not include free movement of people.	Mostly political, uniting Africa to give its nations a bigger voice on the global stage. Backlash against colonial and neocolonial interference in Africa, and therefore has security elements.	Mostly political, to encourage cooperation between member states in order to promote their interests and affairs. Significant security element, with the aim to protect member state sovereignty.	Mostly economic, with a clear aim to promote trade in the region (particularly to protect against Chinese domination). Broader social aims to combat certain issues such as health. Political element via the aim to defend member sovereignty.

Rwandan soldiers boarding an aircraft in support of an AU effort to quell violence in the Central African Republic

Activity

1 Conduct research into other regional blocs, such as the Asia-Pacific Corporation (APEC), Mercosur and the Trans-Pacific Partnership (TTP). Try to identify:
   (a) the type of regionalism
   (b) what countries they include
   (c) how big they are (the populations they represent, the number of states, their combined GDPs etc.)
   (d) their key aims
2 Are there any other regional blocs that you could add to the list? Find other examples to try to form a spread of different types of regionalism (use Figures 8.1 and 8.2 to help you see what examples you need) and then add them to a table like Table 8.3. Remember that the examiners award marks for reference to recent news stories, so it is worth researching current regional organisations and the events affecting them. A good example would be President Trump's withdrawal from the TPP.

Key term

European integration
The level to which the EU is integrated legally, economically, culturally and socially, considering the deepening and widening elements of its formation.

We can see from the examples of regional blocs in Table 8.3 that they do not have the scope or level of **European integration** that makes the EU such a unique example of regionalism. While these regional blocs are still developing and their integration is in some instances deepening and widening, it does seem unlikely that they will ever come to rival the EU model. However, there are arguments on both sides of this debate (see Debate box).

Will regional blocs ever rival the EU?

Yes

- The EU has gradually expanded and developed its role since its origins as the European Coal and Steel Community in 1951. Given that the rise of 'new regionalism' did not emerge until the 1990s, perhaps it is still early days for other regions that may decide to go down a similar path.
- Other regional blocs have moved to expand their remit. Many regional blocs have evolved from being purely economic in nature to now sharing political and security aims (e.g. ASEAN, AU).
- It is hard to predict whether other regional blocs will emerge on the global stage, as they may react in response to power plays in the broader international system. For example, the rise of the AU could be seen as a feature of multipolarity (see page 271) or as a rise in the power of the Global South. On the other hand, were there to be a revival of a dominant hegemony, we may see different forms of 'bandwagoning'.

No

- The EU has had a unique role in promoting cultural values and ideals. It has a clear identity in promoting democracy, peace and security. Arguably this is unique to the EU, given its foundation in the wake of the Second World War, its role in addressing the long-standing rivalry between France and Germany and the all-pervasive feeling of 'never again' in regards to the conflict.
- The EU has played a unique role in promoting certain policies on a global scale. It has pioneered human rights, adopting the ECHR and establishing its own judicial system for its administration (the European Court of Human Rights). The EU has also been instrumental in environmental agreements — for example, it played a key role in the 2009 Copenhagen Agreement (see Chapter 6).
- The EU has a balance of strong powers, but not superpowers, which enables it to 'pool sovereignty' in the absence of a dominant superpower.

European integration: major factors and developments

There are currently 28 members of the EU, including the UK, which will soon begin the process to leave the union since it triggered Article 50 in 2017.

EU formation, its role and objectives

Formation

The EU's formation is best understood chronologically (see Table 8.4). It was formally established in 1993 with the Maastricht Treaty but, as we have seen, its roots lie in the formation of the European Coal and Steel Community (ECSC). From here the group progressed into the European Economic Community (EEC) and finally the EU.

Greece's financial crisis

Following the 2008 global financial crisis, there were fears of a debt crisis among Eurozone members, particularly those dubbed the 'PIIGS' (Portugal, Ireland, Italy, Greece, and Spain). Each of these countries fell into a significant economic recession, which had a knock-on effect that created an overall crisis of confidence. There was particular concern for Greece's future — it was experiencing severe financial trouble due to flouting EU rules on fiscal responsibility, after which it hid the extent of its budgetary issues in an attempt to cover them up.

Therefore, Greece was forced to implement significant spending cuts, as well as to rely on Eurozone bailouts, which became part of the structural adjustment programme (SAP) that the International Monetary Fund (IMF) and EU imposed on the country.

There were further concerns that if Greece defaulted on its loans, it would exacerbate the financial crises in other PIIGS. Germany was especially concerned about Greece's level of debt and the implications this would have for the EU as a whole. It eventually persuaded the EU to call in the IMF in 2011. The EU and the IMF created a loan package, which came with the conditions laid out in the previous SAP. This essentially followed a Washington Consensus approach to boosting economic growth.

Table 8.4 Timeline of EU formation

Year/s	Events
1945–51	The first steps: after the Second World War there was a need for integration and a desire for peace and security. The ECSC was formally introduced in 1951. France and Germany made the initial proposal in an attempt to ease the competition between them by fostering greater cooperation. This community comprised the 'Inner Six' (see page 316). The ECSC was designed to reduce trade barriers on coal and steel and to better coordinate policies over these resources.
1957	The Treaty of Rome (1957) was crucial to European integration and provided the legal basis for the modern EU. This saw the formation of the EEC, essentially the beginning of the common market. Key agreements came into force, such as the Common Agricultural Policy (CAP) and the Common Fisheries Policy (CFP).
1973–79	The UK joined the EEC in 1973. This was the first period of enlargement, with Denmark and Ireland also joining at this time.
1986–92	The Single European Act (1986) prepared for establishing the Single Market, which was completed in 1992. This also saw the abolishment of national vetoes in host areas and a monetary union (some erosion of national sovereignty). The Berlin Wall fell in 1989.
1992/93	The Maastricht Treaty (1993) set up four freedoms of movement: people, goods, capital and services. It also saw the completion of the Single Market. The euro was introduced (although Denmark and the UK opted out of the single currency). Key features of the Maastricht Treaty include: ■ the establishment of the Common Foreign and Security Policy (CFSP), which promotes cooperation in justice and home affairs ■ certain institutions in the EU are strengthened, with more power going to the European Parliament and the European Court of Justice ■ a cohesion fund is set up to help poorer countries to meet the costs of convergence criteria of monetary union (see page 298) ■ the establishment of the subsidiarity principal (upon former prime minister John Major's insistence), which is a general principal of EU law whereby the EU can only act where the action of individual countries is insufficient to the interests of the EU as a whole (a measure to protect the sovereign interests of EU member states)
1999–2002	The euro was introduced in 11 countries and then in Greece in 2001. At this point it was used for commercial transactions only (currency in the form of notes and coins came later, in 2002). This created the Economic Monetary Union (EMU), with the exception of Portugal, Scandinavia and the UK. The European Economic Bank regulates the euro.
2003–8	In 2003, the Treaty of Nice made amendments to both the Maastricht Treaty and the Treaty of Rome. It reformed the institutional structure of the EU, in part to deal with eastward expansion. In 2004, ten more countries joined, with a further two in 2007, making this a notable period of expansion. In 2008, the financial crisis hit Europe.
2009	The Treaty of Lisbon was ratified and came into force in 2009. This was significant in modernising the key EU institutions and making them more efficient. The reforms decreased the number of policy areas in the Council of Ministers where unanimous decisions were needed in order to pass EU laws, representing for some an increase in EU powers and a negative impact on state sovereignty. The treaty also created the positions of President of the European Council and High Representative for Foreign Affairs, which aimed to give the EU more of an independent and influential voice on the world stage.
2008–9, global financial crisis	The so-called PIIGS were in a deep sovereign debt crisis brought on by the global financial crisis and bank bailouts. This led to a crisis of confidence and there was panic on the international market because of the gravity of these debts and the bailouts required to resolve them.
2012–17	In 2012, the EU won the Nobel Peace Prize. In 2013, Croatia joined the EU (the most recent member to be accepted). In 2016, the UK held a referendum to leave the EU and on 29 March 2017 Article 50 was triggered. This period also saw multiple terrorist attacks on EU nation-states and the emergence of the European migrant crisis, putting pressure on the EU's Schengen freedom of movement area.

Activity

Conduct research into the other PIIGS nations (Portugal, Ireland, Italy and Spain). How was the situation in these countries similar/different to that in Greece?

Roles and objectives

The EU's role has changed over time — it began very much as an economic organisation and has increasingly become far more political. As we can see from the timeline of its formation, the EU always had the intention of promoting peace and stability, but in its initial stages it was focused on the trade of coal and oil. Realists argue that this initial focus could be seen as promoting state self-interest, since the objective was clearly primarily economic. However, for liberals, the economic incentive also had a political advantage, with the added bonus that increased economic cooperation would help to create stability, particularly between the long-standing rivals France and Germany, in order to reduce the threat of future conflict.

As time progressed and the economic ties became deeper through the adoption of the Single Market and monetary union, it was clear that the EU was increasingly taking on more of a political role. Various treaties, especially the Maastricht Treaty (1993), saw developments in the EU's key institutions and systems of governance. Increasingly there was a common political agenda and a growing feeling that its institutions should be acting on behalf of the EU as a single entity. During this period, questions of sovereignty were up for debate, with measures such as subsidiarity (the idea that a central authority should perform only those tasks that cannot be performed at local level) demonstrating the clear adoption of a more political role.

The EU has also increasingly taken on more of a security role. After the Treaty of Lisbon (2009) the External Action Service was established, which is the

In response to the increased terror threat, there has been a growing and symbolic sense of a shared European identity: London's Tower Bridge was lit up in the red, white and blue of the French flag after the November 2015 Paris terrorist attacks

EU department that formally implemented the European Security and Defence Policy (ESDP), later called the Common Security and Defence Policy (CSDP). This covers EU defence and military aspects, as well as civilian crisis management, and falls under the jurisdiction of the EU itself.

Furthermore, particularly since the early 2000s, the EU has been increasingly involved in humanitarian work, and has performed operations in Europe itself (the former Yugoslavia), Africa and Asia. While the EU has no standing army, it does have the European Union Force (EUFOR) and the European Union Naval Force (EUNAVFOR), both of which have been involved in interventions with a military focus.

Increasingly, the EU's various intelligence services and armed and police forces are also working collectively in response to the increased terrorism threat. For example, the 2016 attack on Berlin's Christmas market saw Italian police authorities arrest the perpetrator within Italian borders. Furthermore, this has led to a growing and symbolic sense of a shared European identity, with various landmarks across Europe being lit in the colours of the national flags of those nations affected.

Federalism

Federalism suggests that there should be a move towards a centralised federal body that acts on behalf of the regional bloc. It therefore advocates supranationalism, and deeper economic and political integration. This fits the EU model well, since it argues that regionalism under a federalist model is a good way to promote peace and stability, as it prevents state-centrism (states acting purely in their own interests). If states transfer some of their sovereignty to a higher federal body (pooled sovereignty), they reduce the risk of the pursuit of self-interest creating an anarchic system.

The EU is an excellent example of this form of federalism, as it was designed initially to reduce the tensions between France and Germany. It has since developed to such an extent that war between these two nations is now unthinkable.

However, one could argue that the EU is not integrated enough to be considered a federal system — for example, not all EU states have adopted the euro. This alone is incongruous to a truly federal system. Furthermore, states can opt out of agreements or even remove themselves entirely from the system (as seen with Brexit).

Functionalism

The functionalist model arose as a challenge to the idea of federalism. It argues that blocs such as the EU did not emerge to become federalist, but rather to serve specific functions. We can see from the stages of the EU's formation that functionalism is an applicable model. The EU was first set up to establish an agreement over the trading of coal and steel. While it has continued to develop as an economic institution, it has also grown to meet various political and security functions. These functions are better met with collective action, as opposed to individualistic state action. Functionalists are generally positive about the EU's ability to meet these needs effectively.

However, others have argued that, in practice, states have been very reluctant to hand over power to functional bodies, and that these bodies have lacked the legitimacy of sovereign bodies. Furthermore, one could argue that the model is too simplistic and short sighted in relation to the EU, and that the EU has always had longer-term visions than functionalism.

Neofunctionalism

The theory of neofunctionalism sits somewhere between the previous two theories, and argues that regionalism does indeed meet some functional needs but that this spills over into other, broader areas. Usually neofunctionalism begins by addressing economic functions, but leads to some political spill-over. We can certainly see this right from the beginning of the EU, in the form of the coal and steel trade agreement, which had primarily economic goals but also aimed to promote stability within Europe.

Furthermore, the European defence policies of recent years demonstrate that when there is a functional need, the EU develops new policies (for example, to combat terrorism) but that these often morph into longer-term strategic aims (for example, fostering a cosmopolitan identity and encouraging much of Europe to 'band together'). This approach suggests that there is a complex interplay between the economic and political aspects of regionalism.

Establishment and enlargement of the EU's key institutions

Establishment

Figure 8.3 represents the organisation of the key EU institutions (aside from the European Council) and how they interrelate. The role of voters in both national governments and the European Parliament is significant when we consider how democratic the EU is. Furthermore, considering its legislative, executive and judiciary roles helps us to explain how the EU system can be seen as federalist, and to decipher whether or not the EU works intergovernmentally, supranationally or as a combination of the two.

Table 8.5 summarises the major EU institutions and their features.

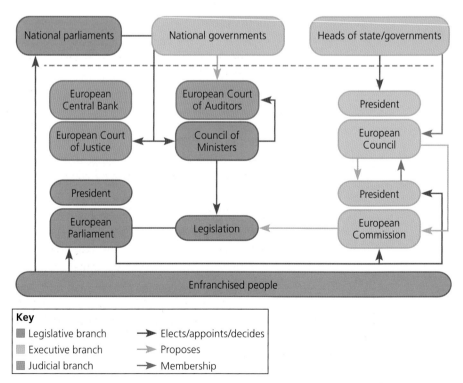

Figure 8.3 How the key EU organisations interrelate

Table 8.5 The major EU institutions and their features

Institution	Key feature
European Council	Informally known as the European Summit.
	One of the EU's intergovernmental institutions.
	A decision-making body, focusing on longer-term decisions.
	Comprises heads of state and foreign ministers. It also includes the president and vice-president of the European Commission.
	Has a permanent full-time president (currently Donald Tusk).
	Meets four or more times a year.
	Offers strategic leadership and is responsible for the EU's longer-term vision, including setting policy guidelines, resolving disputes between member states, agreeing reforms of treaties and steering the EU's foreign policy.
Council of Europe	Also known as the Council of Ministers.
	One of the EU's intergovernmental institutions.
	Also a decision-making body, focusing more on day-to-day or shorter-term decisions.
	Comprises ministers from all 28 member states (pre-Brexit). These ministers are accountable to their own governments.
	The ministers change depending on the issue under discussion and thus act almost like a cabinet.
	The president is a country, not a single person, and this rotates among the members every 6 months.
	Decision making is made through a voting system (this has to be unanimous for decisions on some policy areas, but for other issues is based on a majority voting system known as 'qualified majority voting'). The Treaty of Lisbon increased the number of policy areas where qualified majority voting applies.
European Commission	Often seen as the main executive institution of the EU. It exists to promote and defend the interests of the whole EU.
	The only part of the EU that can propose new laws.
	A supranational organisation.
	The bureaucratic arm of the EU.
	Based in Brussels, Belgium.
	Comprises 28 commissioners (pre-Brexit), one from each EU member state, and a president (currently Jean-Claude Juncker). Commissioners are duty bound to defend and promote the EU's interests, rather than the interests of their home state.
	Responsible for processing legislation and acts as a watchdog for policy implementation.
European Parliament	Made up of Members of the European Parliament (MEPs) from the 28 member states (pre-Brexit). It is the only elected body of the EU, with countries directly electing MEPs every 5 years.
	A supranational organisation.
	Usually located in Strasbourg, France.
	Organised by political group as opposed to nationality. For example, the Europe of Freedom and Democracy political group comprises Eurosceptic parties from across the EU, such as the United Kingdom Independence Party (UKIP).
	Its role has expanded over the years, but its main function remains to scrutinise, rather than create, legislation.
	Its main powers (to reject the EU's budget or dismiss the commission) are in practice too far-reaching for it to implement.
European Court of Justice	Acts as a judicial body, interpreting and adjudicating EU laws and treaties.
	A supranational organisation.
	Comprises 28 judges (pre-Brexit), one for each member state, and eight advocates who advise the courts.
	EU law has primacy over national law, which means that the European Court of Justice has the power to dis-apply domestic laws.
	The Court of First Instance handles certain cases brought by individuals or companies.
European Central Bank	Responsible for the economic governance of the euro, specifically its purchasing power and therefore its price stability (similar to the Bank of England's role with the pound sterling in the UK).
	A supranational organisation.
	Based in Frankfurt, Germany.
	Represents the 19 countries that are in the Eurozone.

Current president of the European Council Donald Tusk

Enlargement

As well as deepening integration (which considers the loss of sovereignty for the wider interests of the EU), there has been much discussion in relation to the widening integration of the EU, in particular to its expansion to include additional member states. As the timeline of the EU's formation demonstrates (see page 311), there have been various waves of enlargement throughout the regional bloc's history.

When it was first established, the EU had only six original members (known as the Inner Six), in contrast to the 28 members of today (pre-Brexit). Since then it has seen several waves of enlargement:

- **Inner Six (1951):** Belgium, France, Germany, Italy, Luxembourg, the Netherlands
- **First Enlargement (1970s):** Denmark, Ireland, the UK (including Gibraltar)
- **Mediterranean Enlargement (1980s):** Greece, Portugal and Spain
- **Northern Enlargement (1990s):** Austria, Finland and Sweden
- **Post-Communist/Eastern Enlargement (2000s):** Czech Republic, Cyprus, Estonia, Hungary, Latvia, Lithuania, Malta, Poland, Slovenia, Slovakia (2004), Bulgaria, Romania (2007), Croatia (2013)

There are many states that are still waiting to join the EU, with the Balkan states, in particular those of the former Yugoslavia, being the main contenders. Some argue that it would be easier for the EU to absorb these states, given that EU funding already makes contributions towards their development. One of the more controversial applicants is Turkey, which has been under negotiation to join since 1987 (see Debate box).

Enlargement on this grand scale has been controversial — Russia, in particular, has seen the EU's growth as antagonistic, given that the EU's border looks increasingly similar to that of NATO's and many of the newer eastern European members were former Russian allies or satellite states. Therefore, the EU, designed to promote peace and security in the region, has had to consider the wider impact of allowing eastern European countries to join and how this could cause conflict with Russia. Furthermore, newer members often have weaker economies, putting pressure on the existing members' economies.

Another issue relates to the significant cultural differences of possible new EU members. Given that the EU has grown to have more of a collective cultural identity, accepting countries that have quite different outlooks (such as Turkey) could prove to be problematic.

Finally, there is the issue of effectiveness — the larger the EU, the larger the base of interests it needs to coordinate. This may make it harder for the EU to form cohesive policies, especially in regards to foreign policy. This is especially problematic when unanimity is called for, for example in the Council of Europe.

Debate

Should Turkey be accepted to the EU?

Yes

- Accepting Turkey to the EU would present an image of inclusivity and diversity (it prevents the EU being seen as a 'Christian Club').
- It would extend the scope of diplomatic relationships, particularly with the middle east.
- It would provide the EU with access to key natural resources, particularly energy.
- It would prevent Turkey from forming greater ties with Russia.
- EU borders would be more in line with those of NATO, which makes sense given the EU's and NATO's defence alliance.

No

- Turkey is a culturally different country to other EU member states.
- It has a poor human rights record, which is in direct contradiction to EU values and would impact the EU's soft power were it to join.
- It has been politically unstable at times and is not seen as overly democratic (again, in direct contradiction to EU values of liberal democracy).
- Many worry that Turkey's connections with the middle east are a concern rather than an asset, therefore leaving the EU vulnerable to Islamic extremism and further immigration from the region.

Key treaties and agreements

Many of the key treaties and agreements within the EU are used as evidence of deepening integration within the regional bloc. They have also evolved the key institutions and extended their powers. However, some agreements have meant that nation-states have had to compromise their national interests for the sake of wider EU interests. This loss of sovereignty is evidence of federalism.

However, one can argue that member states still act in their own interests, in that they can either opt out of certain agreements or ultimately withdraw from the EU, as we have seen with the UK and Brexit. The fact that numerous states opted out from the euro (including Denmark, Sweden and the UK) is evidence that member states retain sovereign control and, therefore, that the EU is not a truly federal system. While this is changing (since the Treaty of Lisbon (2009), it has been mandatory for new member states to adopt the euro), it is still significant that several EU states have been able to maintain this position. Furthermore, certain countries have negotiated their way out of various other agreements, or renegotiated the terms (as the UK did in the 1980s with the CAP).

Table 8.6 The EU's key treaties

Key treaties	Key agreements
Treaty of Rome (1957)	European Economic Community Common Agricultural Policy and Common Fisheries Policy
Maastricht Treaty (1993)	The freedom of movement of goods, services, people and money The principle of subsidiarity European Monetary Union (including the formation of the European Central Bank)
Treaty of Nice (2003)	Single European Act Single Market
Treaty of Lisbon (2009)	Common Security and Defence Policy European Constitution President of the European Council External Action Service and High Representative for Foreign Affairs

Finally, the law of subsidiarity states that the EU can only act when individual nation-states are incapable of acting — in other words, it cannot otherwise impinge upon state sovereignty.

Table 8.6 is a summary of the EU's key treaties and their agreements.

Activity

1 First see what you can remember about the treaties and agreements shown in Table 8.6, and then go back to the EU formation section (page 310) to see how much you have remembered.
2 As an additional activity, conduct research into those treaties and agreements with which you are less familiar.

The Economic and Monetary Union

The process of European integration broadly followed three stages:

1 economic union
2 monetary union
3 political union

As the middle stage of integration, the Economic and Monetary Union (EMU) clearly had both economic and political elements.

The origins of the EMU go back to 1978, when the European Exchange Rate Mechanism (ERM) was established. The ERM was designed to tackle one of the biggest issues with trade in the EU: fluctuating exchange rates. The ERM would reduce exchange rate variability and achieve monetary stability in Europe.

In 1992, the pathway to EMU was agreed under the Maastricht Treaty. It represented a clear move beyond stabilising exchange rates to establishing a single currency. In practice, the EMU is a group of policies aimed at converging the economies of EU member states in three stages (the euro convergence criteria), with each stage designed for progressively closer economic integration. Only once a state participates in the third stage can it adopt the euro as its official currency.

Some EU member states opted out of the single currency (namely Denmark and the UK), but those who qualify today have to meet the euro convergence criteria set out by the Maastricht Treaty as, after the enlargement of the EU in 2004–7, all new EU member states must commit to participate in the third stage in their treaties of accession.

As part of the 1996 Dublin Summit, the Stability and Growth Pact (SGP) was established, which was designed to ensure that EMU members had a strict budgetary discipline and to maintain the EMU's stability. However, the SGP was non-binding and some member states did not comply with the need for budgetary discipline.

The EMU: economic benefits

Membership of the EMU has clear economic benefits:

- It removes obstacles to trade by extending the Single Market. Traders and travellers are free of the constraints of currency conversion rates. This creates a certainty in trade prices, enabling traders to trade on lower profit margins and therefore creating savings and reducing prices.
- There is greater transparency over prices, which benefits producers, cross-border traders and consumers alike.
- The SGP ensures economic stability and thus low inflation.
- The EMU is, in theory, less vulnerable to the world currency markets, allowing the EU to have a greater financial and economic global influence, to the extent that within organisations like the World Bank and IMF, the EU is able to counterbalance the USA.

The euro is the official currency of the Eurozone, which consists of 19 of the 28 (pre-Brexit) EU member states

The EMU: political benefits

There are also many political benefits to membership of the EMU:

- Pooling sovereignty arguably strengthens, rather than weakens, EMU member-state sovereignty. This is arguably especially true in an increasingly globalised world in which national monetary sovereignty is already challenged.
- Before the EMU was established, the Bundesbank (the German Federal Bank), rather than the ECB, controlled EU monetary policy. Many other European countries (especially France) were unhappy with Germany's economic control of the union. The EMU redresses this imbalance.
- Many see the euro as a further step towards a federalist political union, leading to greater integration. This could include harmonising taxes or larger budgets to offset the negative impacts of depressed areas. Furthermore, it also helps to foster the EU's cosmopolitan identity and creates a stronger European identity.

The EMU: drawbacks

Nonetheless, the EMU does have its drawbacks:

- There are economic risks, including the capacity for the ECB to misjudge monetary policy and the potential for EMU governments to ignore, or sidestep, SGP rules. In fact, both France and Germany flouted these rules in the mid-2000s by overspending and exceeding the 3% of GDP limit on a state's budget deficit.
- Policies won't always benefit all states. For example, interest rates that suit some have a negative impact on others.

- The SGP gives EMU member states the ability to employ measures traditionally used to boost weakened economies, for example raising public spending to tackle unemployment.
- Politically, there is the cost to national sovereignty over some key areas of economic and monetary policy, as well as an element of hypocrisy as to how this is enforced among EMU members.
- There is a democratic deficit issue, given that sovereign responsibility to regulate monetary policy is removed and transferred to an unelected independent central body (the ECB).

Debate

Is EMU membership positive or negative?

Positive

- The euro has made free trade even easier within the EU member states that are part of the Eurozone. Exchange rate costs are eliminated when trading between the Eurozone member states and for foreign investors with operations in more than one Eurozone member state.
- The ECB can regulate monetary policy across the EU, making financial conditions more stable and predictable.
- The ECB can offer more stability through the ability of states to pool together to help states that encounter economic difficulty. If Greece had not been a Eurozone member, it is doubtful as to whether it would have received so much financial assistance during its recent debt crisis.

Negative

- Some states lose out, as they are supporting weaker economies (perhaps even responding when weaker economies have made poor decisions in respect of managing their own economies and getting into debt).
- There is a loss of sovereignty for EMU members. Individual member states are less able to change their monetary policy in order to respond to economic conditions within their own state (for example, by raising or lowering interest rates).
- There is a democratic deficit, given that domestic citizens of EMU member states do not have a direct say over monetary policy. The Fiscal Compact also limits states' choices on their public spending, by requiring states to balance their budgets.

Supranational vs intergovernmental approaches

When arguing whether the EU is a supranational or intergovernmental organisation, it is worth considering how its key organisations fit into the two categories (see Table 8.7).

Table 8.7 EU organisations: intergovernmental or supranational?

Organisation	Intergovernmental or supranational?
European Council	Intergovernmental, because each member state is represented within the European Council and is acting on its own behalf. Therefore, heads of state and foreign ministers retain a reasonable amount of control in steering the overall direction of the EU on behalf of their own sovereign interests.
Council of Europe	Intergovernmental, since MEPs represent their own country and therefore their country's sovereign interests in shorter-term decision making within the EU and on specific issues.
European Commission	Supranational, given that it essentially acts as an executive with a legislative role. The laws and policies it oversees act in the interests of the EU as a whole as opposed to its individual sovereign members.
European Parliament	Supranational since, while member-state domestic populations elect MEPs to office, the parliament's role is to scrutinise legislation on behalf of EU, rather than national, interests.
European Court of Justice	Supranational, given that it has the ability to pass legislation that can override the laws of national governments.
European Central Bank	Supranational, since it oversees monetary regulation on behalf of EMU countries, which is traditionally seen as a key role for sovereign states.

The European Parliament Building in Strasbourg

Debate

Is the EU a supranational/federal institution?

Yes

- There are more supranational organisations in the EU. Their powers are significant (e.g. the European Court of Justice can make laws that have primacy over national laws, the ECB controls monetary policies for EMU members).
- EU institutions gain more power through its various agreements and treaties.
- There is now a clear EU figurehead (Donald Tusk, former President of Poland and current President of the European Council).
- The EU's role has adapted and moved from a primarily economic agreement to more of a political and strategic alliance.
- It acts on a global stage with a significant amount of structural and diplomatic power. It has a significant influence over certain global issues (e.g. the environment, human rights) and an important role in various IGOs and NGOs.

No

- The most significant organisations are intergovernmental — that is, the decision-making bodies (the European Council and the Council of Europe). Ultimately these bodies steer the direction of the EU as a whole, while ensuring that national interests are represented.
- The principle of subsidiarity ensures that states retain their sovereignty in most situations.
- States can ultimately withdraw from certain agreements (e.g. not all states are party to the single currency), or decide to withdraw from the EU altogether, which demonstrates that ultimately the EU is still state-centric.
- The EU lacks the central authority required of a federalist system.
- It lacks a cohesive foreign policy and, due to its diverse membership, is unlikely to form one.

The EU as an international body/global actor

The former US secretary of state Henry Kissinger (in office as secretary of state between 1973 and 1977) once asked the question, 'Who do I call if I want to speak to Europe?' on a matter of international importance. Traditionally, the USA has relied heavily on France, Germany and the UK as the most powerful voices in Europe and therefore the most reliable and influential European governments to work with on issues of major significance.

The EU has increasingly attempted to expand its role from a regional body coordinating policy within Europe to a regional body with power and influence

Key term

Global actor A power or entity (e.g. a collection of states) that has a significant presence on the international stage, participates or acts in international affairs and is considered to have influence over states and the international system in general.

as a **global actor** in its own right. For some, the idea that the EU acts as a spokesperson for the peoples and governments of EU member states is a controversial one, and represents a threat to individual member states' sovereignty and their ability to conduct their own, independent foreign policy. Others see a useful role in the EU gaining influence as a more independent and unified voice on the world stage, perhaps at last answering Kissinger's famous question.

Constraints and obstacles affecting the EU's influence in global politics

Political

The EU has had a number of political obstacles to contend with. While there have been some clear political benefits, the EU as a regional bloc and organisation has faced significant challenges.

The most obvious political challenge is the impingement of sovereignty. This issue was especially brought to the fore when the UK voted in the 2016 Referendum to leave the EU, but it has been an element of tension throughout the EU's history. The issue of state sovereignty fuels the debates around freedom of movement, particularly in the wake of the European migrant crisis.

There is also the issue of a democratic deficit, in that the EU lacks basic democratic principles. As citizens of democratic countries, EU citizens should have the ability to vote over its more supranational elements and institutions, but in reality they do not — the European Parliament is the only elected body within the EU and it is not a decision-making body. This is especially problematic given that the EU promotes the liberal values of democracy and freedom, and some would argue that this aspect of EU governance has even damaged its soft power.

Economic

In many ways, the EU has been a great economic success, but there have also been some significant economic drawbacks. The 2008 global financial crisis hit Europe especially hard (in particular the PIIGS states), and demonstrated that the EU was not immune to fluctuating global markets. The PIIGS economies have still not yet fully recovered, and the bailout of these national economies has been expensive for other EU member states.

Furthermore, expansion has created an economic strain on EU countries because the newer members tend to have weaker economies, thereby creating an economic burden on the stronger states. Additionally, not all EU member states have accepted the euro and of those that have, there have been winners and losers. Germany has done well from having a devalued currency, which has made its exports more appealing to the global market, while other countries, such as Italy, which would ordinarily have used methods such as devaluation to overcome recession, have been prevented from doing so. There has also been significant disagreement over policies such as the CAP, demonstrating the difficulty in an organisation of 28 member states (pre-Brexit) of reaching agreement on matters of trade.

Structural

There are some obvious overlaps with broader political obstacles when it comes to the EU's structural power. How much political power does the EU really have on the global stage? Can it be seen as a superpower? Many have argued that it cannot, given that there is a lack of a central authority or a clear figurehead in the same way as exists in superpower nation-states.

Furthermore, the EU has such a diverse set of interests (both politically and culturally) that at times it has been a challenge to agree on cohesive policies — this is especially true in the case of foreign policy. This again hampers the EU's ability to act as a unified player on the global stage. Its continued expansion has exacerbated this issue and arguably made it less effective.

It can also be argued that the UK's decision to leave the EU has proved detrimental to the EU's structural power, especially when seeing Europe as a counterbalance to the USA in organisations such as the World Bank and the IMF. The UK is one of the key EU powers, and its 'special relationship' with the USA has helped to bolster the EU's overall influence on the international stage. However, President Trump has made it clear that he would like a US–UK alliance, rather than an EU alliance, which in part formed the rationale behind the 'Leave' campaign. The extent of Brexit's impact on the EU's global influence remains to be seen.

Military

One of the EU's most significant weaknesses is its lack of a central military power. The EU employs forces primarily for humanitarian intervention, but it does not have a central standing army. The EU relies on NATO (which has a very similar membership to the EU) for defence, but this has led to some seeing the EU as the USA's military puppet. This was highlighted during the war in the former Yugoslavia, and especially in Kosovo, during which NATO had to step in to end the conflict. The EU was largely seen as weak for allowing the largest genocide since the Second World War to happen in its own back yard.

Debate

Can the EU be considered to be a superpower?

Yes
- **Economic power:** the EU has significantly increased its economic power by unifying its currency and establishing the largest free-trade area in the world.
- **Structural power:** the EU has been highly influential in global institutions, particularly in relation to certain issues such as human rights and the environment.
- **Soft power:** the EU has a significant influence over other states, with many countries still very keen to join it (e.g. other Balkan states, Turkey).
- **Organisation:** the EU has made changes to its structure in efforts to become more efficient, strengthening the role of its institutions and giving it a clear figurehead (Donald Tusk).

No
- **Economic:** the EU has not been immune to fluctuating global markets and was a major victim of the global financial crisis.
- **Lack of military power:** the EU has no standing army and has been seen as the USA's puppet, given its reliance on NATO for defence.
- **Lacks cohesion:** given its diverse range of members and therefore interests, the EU does not have a clear foreign policy, which also hampers its structural power within global organisations.
- **Lack of central authority:** arguably there is no clear central authority and its 'leaders' act more as chairpersons or managers.

Activity

'Evaluate the extent to which the EU is a superpower.'
Think back to the key features of a superpower and write a conclusion to the above essay question. You should try to include the key features of a superpower in your answer and justify (back up) your argument with what you believe to be the most compelling argument. Try not to sit on the fence — there is no right or wrong answer, as long as you can evidence it.

Furthermore, the EU has developed a common security policy, but it has been susceptible to national security failures, with a number of terrorist attacks taking place across Europe in recent years.

Regionalism and global issues

Increasingly, regionalism has a part to play in global issues. This is partly due to the supranational element of regionalism, and the role that regional blocs play in governance (at state, regional and global levels). Some key synoptic areas to consider are conflict, poverty, human rights and the environment. It is important to consider what influences and impacts regionalism has had in these areas.

Conflict

Regionalism can generally be seen to promote peace and security. It can be associated with the liberal idea of democratic peace theory, given that where there is political regionalism, there is a tendency towards multilateral cooperation, which goes hand in hand with democracy. As globalisation and regionalism have spread, there has been a simultaneous spread of democracy, leading political scientist Francis Fukuyama to say that liberal democracies are the end of political evolution, as they are the ultimate political system. Democratic peace theory argues that democracies are unlikely to go to war with one another. The EU is an excellent example of this, with countries such as France and Germany — former longstanding rivals with complex histories of conflict — now so unlikely to go to war with one another that we can describe it as unthinkable.

The reduction in conflict is not just down to political regionalism — we could also make the neoliberal argument that economic cooperation is a very effective way to promote peace and stability. If states are economically reliant on one another there is very little incentive for them to go to war with each other. Indeed, this feeds into the arguments of British academic Mary Kaldor, who highlights that increasingly war is not centred on states in the traditional sense (the 'New War' thesis, see page 196). Regionalism tends to unite like-minded countries, but it can also create alliances between states that might not otherwise cooperate.

A 2017 study by PricewaterhouseCoopers estimated that China will overtake the USA as the world's largest economy by around 2020

That said, regional blocs can be quite inward looking, with isolationist agendas that could arguably lead to conflict. For example, the ASEAN is keen to temper China's dominance in Asia. Furthermore, if regionalism becomes increasingly linked to ideology, there is potential for conflict — the Cold War was essentially a conflict between two ideologically focused regional blocs.

Poverty

Regionalism has had an impact on poverty in terms of how regional blocs have addressed this concern, both within their own regions and globally. First, there is greater cooperation and both economic and political incentive to tackle the issue of poverty within regional blocs. A good example has been the EU and its attempts to address issues of poverty, particularly in the former Yugoslavian states, to better align those state populations and economies with the rest of Europe. Second, regional blocs dealing with significant levels of poverty (for example, the AU) have a voice in global institutions in regards to their own development.

Regionalism can also be seen to promote international cooperation in the areas of aid and development external to regions (demonstrating the 'building blocks to globalisation' argument, see page 305). The EU has a clear identity of promoting liberal values and has therefore invested heavily in funding aid programmes abroad, and is deeply involved in global strategies to reduce poverty. Initiatives such as the UN's Sustainable Development Goals can be much more effective if regional alliances can help implement them.

Human rights

Similar to poverty, regional cooperation is advantageous to human rights at both the regional and the global level. Regionalism promotes human rights within regional blocs (e.g. the ECHR in the case of the EU). The EU has also encouraged freedom of movement and has had a significant role in taking in asylum seekers from north Africa and the middle east (albeit, controversially).

There has also been a benefit to human rights on a global scale, with regionalism helping to promote a more global appreciation of liberal values and freedoms, thereby reinforcing the UN's Charter of Human Rights. This fits in with ideas of cosmopolitanism and identities that extend beyond nation-states.

> **Synoptic links**
>
> The idea that the EU promotes human rights links to that of liberalism from Component 1. The EU promotes and upholds the ideals of legal equality and equal opportunity. Consider 'key thinkers', such as Professor of Government at Harvard University Jeffry Frieden, in relation to this. Frieden specifically refers to gender rights in his writing, but the concept could be extended to other groups also.

The environment

Climate change is a modern-day concern that has posed a challenge to state-centric politics, given that it cannot be tackled at state level. Action is needed at state, regional and global level, and regionalism has offered a crucial link between the state and the global in that it can help to make global governance more effective (this again forms part of the 'building blocks' argument). The EU has led the way in terms of agreeing at regional level what could not be agreed at international level. It has also been highly influential at international summits such as the 2015 Paris Agreement, which was a UN initiative within which the EU played a fundamental role.

Arguably, another advantage of a regional approach to environmental issues is that there is potential to better deal with the different needs of regions when developing international environmental policies. This is a liberal argument, and one that realists would see as unrealistic. Many have argued that it is unfair to impose the same climate change restrictions as those on already-industrialised nation-states on developing countries that are still industrialising. Some even see this as part of a neo-imperialistic agenda to maintain an international hierarchy and prevent these states from developing. Others have argued that as we have seen a progression in technology, scientific collaboration and access to evidence, we can better react to climate change, in a way that we could not during the period in which developed countries were industrialising.

In any case, if these issues are to be reconciled, it may well be easier to do this through collective regional voices, as opposed to employing a state-based approach.

Synoptic links

The idea that the environment is an issue beyond the capacity of individual states and that a more holistic approach is required to solve it relates to the theories of ecologist Rachel Carson, in Component 2's ecologism option. Furthermore, the idea of greener technologies links to the concept of 'green capitalism'.

Activity

Close the textbook and put your notes away. Draw a concept map of the synoptic links in this topic in order to see how much you can remember, or if there is anything that you can add to the links. Once you have listed as many items as you can, go back and check your concept map against the links presented in the textbook — are there areas you were unsure on? This should help you to form a plan for revision.

Other issues

Globalisation

There is a clear link between regionalism and globalisation. While there is debate over the extent to which regionalism is a help or a hindrance to globalisation, there is no doubt that it has emerged alongside globalisation and that the two are most certainly intertwined.

Therefore, we see the same debates that relate to globalisation coming up in the topic of regionalism, including:

- widening and deepening integration
- the challenges to state sovereignty
- the implications for issues larger than the state

Power and developments

There is a clear link between regionalism and the Power and developments component. It is important to consider the role that regional blocs play in international relations, which is becoming an increasing feature of a globalised world. As the world has become more interconnected, we have seen a decline in the traditional, state-centric approach to international relations and an increased move towards pooled sovereignty.

What you should know

Having read this chapter you should have knowledge and understanding of the following:

- Regionalism has been increasing in the post-1945 world order, as states try to find ways of cooperating with their nearest neighbours on issues of common concern. Regionalism can often be less prone to gridlock and disagreement than global governance on an international level.
- The European Union (EU) is the world's most comprehensive and extensive regional organisation in terms of both the number of member states and the amount of policy areas that it deals with ('widening and deepening' throughout its history). The EU's primary role has been to deepen economic and trading partnerships with Europe, through a single market and single currency.
- Regionalism can present challenges for state sovereignty, particularly in regional organisations that have supranational decision-making powers, because in these cases the organisation can force member states to comply with decisions that a member state might not have agreed to. The EU is the most powerful regional organisation in terms of the powers that it has over its member states. Arguments that the EU represented an excessive loss of control and sovereignty were a key part of the successful 'Leave' campaign in the 2016 Referendum on the UK's membership of the EU.
- Regional organisations can focus on economic matters and trade, security, development or human rights. Most regional organisations focus on economic and trade cooperation, such as the North American Free Trade Agreement and the Association of Southeast Asian Nations. Regional blocs, such as the Arab League and the African Union, are useful ways for states within a region to have more influence together than individual states would alone. This pooling of sovereignty can be argued to increase, rather than decrease, a state's power and influence on the world stage.

Further reading

Dixon, H. (2014) *The In/Out Question: Why Britain Should Stay in the EU and Fight to Make it Better.* CreateSpace Independent Publishing Platform.

Fawn, R. (ed.) (2010) *Globalising the Regional, Regionalising the Global.* Cambridge University Press.

Peet, J. & La Guardia, A. (2014) *Unhappy Union: How the Euro Crisis — and Europe — can be Fixed.* Economist Books.

Rosamond, B. (2000) *Theories of European Integration.* Palgrave Macmillan.

Exam focus

Section A

1 Examine, using examples, the differences between economic and political regionalism. *[12 marks]*

2 Examine the implications of the debt crisis for the future of the Economic Monetary Union and the EU. *[12 marks]*

3 Examine the benefits for EU members of EU integration. *[12 marks]*

4 Examine what the key driving forces behind EU expansion are. *[12 marks]*

Section C

1 Evaluate the extent to which the EU has been a model for regionalism around the world. *[30 marks]*

2 Evaluate the extent to which the EU can be considered a superpower. *[30 marks]*

3 Evaluate the extent to which the EU is a federalist system. *[30 marks]*

4 Evaluate how desirable EU integration is. *[30 marks]*

Index

Page numbers in **bold** refer to key term definitions

D

E